VOLUME 002

Amazing_Agent
LUNA

art by Shiei

story by Nunzio DeFilippis
and Christina Weir

[CONFIDENTIAL]

AMAZING AGENT LUNA
VOLUME 2

Staff Credits:

Art: Carmela "Shiei" Doneza

Story: Nunzio DeFilippis & Christina Weir

Tones: Jay Jimenez

Background Assists: Roland Amago

Letters and Graphic Design: Nicky Lim

Editor: Jason DeAngelis

Publisher: Seven Seas Entertainment

Visit us online at www.gomanga.com.

ISBN 1-933164-04-2

Manufactured in the United States of America

First printing: July, 2005

10 9 8 7 6 5 4 3 2 1

Seven Seas

NEW WORLDS AT YOUR FINGERTIPS
www.gomanga.com

AMAZING AGENT LUNA - VOLUME 2

File 07
FAMILY WEEK 6

File 08
UNEXPECTED ARRIVALS 33

File 09
BONDING 77

File 10
MEMORIES 129

LUNA'S FAMILY ALBUM 167

OMAKE 186

FAN ART 190

OPERATIONAL STATUS REPORT

FILE NO. 012-a

PORT PRODUCED AT	DATE PRODUCED	FILE PROCESSED BY	NATURE OF REPORT
OB - 05i2			[CLASSIFIED]

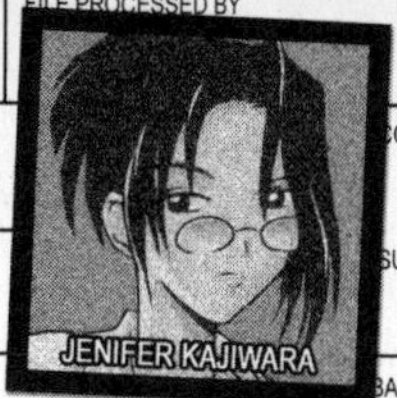
JENIFER KAJIWARA

ERATION

HIGH SCHOOL

CONTROL AGENT

Jennifer Kajiwara

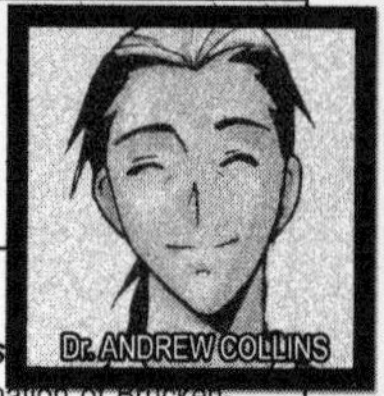
Dr. ANDREW COLLINS

ERATIVE

Agent Luna

SUPPORT AGENT

Dr. Andrew Collins

SION CATEGORY

ubset of **PROJECT LUNA** – a classified project in hich a girl was genetically engineered and raised to erve as the ultimate secret agent. There is currently nly one agent as a part of this project: Agent Luna, ow age 16.

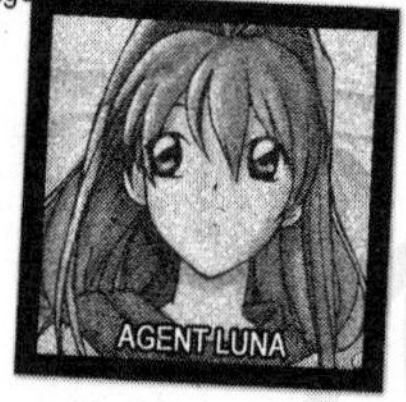
AGENT LUNA

BACKGROUND

Count Heinrich Von Brucken ***(s*** ***and photo)***, ruler of the rogue nation of Brucken-stein, has launched a new plan called Project Scion. His notes on this project contained detailed files on the student body of Nobel High. Nobel High is a private high school run by the United Nations. The students are the children of diplomats, leaders, and scientists from around the world.

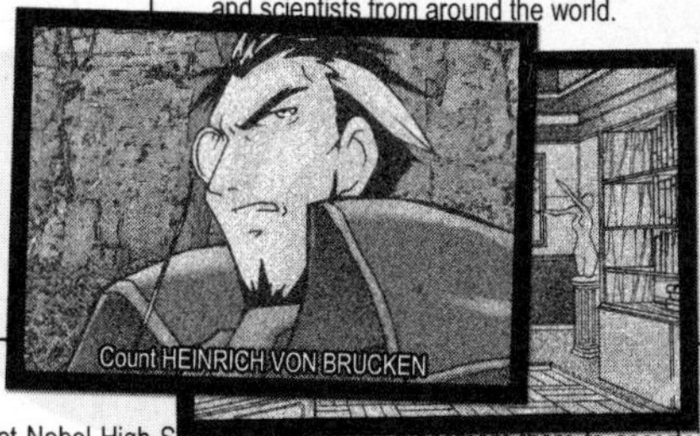
Count HEINRICH VON BRUCKEN

SION OBJECTIVE

Agent Luna is to pose as a new student at Nobel High School, and use her placement there to ascertain the objectives of Project Scion and thwart this Project if at all possible.

ONDARY OBJECTIVES

Concerns have been raised about Agent Luna's ability to function during adolescence. Having been genetically engineered and raised by the government, she has not been fully tested in an environment suited to her status as a teenager. Dr. Andrew Collins, a psychologist, has been assigned to assess her progress in this area.

ER

Agent Luna has been tasked to infiltrate the school as Luna Collins, daughter of Dr. Andrew Collins and Jennifer Kajiwara. Dr. Collins' story is factual, with his recent employment with the Agency kept out of his records. The background of Agent Kajiwara, Agent Luna's Control Agent, has been purged to list her as a secretary at the National Institute of Health.

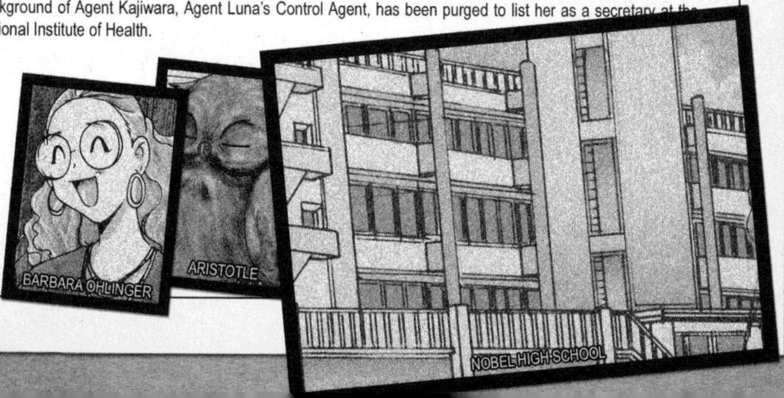
BARBARA OHLINGER
ARISTOTLE
NOBEL HIGH SCHOOL

VOLUME 002

OPERATIONAL STATUS REPORT

FILE NO.

REPORT PRODUCED AT	DATE PRODUCED	FILE PROCESSED BY	NATURE OF REPORT
OB - 05i2		Jennifer Kajiwara	[CLASSIFIED

OPERATIONAL STATUS

Agent Luna has successfully infiltrated the school and is considered a normal teenage girl by the faculty there She has been accepted as a new student by Principal Barbara Ohlinger ***(see attached file and photo)*** and he many teachers. She has had clashes with physical education teacher Mark Dreyfus ***(see attached file anc photo)***. Dreyfus' background is attached – his record is clean, and his problems with Luna are not related tc Project Scion, though if she continues to draw his ire, we may be at risk of Dreyfus discovering her secret.

On the primary objective, Luna has uncovered elements of Project Scion, but not the larger picture. Although we still don't know why the Count had files on many of the students at Nobel High, we are still very much convincec that his Project Scion has something to do with the school. Our suspicions were further increased when we discovered his son Jonah Von Brucken ***(see attached file and photo)*** was recently enrolled there as a student

Additionally, Luna's science teacher Dr. Talia Warren ***(see attached file and photo)***, has been exposed as a agent of Bruckenstein. Her actions are harder to explain than her loyalties, however. Warren kidnapped Aristotle the school mascot owl ***(see attached file and photo)***, and made genetic duplicates. In an attempt to give then heightened strength, Warren made the owls larger than the original, though Agent Luna reports that this was a side effect Warren had hoped to fix. Luna rescued the owl, captured the duplicates, raided Warren's lab, and gc the rogue scientist arrested.

However, in the wake of Warren's arrest, she was replaced by Professor Yves Tromperie ***(see attached file an photo)***, a known associate of Von Brucken's, who has been hired by the Count to work on Project Scion Obviously, this work continues and Project Scion is still a threat. Warren has yet to reveal the details of Scion and we have no intel of Tromperie's objectives since his arrival at the school. We are continuing to monitor him

On our secondary objective, Dr. Andrew Collins (I feel the need to restate my protestations about his assignmer to the case) initially had some reservations about Luna's ability to deal with high school. However, he is please to see she has made several friends – Francesca Aldana and Oliver Riggs ***(see attached files and photos,*** He also notes that she has even made a school rival in Elizabeth Westbrook ***(see attached file and photo)***. fail to see why this is worthy of note (or why this secondary objective is part of the mission parameters at all), bu he tells me it merely indicates that Luna is experiencing all aspects of teenage life and that in the long run this i beneficial to her development.

We do believe that Luna's continued presence at Nobel High will prove useful. She has developed th beginnings of a bond with Jonah Von Brucken and I believe a continued association might provide us with som clues about what Count Von Brucken has planned next. While I am concerned about the risk of emotiona considerations jeopardizing her objectivity in dealing with the son of our enemy, I feel this has the potential t lead us to greater intel on Von Brucken and Project Scion.

In short, I conclude the operation merits continuation and Luna be kept undercover at Nobel High.

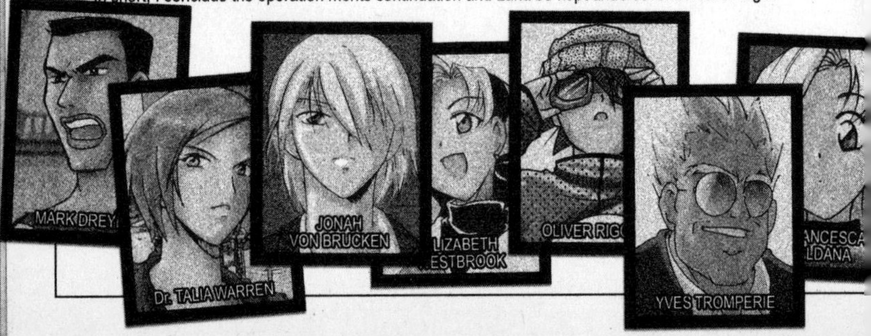
MARK DREY
JONAH VON BRUCKEN
LIZABETH ESTBROOK
OLIVER RIGG
ANCESCA LDANA
Dr. TALIA WARREN
YVES TROMPERIE

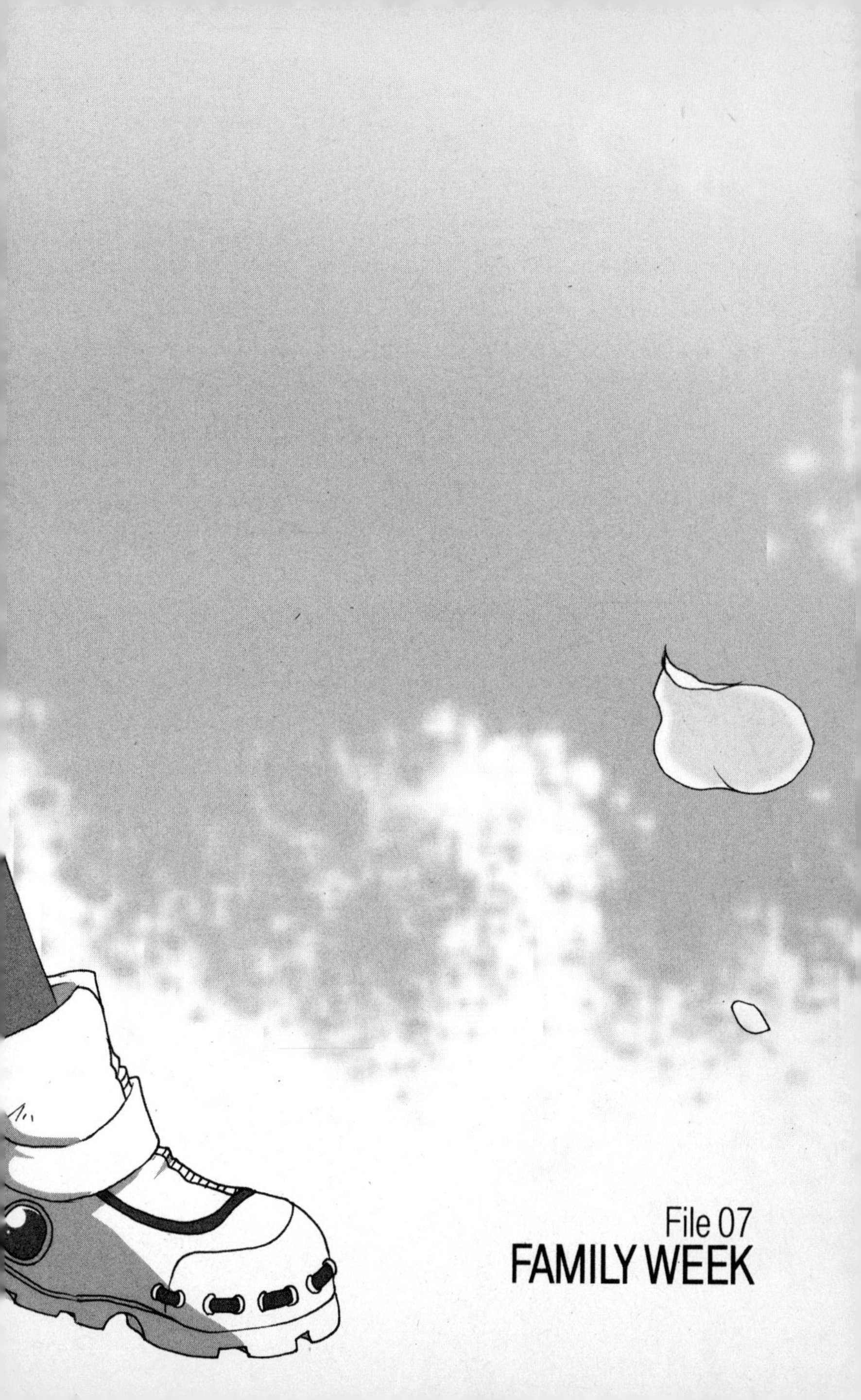
File 07
FAMILY WEEK

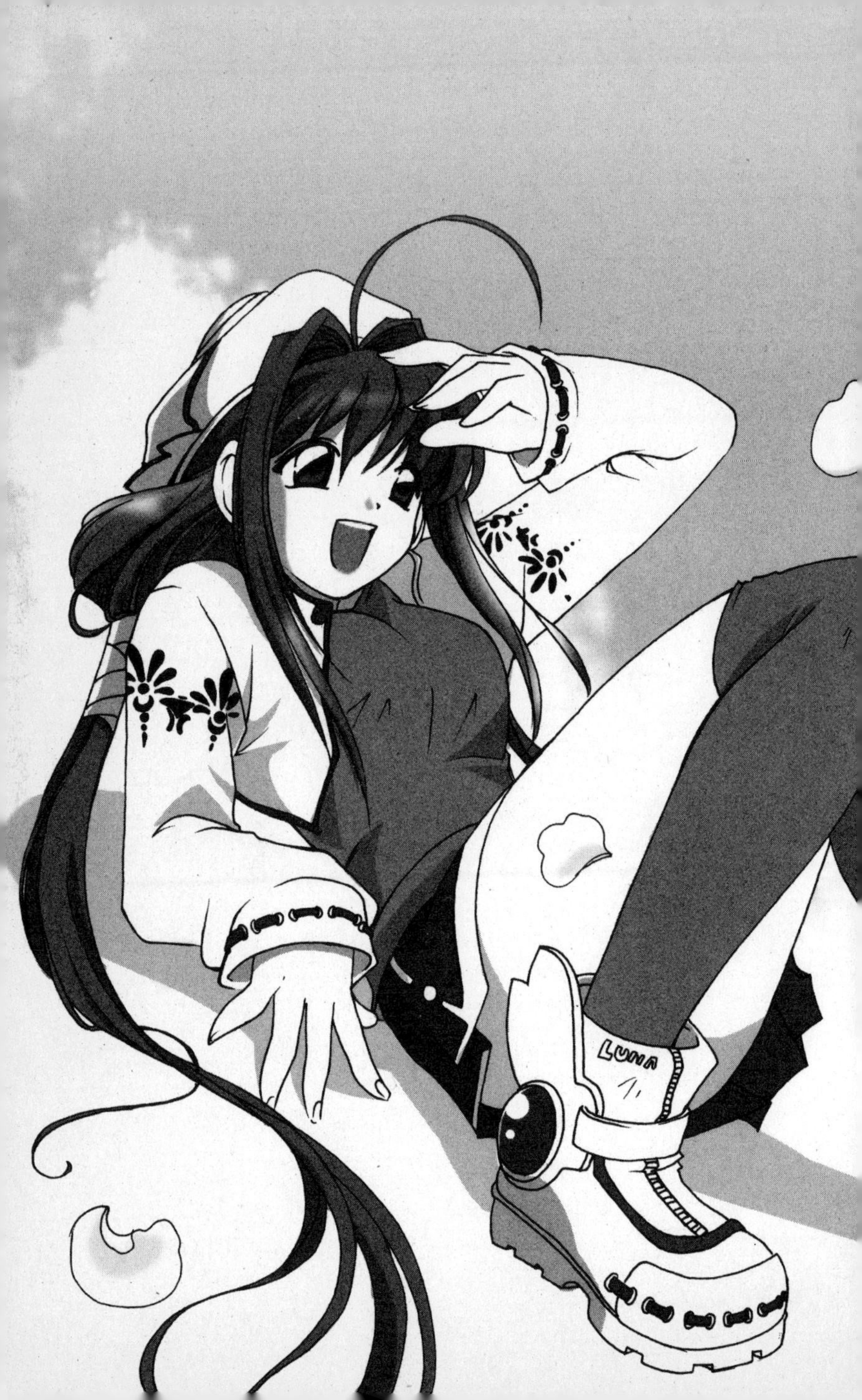
LUNA

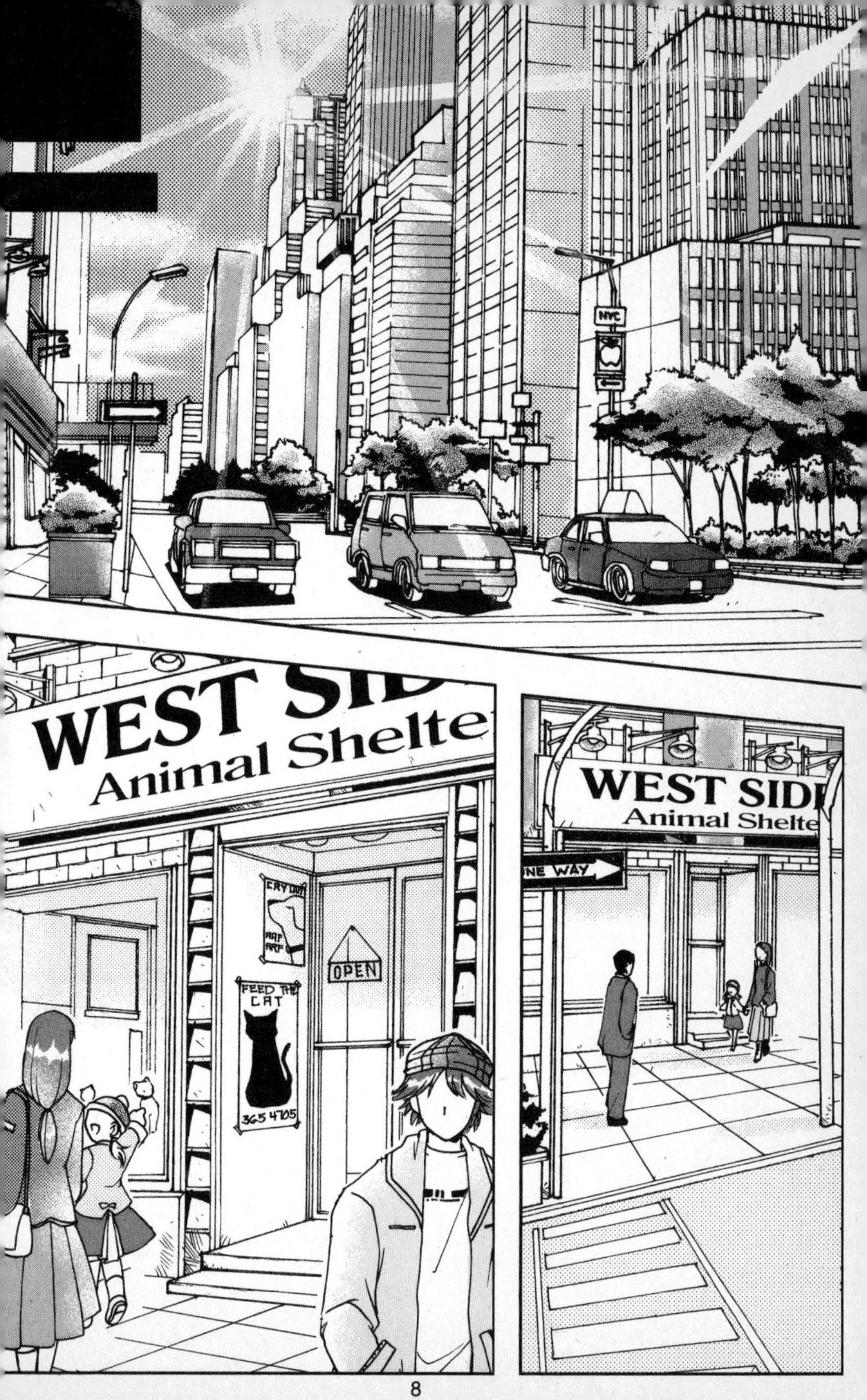
[redacted]
NYC
WEST SID
Animal Shelte
NE WAY
WEST SID
Animal Shelte
CRY OUT
ARF ARF
OPEN
FEED THE CAT
365 4705

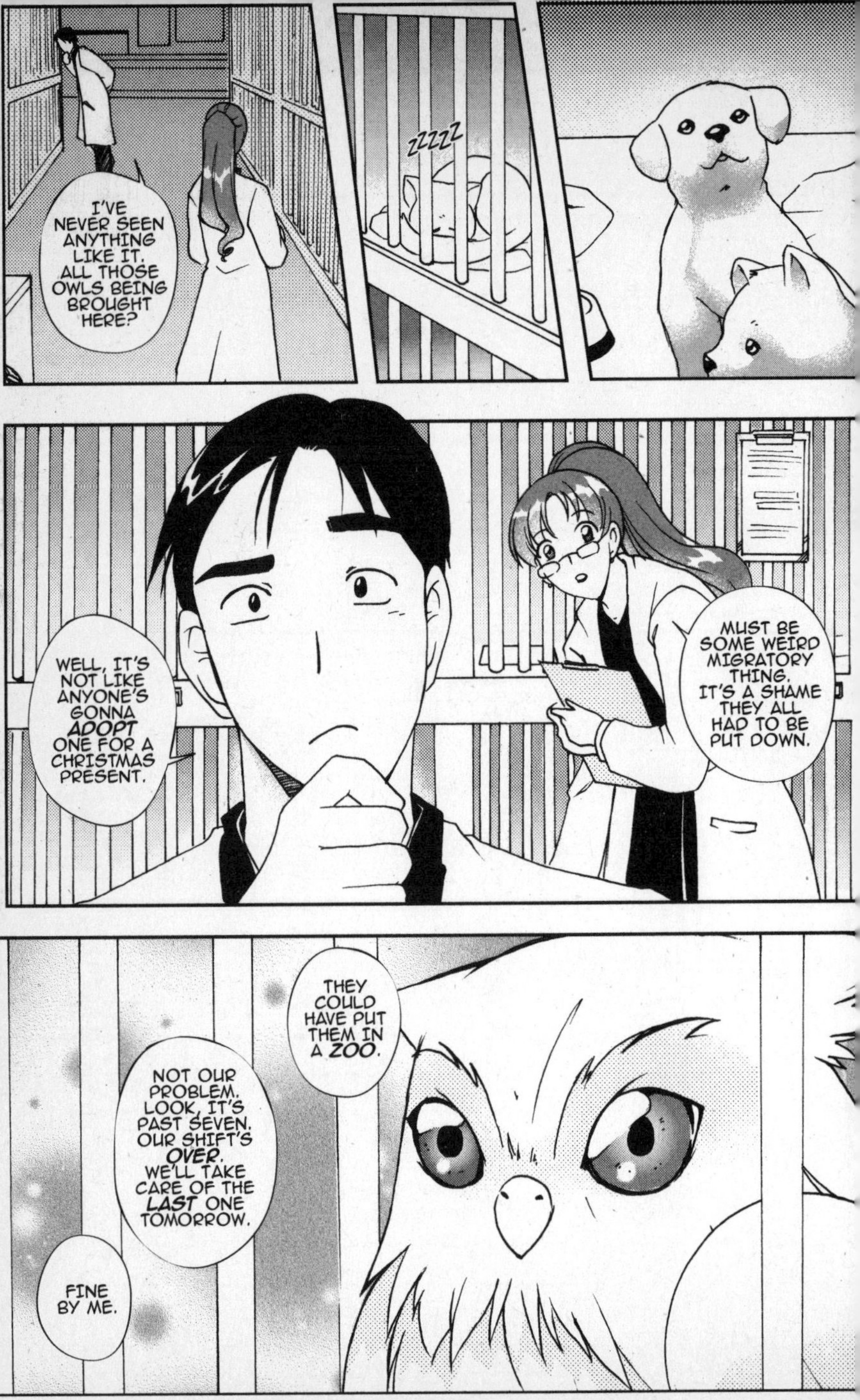
ZZZZZ
I'VE NEVER SEEN ANYTHING LIKE IT. ALL THOSE OWLS BEING BROUGHT HERE?
MUST BE SOME WEIRD MIGRATORY THING. IT'S A SHAME THEY ALL HAD TO BE PUT DOWN.
WELL, IT'S NOT LIKE ANYONE'S GONNA ADOPT ONE FOR A CHRISTMAS PRESENT.
THEY COULD HAVE PUT THEM IN A ZOO.
NOT OUR PROBLEM. LOOK, IT'S PAST SEVEN. OUR SHIFT'S OVER. WE'LL TAKE CARE OF THE LAST ONE TOMORROW.
FINE BY ME.

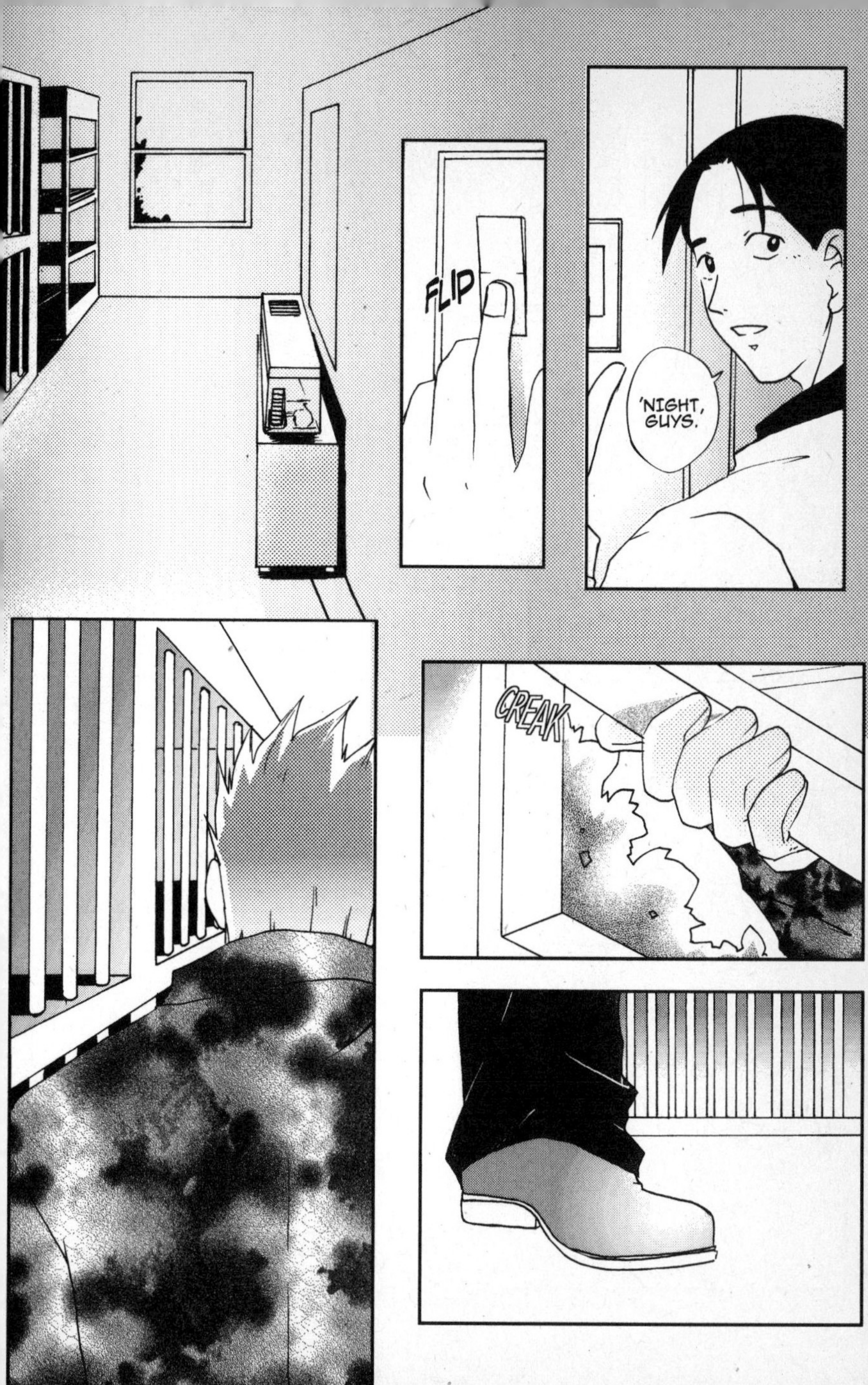
'NIGHT, GUYS.'
FLIP
CREAK

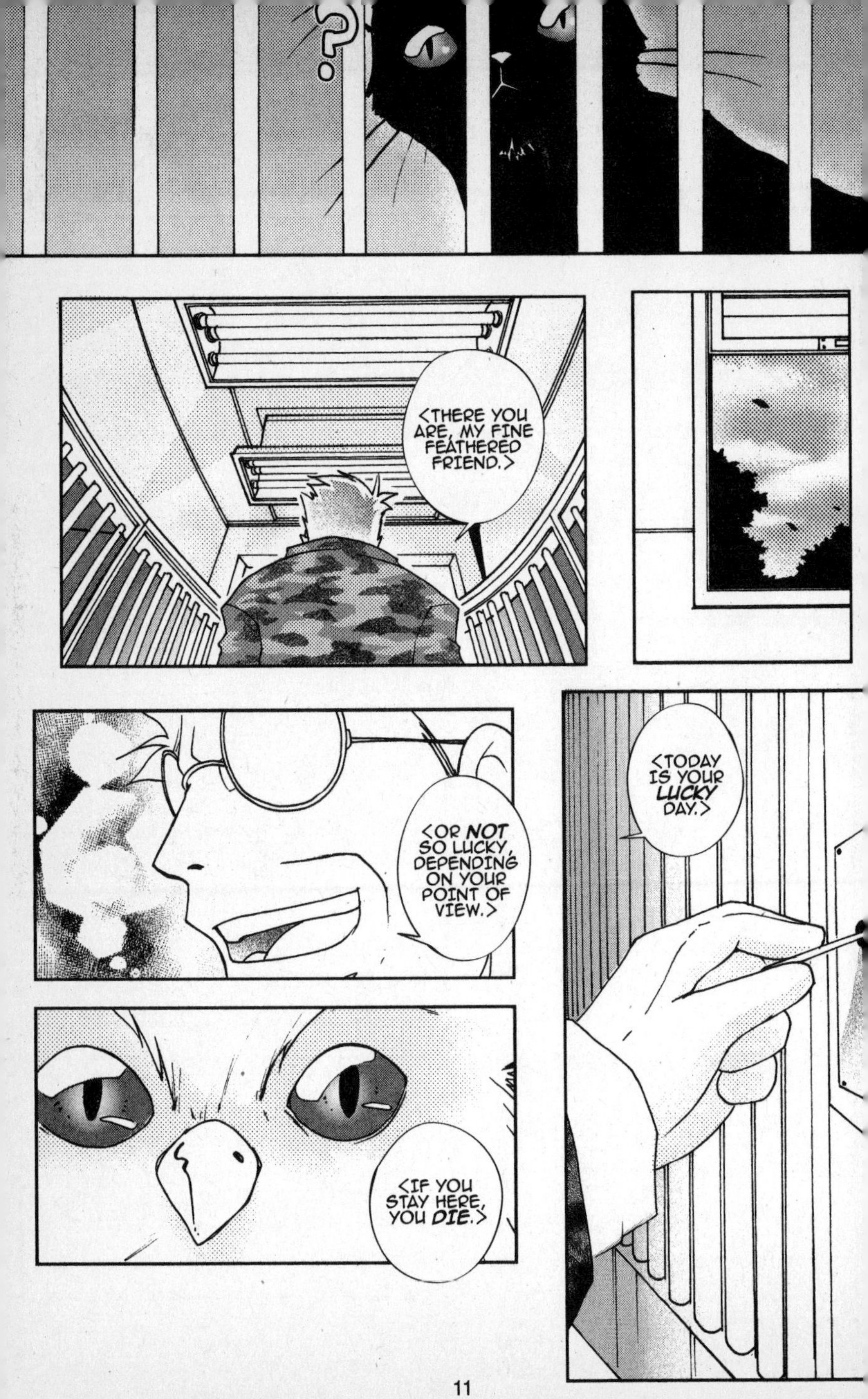
?
<THERE YOU ARE, MY FINE FEATHERED FRIEND.>
<TODAY IS YOUR LUCKY DAY.>
<OR NOT SO LUCKY, DEPENDING ON YOUR POINT OF VIEW.>
<IF YOU STAY HERE, YOU DIE.>

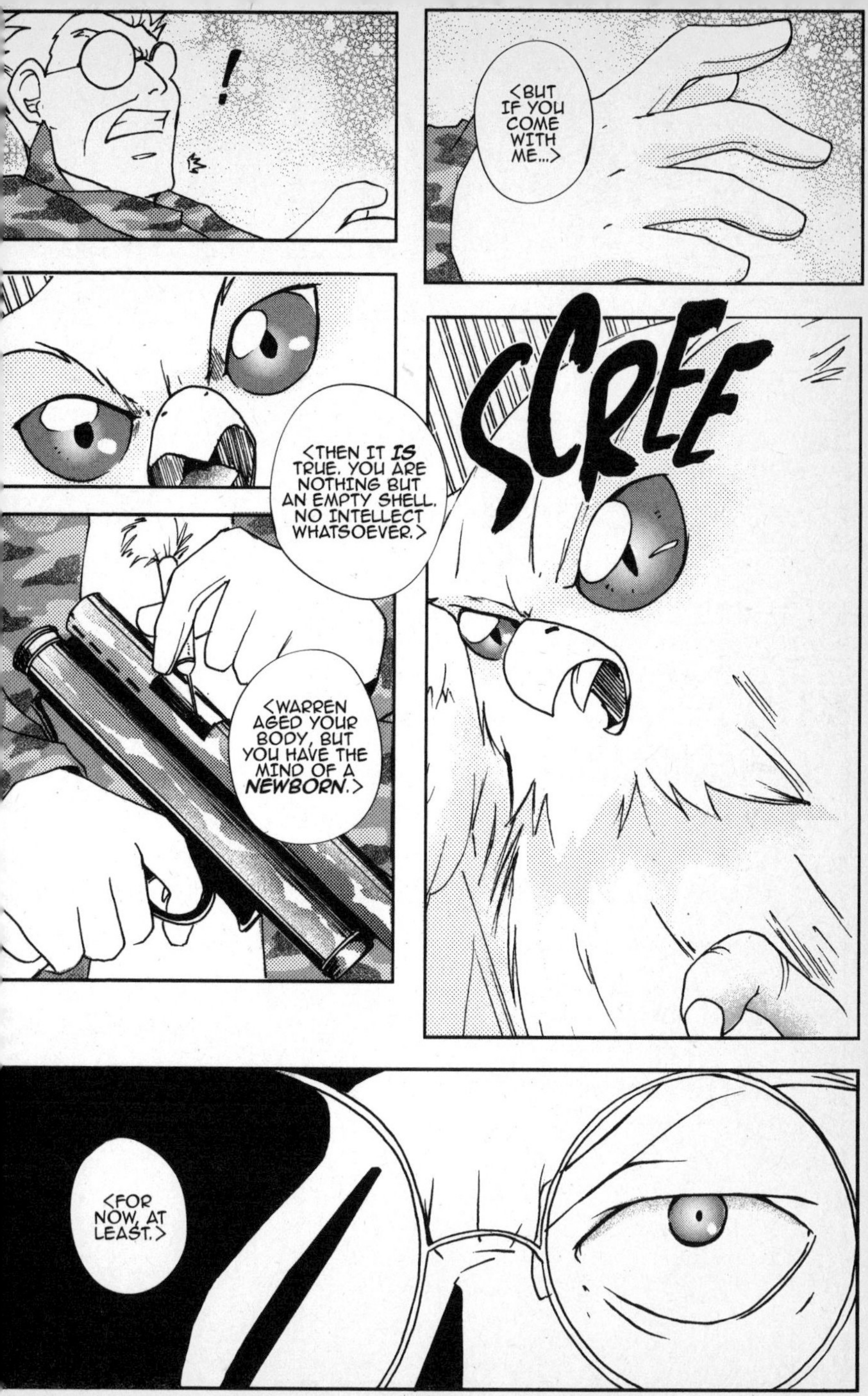

<BUT IF YOU COME WITH ME...>
!
SCREE
<THEN IT IS TRUE. YOU ARE NOTHING BUT AN EMPTY SHELL. NO INTELLECT WHATSOEVER.>
<WARREN AGED YOUR BODY, BUT YOU HAVE THE MIND OF A NEWBORN.>
<FOR NOW, AT LEAST.>

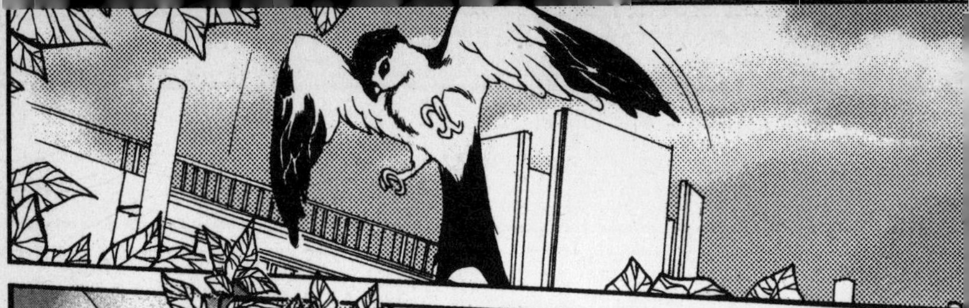

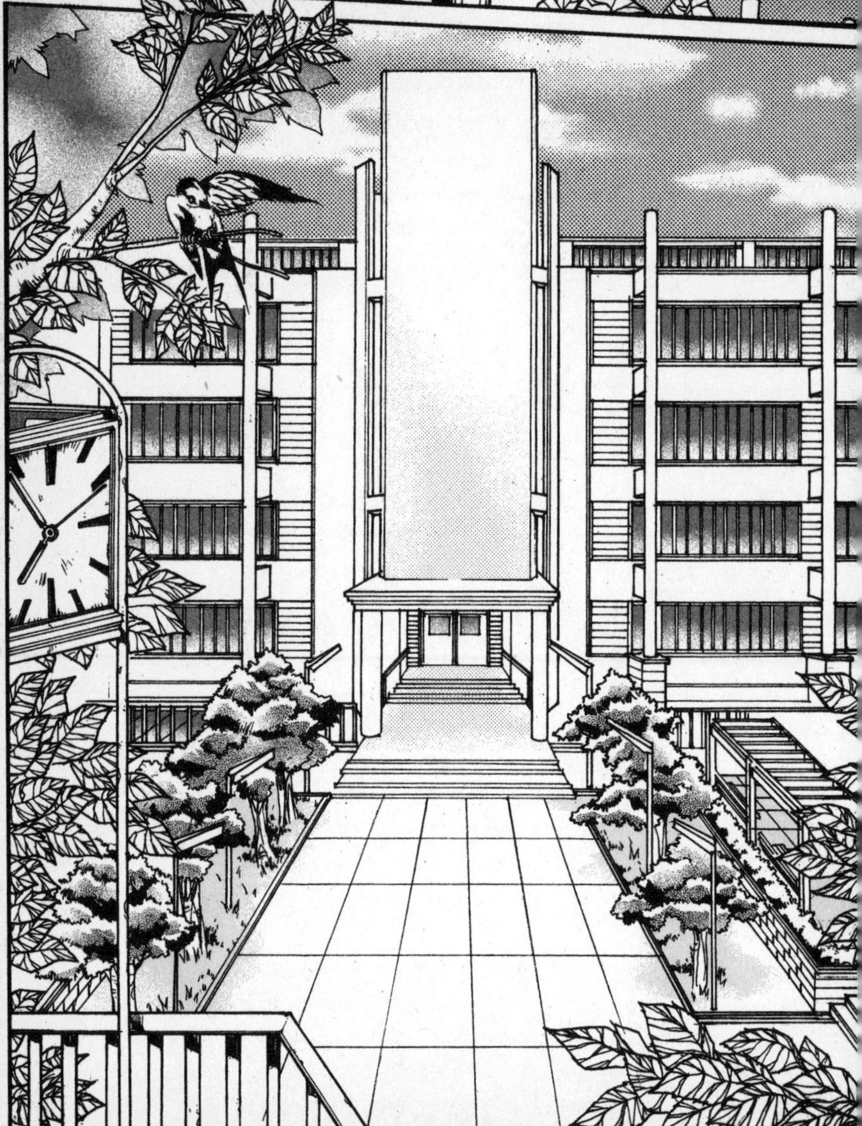

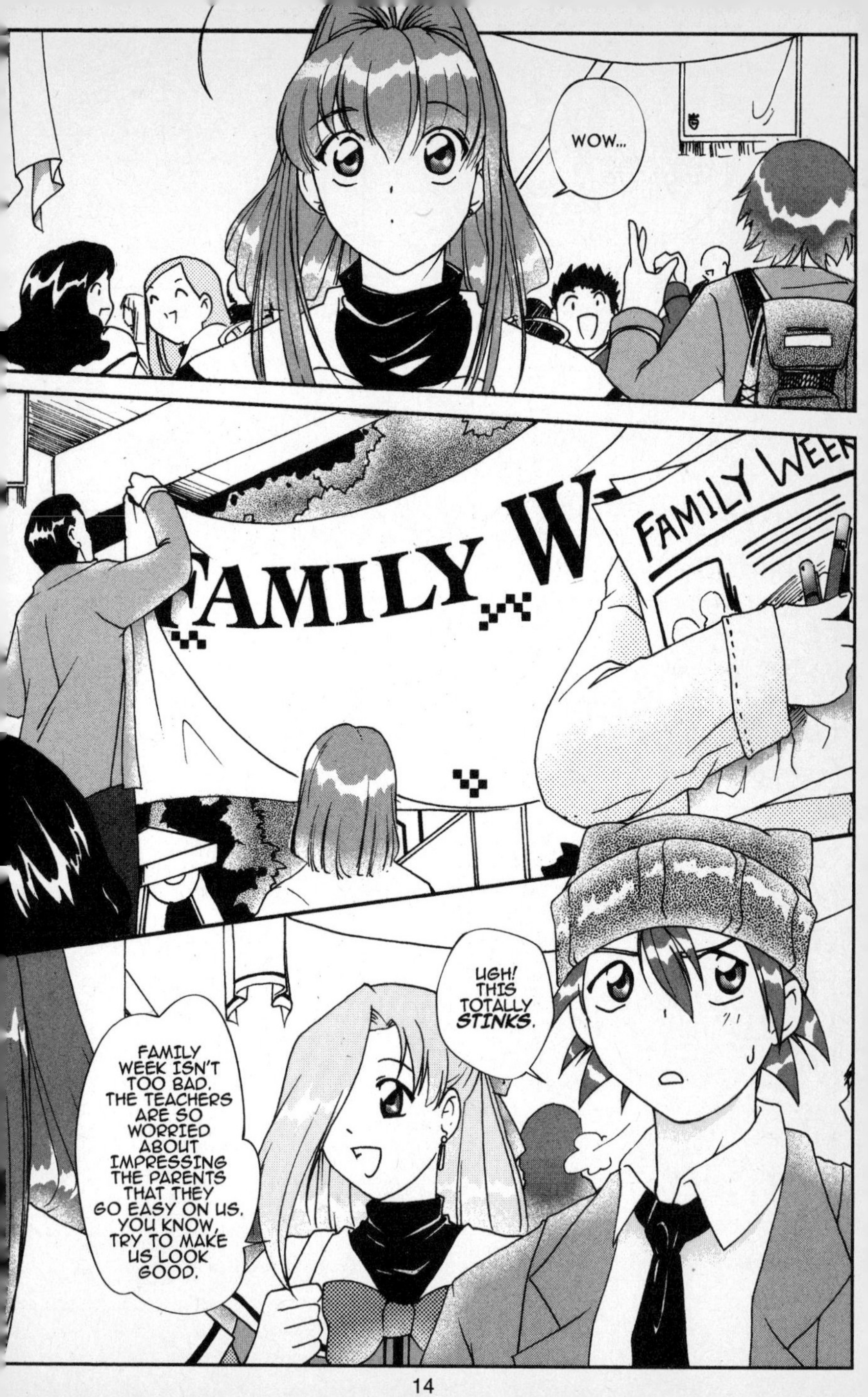
WOW...
FAMILY WEE
FAMILY
FAMILY W
UGH! THIS TOTALLY **STINKS**.
FAMILY WEEK ISN'T TOO BAD. THE TEACHERS ARE SO WORRIED ABOUT IMPRESSING THE PARENTS THAT THEY GO EASY ON US. YOU KNOW, TRY TO MAKE US LOOK GOOD.

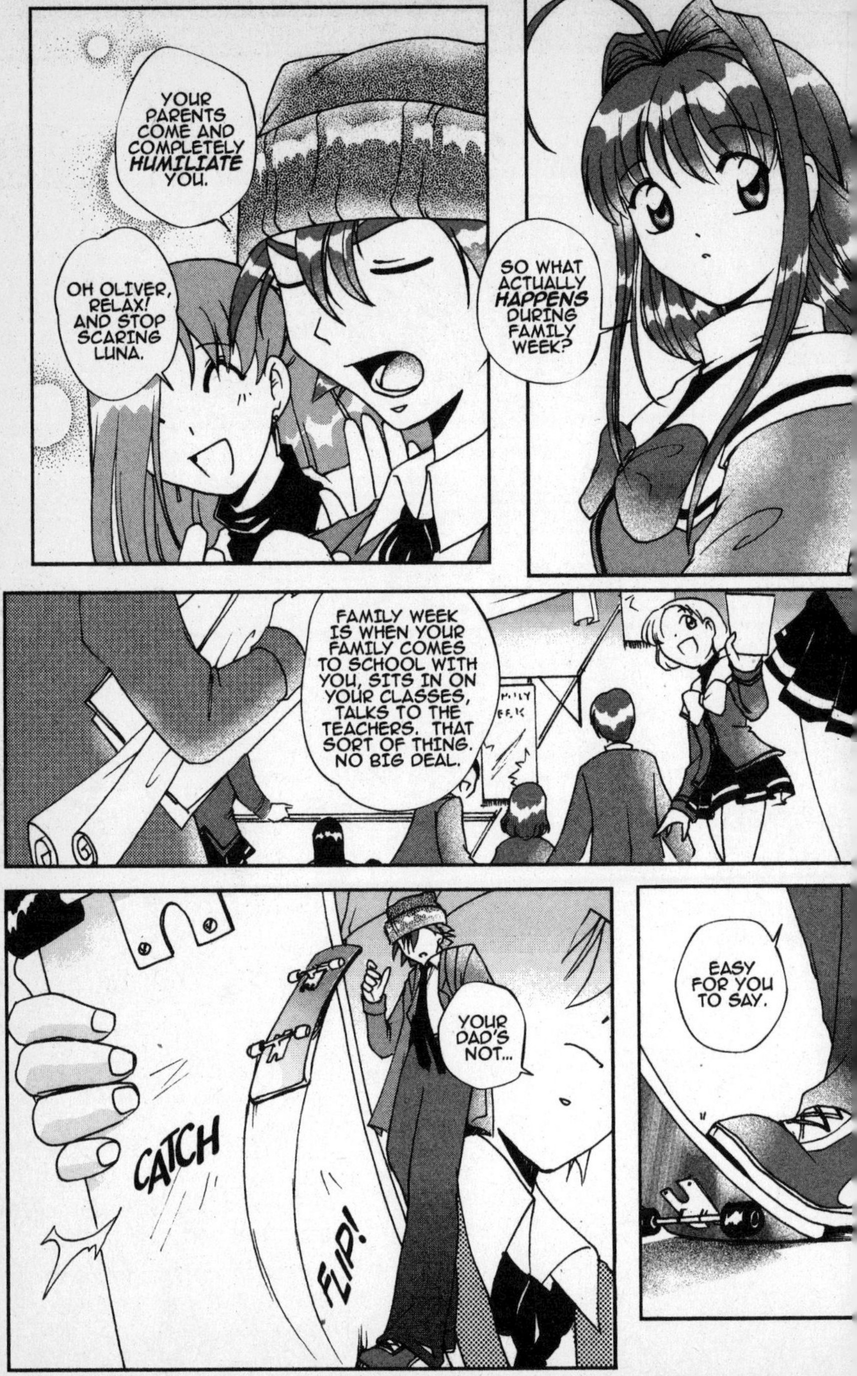
SO WHAT ACTUALLY **HAPPENS** DURING FAMILY WEEK?
YOUR PARENTS COME AND COMPLETELY ***HUMILIATE*** YOU.
OH OLIVER, RELAX! AND STOP SCARING LUNA.
FAMILY WEEK IS WHEN YOUR FAMILY COMES TO SCHOOL WITH YOU, SITS IN ON YOUR CLASSES, TALKS TO THE TEACHERS. THAT SORT OF THING. NO BIG DEAL.
EASY FOR YOU TO SAY.
YOUR DAD'S NOT...
CATCH
FLIP!

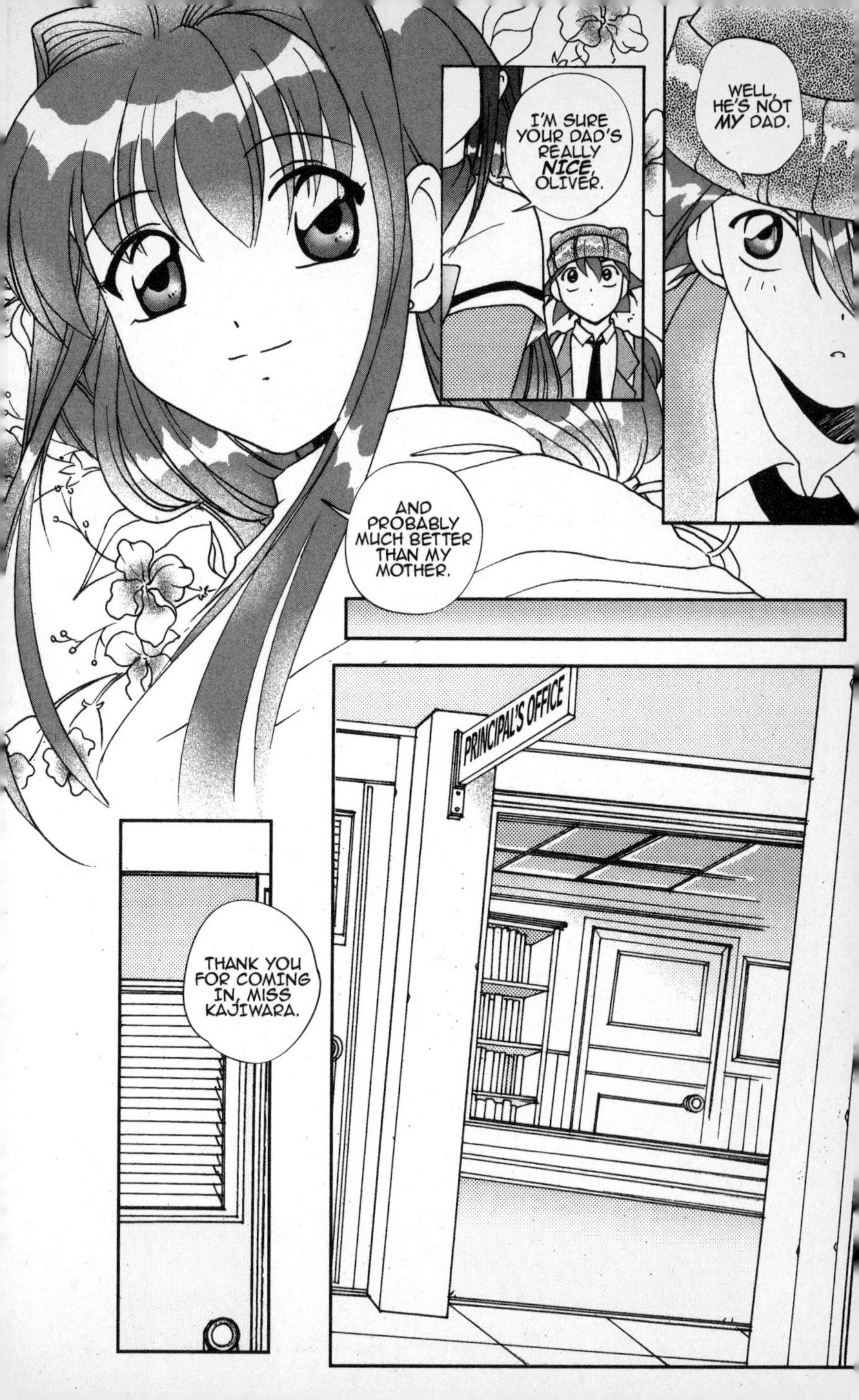
I'M SURE YOUR DAD'S REALLY NICE, OLIVER.
WELL, HE'S NOT MY DAD.
AND PROBABLY MUCH BETTER THAN MY MOTHER.
THANK YOU FOR COMING IN, MISS KAJIWARA.
PRINCIPAL'S OFFICE

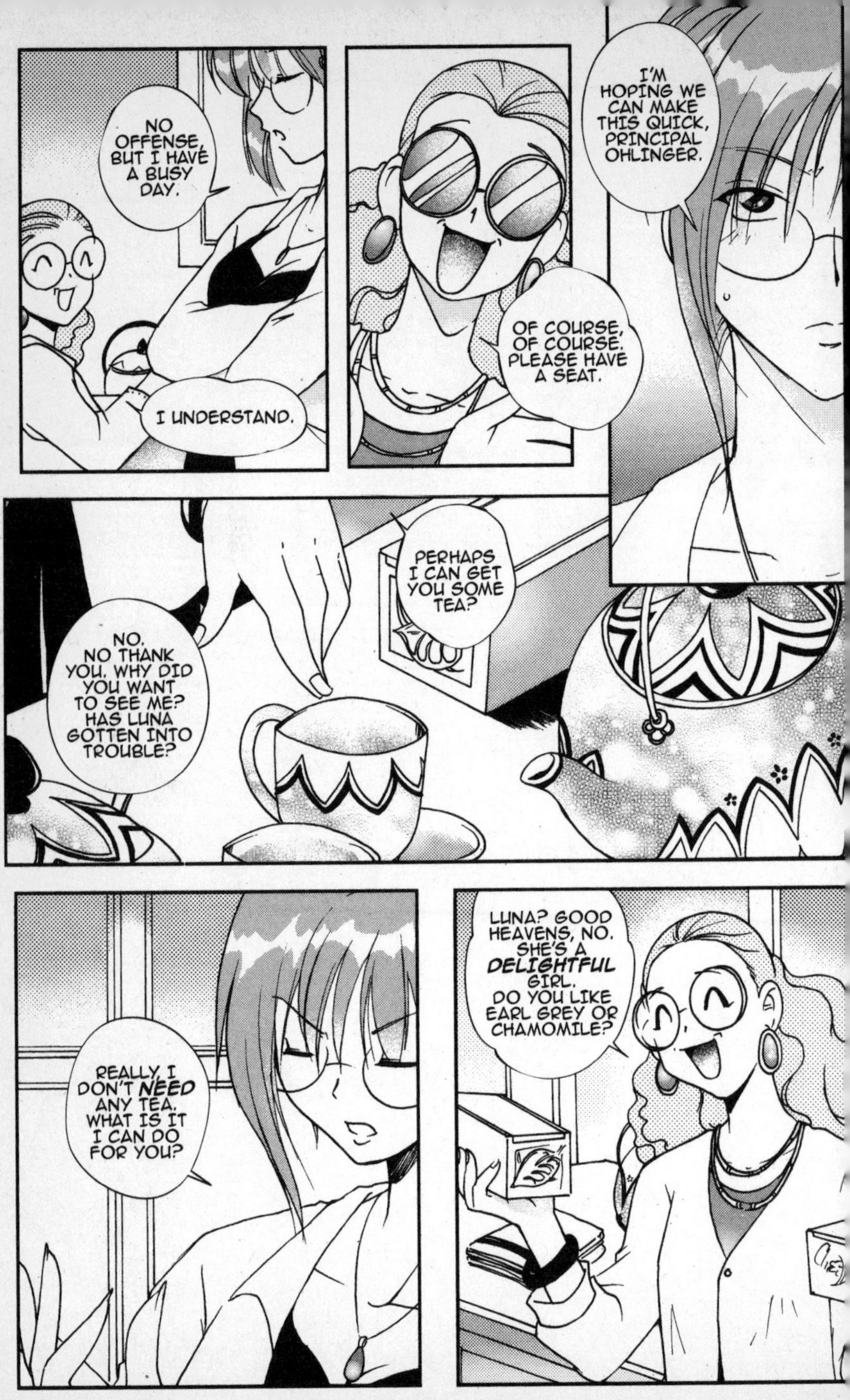
I'M HOPING WE CAN MAKE THIS QUICK, PRINCIPAL OHLINGER.
OF COURSE, OF COURSE. PLEASE HAVE A SEAT.
NO OFFENSE, BUT I HAVE A BUSY DAY.
I UNDERSTAND.
PERHAPS I CAN GET YOU SOME TEA?
NO. NO THANK YOU. WHY DID YOU WANT TO SEE ME? HAS LUNA GOTTEN INTO TROUBLE?
LUNA? GOOD HEAVENS, NO. SHE'S A ***DELIGHTFUL*** GIRL. DO YOU LIKE EARL GREY OR CHAMOMILE?
REALLY, I DON'T ***NEED*** ANY TEA. WHAT IS IT I CAN DO FOR YOU?

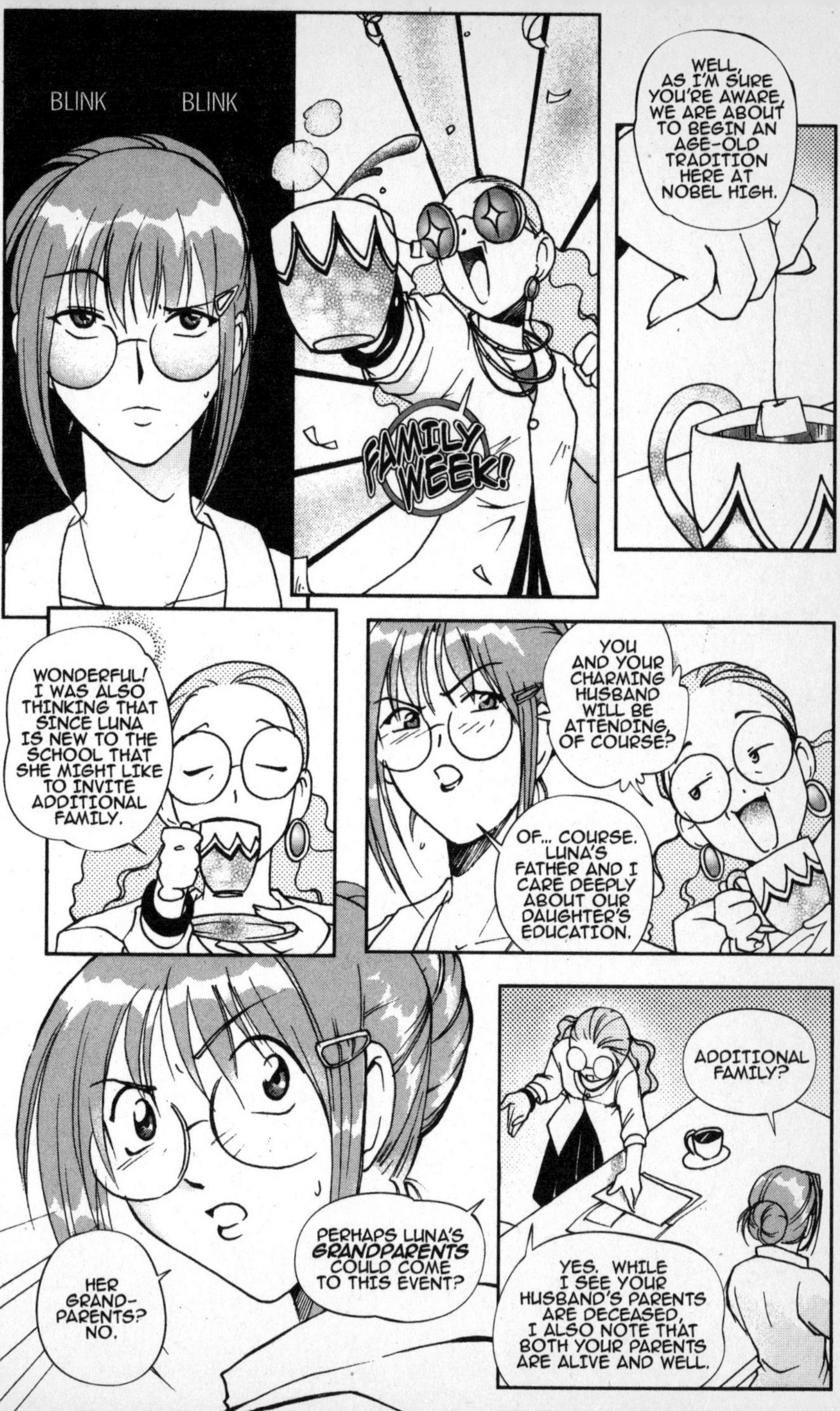
WELL, AS I'M SURE YOU'RE AWARE, WE ARE ABOUT TO BEGIN AN AGE-OLD TRADITION HERE AT NOBEL HIGH.
FAMILY WEEK!
BLINK
BLINK
YOU AND YOUR CHARMING HUSBAND WILL BE ATTENDING, OF COURSE?
OF... COURSE. LUNA'S FATHER AND I CARE DEEPLY ABOUT OUR DAUGHTER'S EDUCATION.
WONDERFUL! I WAS ALSO THINKING THAT SINCE LUNA IS NEW TO THE SCHOOL THAT SHE MIGHT LIKE TO INVITE ADDITIONAL FAMILY.
ADDITIONAL FAMILY?
YES. WHILE I SEE YOUR HUSBAND'S PARENTS ARE DECEASED, I ALSO NOTE THAT BOTH YOUR PARENTS ARE ALIVE AND WELL.
PERHAPS LUNA'S ***GRANDPARENTS*** COULD COME TO THIS EVENT?
HER GRAND-PARENTS? NO.

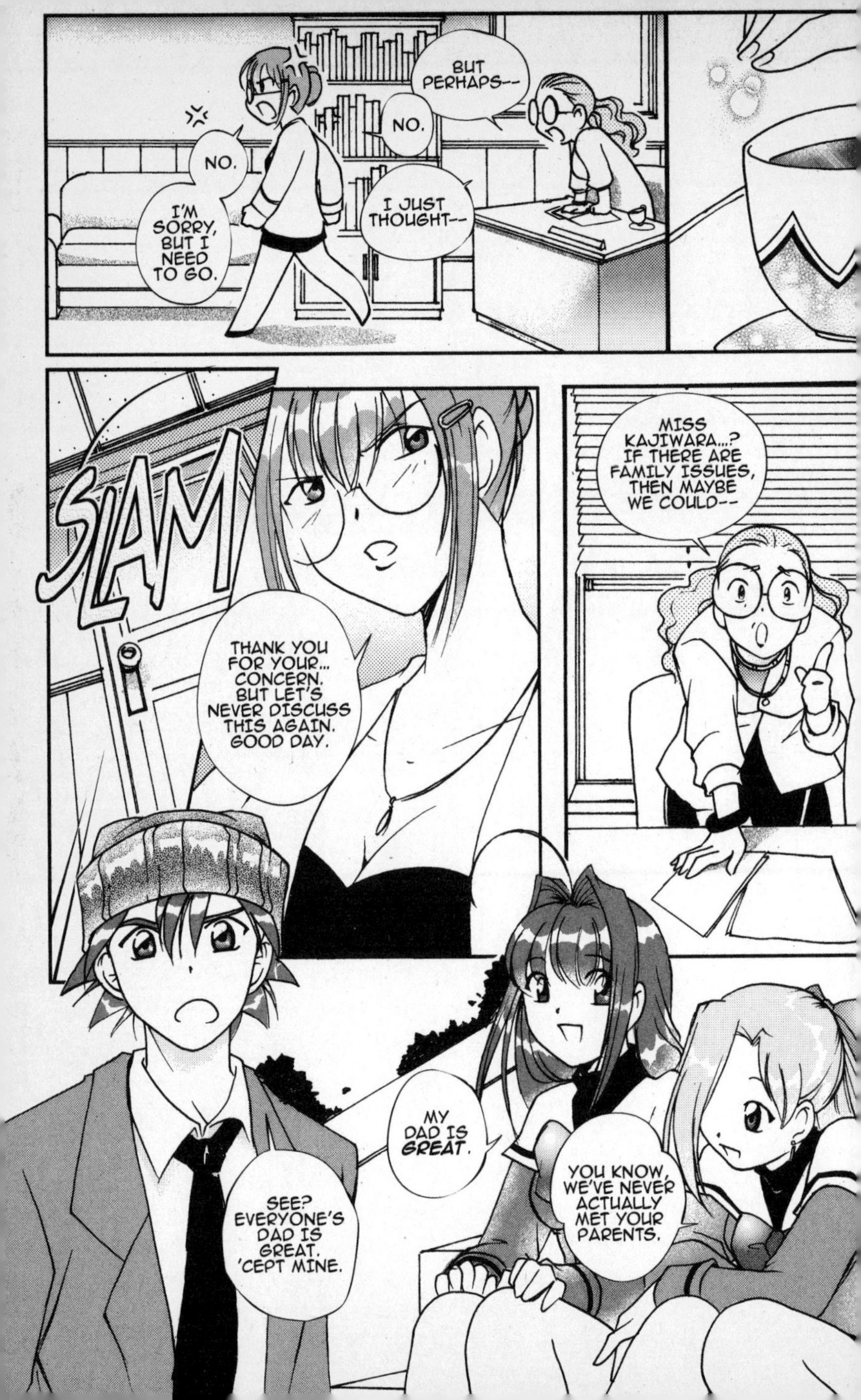
BUT PERHAPS--
NO.
I JUST THOUGHT--
NO.
I'M SORRY, BUT I NEED TO GO.
MISS KAJIWARA...? IF THERE ARE FAMILY ISSUES, THEN MAYBE WE COULD--
SLAM
THANK YOU FOR YOUR... CONCERN. BUT LET'S NEVER DISCUSS THIS AGAIN. GOOD DAY.
YOU KNOW, WE'VE NEVER ACTUALLY MET YOUR PARENTS.
MY DAD IS *GREAT*.
SEE? EVERYONE'S DAD IS GREAT. 'CEPT MINE.

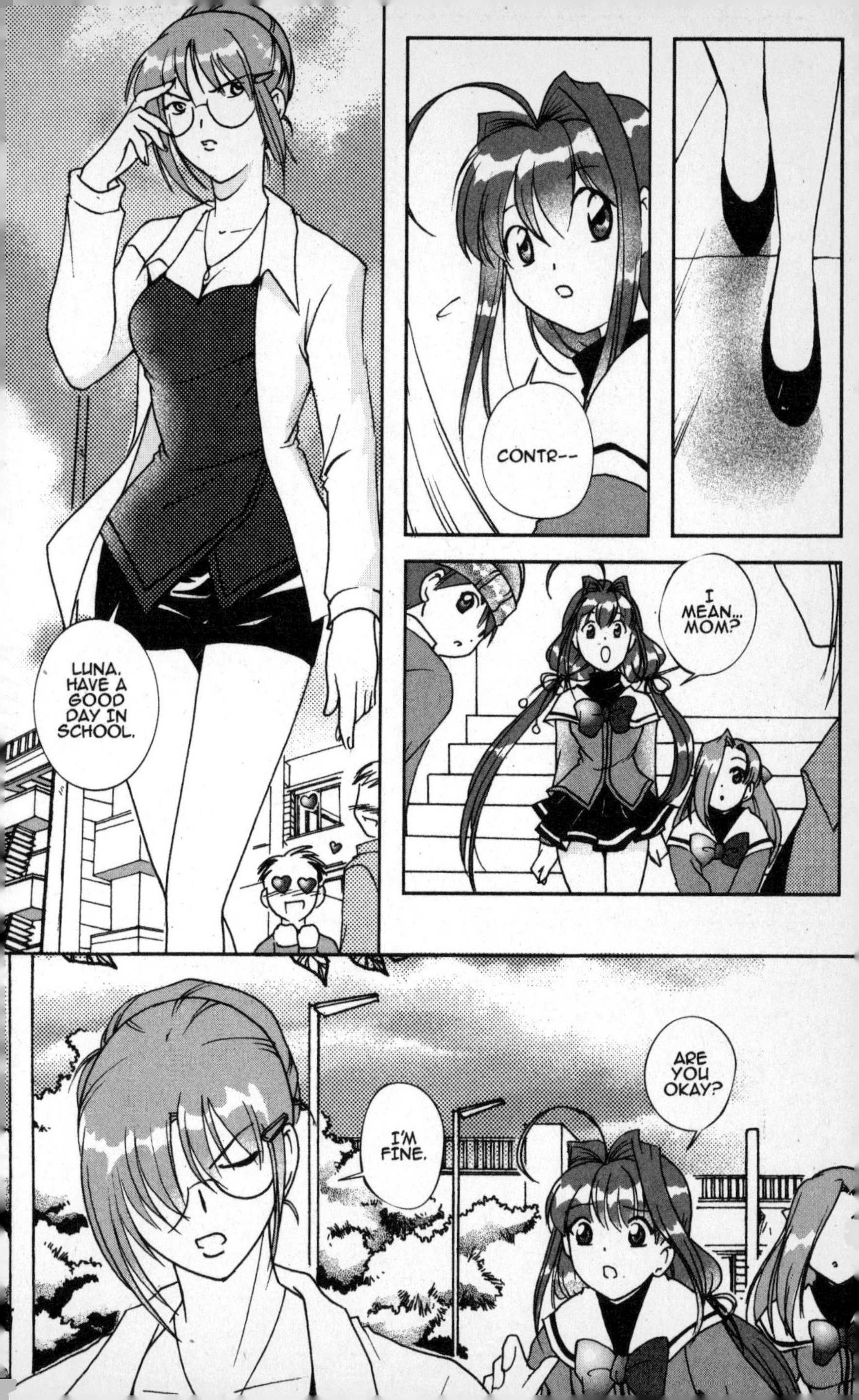
CONTR--
I MEAN... MOM?
LUNA, HAVE A GOOD DAY IN SCHOOL.
ARE YOU OKAY?
I'M FINE.

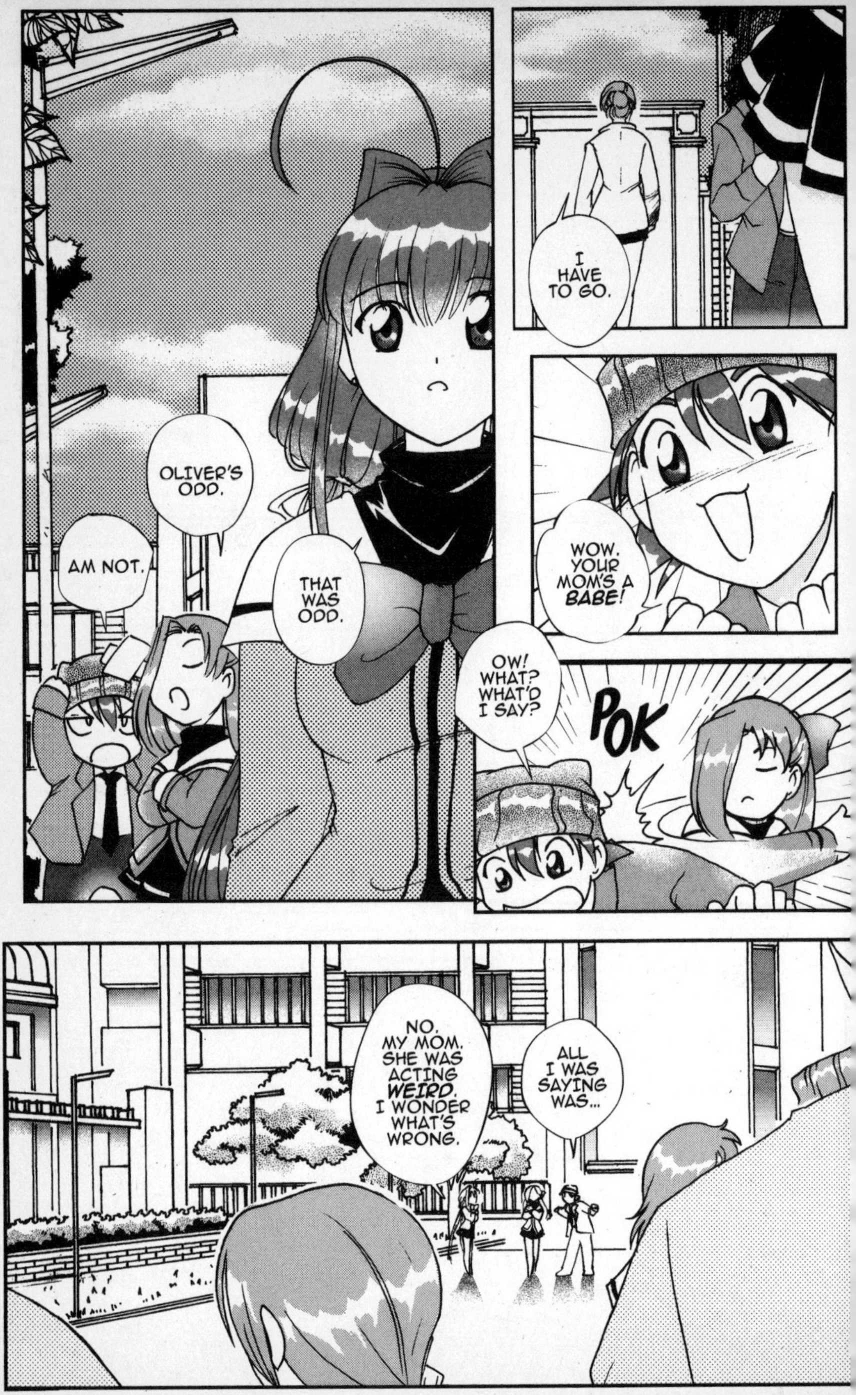
I HAVE TO GO.
WOW. YOUR MOM'S A BABE!
OW! WHAT? WHAT'D I SAY?
POK
THAT WAS ODD.
OLIVER'S ODD.
AM NOT.
ALL I WAS SAYING WAS...
NO. MY MOM. SHE WAS ACTING WEIRD. I WONDER WHAT'S WRONG.

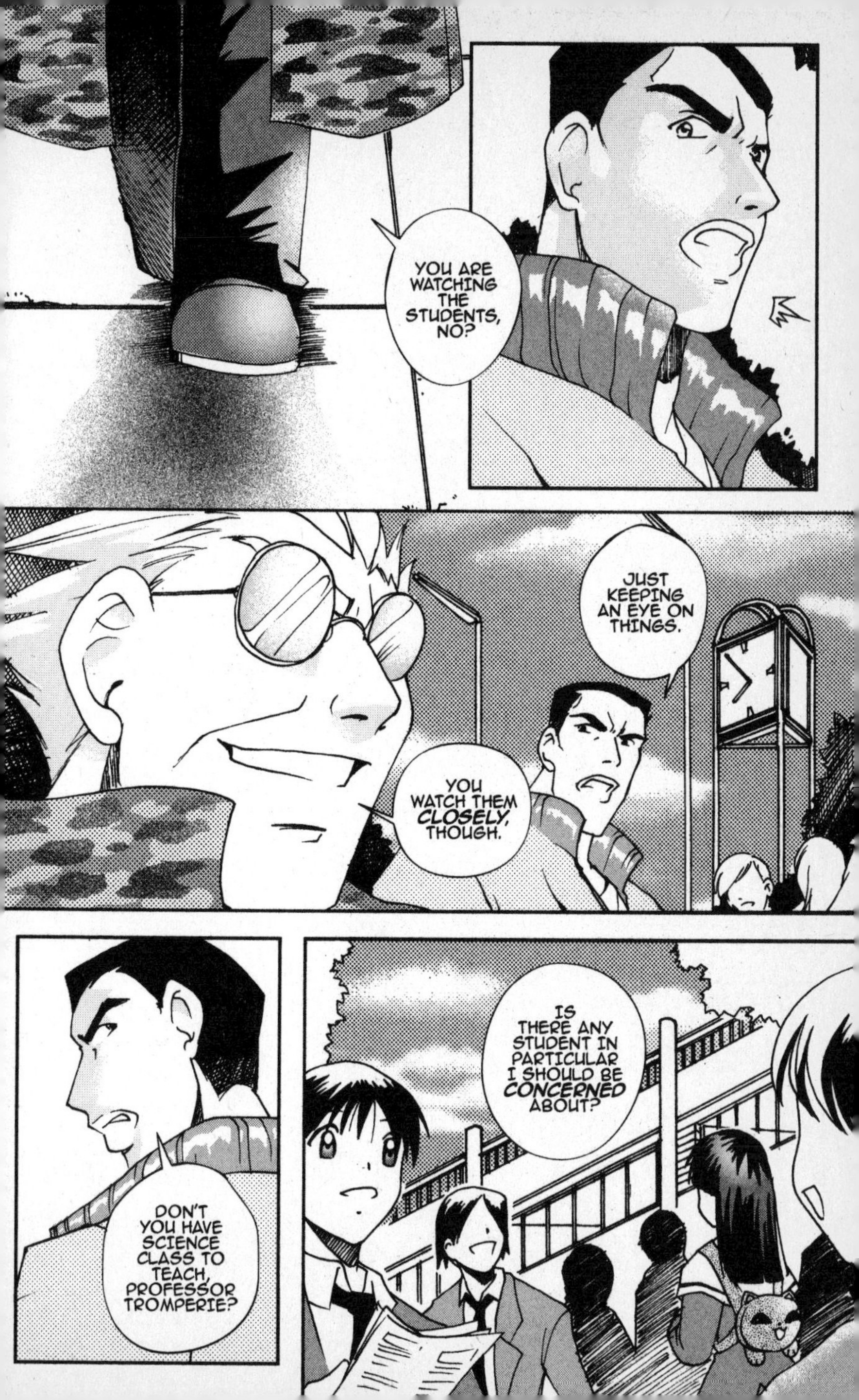
YOU ARE WATCHING THE STUDENTS, NO?
JUST KEEPING AN EYE ON THINGS.
YOU WATCH THEM *CLOSELY*, THOUGH.
IS THERE ANY STUDENT IN PARTICULAR I SHOULD BE *CONCERNED* ABOUT?
DON'T YOU HAVE SCIENCE CLASS TO TEACH, PROFESSOR TROMPERIE?

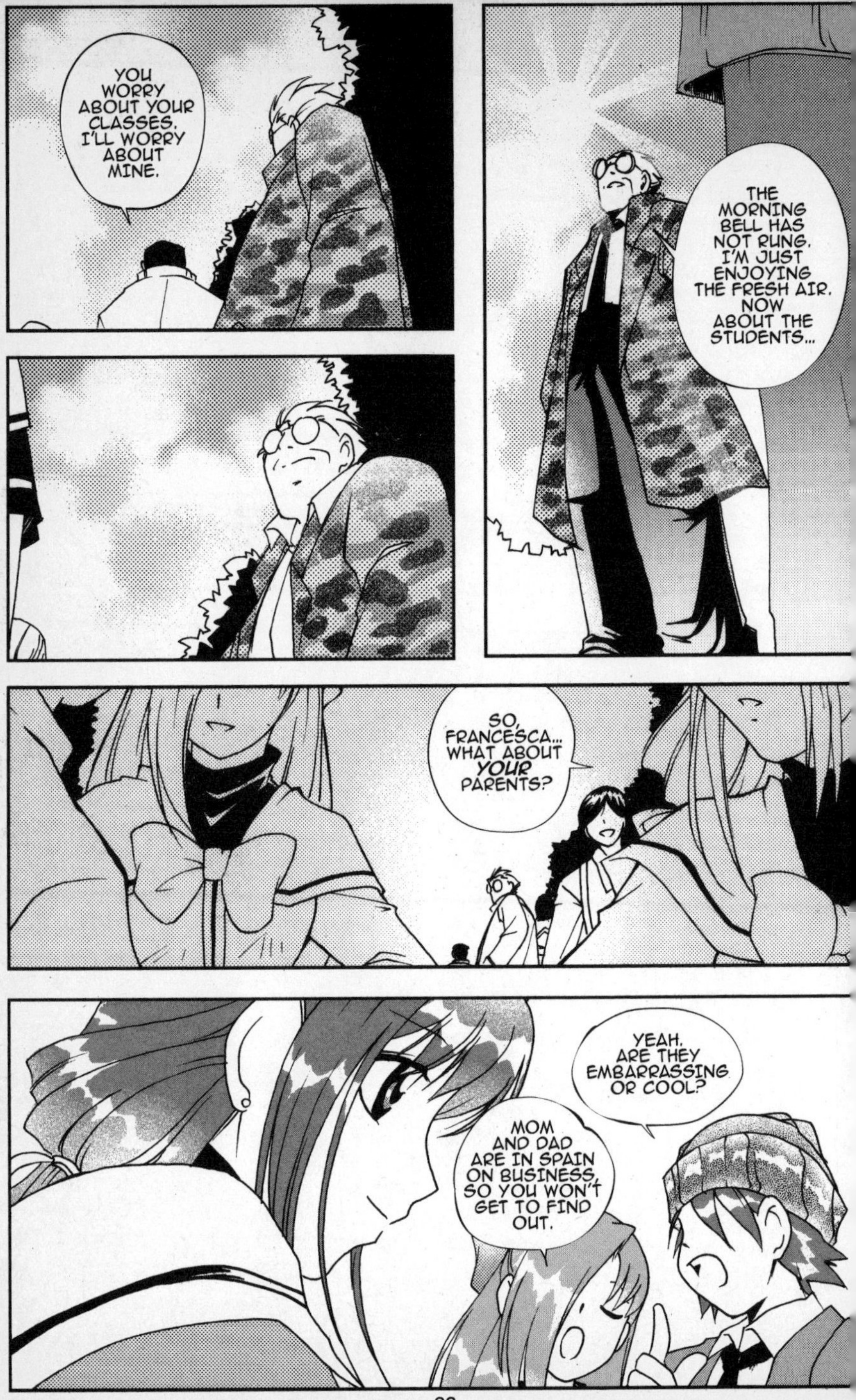
THE MORNING BELL HAS NOT RUNG. I'M JUST ENJOYING THE FRESH AIR. NOW ABOUT THE STUDENTS...
YOU WORRY ABOUT YOUR CLASSES. I'LL WORRY ABOUT MINE.
SO, FRANCESCA... WHAT ABOUT *YOUR* PARENTS?
YEAH. ARE THEY EMBARRASSING OR COOL?
MOM AND DAD ARE IN SPAIN ON BUSINESS, SO YOU WON'T GET TO FIND OUT.

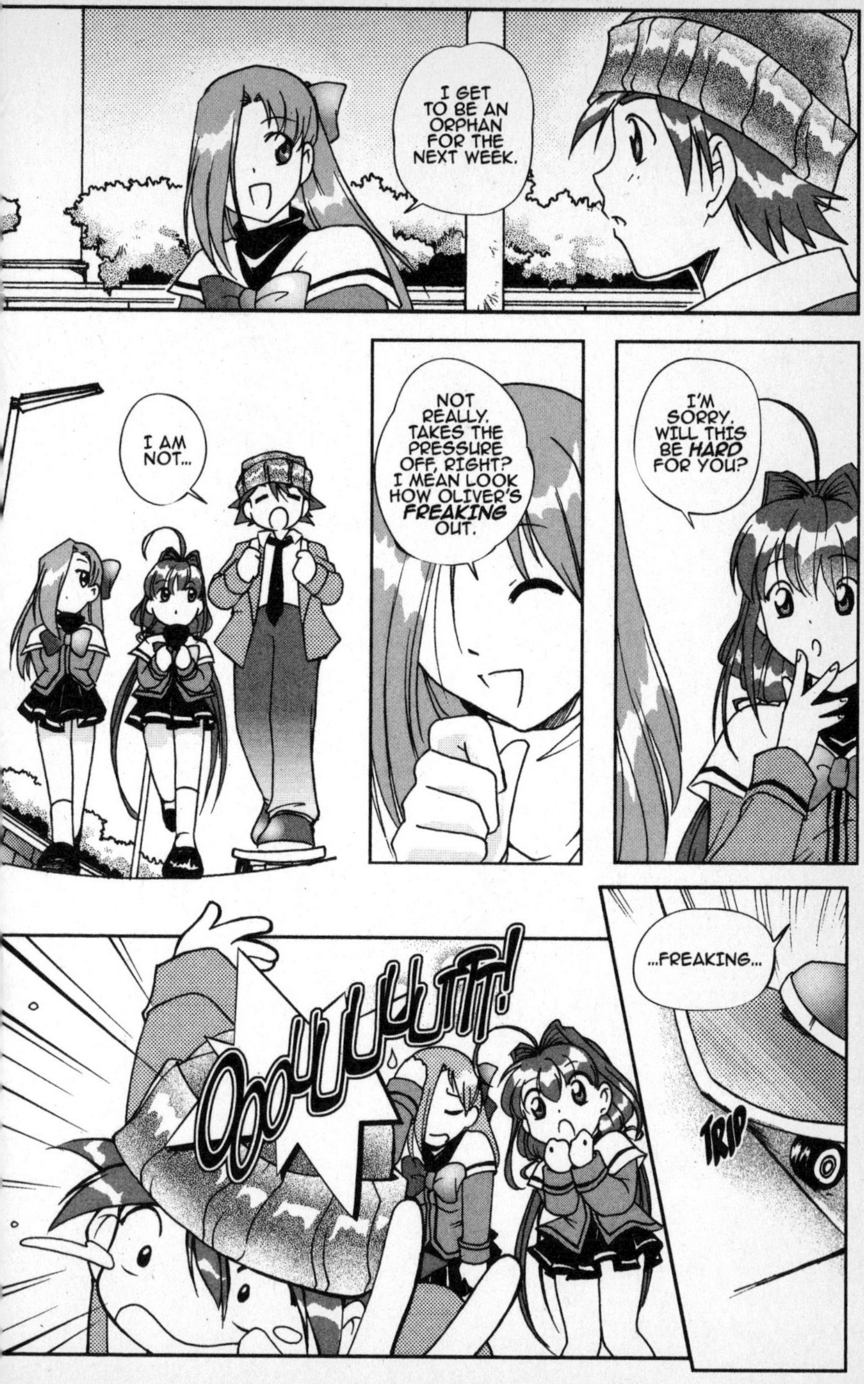
I GET TO BE AN ORPHAN FOR THE NEXT WEEK.
I'M SORRY. WILL THIS BE ***HARD*** FOR YOU?
NOT REALLY. TAKES THE PRESSURE OFF, RIGHT? I MEAN LOOK HOW OLIVER'S ***FREAKING*** OUT.
I AM NOT...
...FREAKING...
TRIP
OOOUUUUUTTT!

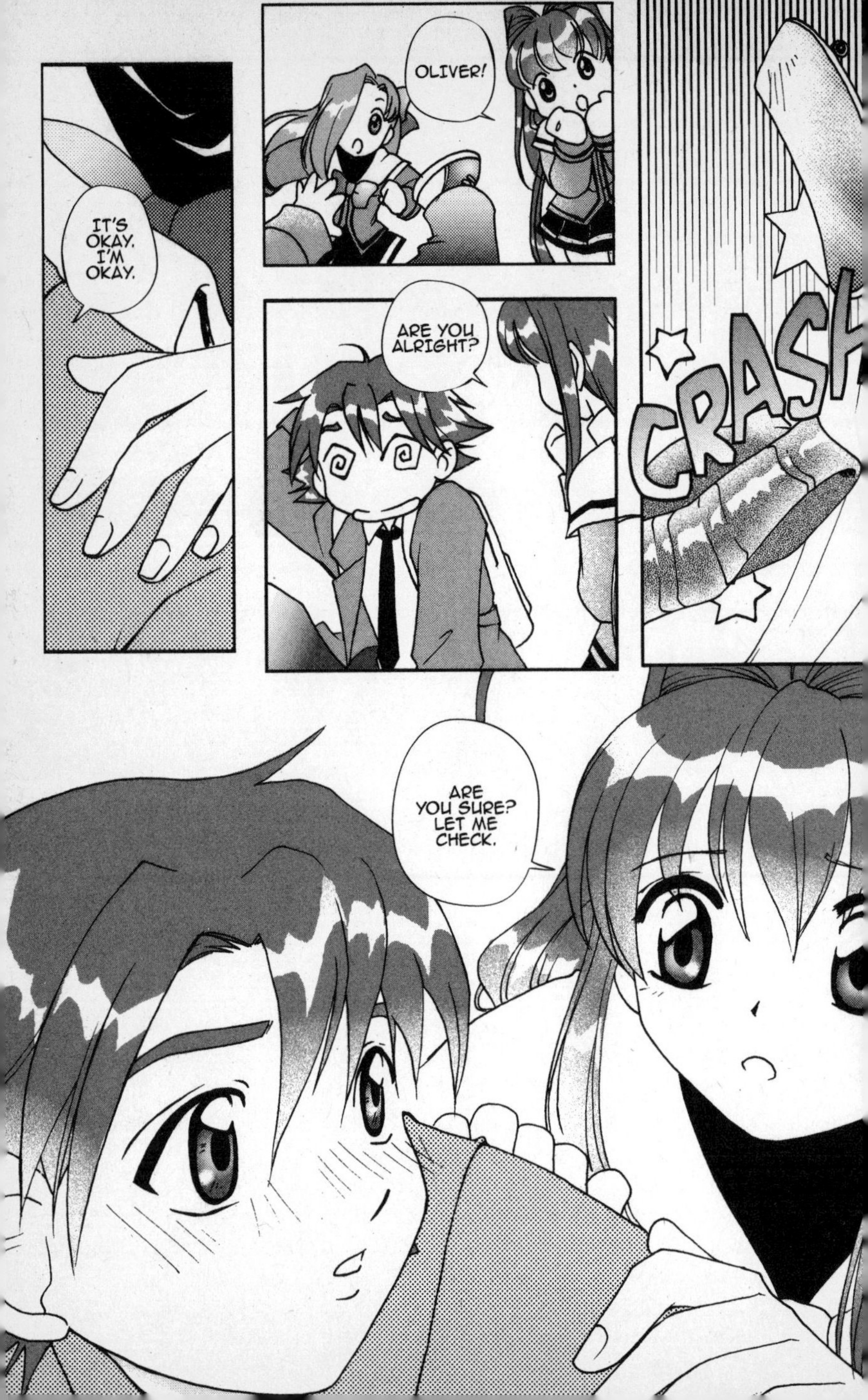
CRASH
OLIVER!
ARE YOU ALRIGHT?
IT'S OKAY. I'M OKAY.
ARE YOU SURE? LET ME CHECK.

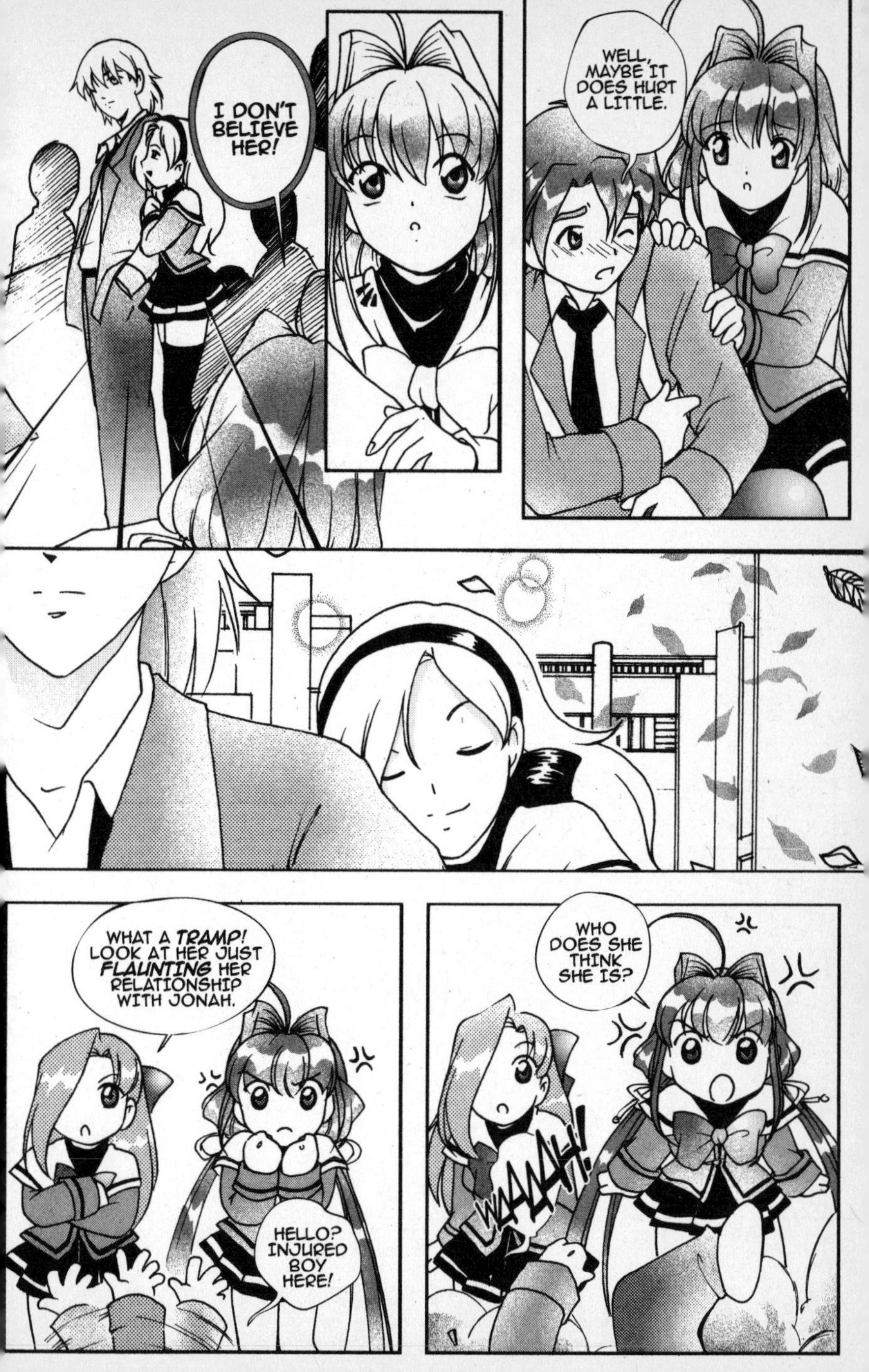
WELL, MAYBE IT DOES HURT A LITTLE.
I DON'T BELIEVE HER!
WHO DOES SHE THINK SHE IS?
WAAAH!
WHAT A *TRAMP!* LOOK AT HER JUST *FLAUNTING* HER RELATIONSHIP WITH JONAH.
HELLO? INJURED BOY HERE!

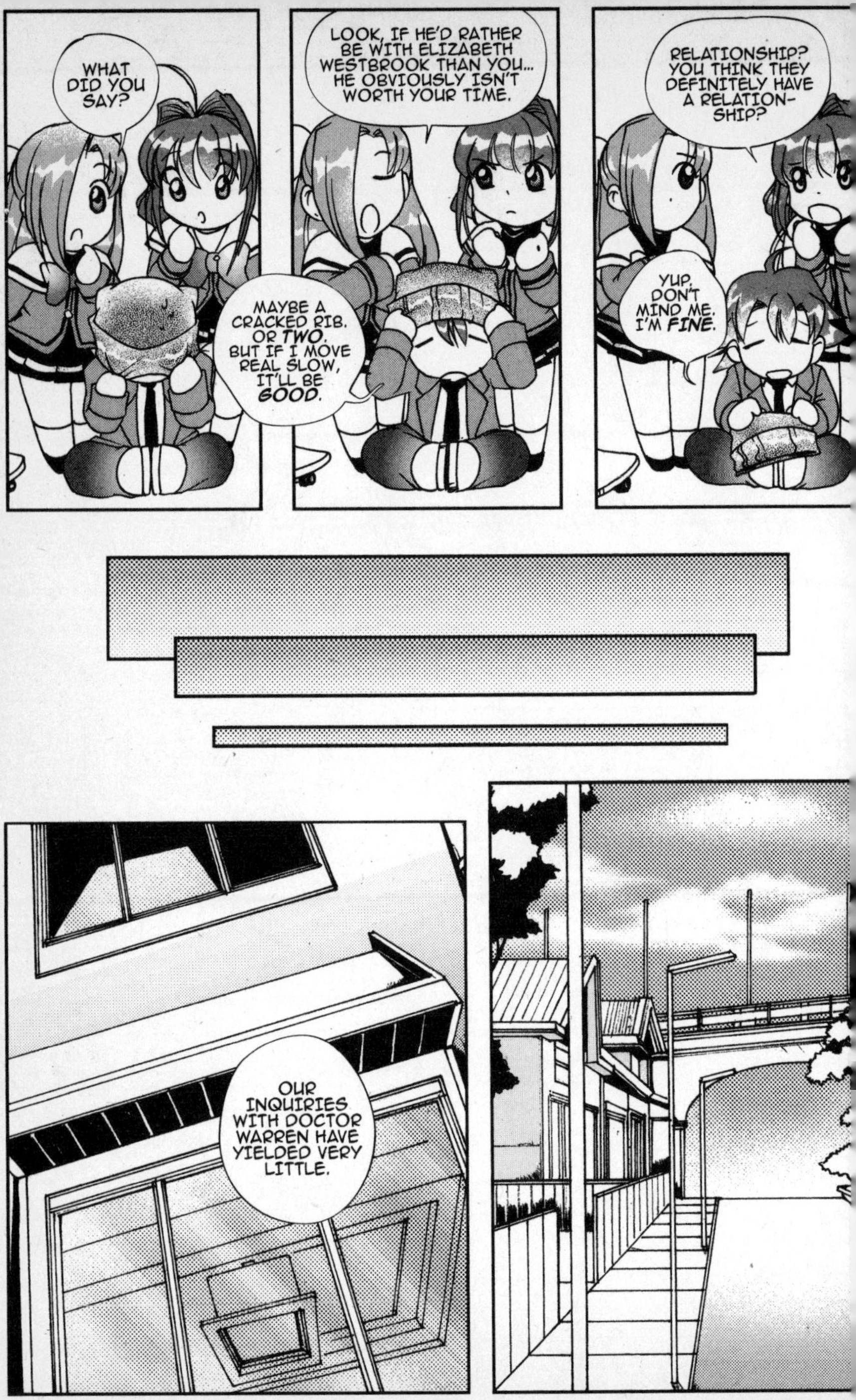
RELATIONSHIP? YOU THINK THEY DEFINITELY HAVE A RELATIONSHIP?
YUP. DON'T MIND ME. I'M **FINE**.
LOOK, IF HE'D RATHER BE WITH ELIZABETH WESTBROOK THAN YOU... HE OBVIOUSLY ISN'T WORTH YOUR TIME.
MAYBE A CRACKED RIB. OR **TWO**. BUT IF I MOVE REAL SLOW, IT'LL BE **GOOD**.
WHAT DID YOU SAY?
OUR INQUIRIES WITH DOCTOR WARREN HAVE YIELDED VERY LITTLE.

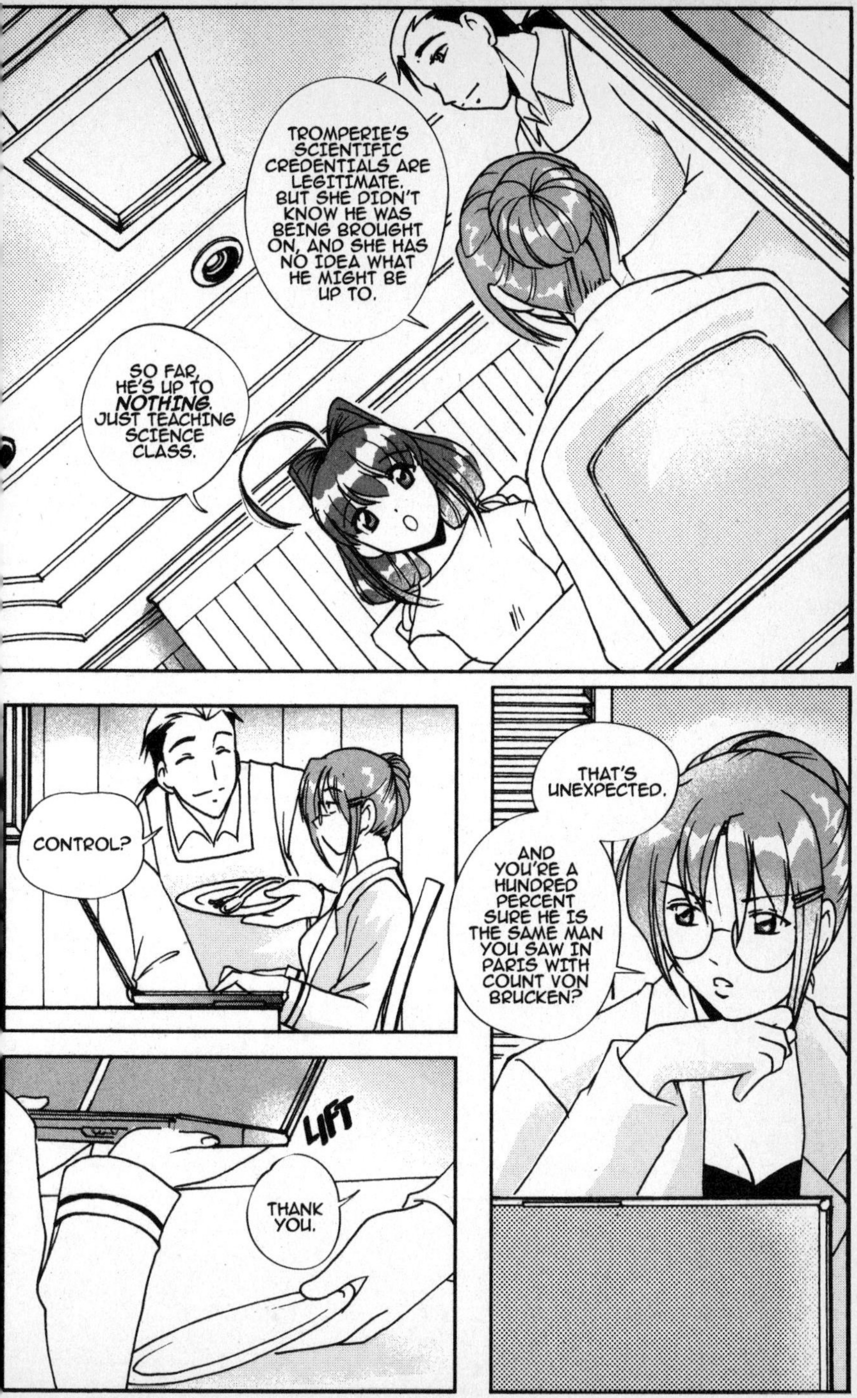
TROMPERIE'S SCIENTIFIC CREDENTIALS ARE LEGITIMATE. BUT SHE DIDN'T KNOW HE WAS BEING BROUGHT ON, AND SHE HAS NO IDEA WHAT HE MIGHT BE UP TO.
SO FAR, HE'S UP TO *NOTHING*. JUST TEACHING SCIENCE CLASS.
THAT'S UNEXPECTED.
AND YOU'RE A HUNDRED PERCENT SURE HE IS THE SAME MAN YOU SAW IN PARIS WITH COUNT VON BRUCKEN?
CONTROL?
LIFT
THANK YOU.

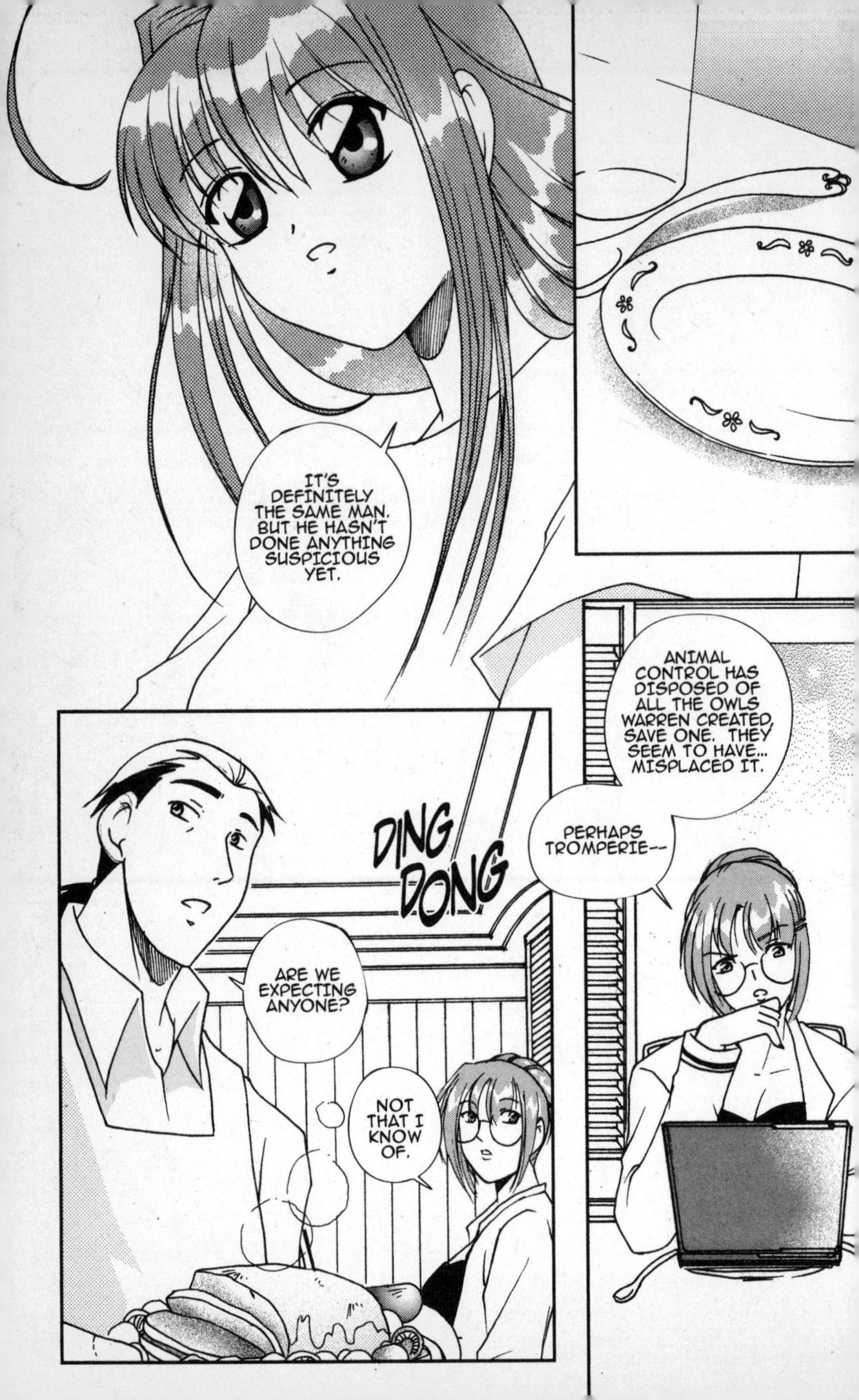
IT'S DEFINITELY THE SAME MAN. BUT HE HASN'T DONE ANYTHING SUSPICIOUS YET.
ANIMAL CONTROL HAS DISPOSED OF ALL THE OWLS WARREN CREATED, SAVE ONE. THEY SEEM TO HAVE... MISPLACED IT.
PERHAPS TROMPERIE--
DING DONG
ARE WE EXPECTING ANYONE?
NOT THAT I KNOW OF.

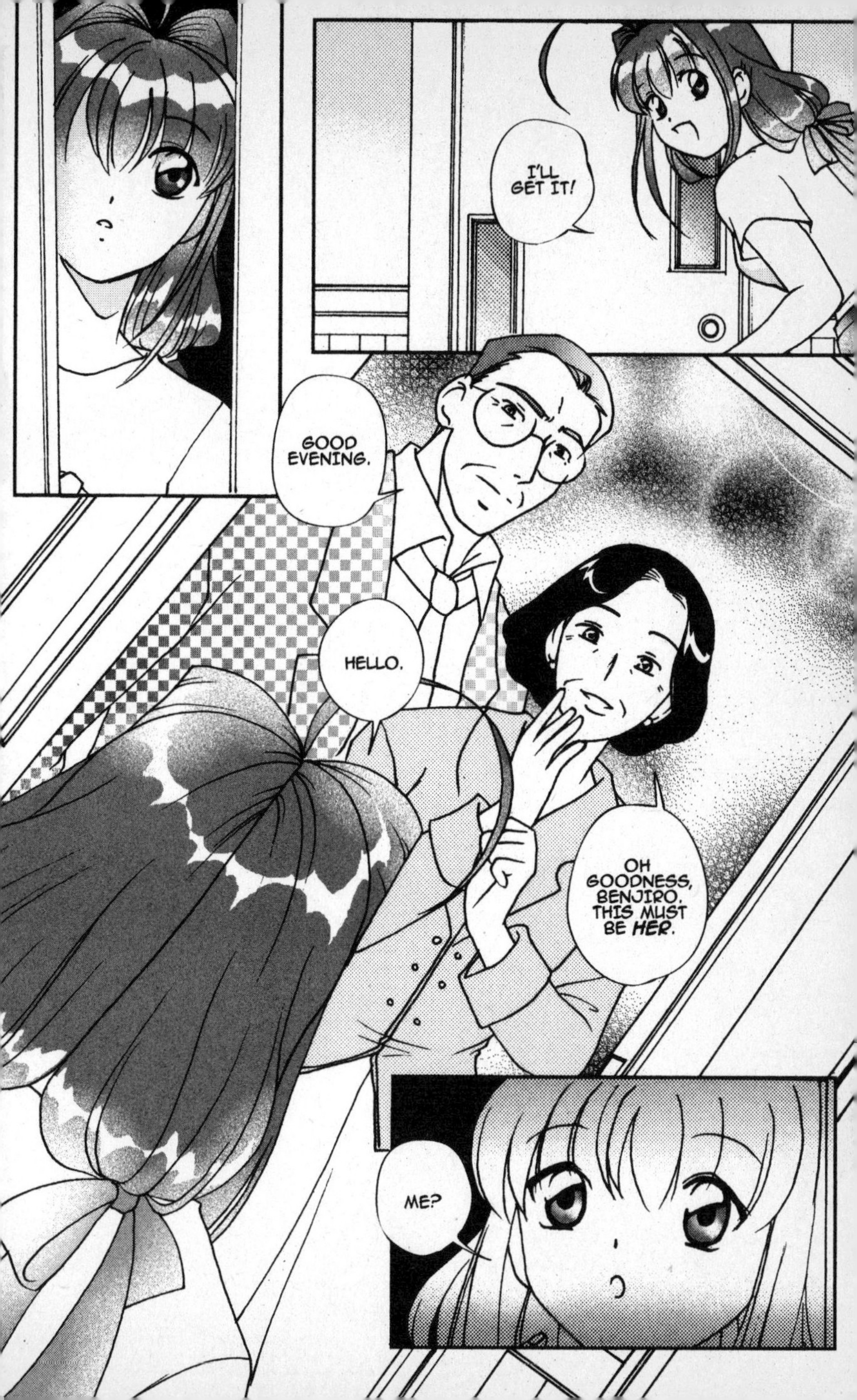
I'LL GET IT!
GOOD EVENING.
HELLO.
OH GOODNESS, BENJIRO. THIS MUST BE *HER*.
ME?

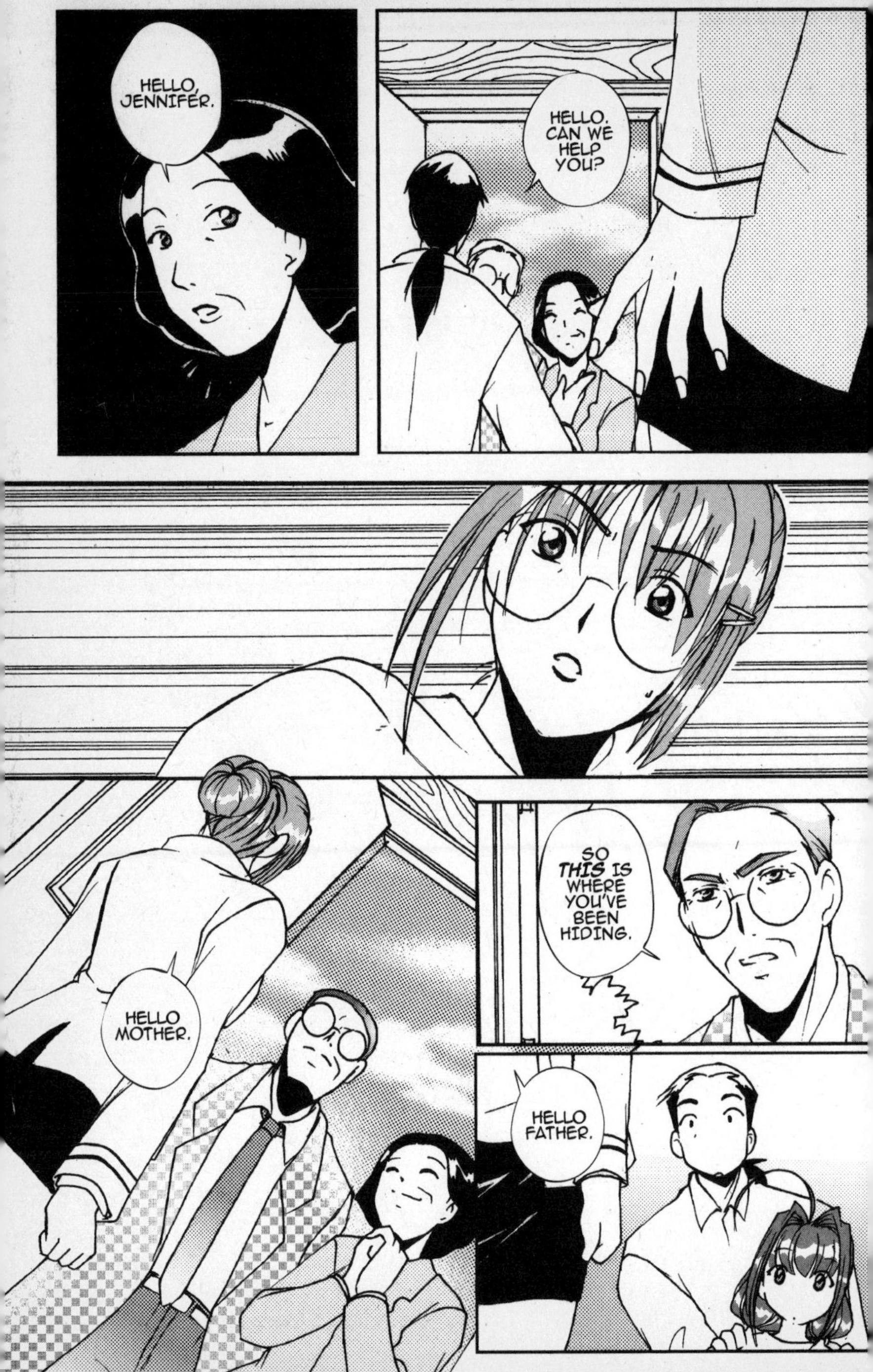
HELLO. CAN WE HELP YOU?
HELLO, JENNIFER.
SO *THIS* IS WHERE YOU'VE BEEN HIDING.
HELLO FATHER.
HELLO MOTHER.

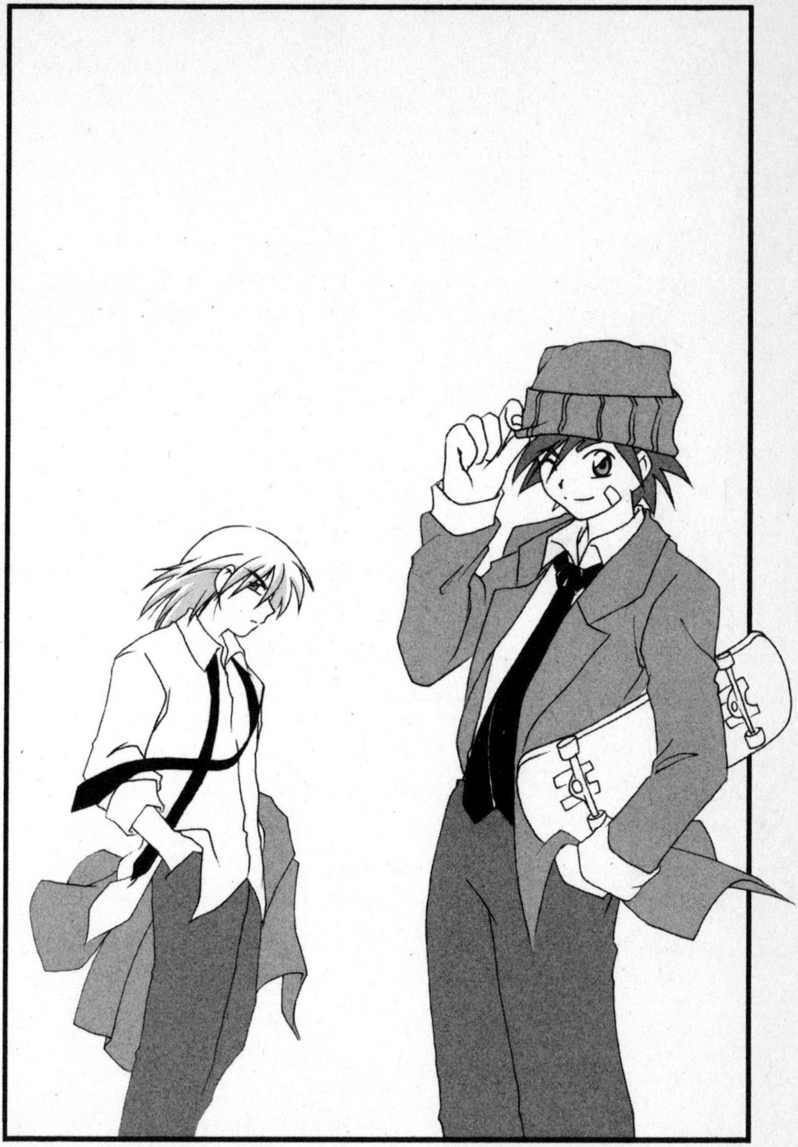

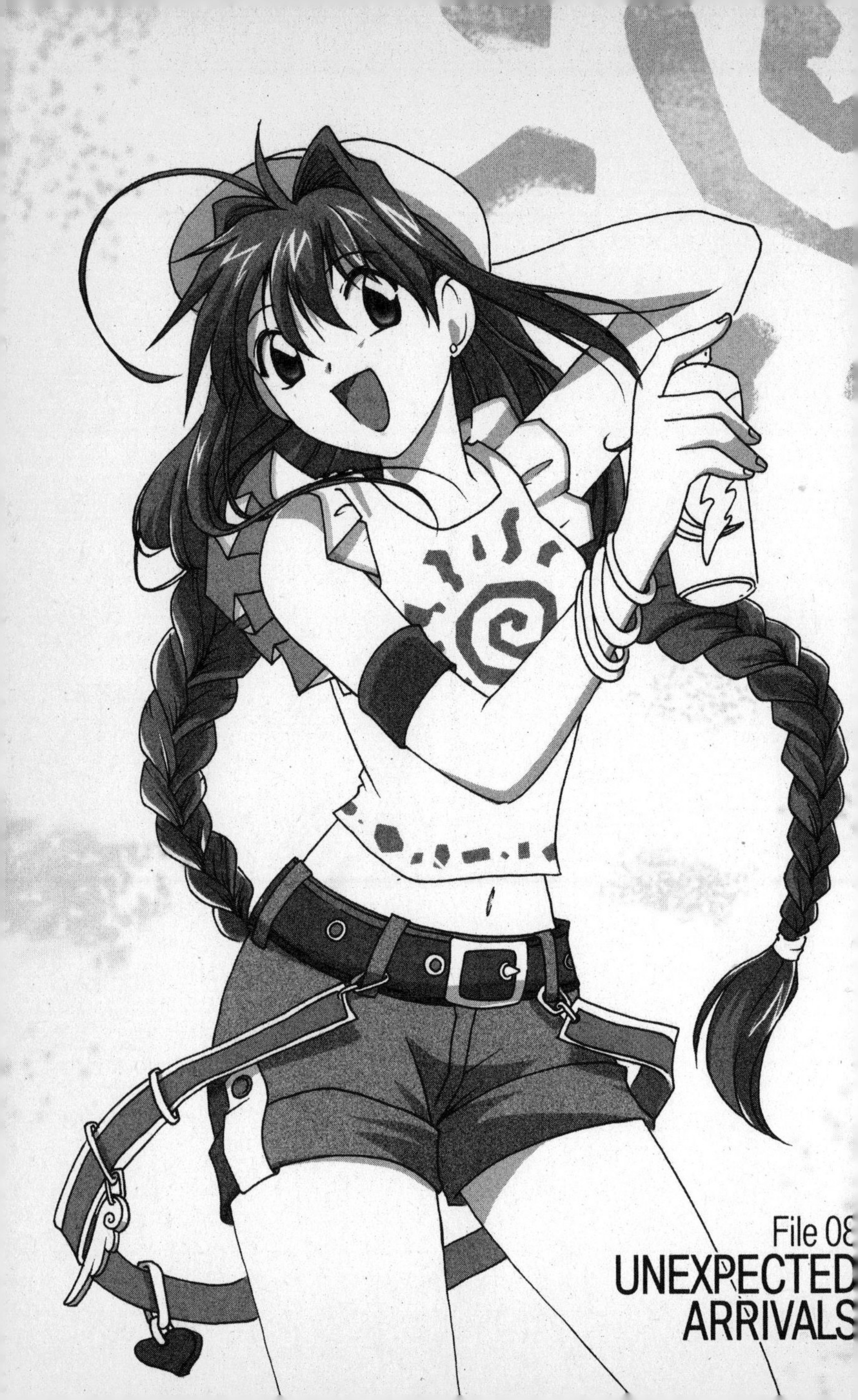

File 08
UNEXPECTED ARRIVALS

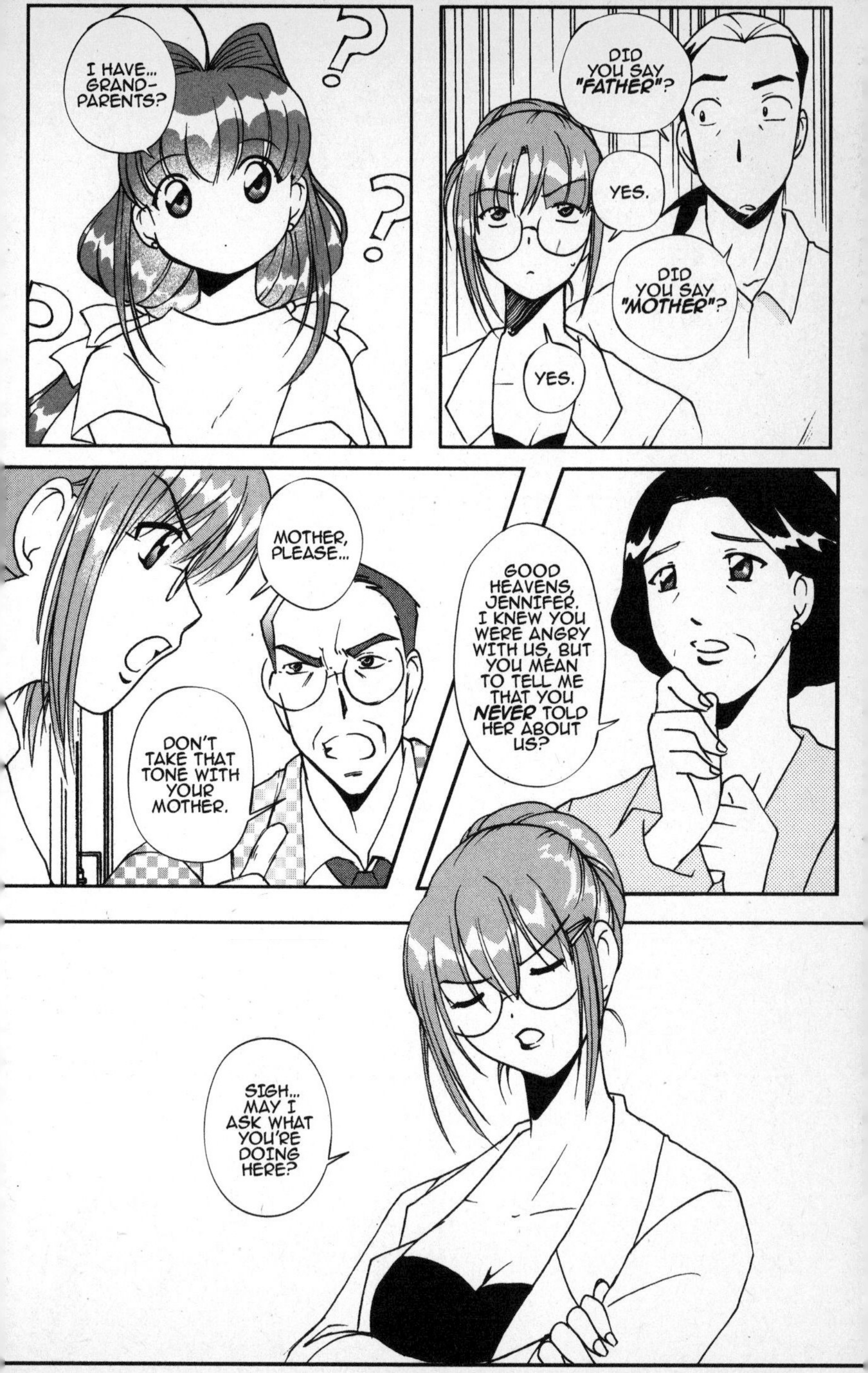
DID YOU SAY "FATHER"?
YES.
DID YOU SAY "MOTHER"?
YES.
I HAVE... GRAND-PARENTS?
GOOD HEAVENS, JENNIFER. I KNEW YOU WERE ANGRY WITH US, BUT YOU MEAN TO TELL ME THAT YOU NEVER TOLD HER ABOUT US?
MOTHER, PLEASE...
DON'T TAKE THAT TONE WITH YOUR MOTHER.
SIGH... MAY I ASK WHAT YOU'RE DOING HERE?

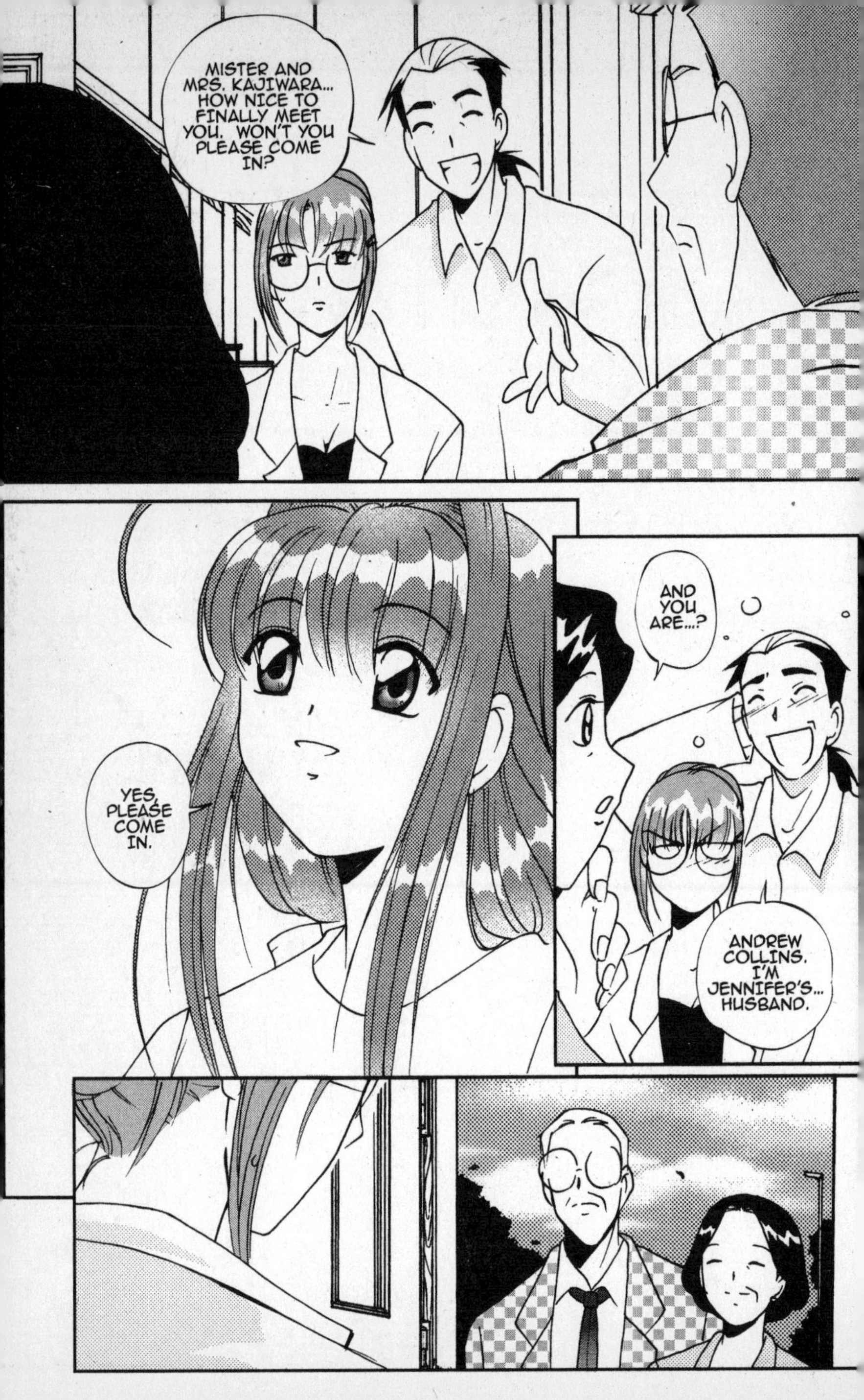
MISTER AND MRS. KAJIWARA... HOW NICE TO FINALLY MEET YOU. WON'T YOU PLEASE COME IN?
AND YOU ARE...?
ANDREW COLLINS. I'M JENNIFER'S... HUSBAND.
YES, PLEASE COME IN.

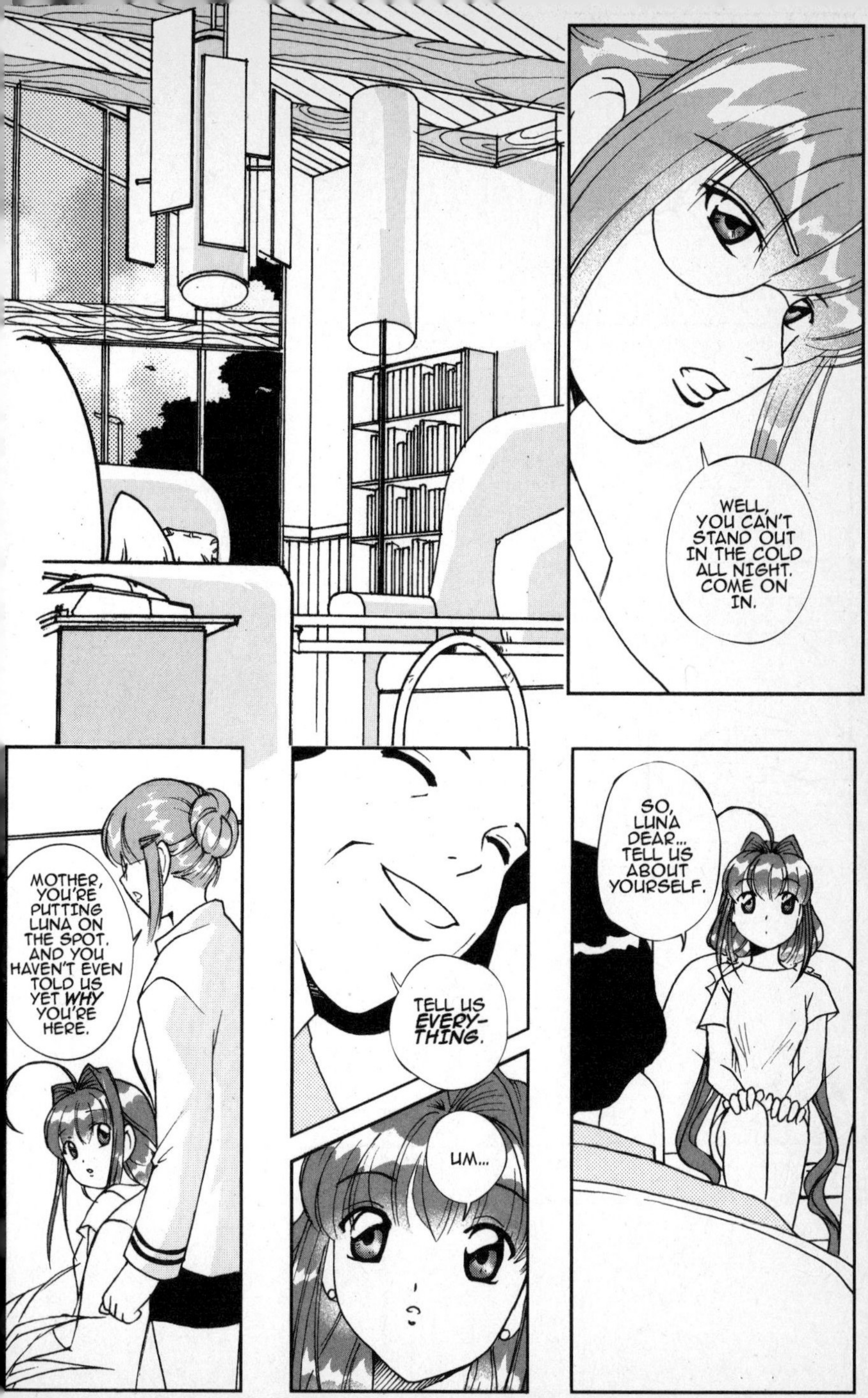
WELL, YOU CAN'T STAND OUT IN THE COLD ALL NIGHT. COME ON IN.
SO, LUNA DEAR... TELL US ABOUT YOURSELF.
TELL US *EVERYTHING*.
UM...
MOTHER, YOU'RE PUTTING LUNA ON THE SPOT. AND YOU HAVEN'T EVEN TOLD US YET *WHY* YOU'RE HERE.

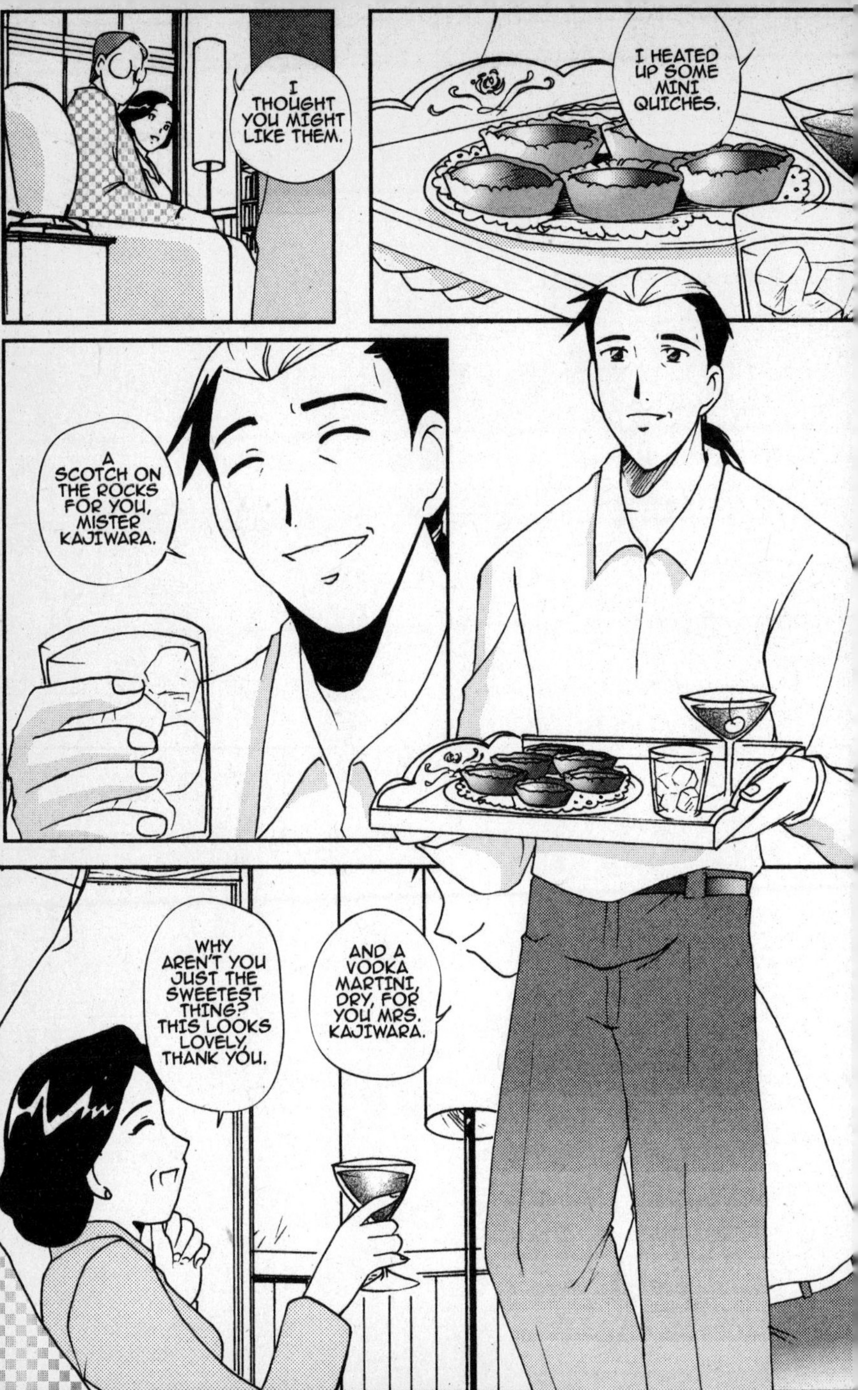
I HEATED UP SOME MINI QUICHES.
I THOUGHT YOU MIGHT LIKE THEM.
A SCOTCH ON THE ROCKS FOR YOU, MISTER KAJIWARA.
AND A VODKA MARTINI, DRY, FOR YOU MRS. KAJIWARA.
WHY AREN'T YOU JUST THE SWEETEST THING? THIS LOOKS LOVELY, THANK YOU.

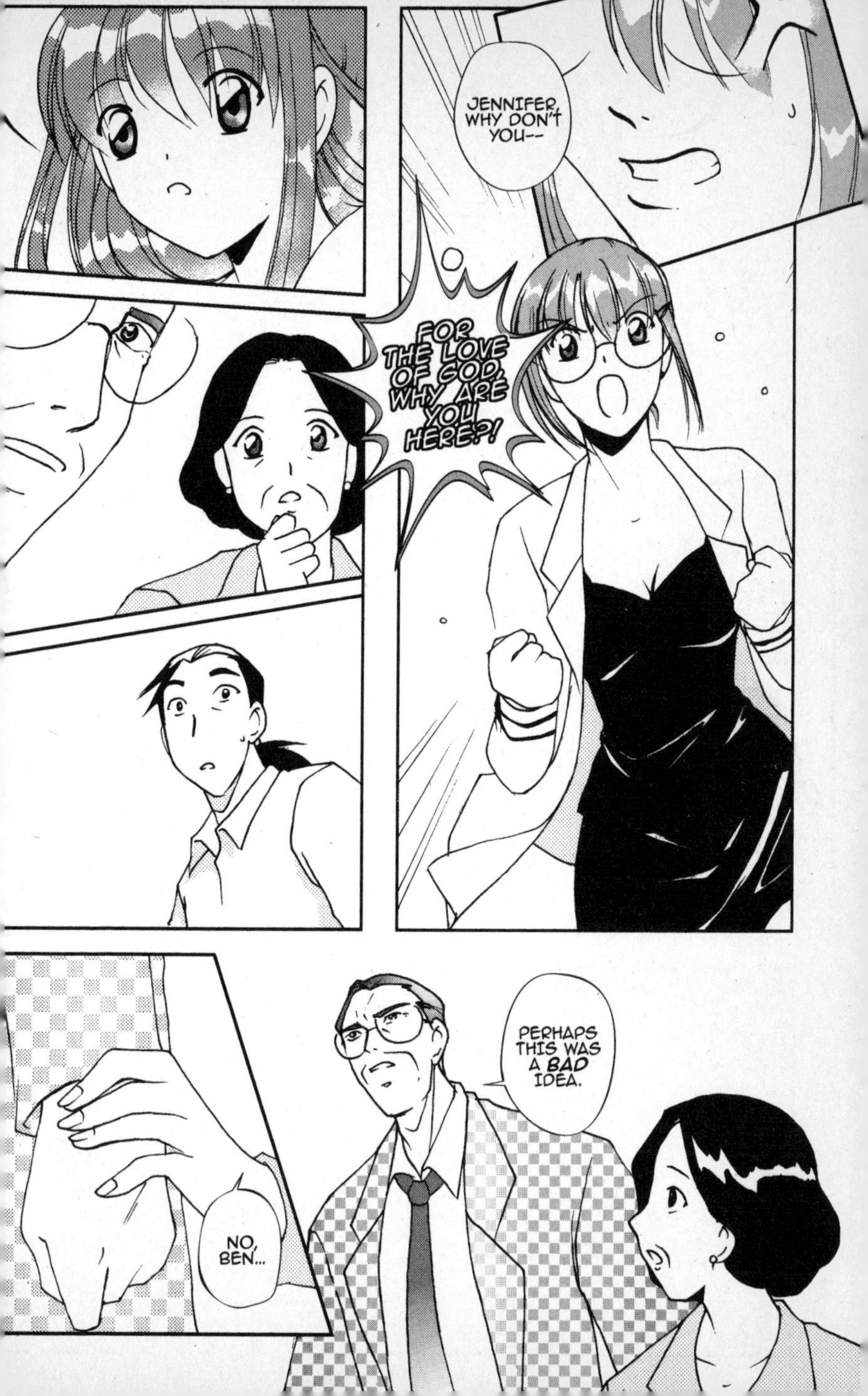
JENNIFER, WHY DON'T YOU--
FOR THE LOVE OF GOD, WHY ARE YOU HERE?!
PERHAPS THIS WAS A *BAD* IDEA.
NO, BEN...

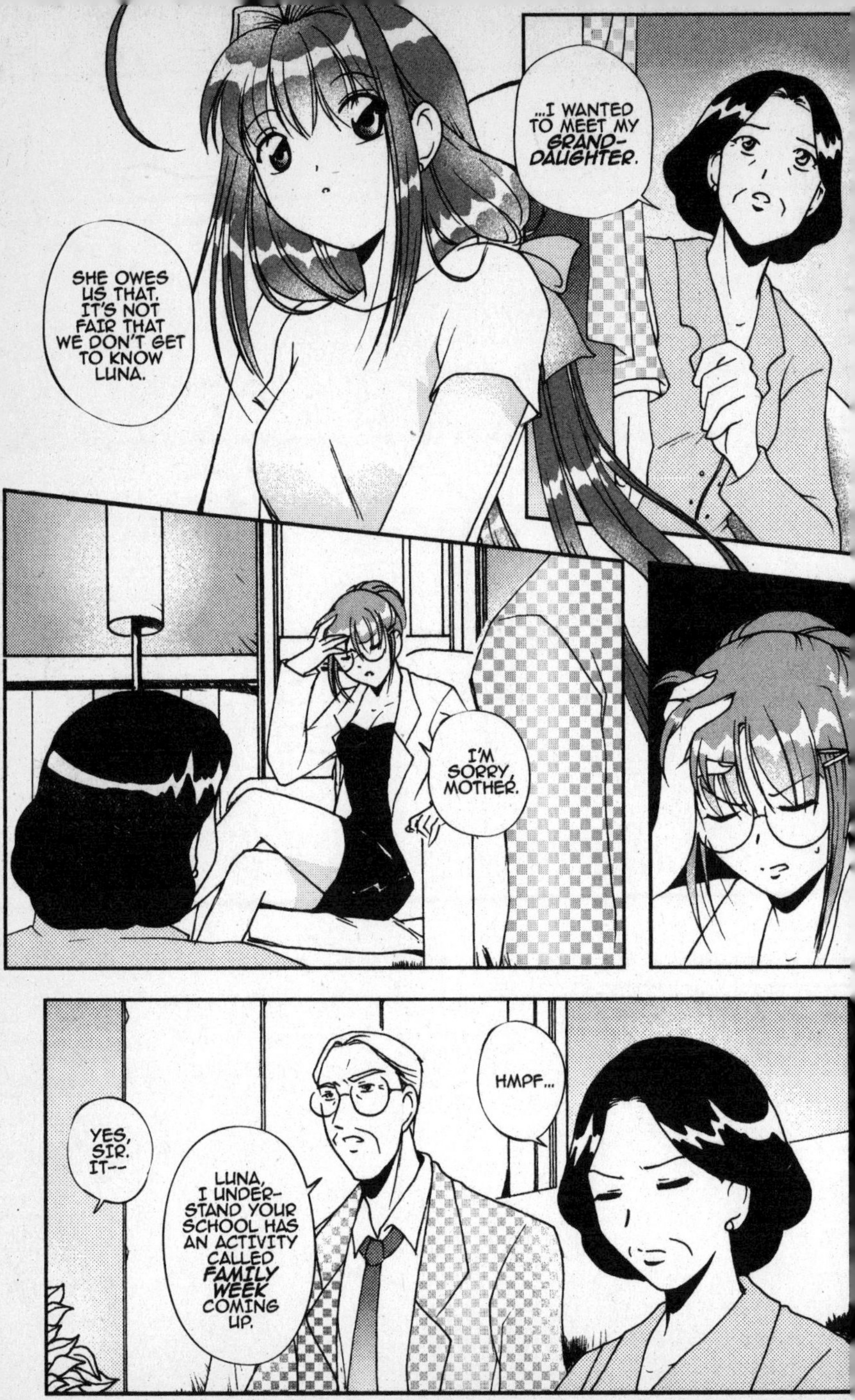
...I WANTED TO MEET MY GRAND-DAUGHTER.
SHE OWES US THAT. IT'S NOT FAIR THAT WE DON'T GET TO KNOW LUNA.
I'M SORRY, MOTHER.
HMPF...
LUNA, I UNDERSTAND YOUR SCHOOL HAS AN ACTIVITY CALLED FAMILY WEEK COMING UP.
YES, SIR. IT--

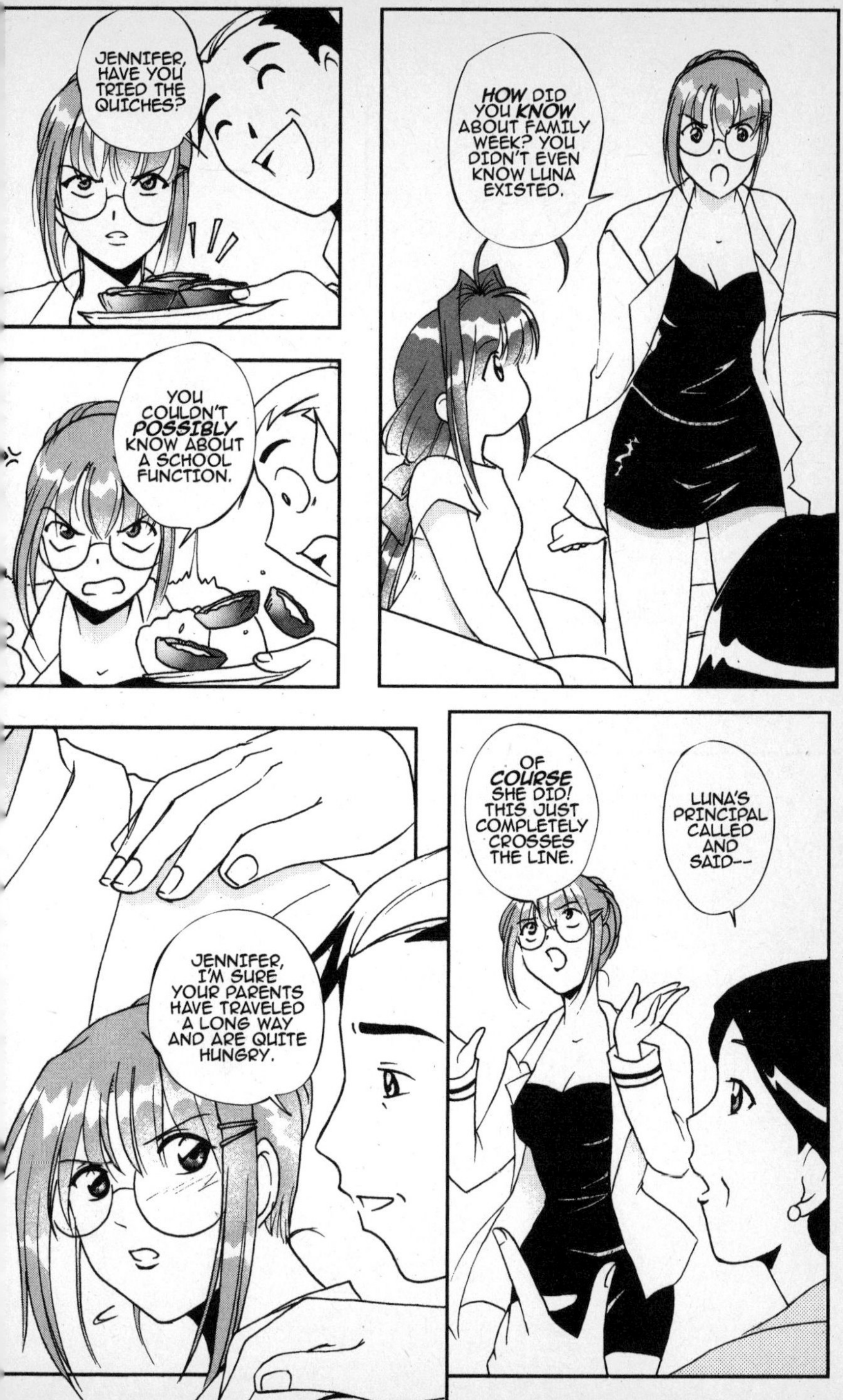
HOW DID YOU KNOW ABOUT FAMILY WEEK? YOU DIDN'T EVEN KNOW LUNA EXISTED.
JENNIFER, HAVE YOU TRIED THE QUICHES?
YOU COULDN'T POSSIBLY KNOW ABOUT A SCHOOL FUNCTION.
LUNA'S PRINCIPAL CALLED AND SAID--
OF COURSE SHE DID! THIS JUST COMPLETELY CROSSES THE LINE.
JENNIFER, I'M SURE YOUR PARENTS HAVE TRAVELED A LONG WAY AND ARE QUITE HUNGRY.

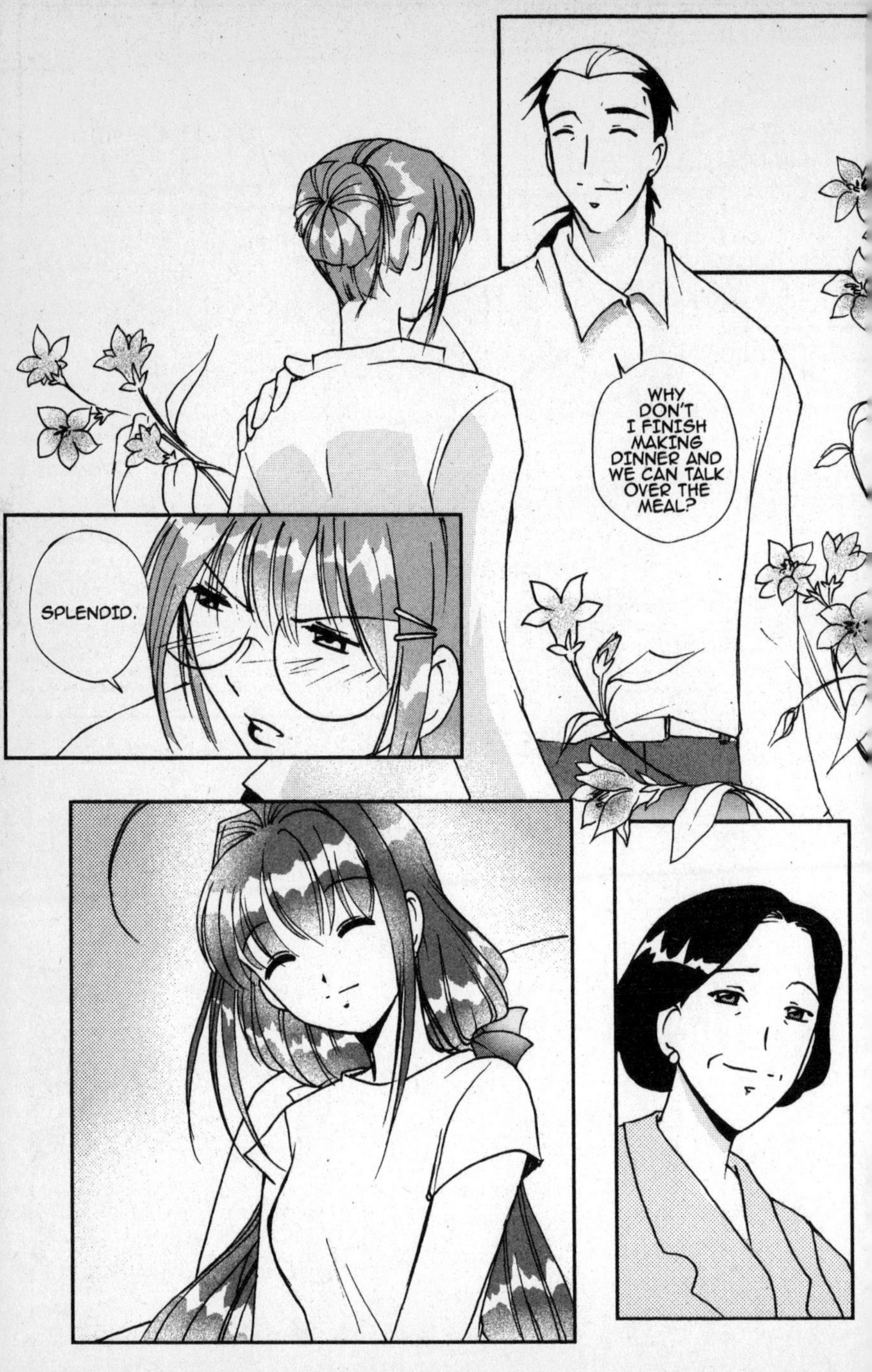
WHY DON'T I FINISH MAKING DINNER AND WE CAN TALK OVER THE MEAL?
SPLENDID.

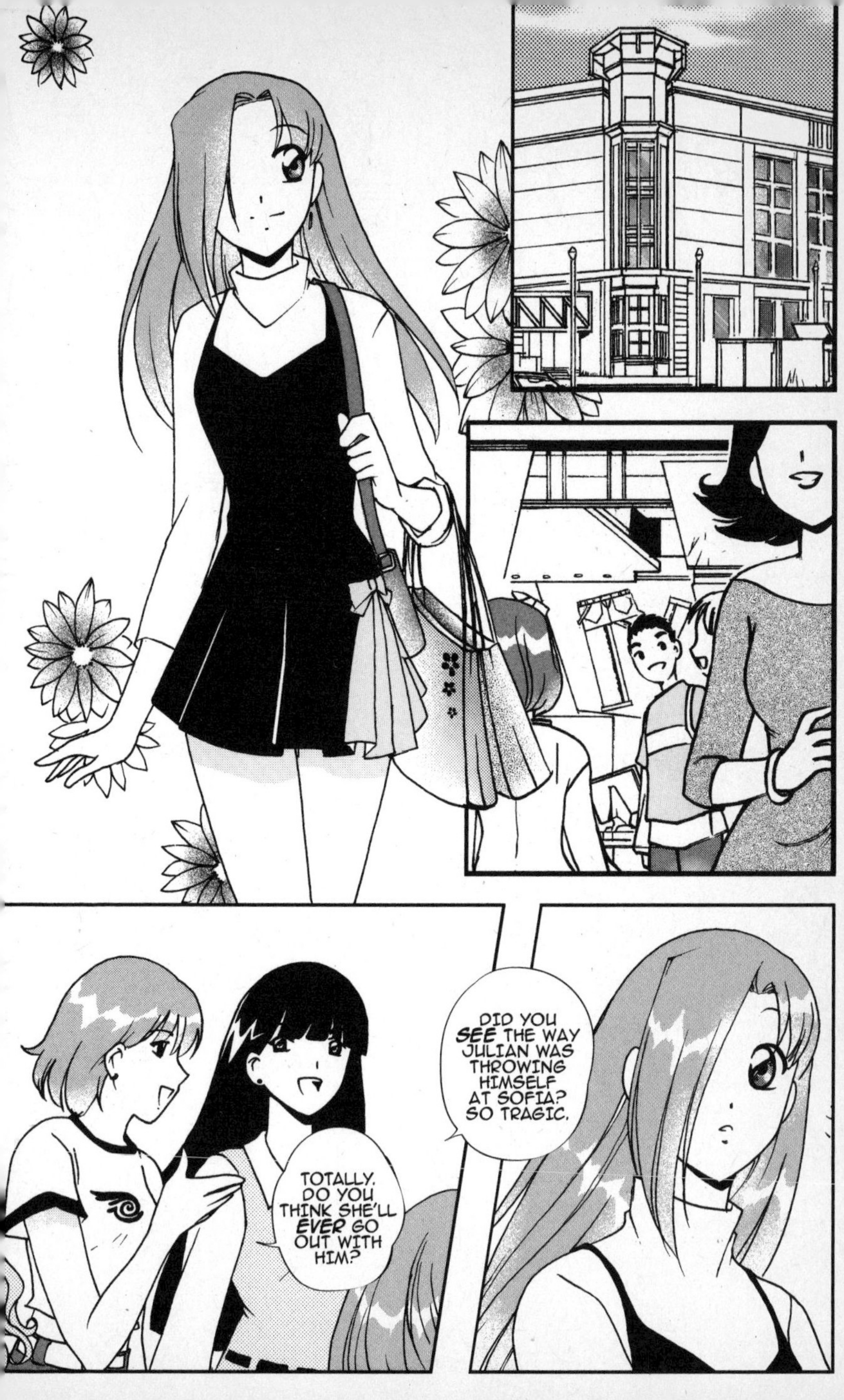
DID YOU SEE THE WAY JULIAN WAS THROWING HIMSELF AT SOFIA? SO TRAGIC.
TOTALLY. DO YOU THINK SHE'LL EVER GO OUT WITH HIM?

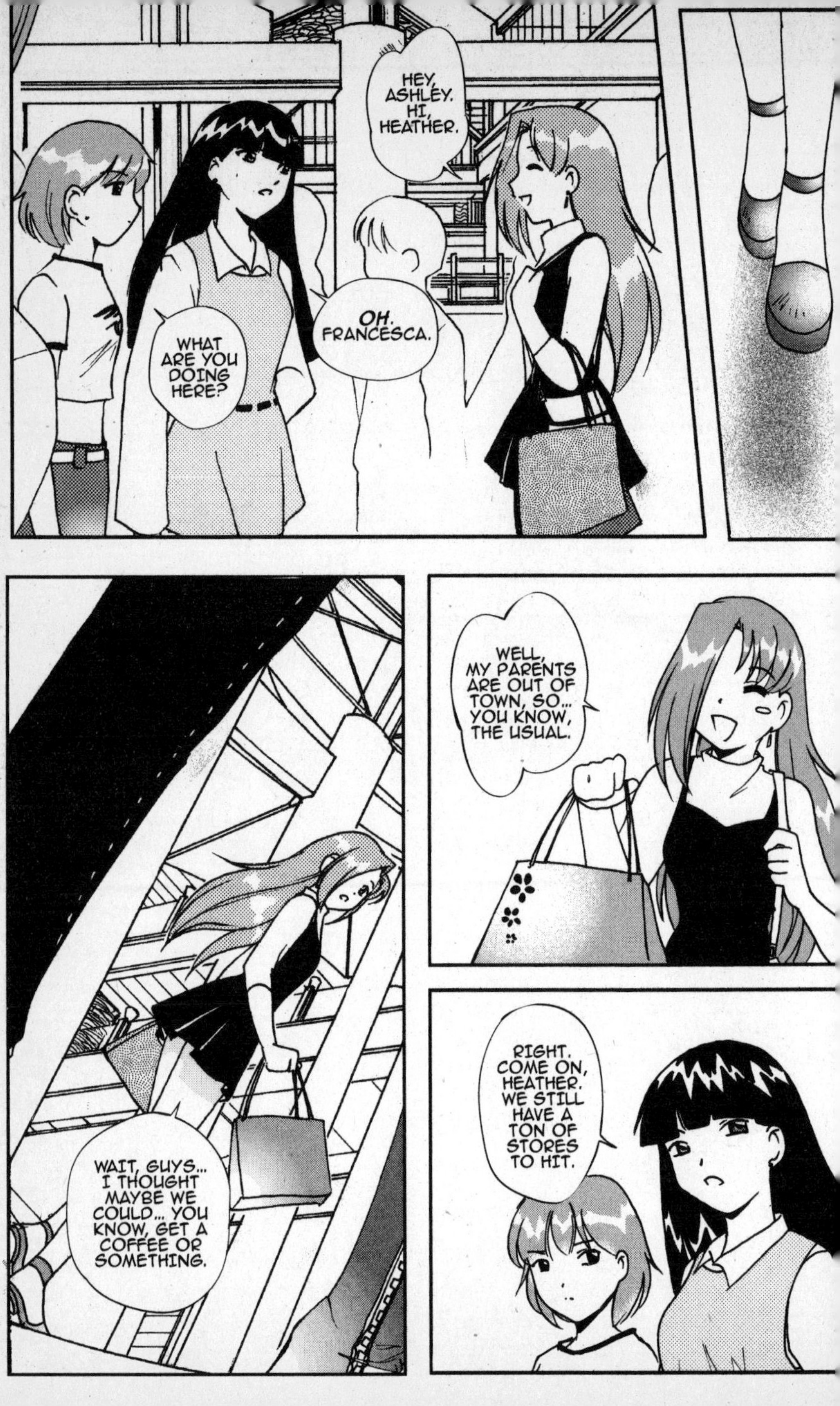
HEY, ASHLEY. HI, HEATHER.
OH. FRANCESCA.
WHAT ARE YOU DOING HERE?
WELL, MY PARENTS ARE OUT OF TOWN, SO... YOU KNOW, THE USUAL.
RIGHT. COME ON, HEATHER. WE STILL HAVE A TON OF STORES TO HIT.
WAIT, GUYS... I THOUGHT MAYBE WE COULD... YOU KNOW, GET A COFFEE OR SOMETHING.

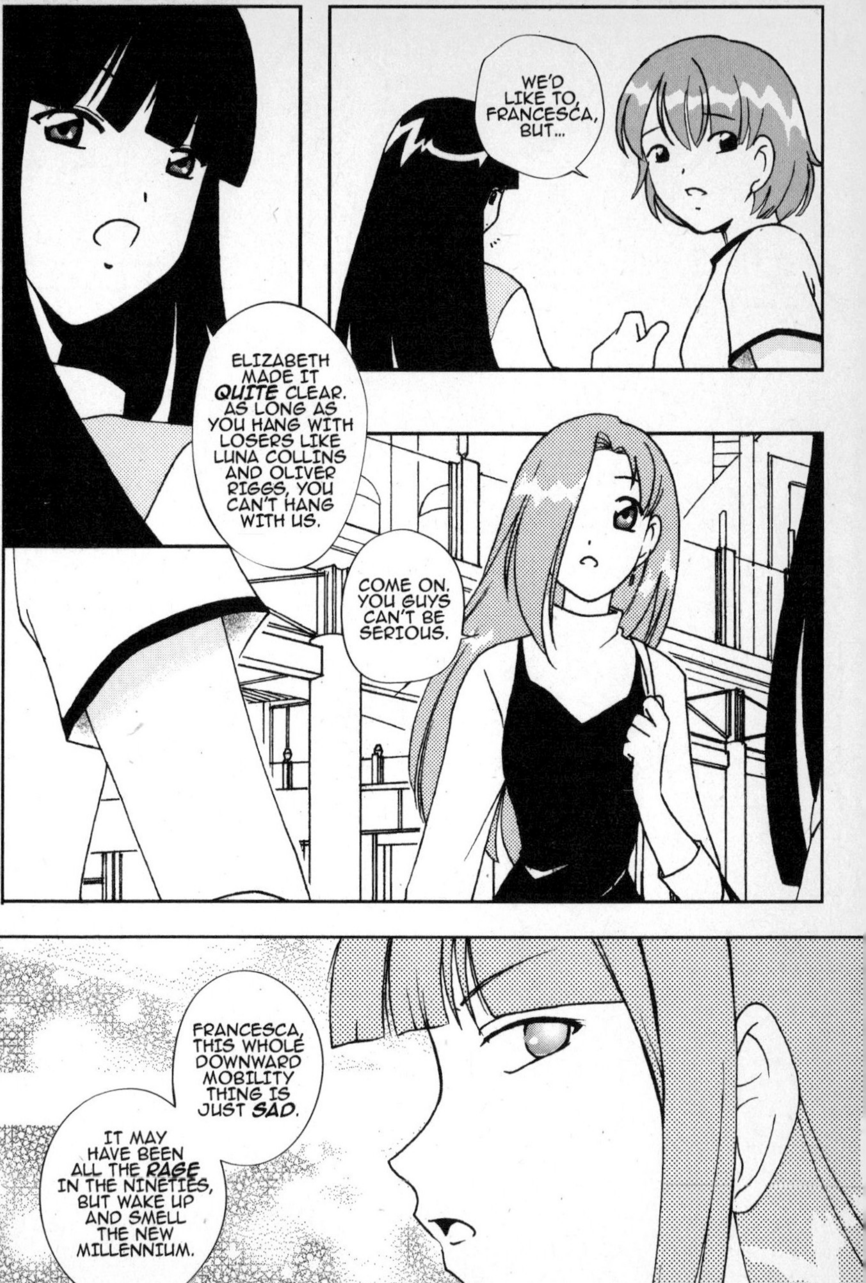
WE'D LIKE TO, FRANCESCA, BUT...
ELIZABETH MADE IT *QUITE* CLEAR. AS LONG AS YOU HANG WITH LOSERS LIKE LUNA COLLINS AND OLIVER RIGGS, YOU CAN'T HANG WITH US.
COME ON. YOU GUYS CAN'T BE SERIOUS.
FRANCESCA, THIS WHOLE DOWNWARD MOBILITY THING IS JUST *SAD*.
IT MAY HAVE BEEN ALL THE *RAGE* IN THE NINETIES, BUT WAKE UP AND SMELL THE NEW MILLENNIUM.

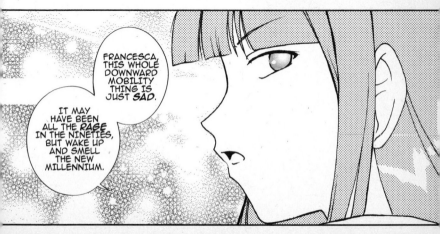

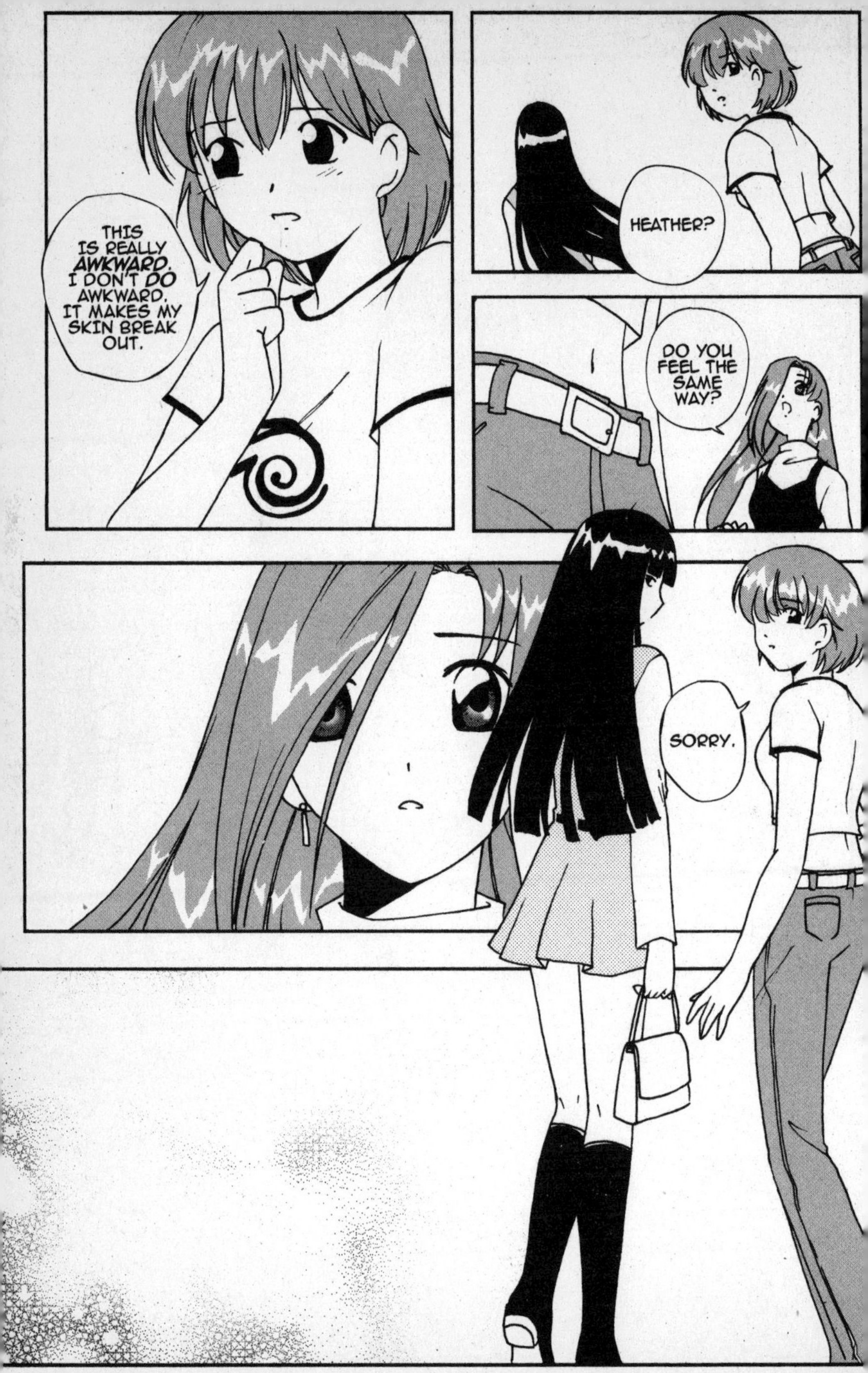
HEATHER?
DO YOU FEEL THE SAME WAY?
THIS IS REALLY AWKWARD. I DON'T DO AWKWARD. IT MAKES MY SKIN BREAK OUT.
SORRY.

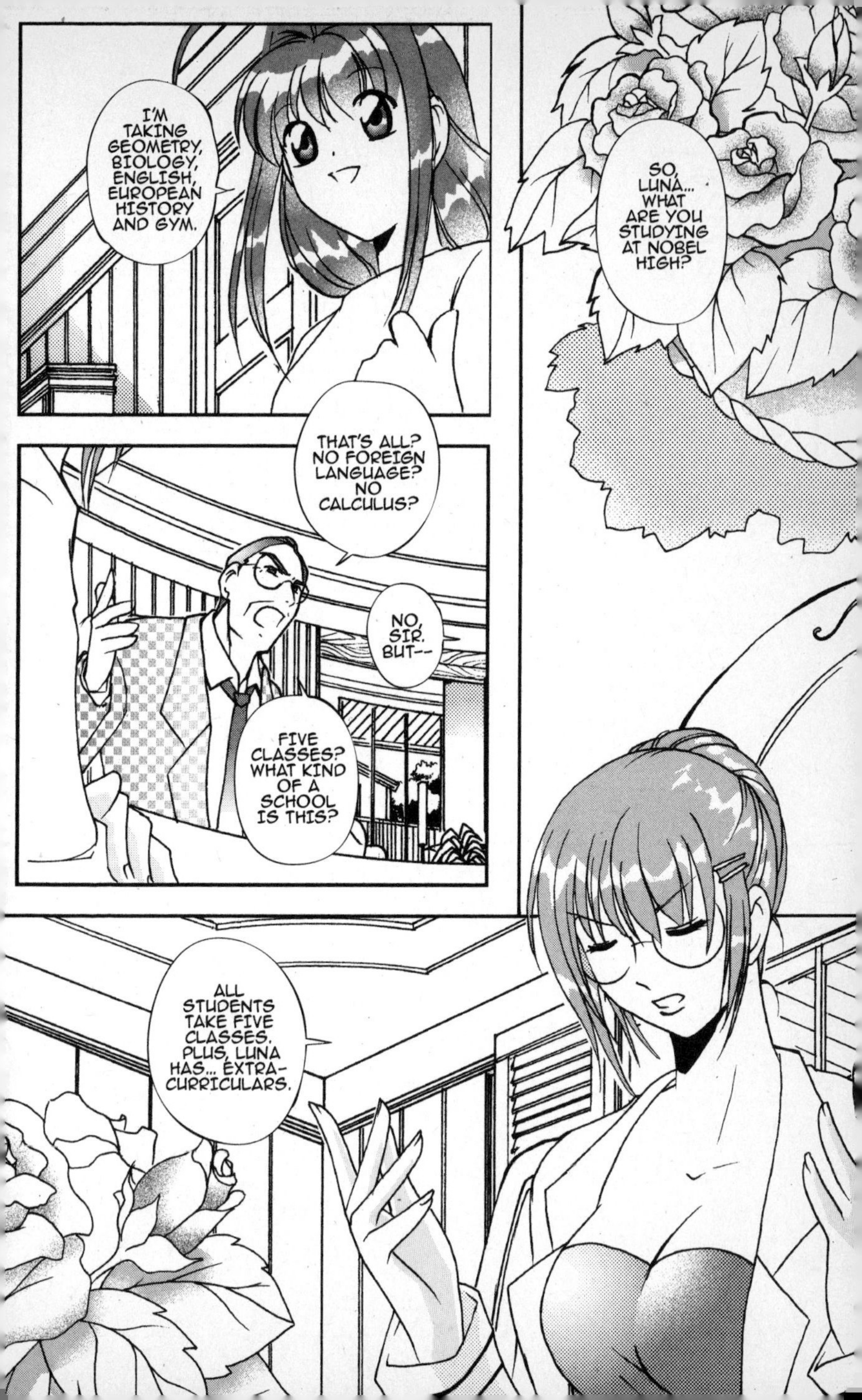
SO, LUNA... WHAT ARE YOU STUDYING AT NOBEL HIGH?
I'M TAKING GEOMETRY, BIOLOGY, ENGLISH, EUROPEAN HISTORY AND GYM.
THAT'S ALL? NO FOREIGN LANGUAGE? NO CALCULUS?
NO, SIR. BUT--
FIVE CLASSES? WHAT KIND OF A SCHOOL IS THIS?
ALL STUDENTS TAKE FIVE CLASSES. PLUS, LUNA HAS... EXTRA-CURRICULARS.

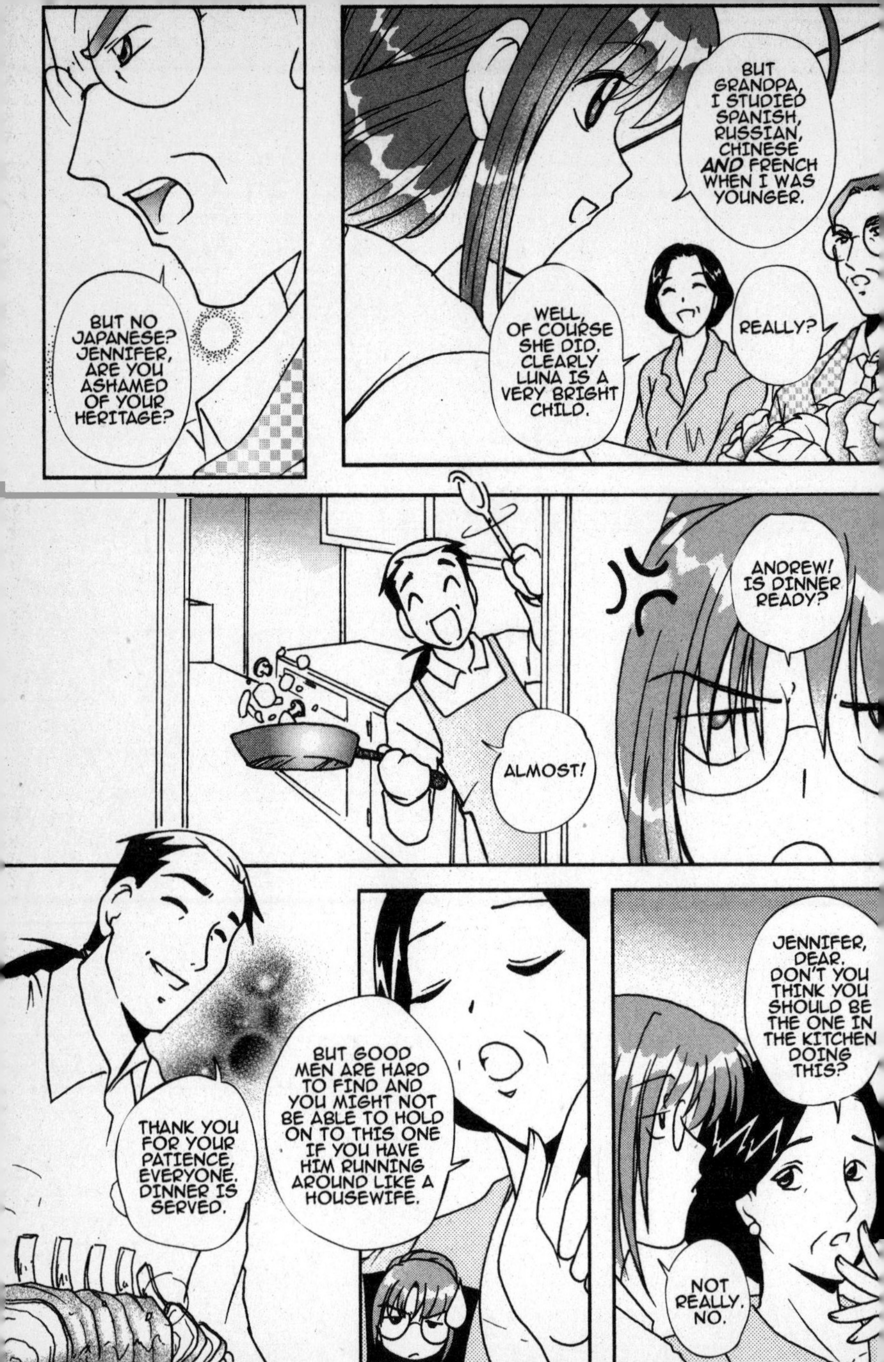
BUT GRANDPA, I STUDIED SPANISH, RUSSIAN, CHINESE AND FRENCH WHEN I WAS YOUNGER.
REALLY?
WELL, OF COURSE SHE DID. CLEARLY LUNA IS A VERY BRIGHT CHILD.
BUT NO JAPANESE? JENNIFER, ARE YOU ASHAMED OF YOUR HERITAGE?
ANDREW! IS DINNER READY?
ALMOST!
JENNIFER, DEAR. DON'T YOU THINK YOU SHOULD BE THE ONE IN THE KITCHEN DOING THIS?
NOT REALLY. NO.
BUT GOOD MEN ARE HARD TO FIND AND YOU MIGHT NOT BE ABLE TO HOLD ON TO THIS ONE IF YOU HAVE HIM RUNNING AROUND LIKE A HOUSEWIFE.
THANK YOU FOR YOUR PATIENCE, EVERYONE. DINNER IS SERVED.

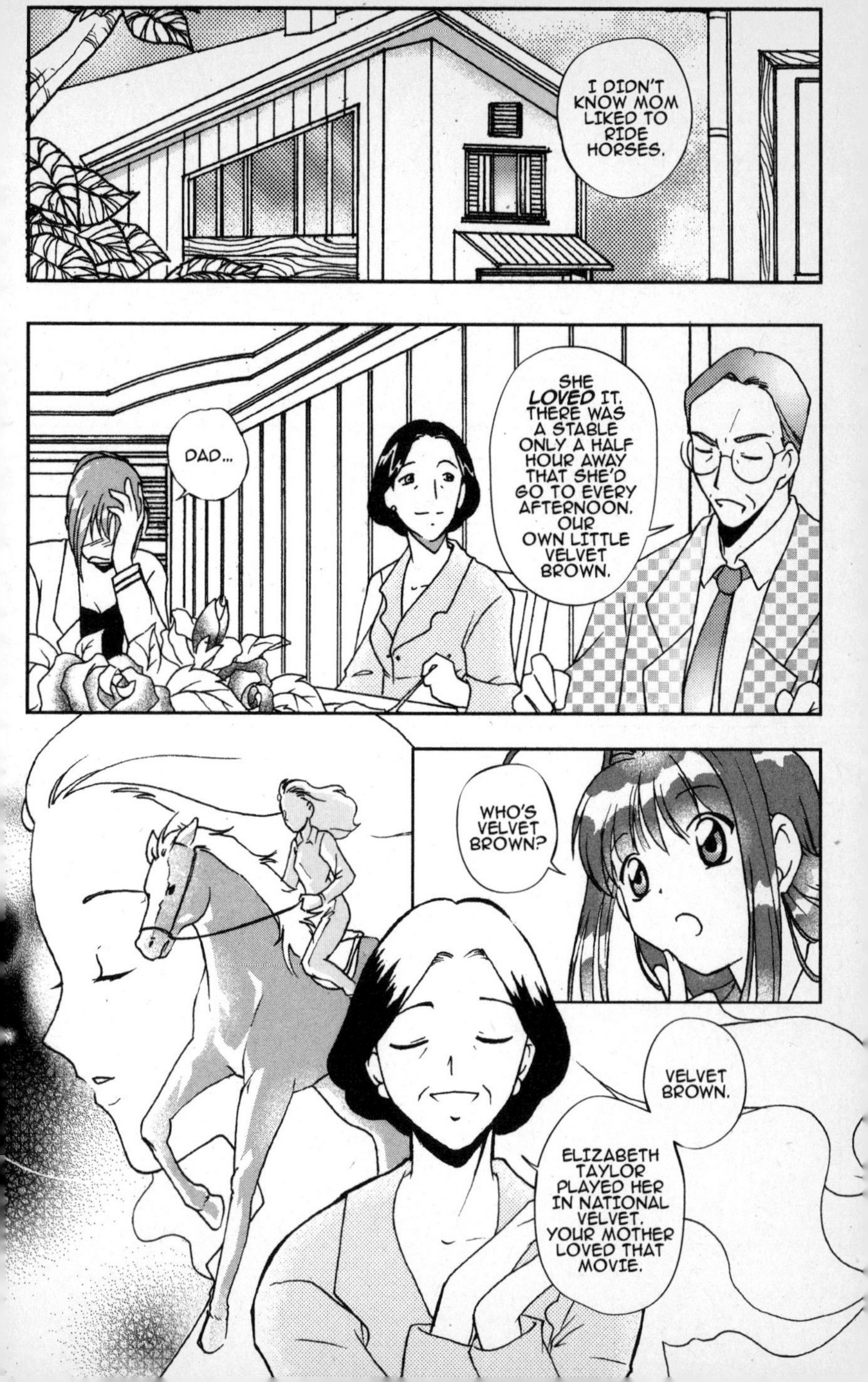
I DIDN'T KNOW MOM LIKED TO RIDE HORSES.
SHE *LOVED* IT. THERE WAS A STABLE ONLY A HALF HOUR AWAY THAT SHE'D GO TO EVERY AFTERNOON. OUR OWN LITTLE VELVET BROWN.
DAD...
WHO'S VELVET BROWN?
VELVET BROWN.
ELIZABETH TAYLOR PLAYED HER IN NATIONAL VELVET. YOUR MOTHER LOVED THAT MOVIE.

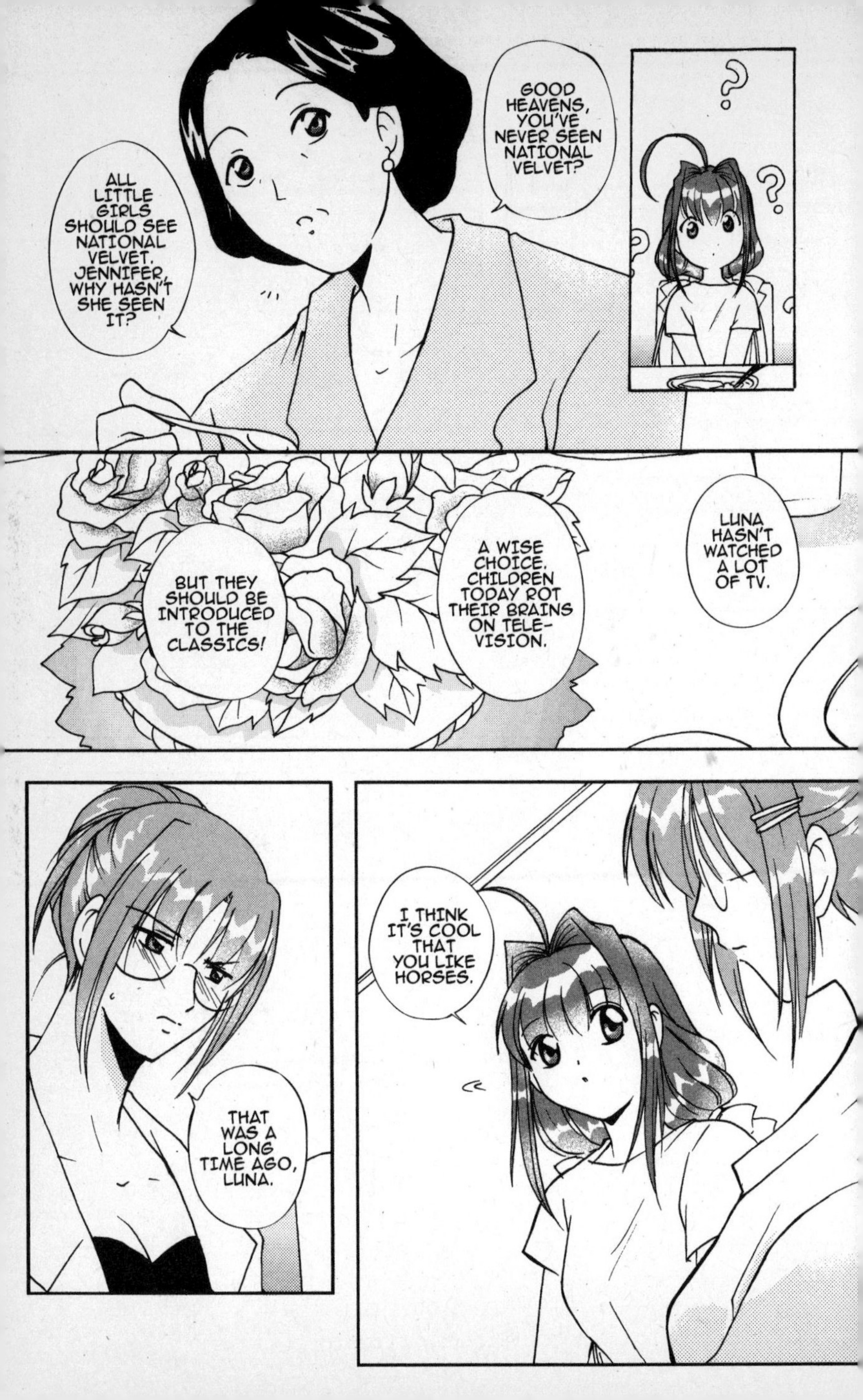
GOOD HEAVENS, YOU'VE NEVER SEEN NATIONAL VELVET?
ALL LITTLE GIRLS SHOULD SEE NATIONAL VELVET. JENNIFER, WHY HASN'T SHE SEEN IT?
LUNA HASN'T WATCHED A LOT OF TV.
A WISE CHOICE. CHILDREN TODAY ROT THEIR BRAINS ON TELE-VISION.
BUT THEY SHOULD BE INTRODUCED TO THE CLASSICS!
I THINK IT'S COOL THAT YOU LIKE HORSES.
THAT WAS A LONG TIME AGO, LUNA.

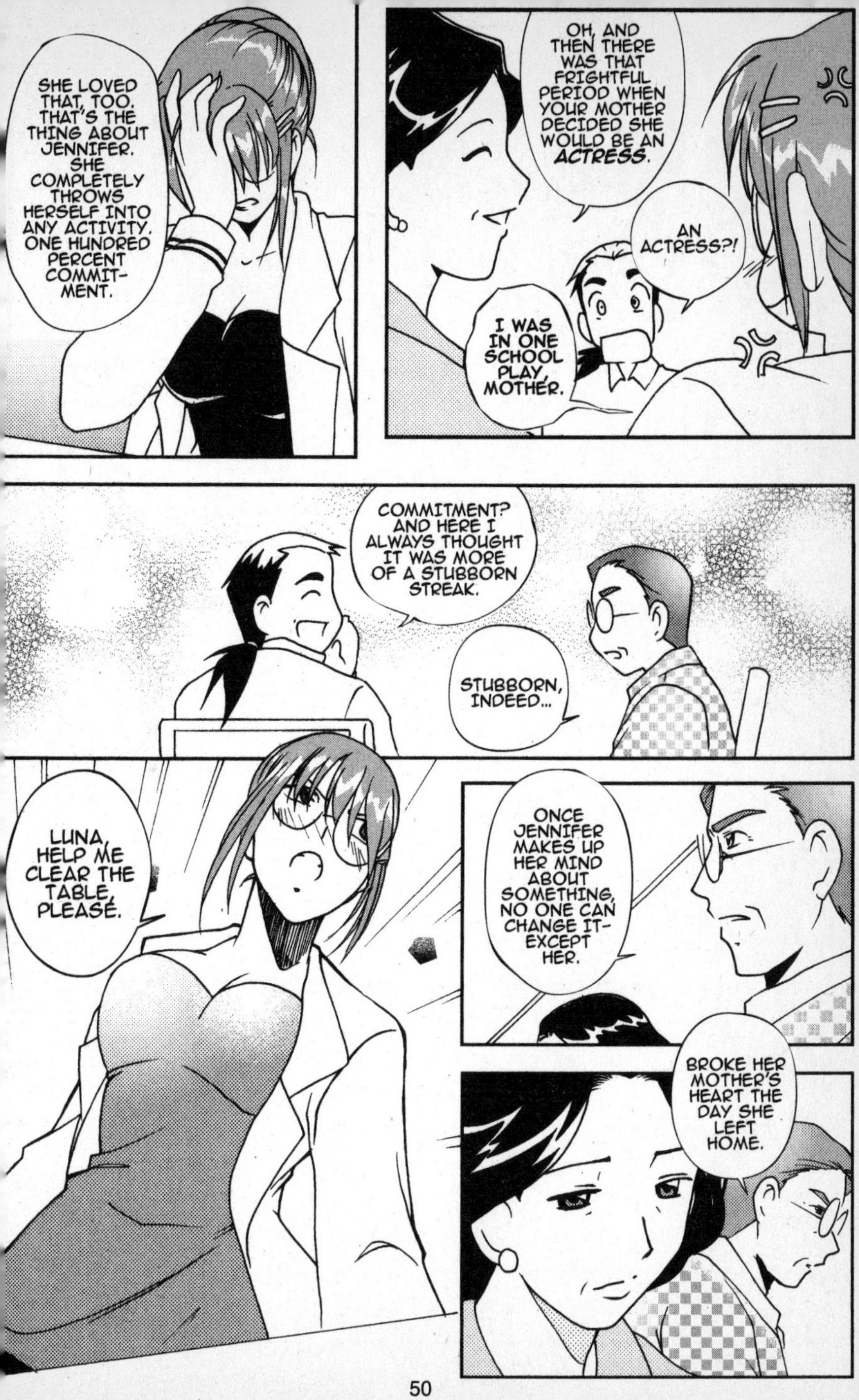
OH, AND THEN THERE WAS THAT FRIGHTFUL PERIOD WHEN YOUR MOTHER DECIDED SHE WOULD BE AN ***ACTRESS***.
AN ACTRESS?!
I WAS IN ONE SCHOOL PLAY, MOTHER.
SHE LOVED THAT, TOO. THAT'S THE THING ABOUT JENNIFER. SHE COMPLETELY THROWS HERSELF INTO ANY ACTIVITY. ONE HUNDRED PERCENT COMMIT-MENT.
COMMITMENT? AND HERE I ALWAYS THOUGHT IT WAS MORE OF A STUBBORN STREAK.
STUBBORN, INDEED...
ONCE JENNIFER MAKES UP HER MIND ABOUT SOMETHING, NO ONE CAN CHANGE IT-EXCEPT HER.
BROKE HER MOTHER'S HEART THE DAY SHE LEFT HOME.
LUNA, HELP ME CLEAR THE TABLE, PLEASE.

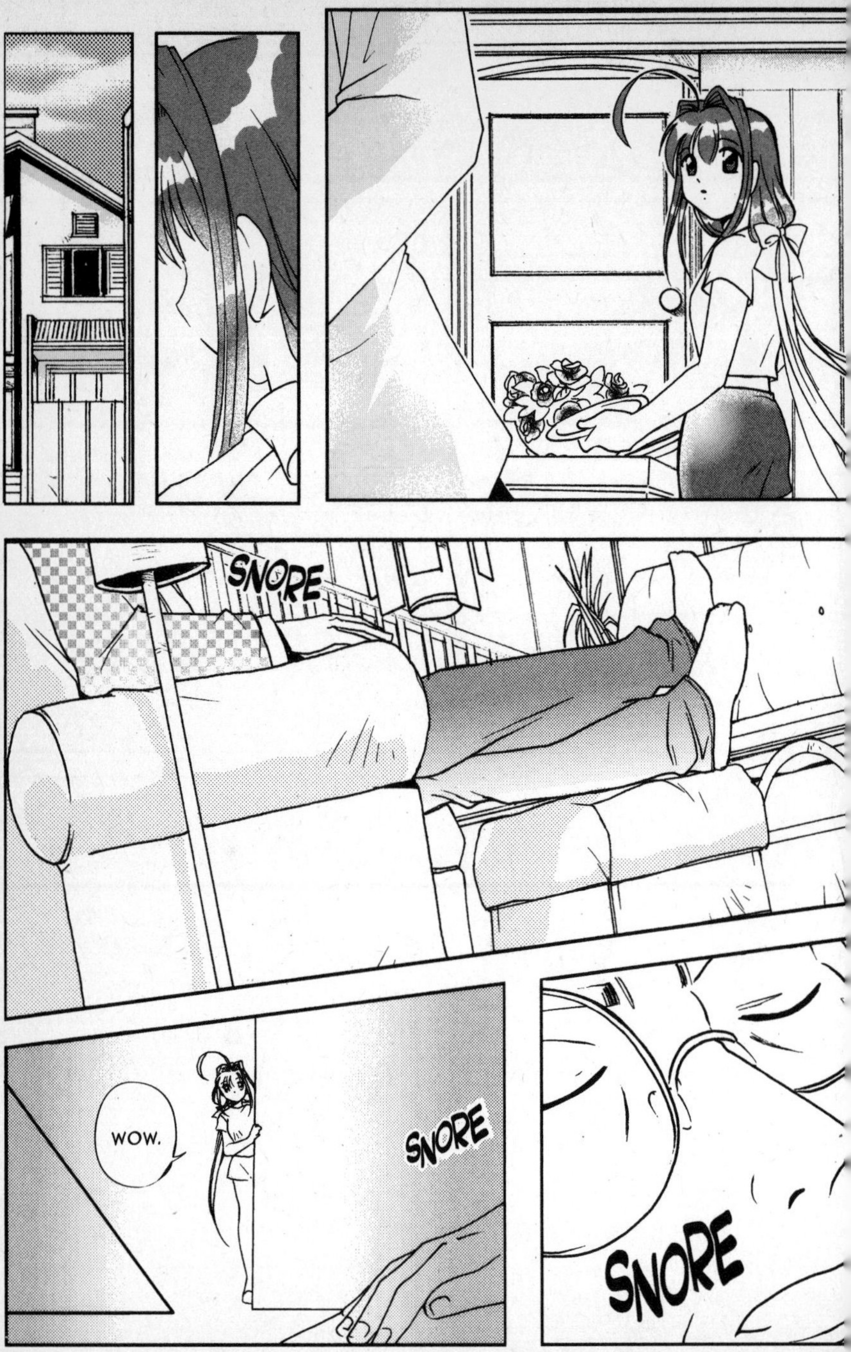
SNORE
SNORE
SNORE
WOW.

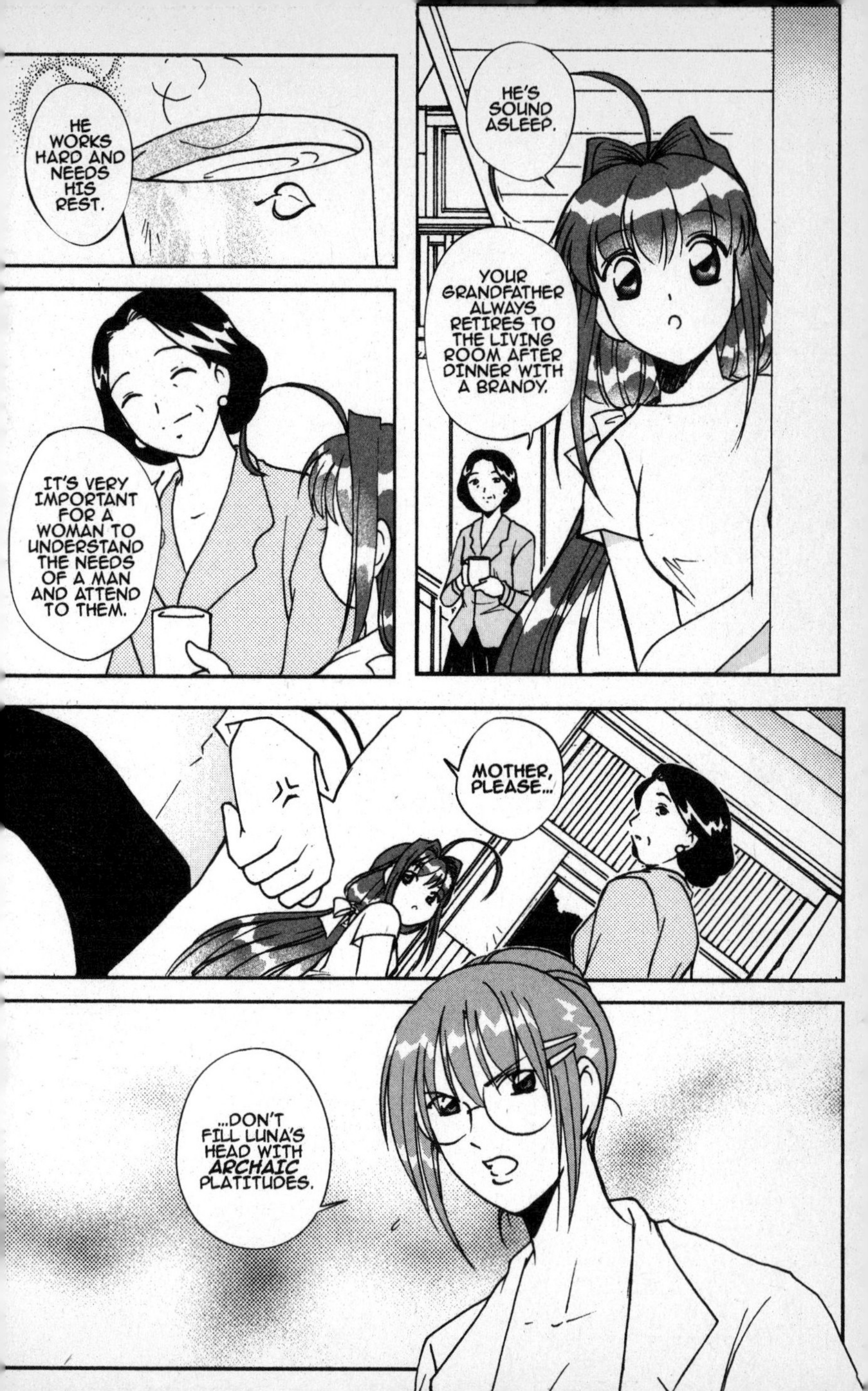
HE'S SOUND ASLEEP.
YOUR GRANDFATHER ALWAYS RETIRES TO THE LIVING ROOM AFTER DINNER WITH A BRANDY.
HE WORKS HARD AND NEEDS HIS REST.
IT'S VERY IMPORTANT FOR A WOMAN TO UNDERSTAND THE NEEDS OF A MAN AND ATTEND TO THEM.
MOTHER, PLEASE...
...DON'T FILL LUNA'S HEAD WITH ARCHAIC PLATITUDES.

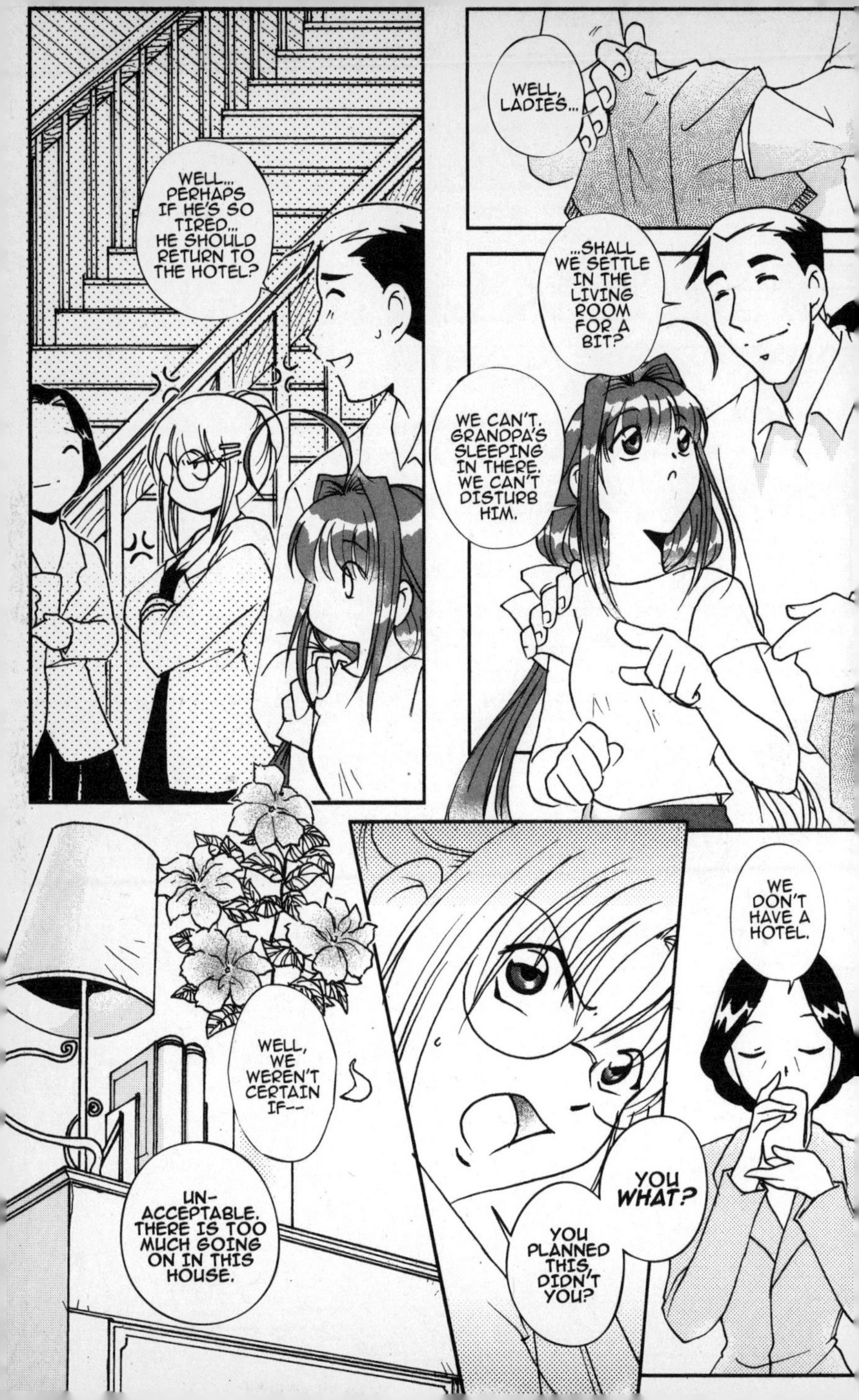
WELL, LADIES...
...SHALL WE SETTLE IN THE LIVING ROOM FOR A BIT?
WE CAN'T. GRANDPA'S SLEEPING IN THERE. WE CAN'T DISTURB HIM.
WELL... PERHAPS IF HE'S SO TIRED... HE SHOULD RETURN TO THE HOTEL?
WE DON'T HAVE A HOTEL.
YOU *WHAT?*
YOU PLANNED THIS, DIDN'T YOU?
WELL, WE WEREN'T CERTAIN IF--
UN-ACCEPTABLE. THERE IS TOO MUCH GOING ON IN THIS HOUSE.

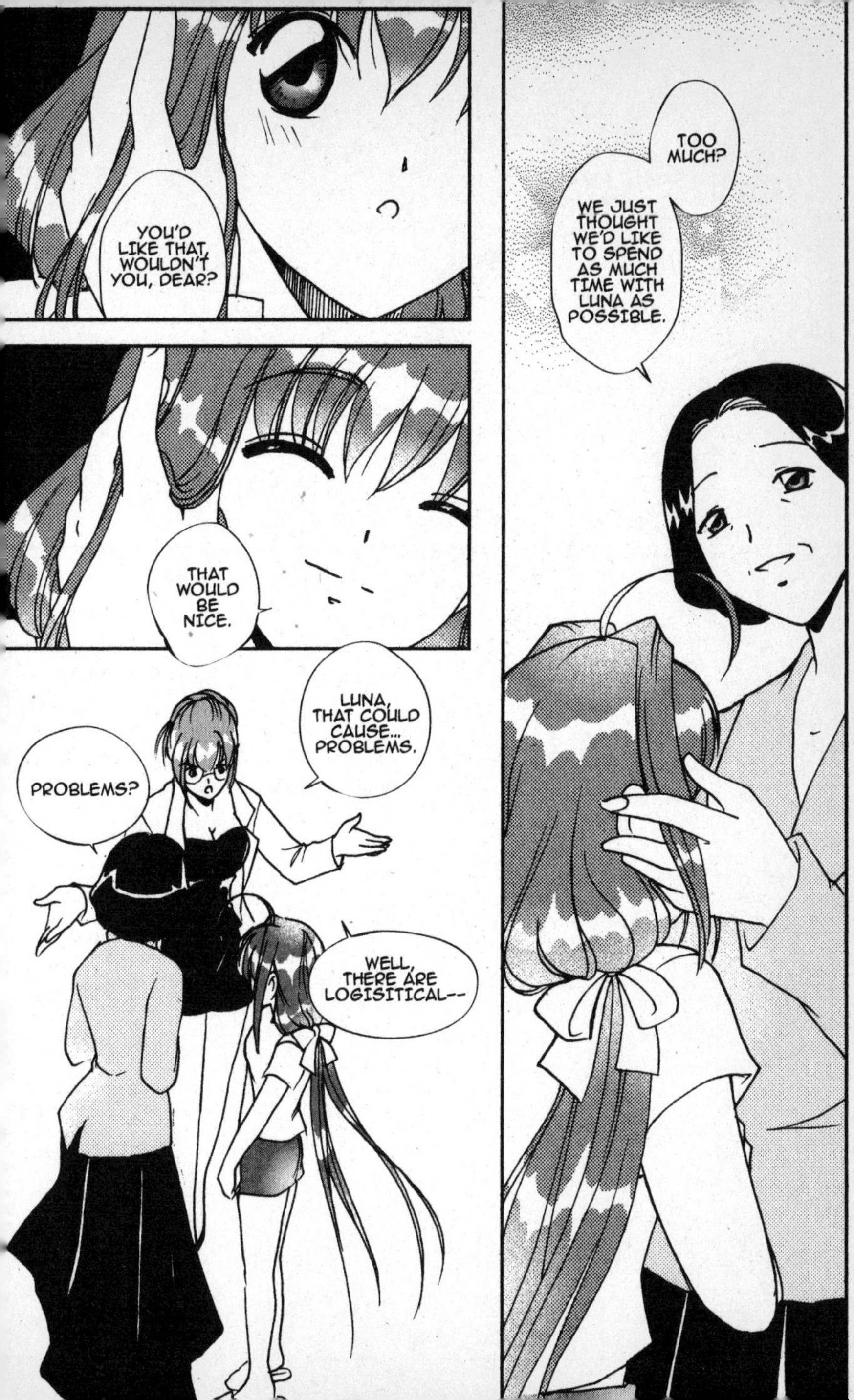
TOO MUCH?
WE JUST THOUGHT WE'D LIKE TO SPEND AS MUCH TIME WITH LUNA AS POSSIBLE.
YOU'D LIKE THAT, WOULDN'T YOU, DEAR?
THAT WOULD BE NICE.
LUNA, THAT COULD CAUSE... PROBLEMS.
PROBLEMS?
WELL, THERE ARE LOGISITICAL--

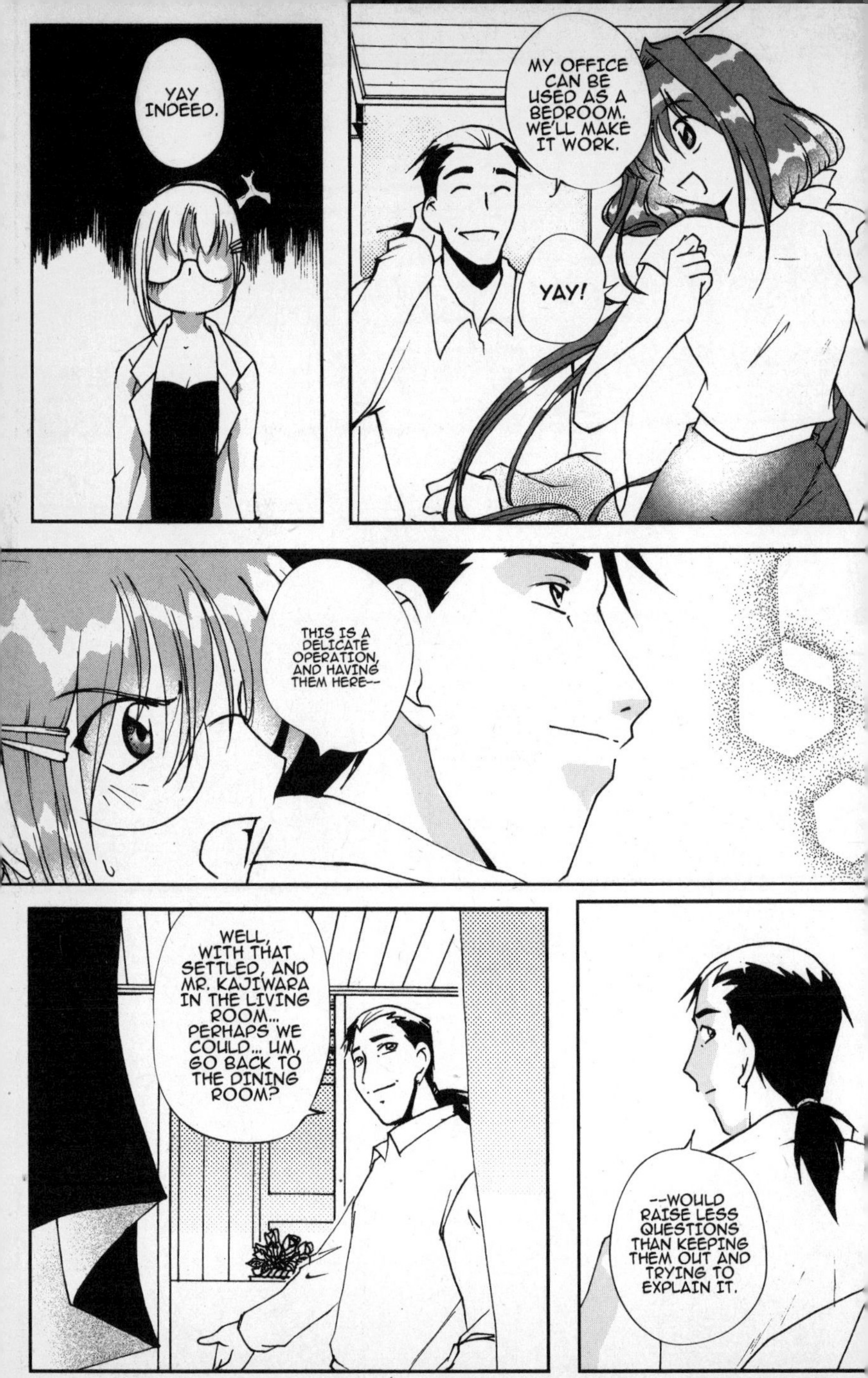
MY OFFICE CAN BE USED AS A BEDROOM. WE'LL MAKE IT WORK.
YAY!
YAY INDEED.
THIS IS A DELICATE OPERATION, AND HAVING THEM HERE--
--WOULD RAISE LESS QUESTIONS THAN KEEPING THEM OUT AND TRYING TO EXPLAIN IT.
WELL, WITH THAT SETTLED, AND MR. KAJIWARA IN THE LIVING ROOM... PERHAPS WE COULD... UM, GO BACK TO THE DINING ROOM?

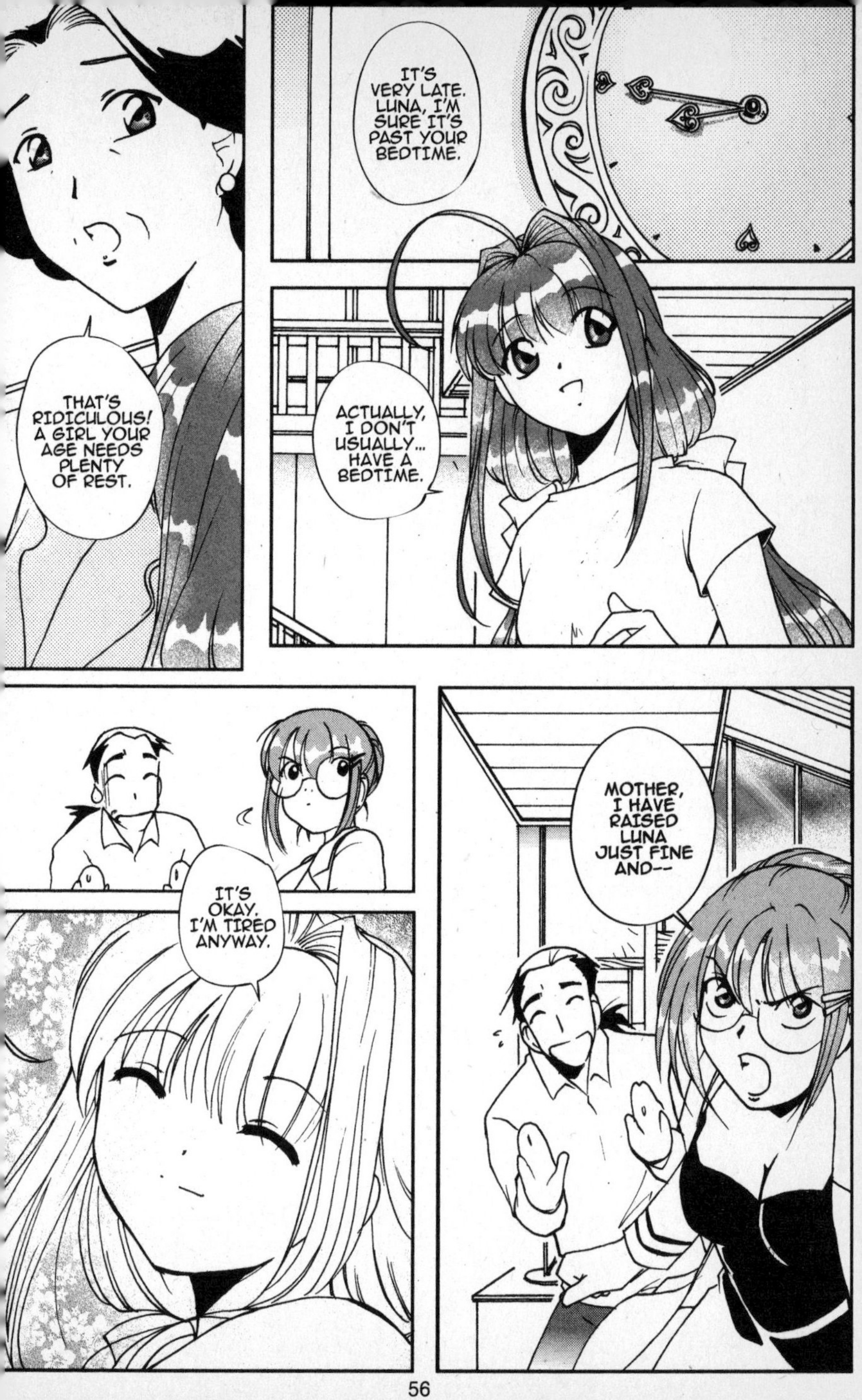
IT'S VERY LATE. LUNA, I'M SURE IT'S PAST YOUR BEDTIME.
ACTUALLY, I DON'T USUALLY... HAVE A BEDTIME.
THAT'S RIDICULOUS! A GIRL YOUR AGE NEEDS PLENTY OF REST.
MOTHER, I HAVE RAISED LUNA JUST FINE AND--
IT'S OKAY. I'M TIRED ANYWAY.

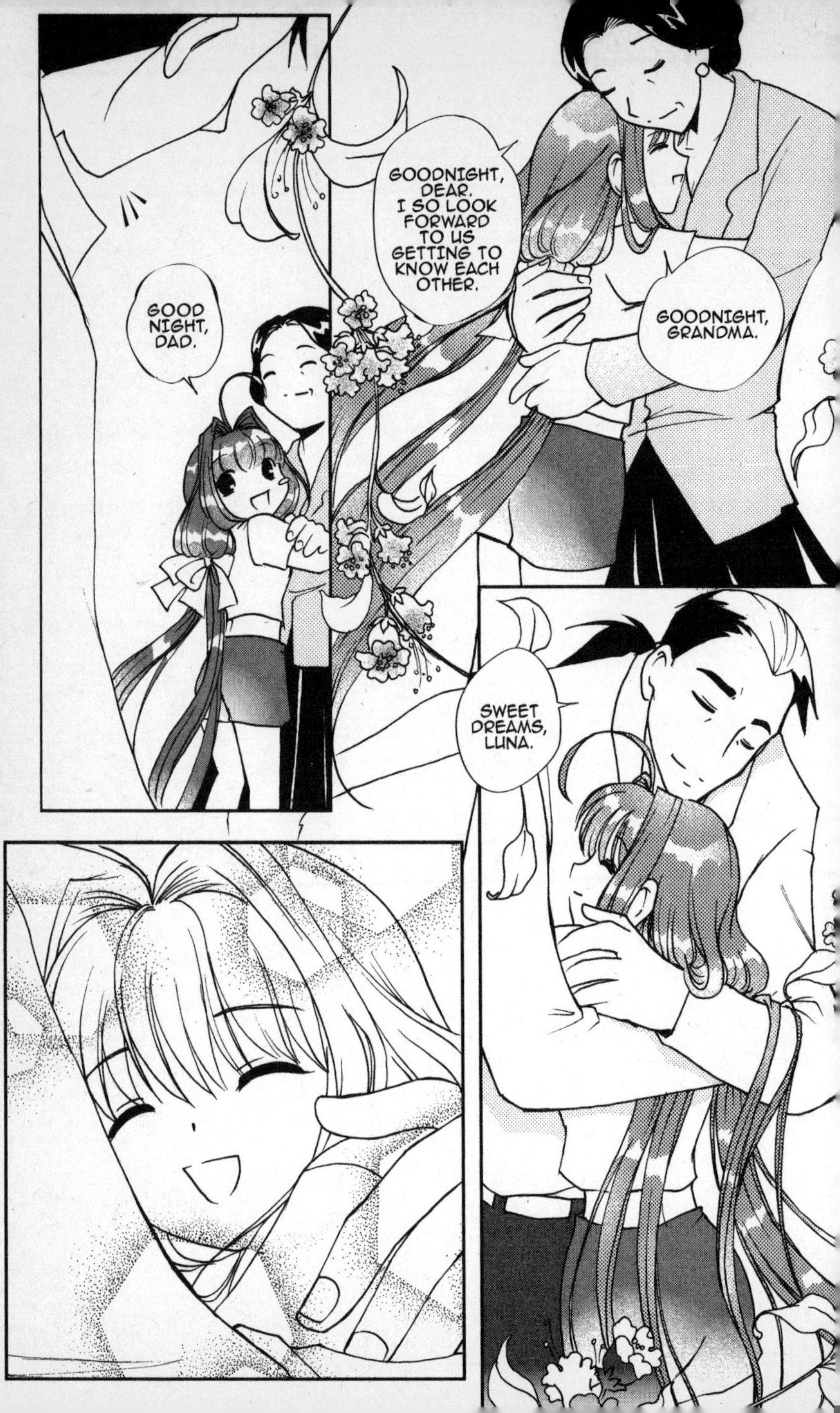
GOODNIGHT, GRANDMA.
GOODNIGHT, DEAR. I SO LOOK FORWARD TO US GETTING TO KNOW EACH OTHER.
GOOD NIGHT, DAD.
SWEET DREAMS, LUNA.

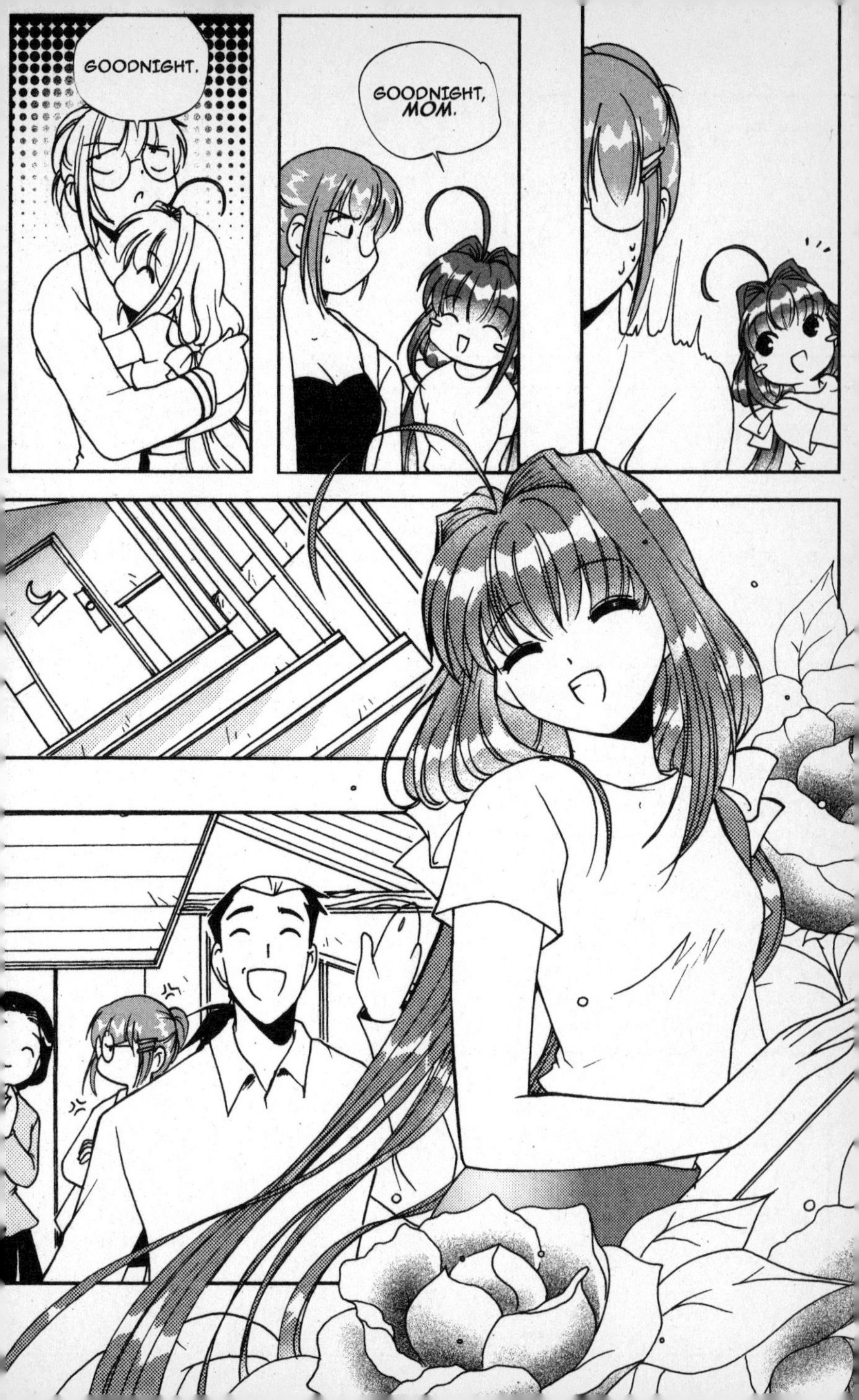
GOODNIGHT, MOM.
GOODNIGHT.

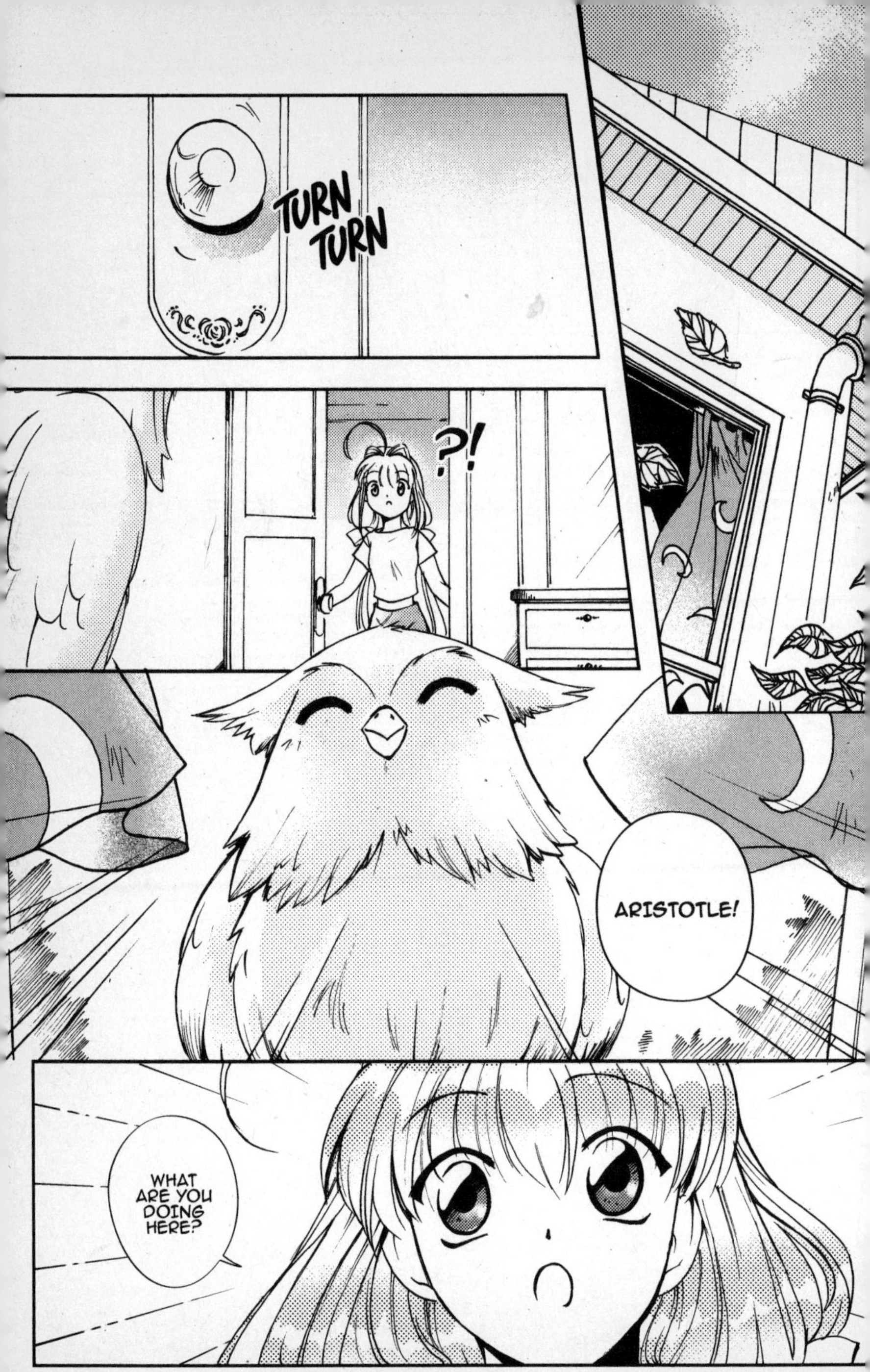
TURN TURN
?!
ARISTOTLE!
WHAT ARE YOU DOING HERE?

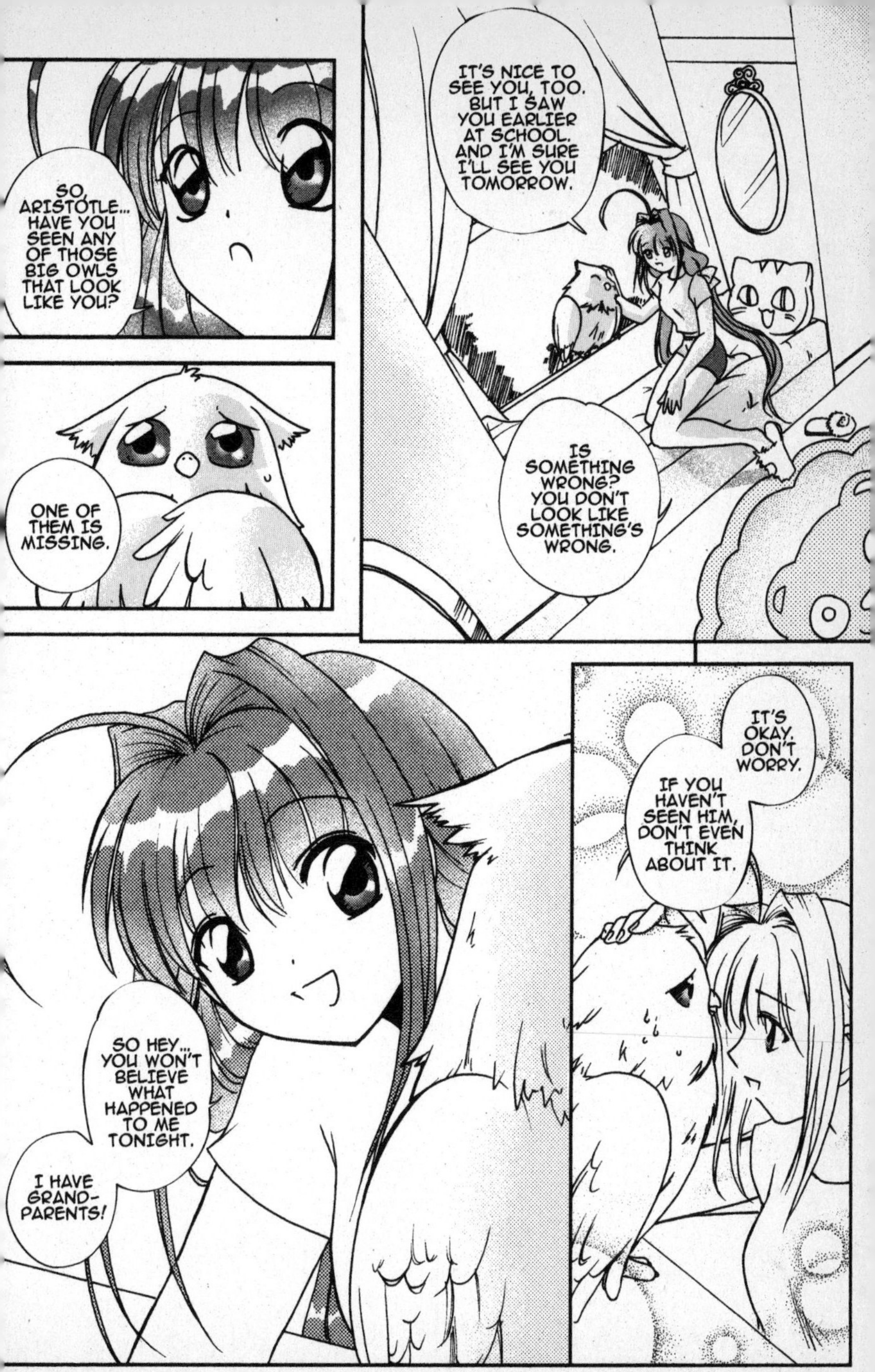
IT'S NICE TO SEE YOU, TOO. BUT I SAW YOU EARLIER AT SCHOOL. AND I'M SURE I'LL SEE YOU TOMORROW.
IS SOMETHING WRONG? YOU DON'T LOOK LIKE SOMETHING'S WRONG.
SO, ARISTOTLE... HAVE YOU SEEN ANY OF THOSE BIG OWLS THAT LOOK LIKE YOU?
ONE OF THEM IS MISSING.
IT'S OKAY. DON'T WORRY.
IF YOU HAVEN'T SEEN HIM, DON'T EVEN THINK ABOUT IT.
SO HEY... YOU WON'T BELIEVE WHAT HAPPENED TO ME TONIGHT.
I HAVE GRAND-PARENTS!

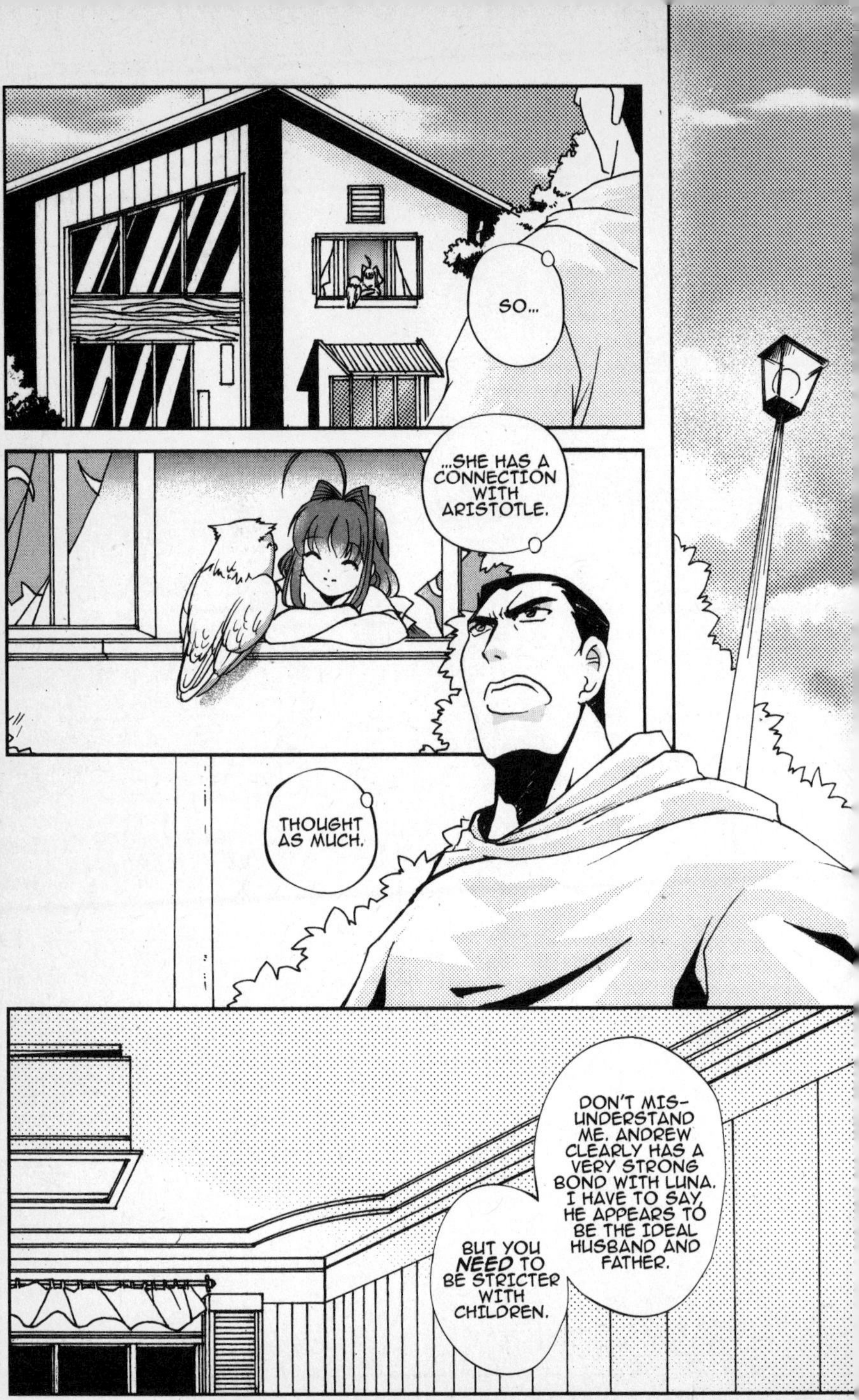
SO...
...SHE HAS A CONNECTION WITH ARISTOTLE.
THOUGHT AS MUCH.
DON'T MIS-UNDERSTAND ME. ANDREW CLEARLY HAS A VERY STRONG BOND WITH LUNA. I HAVE TO SAY, HE APPEARS TO BE THE IDEAL HUSBAND AND FATHER.
BUT YOU ***NEED*** TO BE STRICTER WITH CHILDREN.

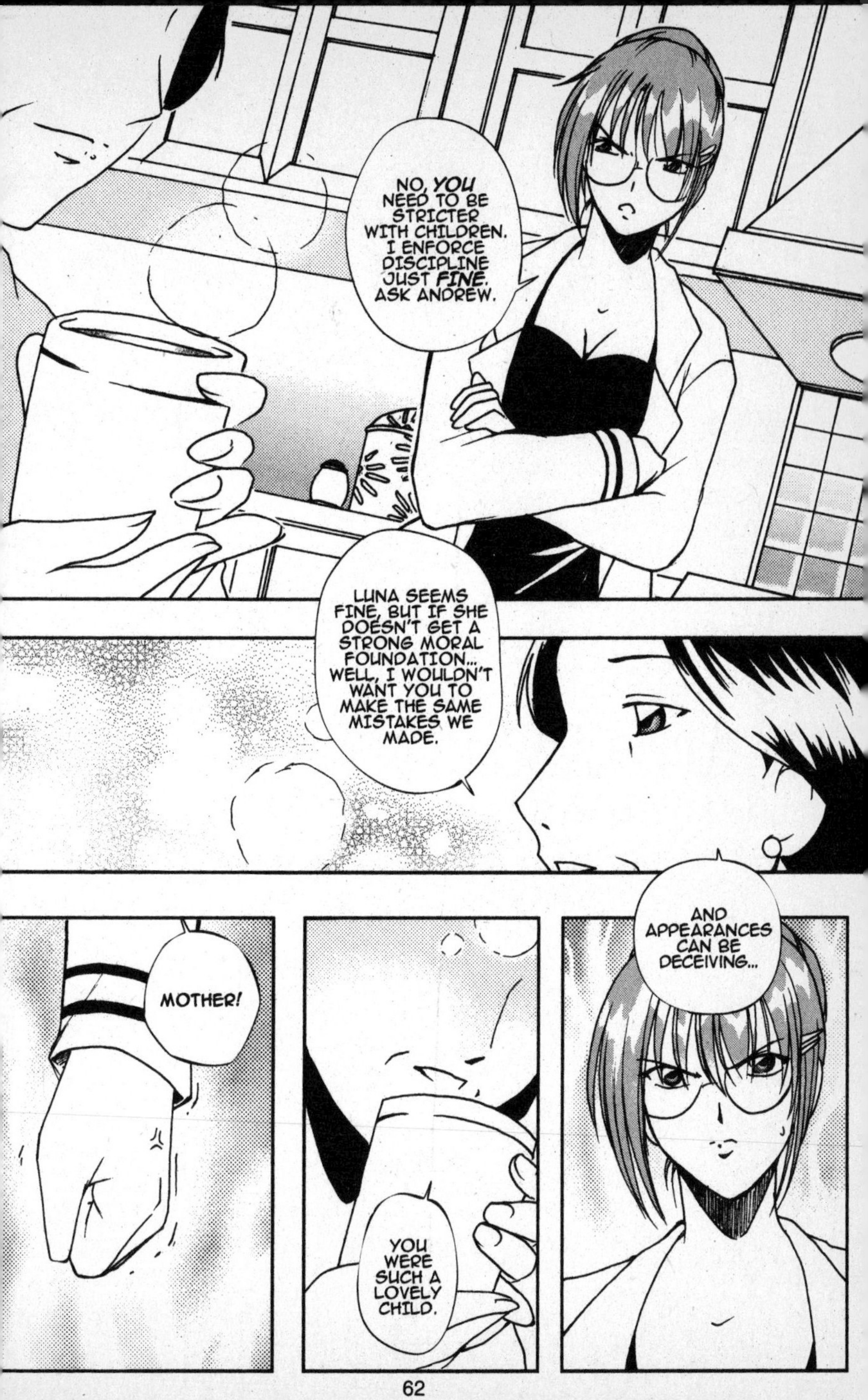
NO, *YOU* NEED TO BE STRICTER WITH CHILDREN. I ENFORCE DISCIPLINE JUST *FINE*. ASK ANDREW.
LUNA SEEMS FINE, BUT IF SHE DOESN'T GET A STRONG MORAL FOUNDATION... WELL, I WOULDN'T WANT YOU TO MAKE THE SAME MISTAKES WE MADE.
AND APPEARANCES CAN BE DECEIVING...
YOU WERE SUCH A LOVELY CHILD.
MOTHER!

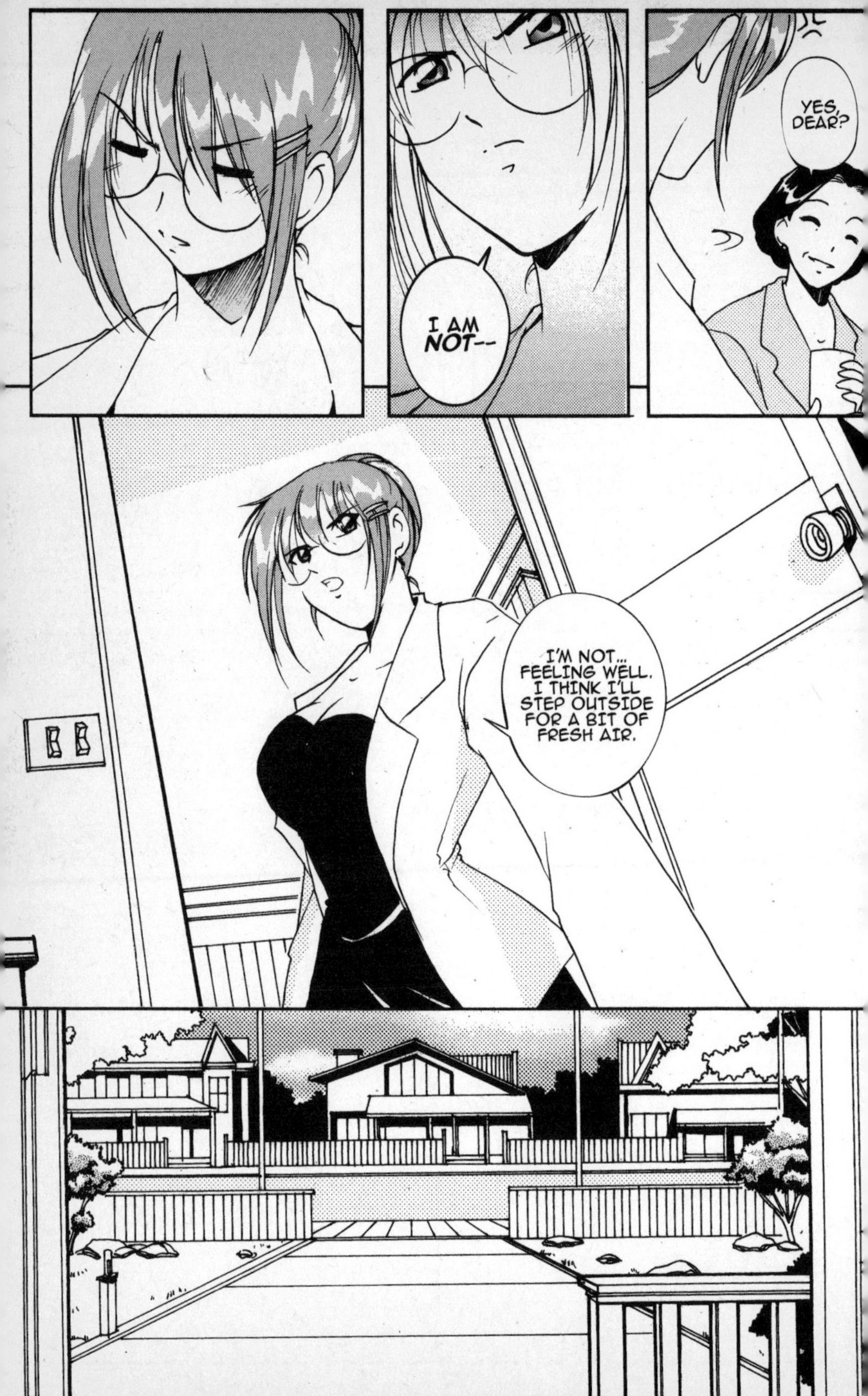
YES, DEAR?
I AM NOT--
I'M NOT... FEELING WELL. I THINK I'LL STEP OUTSIDE FOR A BIT OF FRESH AIR.

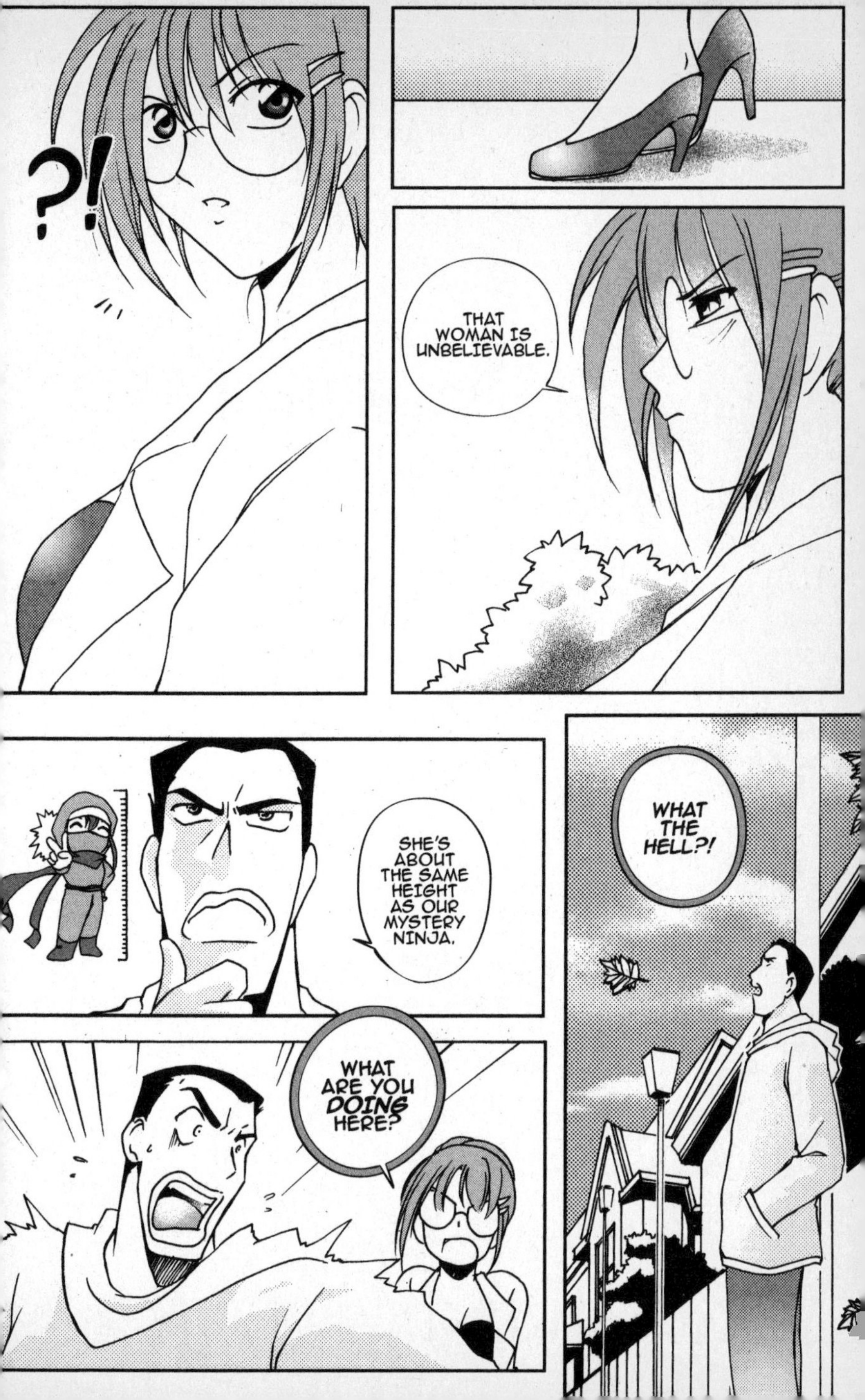
THAT WOMAN IS UNBELIEVABLE.
?!
WHAT THE HELL?!
SHE'S ABOUT THE SAME HEIGHT AS OUR MYSTERY NINJA.
WHAT ARE YOU *DOING* HERE?

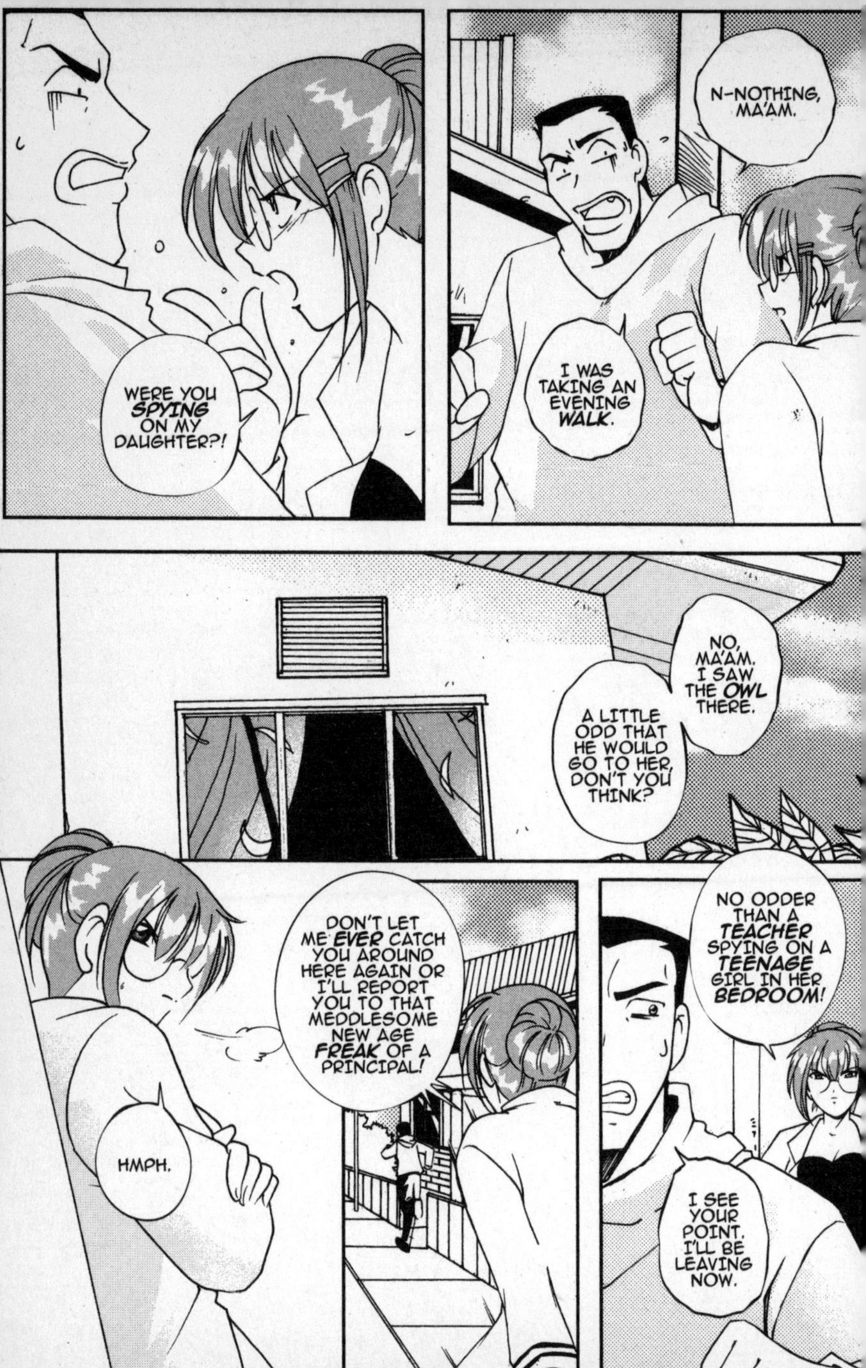
N-NOTHING, MA'AM.
I WAS TAKING AN EVENING WALK.
WERE YOU SPYING ON MY DAUGHTER?!
NO, MA'AM. I SAW THE OWL THERE.
A LITTLE ODD THAT HE WOULD GO TO HER, DON'T YOU THINK?
NO ODDER THAN A TEACHER SPYING ON A TEENAGE GIRL IN HER BEDROOM!
I SEE YOUR POINT. I'LL BE LEAVING NOW.
DON'T LET ME EVER CATCH YOU AROUND HERE AGAIN OR I'LL REPORT YOU TO THAT MEDDLESOME NEW AGE FREAK OF A PRINCIPAL!
HMPH.

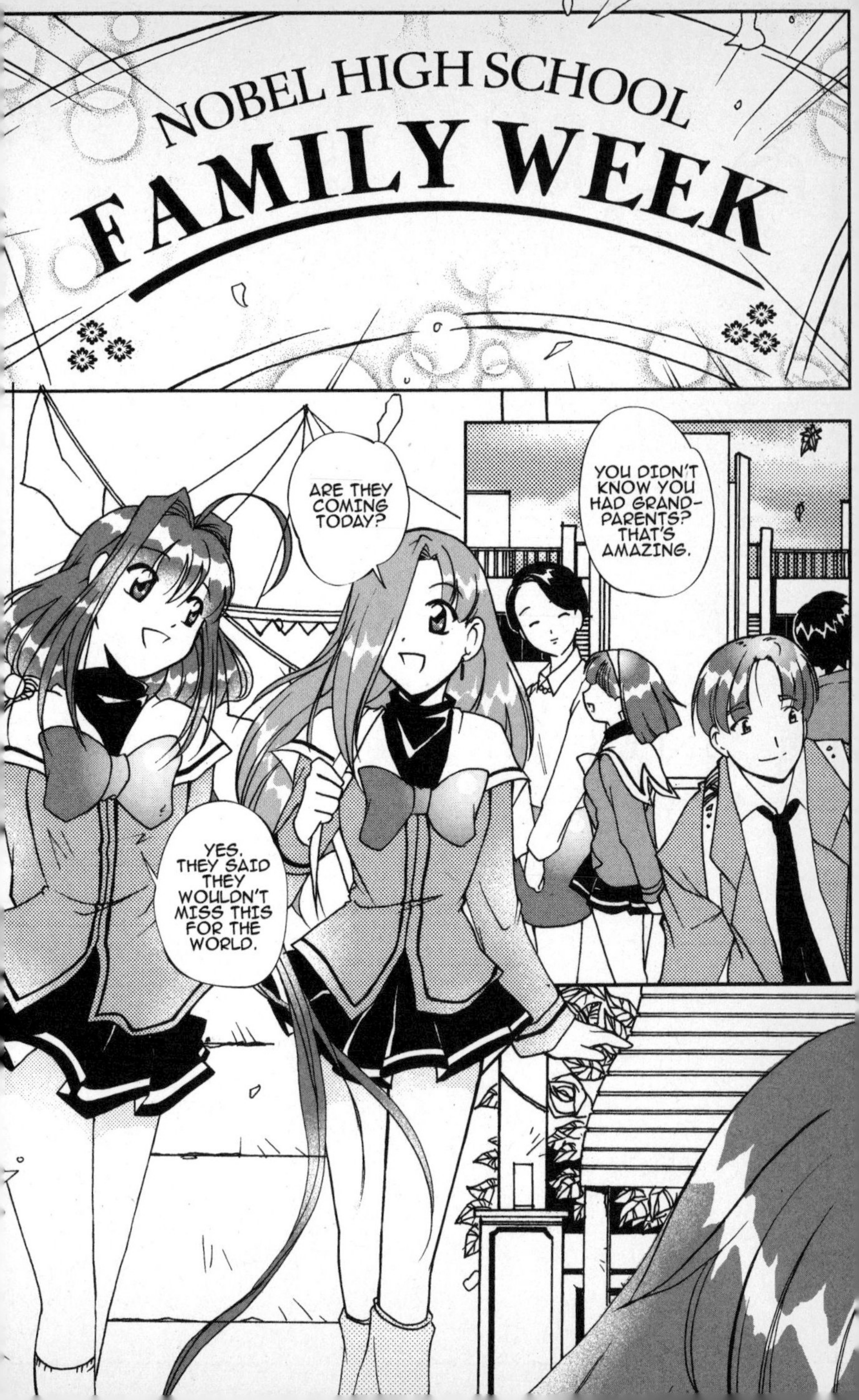
NOBEL HIGH SCHOOL
FAMILY WEEK
YOU DIDN'T KNOW YOU HAD GRAND-PARENTS? THAT'S AMAZING.
ARE THEY COMING TODAY?
YES. THEY SAID THEY WOULDN'T MISS THIS FOR THE WORLD.

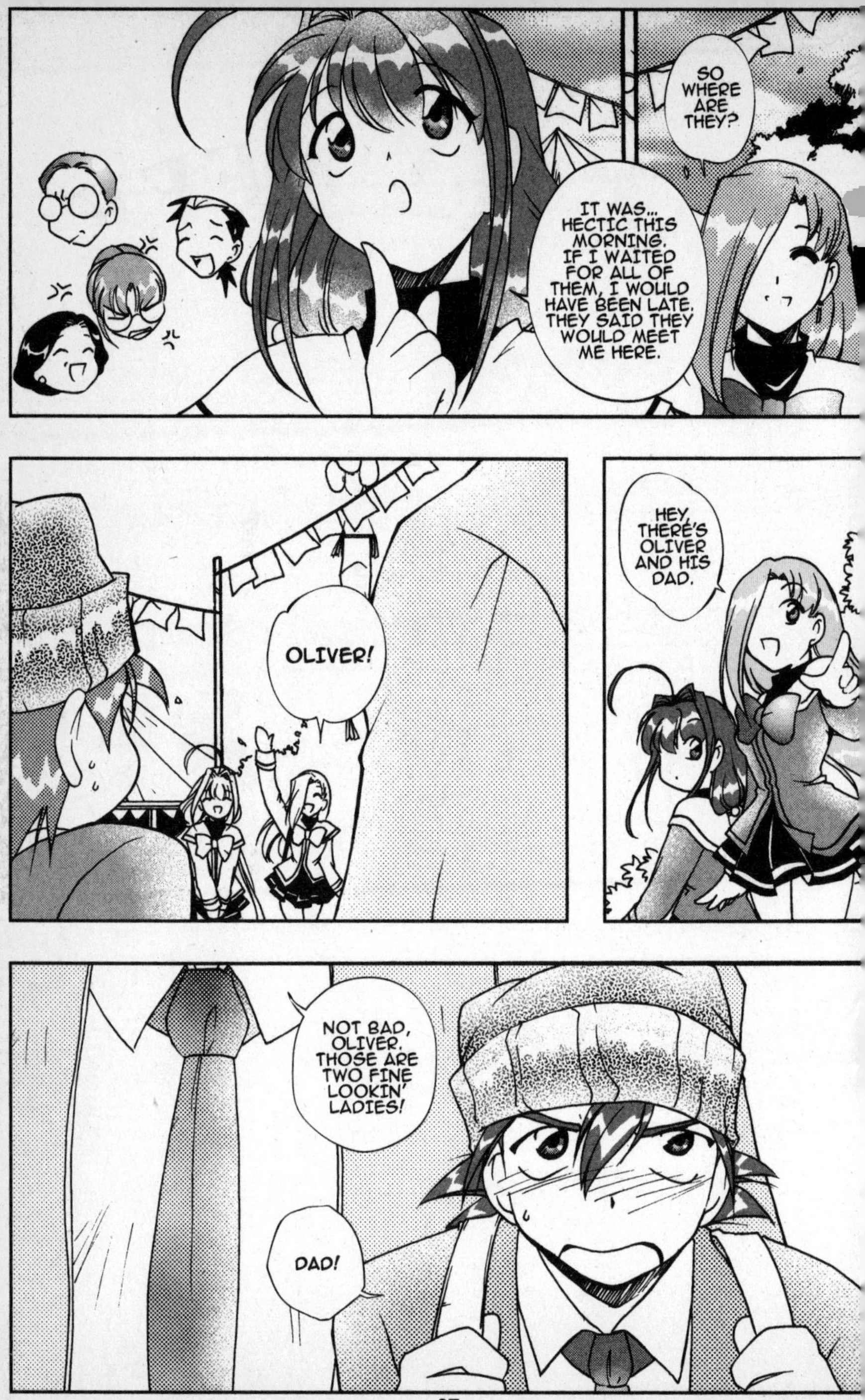
SO WHERE ARE THEY?
IT WAS... HECTIC THIS MORNING. IF I WAITED FOR ALL OF THEM, I WOULD HAVE BEEN LATE. THEY SAID THEY WOULD MEET ME HERE.
HEY, THERE'S OLIVER AND HIS DAD.
OLIVER!
NOT BAD, OLIVER. THOSE ARE TWO FINE LOOKIN' LADIES!
DAD!

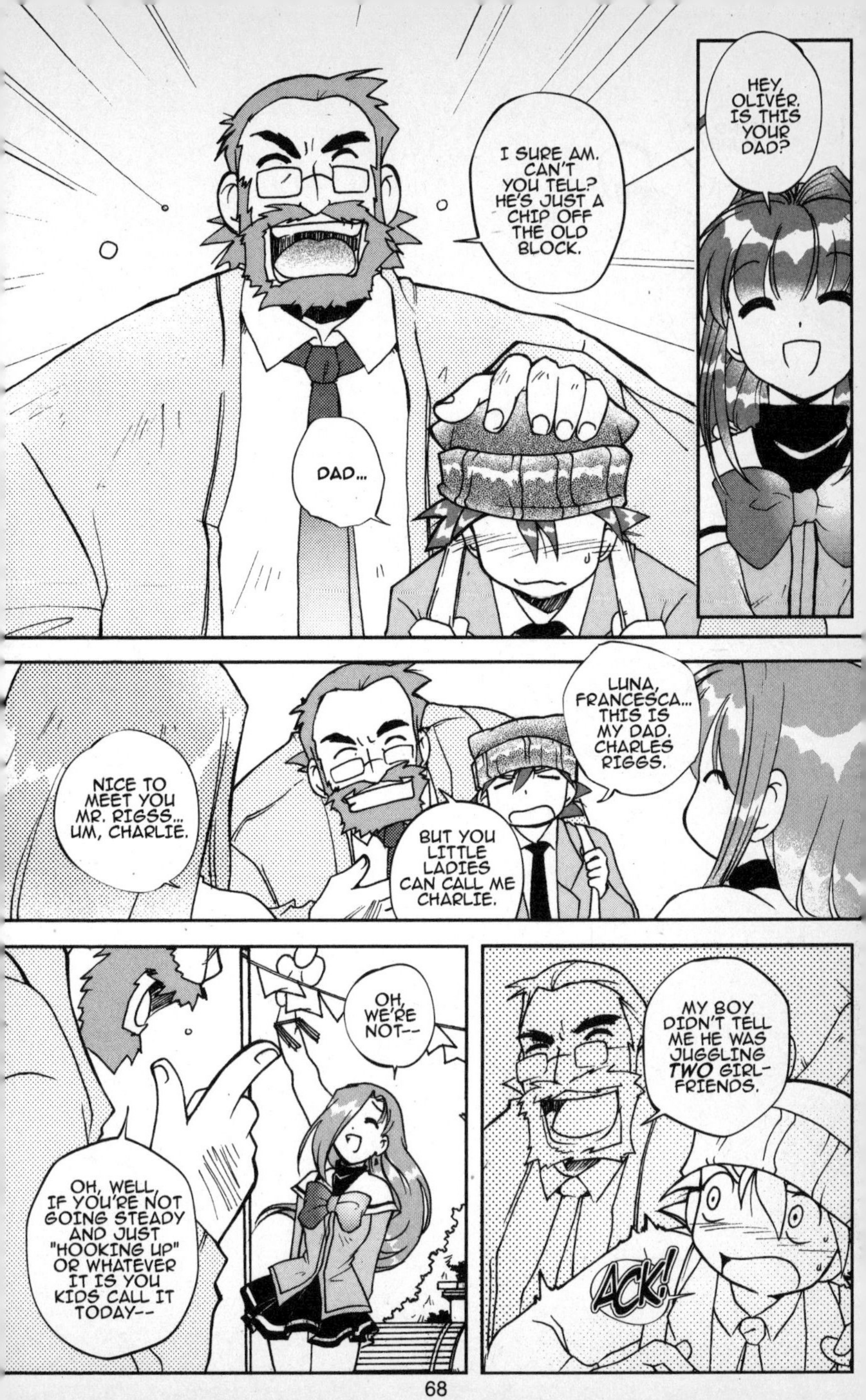
HEY, OLIVER. IS THIS YOUR DAD?
I SURE AM. CAN'T YOU TELL? HE'S JUST A CHIP OFF THE OLD BLOCK.
DAD...
LUNA, FRANCESCA... THIS IS MY DAD. CHARLES RIGGS.
BUT YOU LITTLE LADIES CAN CALL ME CHARLIE.
NICE TO MEET YOU MR. RIGSS... UM, CHARLIE.
MY BOY DIDN'T TELL ME HE WAS JUGGLING **TWO** GIRL-FRIENDS.
ACK!
OH, WE'RE NOT--
OH, WELL, IF YOU'RE NOT GOING STEADY AND JUST "HOOKING UP" OR WHATEVER IT IS YOU KIDS CALL IT TODAY--

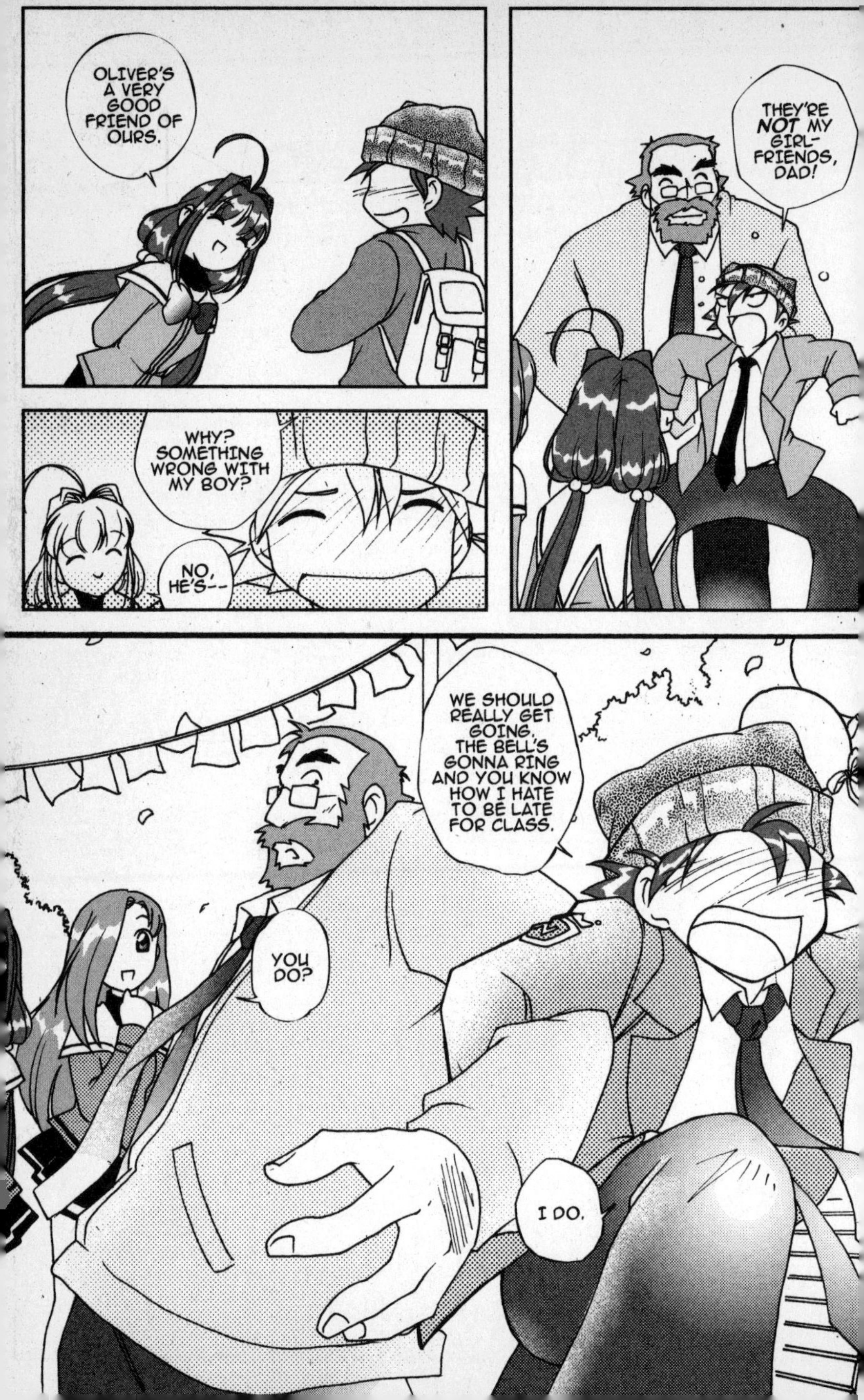
THEY'RE NOT MY GIRL-FRIENDS, DAD!
OLIVER'S A VERY GOOD FRIEND OF OURS.
WHY? SOMETHING WRONG WITH MY BOY?
NO, HE'S--
WE SHOULD REALLY GET GOING. THE BELL'S GONNA RING AND YOU KNOW HOW I HATE TO BE LATE FOR CLASS.
YOU DO?
I DO.

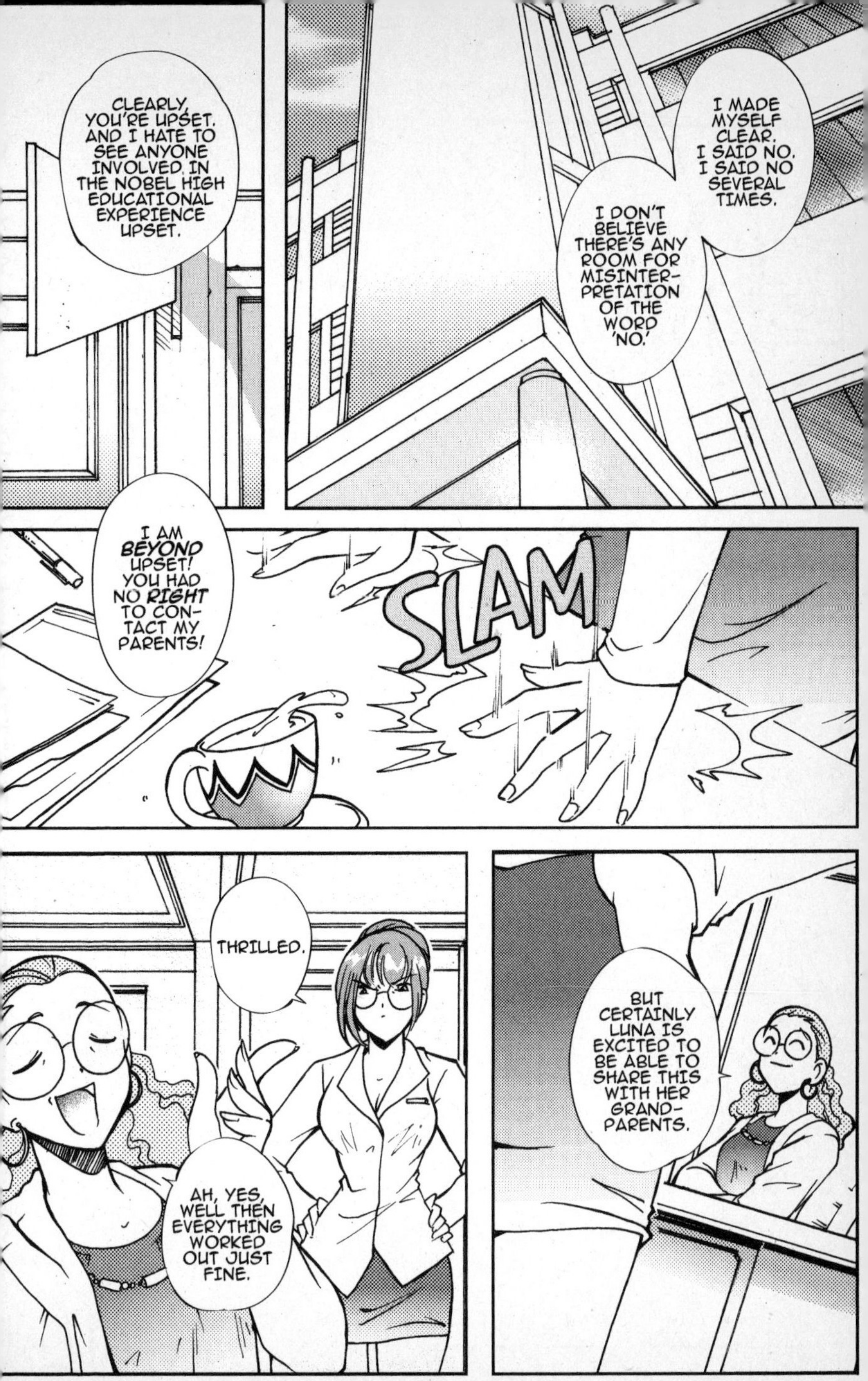
I MADE MYSELF CLEAR. I SAID NO. I SAID NO SEVERAL TIMES.
I DON'T BELIEVE THERE'S ANY ROOM FOR MISINTER-PRETATION OF THE WORD 'NO.'
CLEARLY, YOU'RE UPSET. AND I HATE TO SEE ANYONE INVOLVED IN THE NOBEL HIGH EDUCATIONAL EXPERIENCE UPSET.
SLAM
I AM *BEYOND* UPSET! YOU HAD NO *RIGHT* TO CON-TACT MY PARENTS!
BUT CERTAINLY LUNA IS EXCITED TO BE ABLE TO SHARE THIS WITH HER GRAND-PARENTS.
THRILLED.
AH, YES, WELL THEN EVERYTHING WORKED OUT JUST FINE.

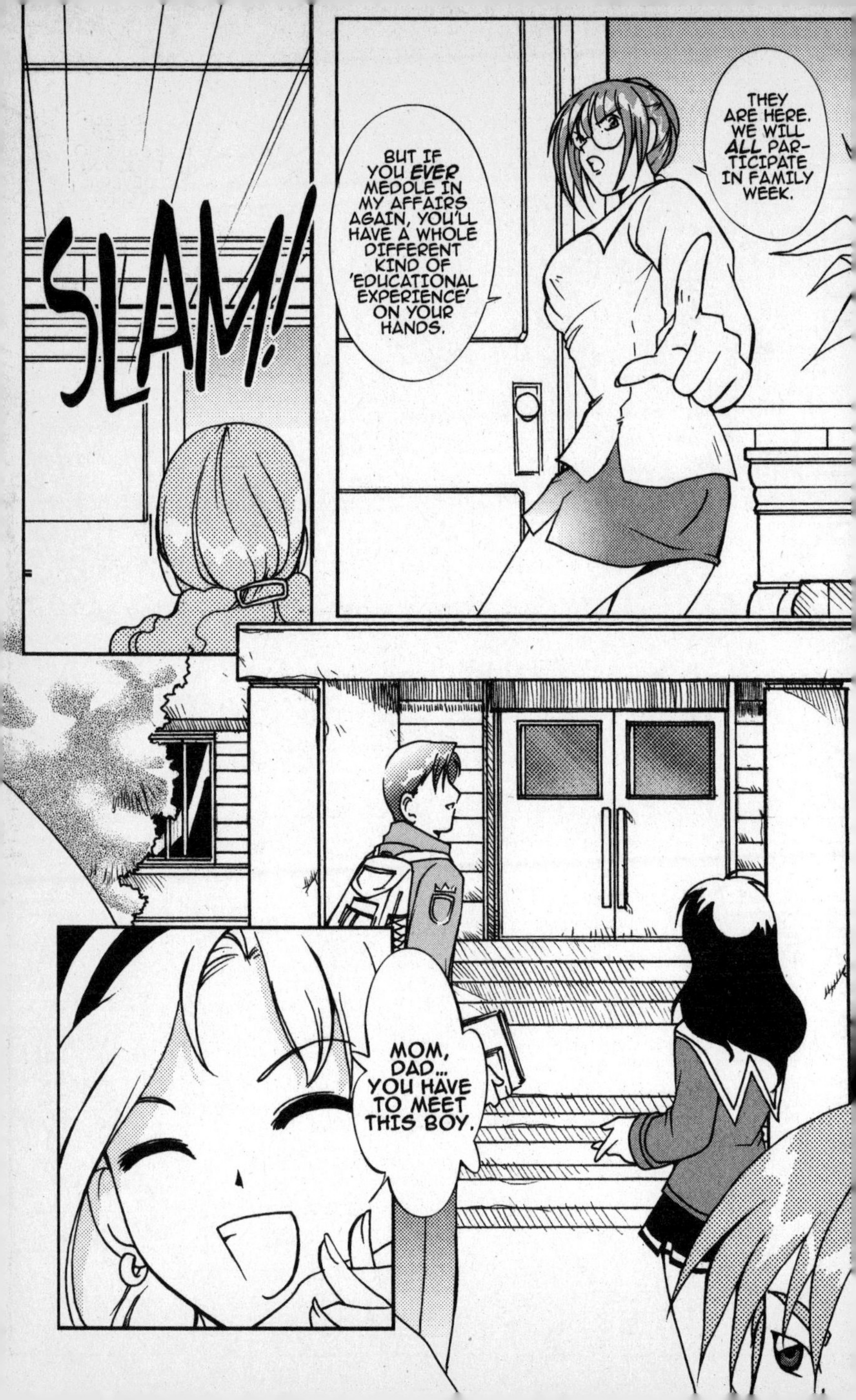
THEY ARE HERE. WE WILL ALL PARTICIPATE IN FAMILY WEEK.
BUT IF YOU EVER MEDDLE IN MY AFFAIRS AGAIN, YOU'LL HAVE A WHOLE DIFFERENT KIND OF 'EDUCATIONAL EXPERIENCE' ON YOUR HANDS.
SLAM!
MOM, DAD... YOU HAVE TO MEET THIS BOY.

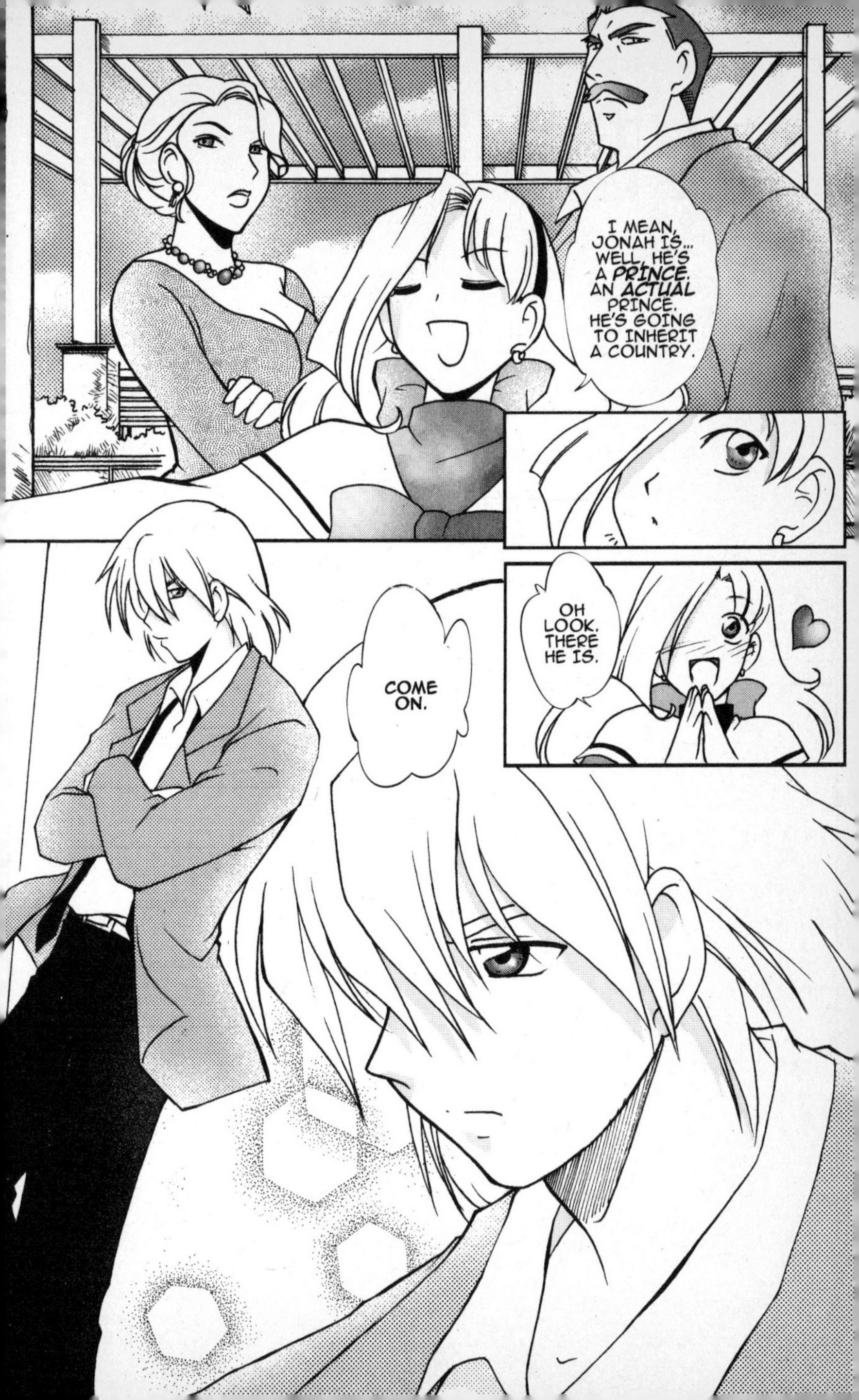
I MEAN, JONAH IS... WELL, HE'S A PRINCE. AN ACTUAL PRINCE. HE'S GOING TO INHERIT A COUNTRY.
OH LOOK. THERE HE IS.
COME ON.

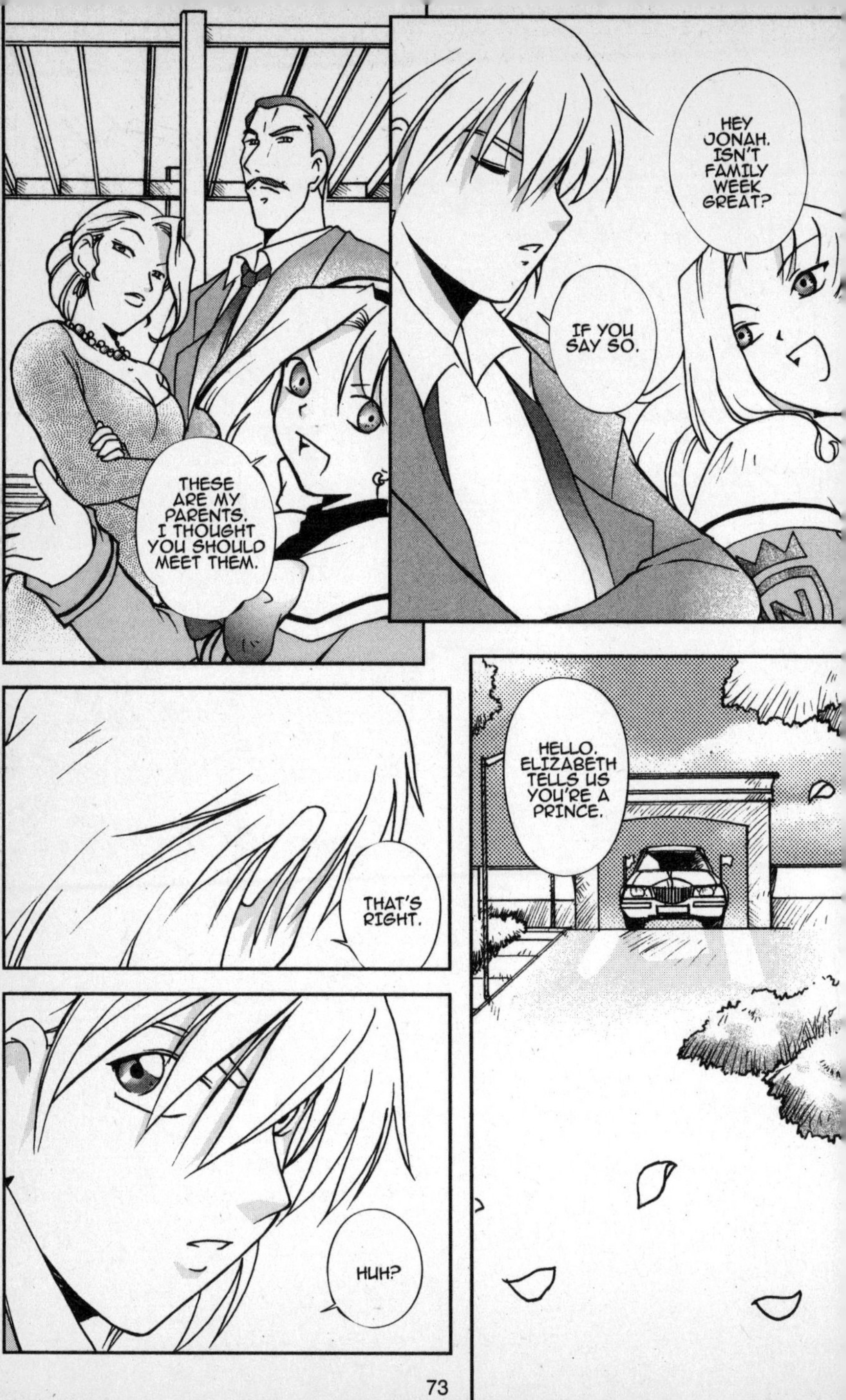
HEY JONAH. ISN'T FAMILY WEEK GREAT?
IF YOU SAY SO.
THESE ARE MY PARENTS. I THOUGHT YOU SHOULD MEET THEM.
HELLO. ELIZABETH TELLS US YOU'RE A PRINCE.
THAT'S RIGHT.
HUH?

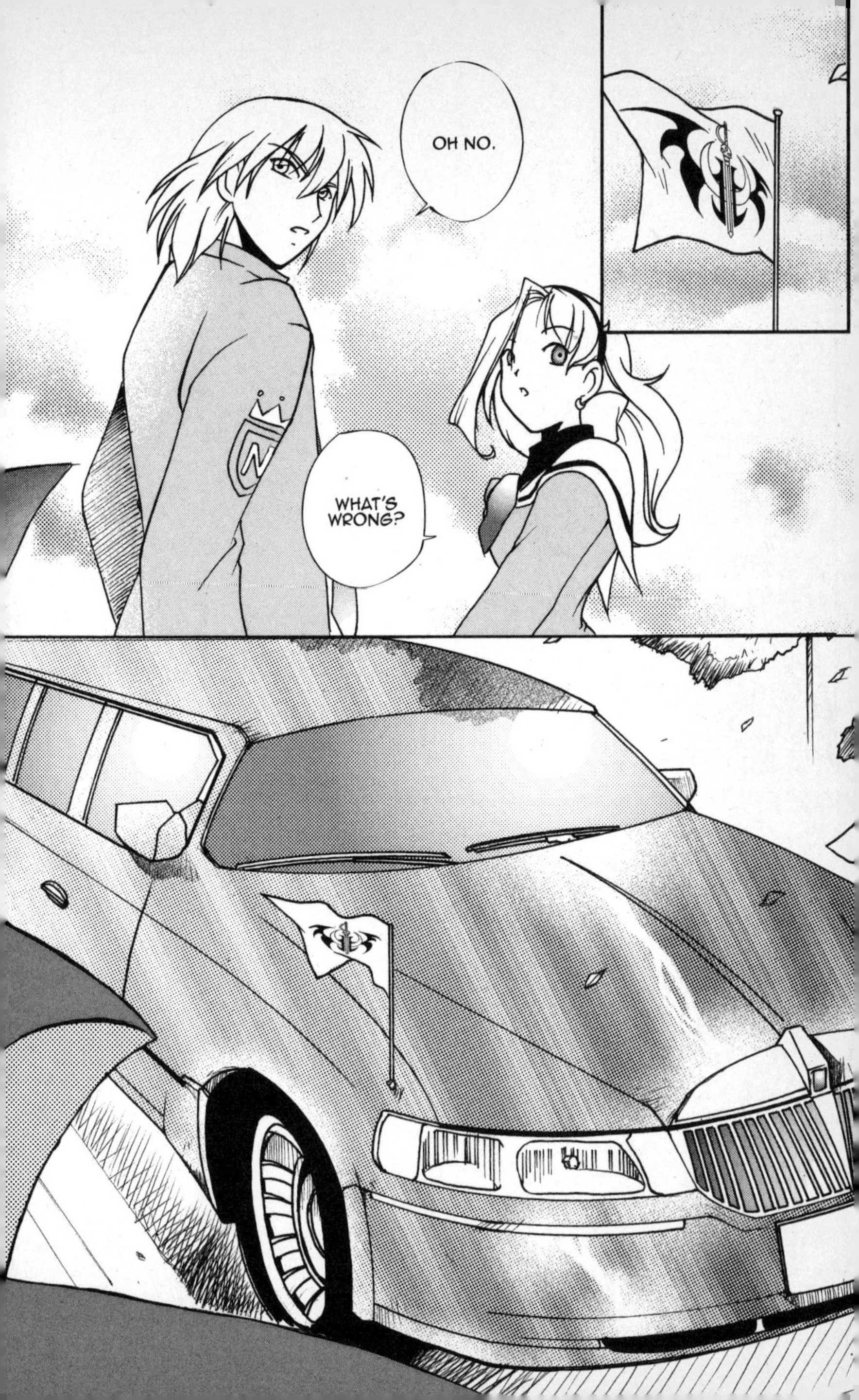
OH NO.
WHAT'S WRONG?

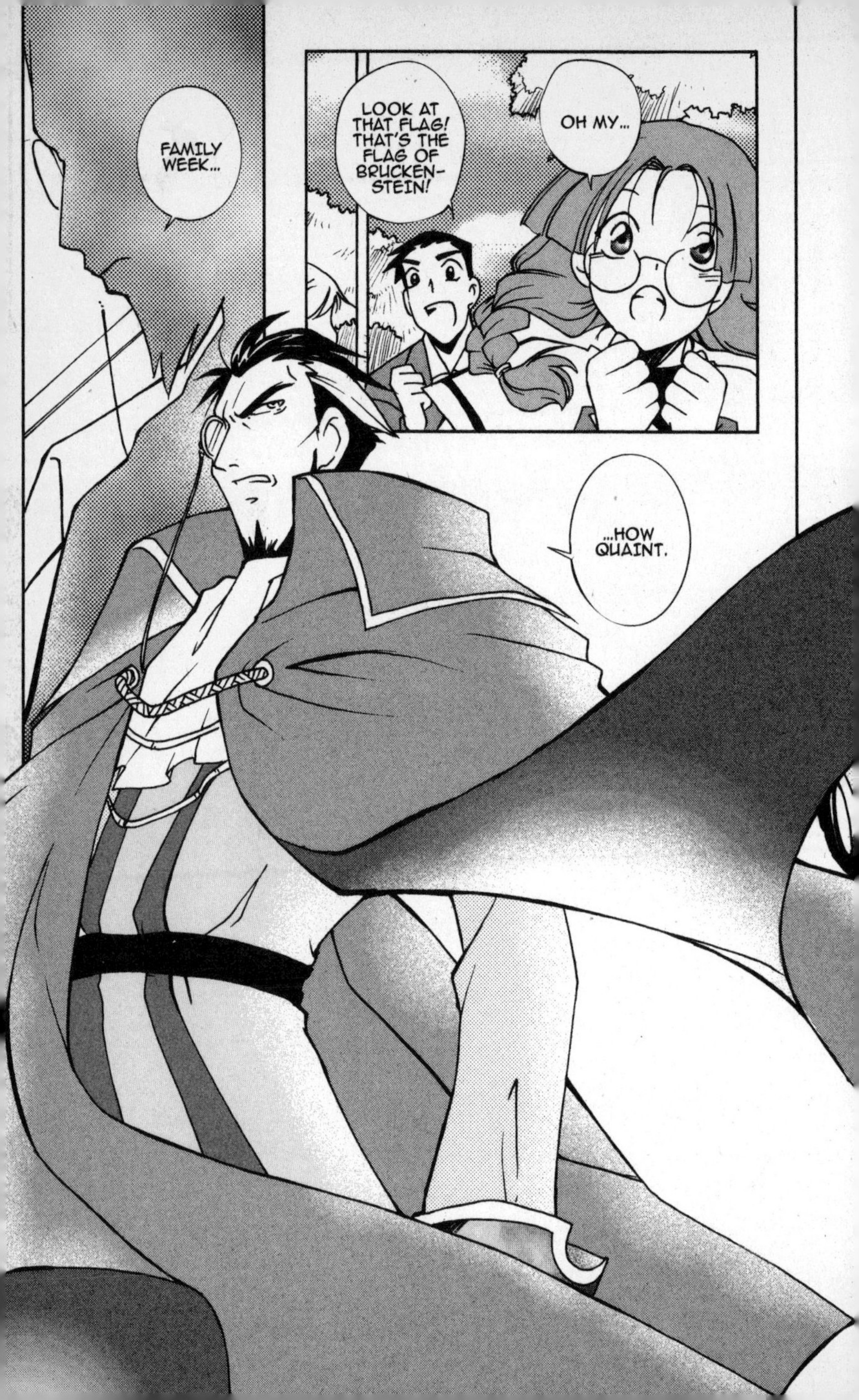
OH MY...
LOOK AT THAT FLAG! THAT'S THE FLAG OF BRUCKEN-STEIN!
FAMILY WEEK...
...HOW QUAINT.

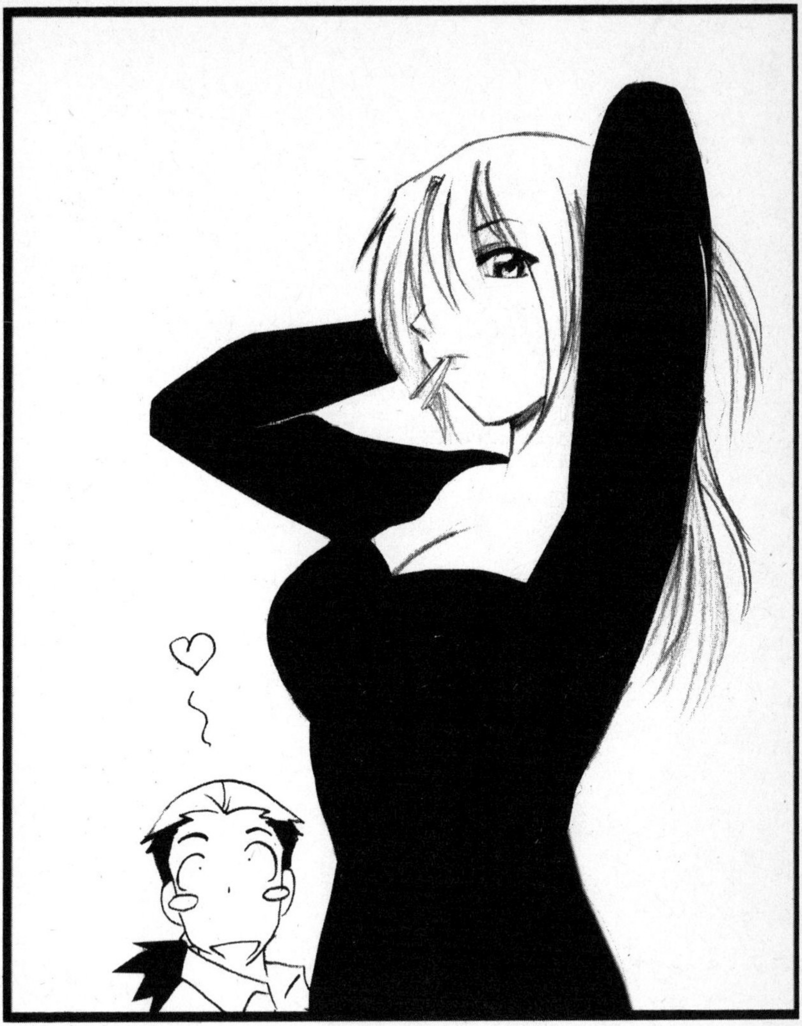

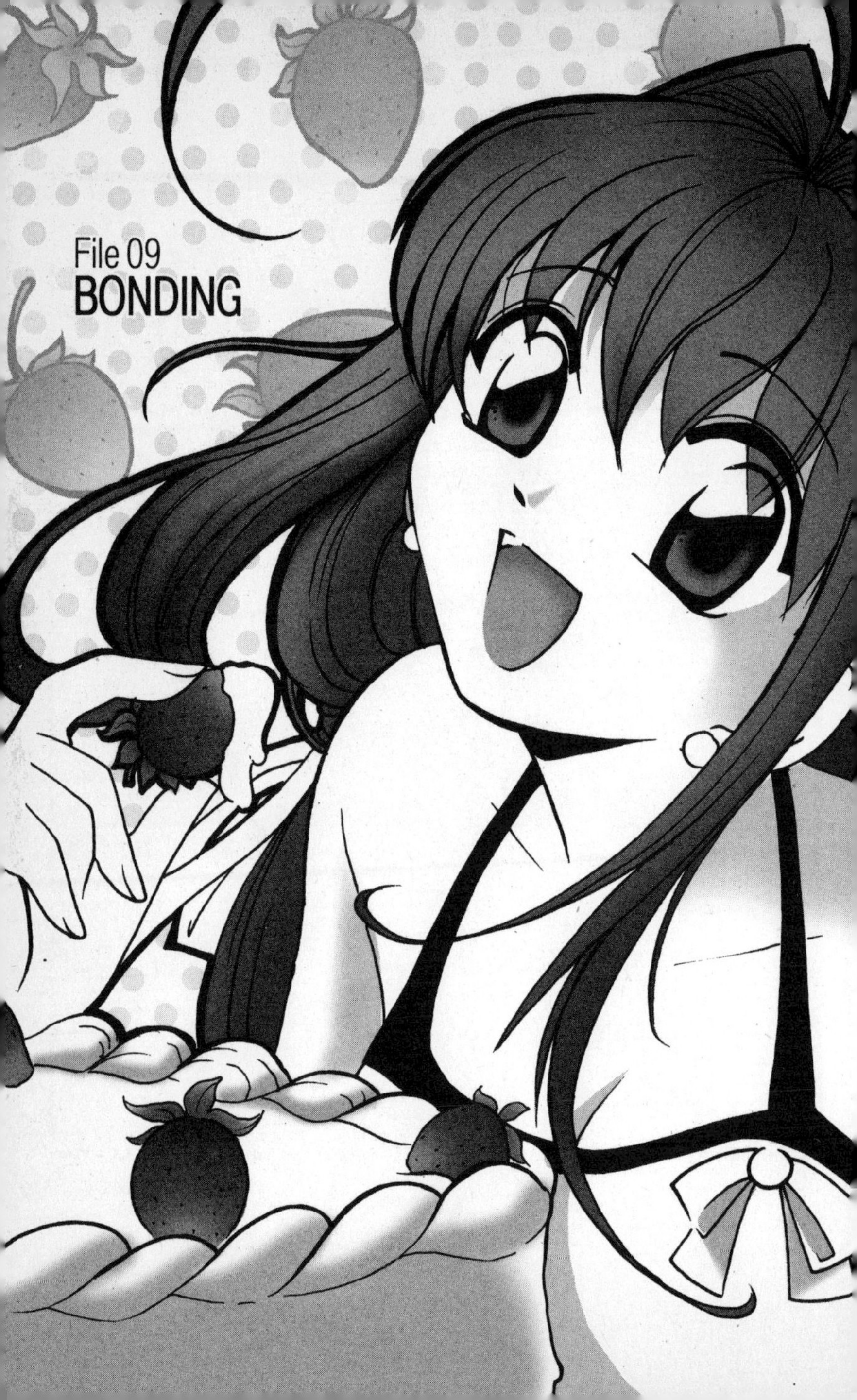
File 09
BONDING

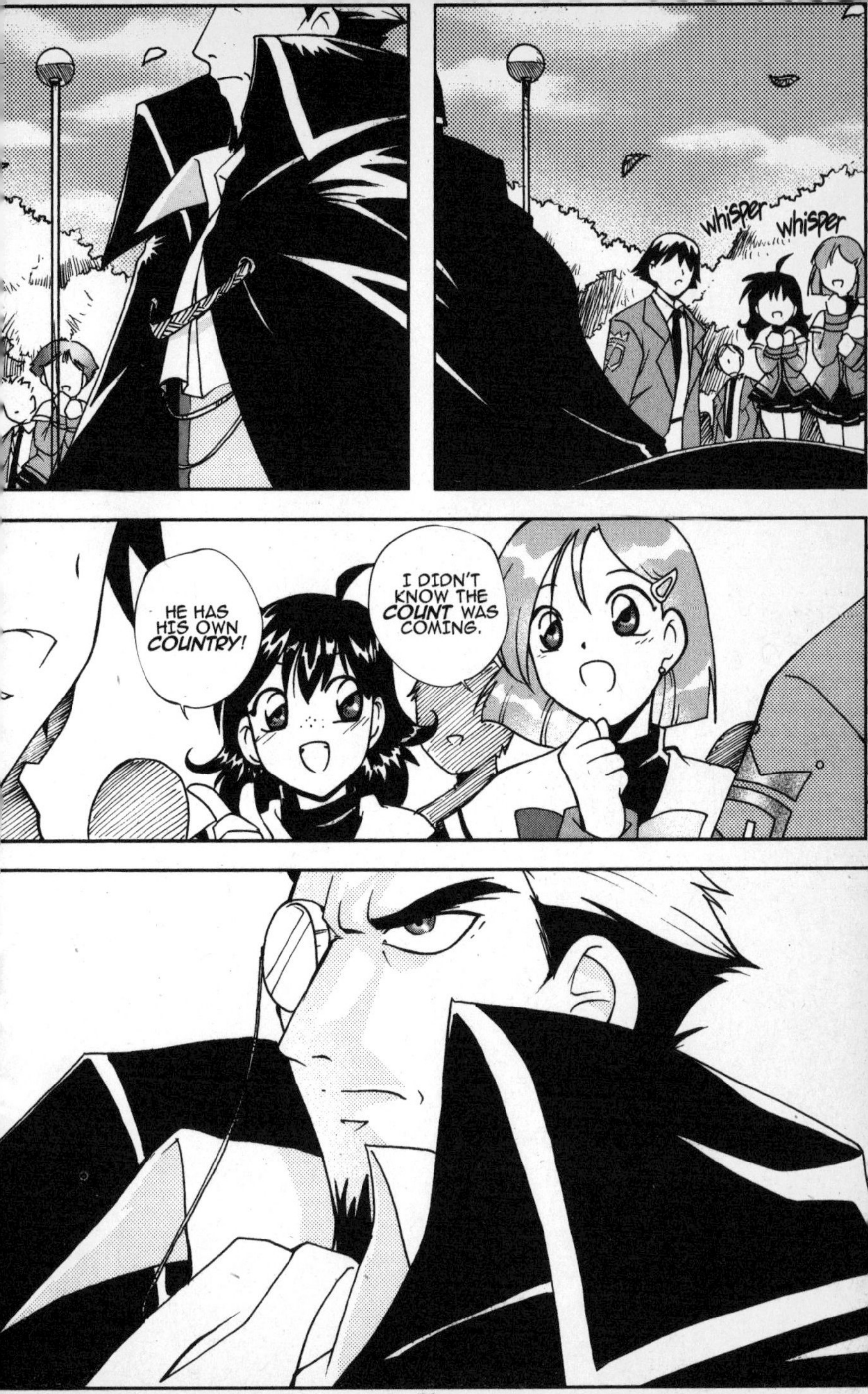
whisper
whisper
I DIDN'T KNOW THE COUNT WAS COMING.
HE HAS HIS OWN COUNTRY!

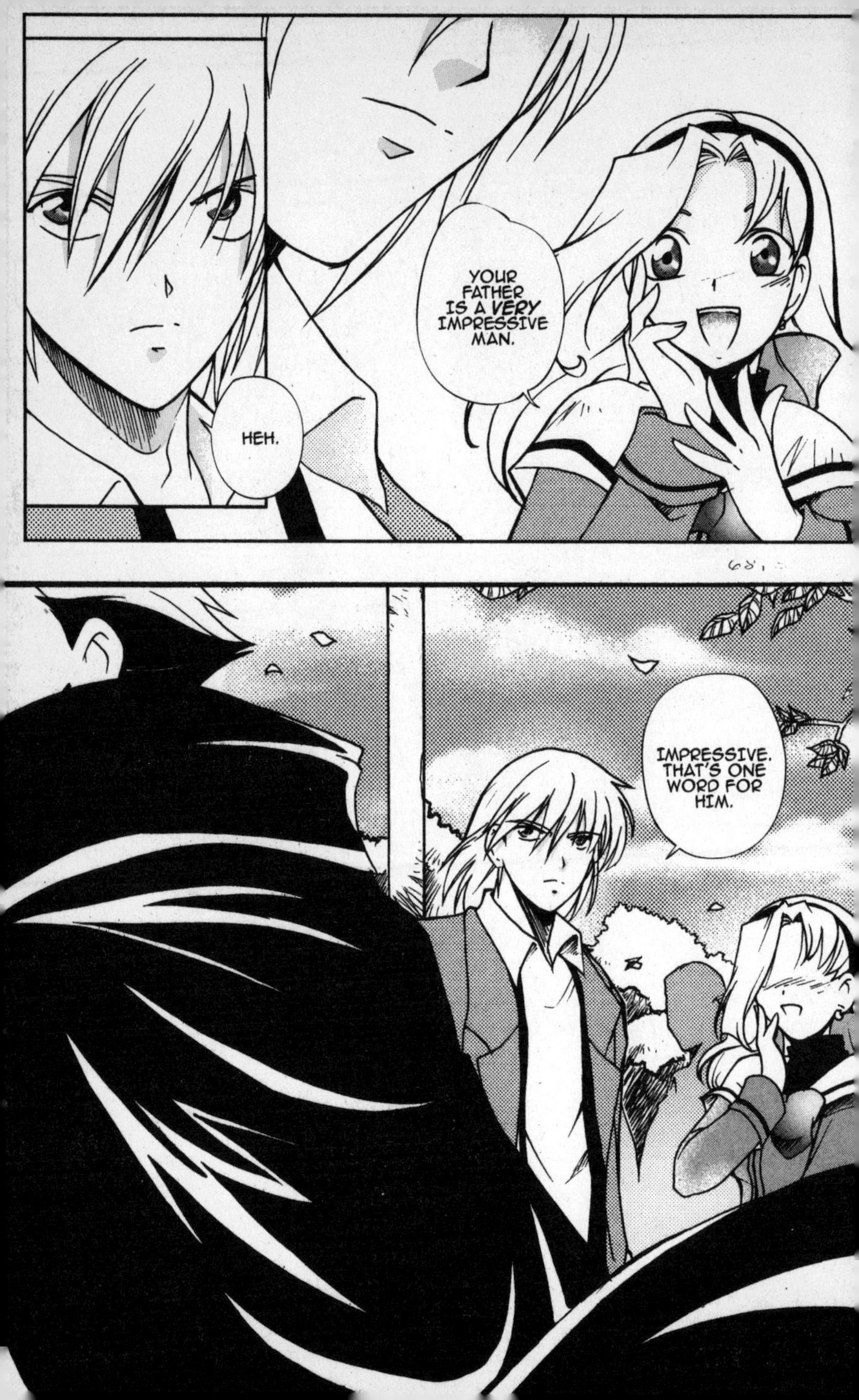
YOUR FATHER IS A *VERY* IMPRESSIVE MAN.
HEH.
IMPRESSIVE. THAT'S ONE WORD FOR HIM.

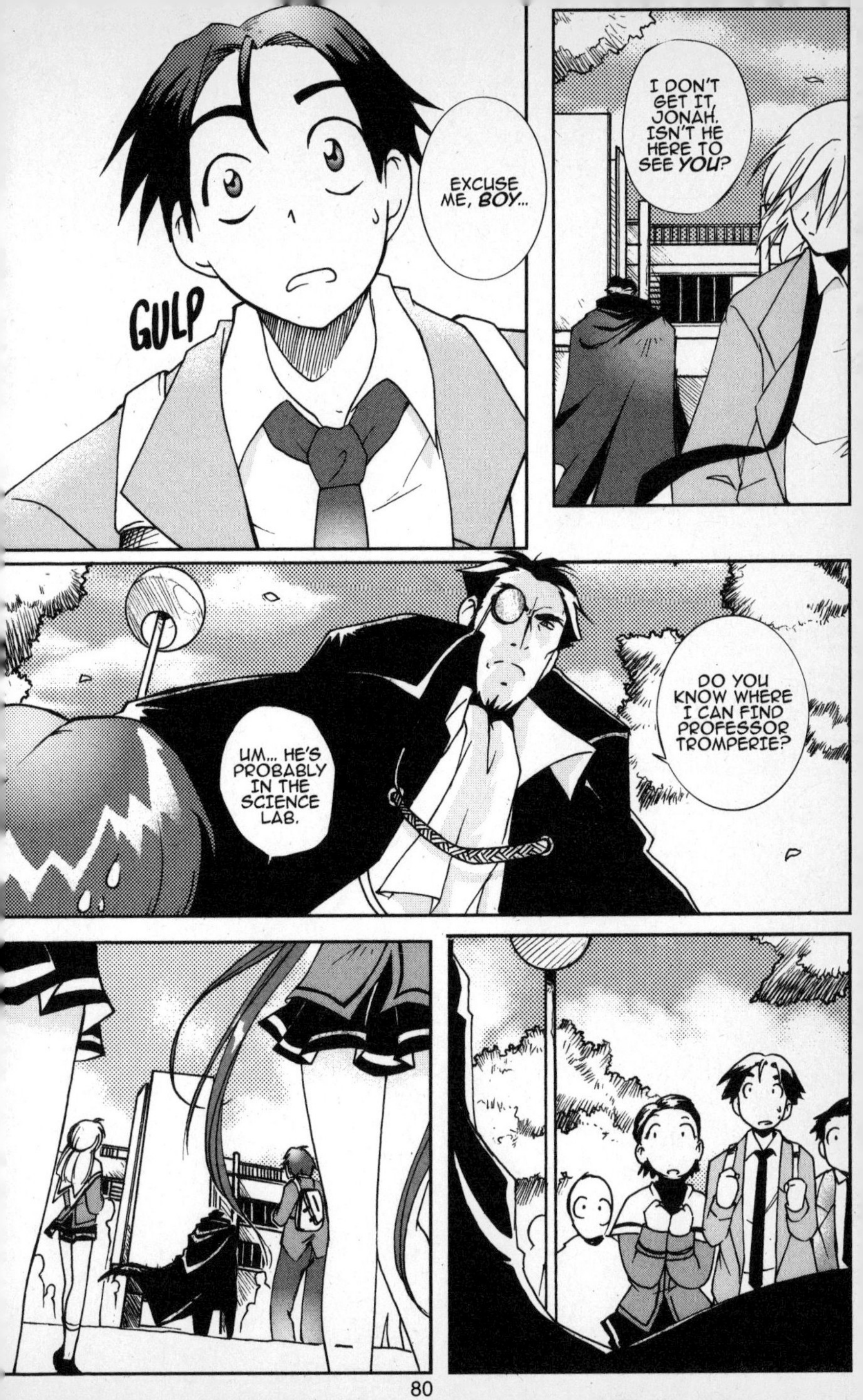
I DON'T GET IT, JONAH. ISN'T HE HERE TO SEE *YOU*?
EXCUSE ME, *BOY*...
GULP
DO YOU KNOW WHERE I CAN FIND PROFESSOR TROMPERIE?
UM... HE'S PROBABLY IN THE SCIENCE LAB.

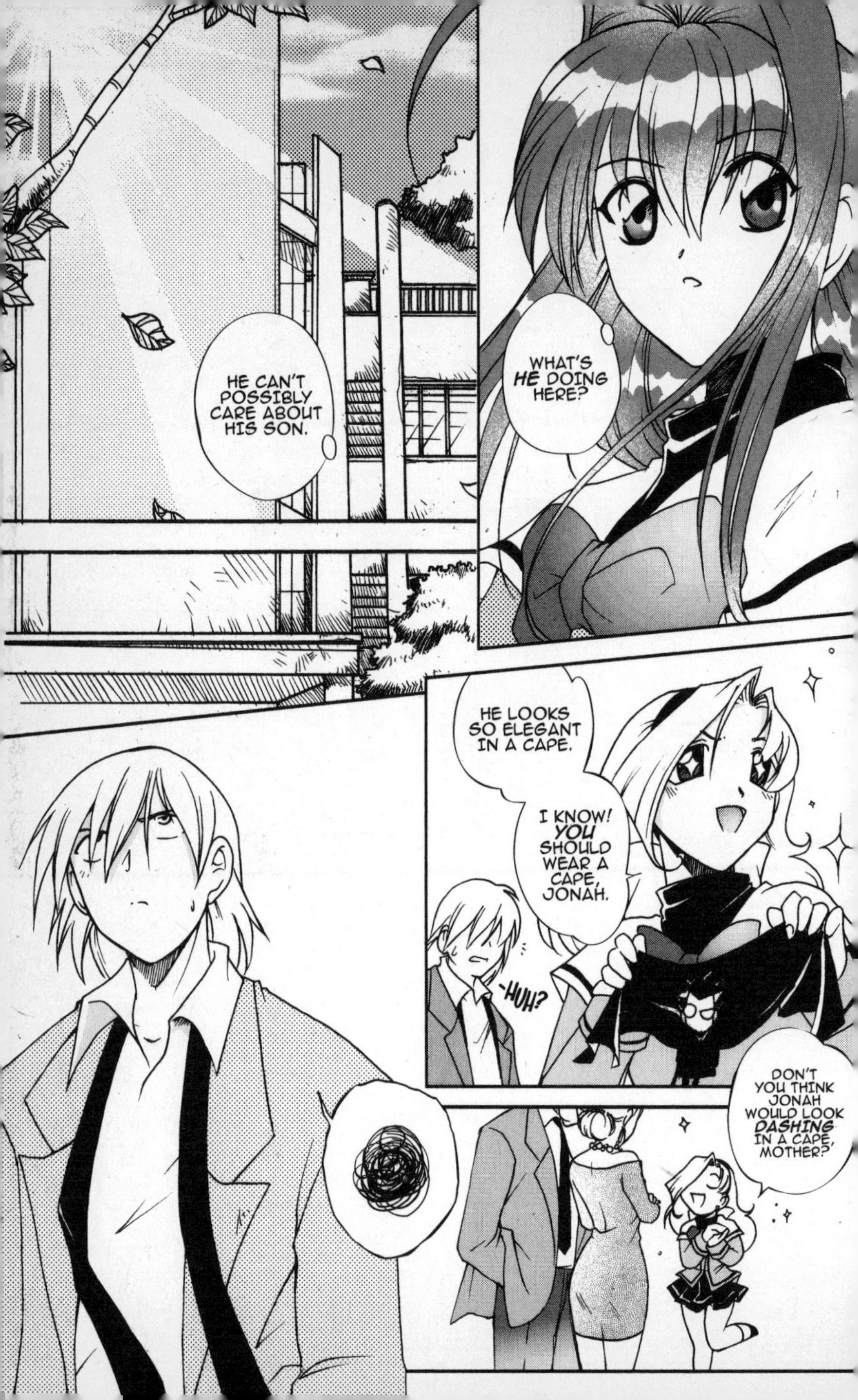
WHAT'S HE DOING HERE?
HE CAN'T POSSIBLY CARE ABOUT HIS SON.
HE LOOKS SO ELEGANT IN A CAPE.
I KNOW! YOU SHOULD WEAR A CAPE, JONAH.
-HUH?
DON'T YOU THINK JONAH WOULD LOOK DASHING IN A CAPE, MOTHER?

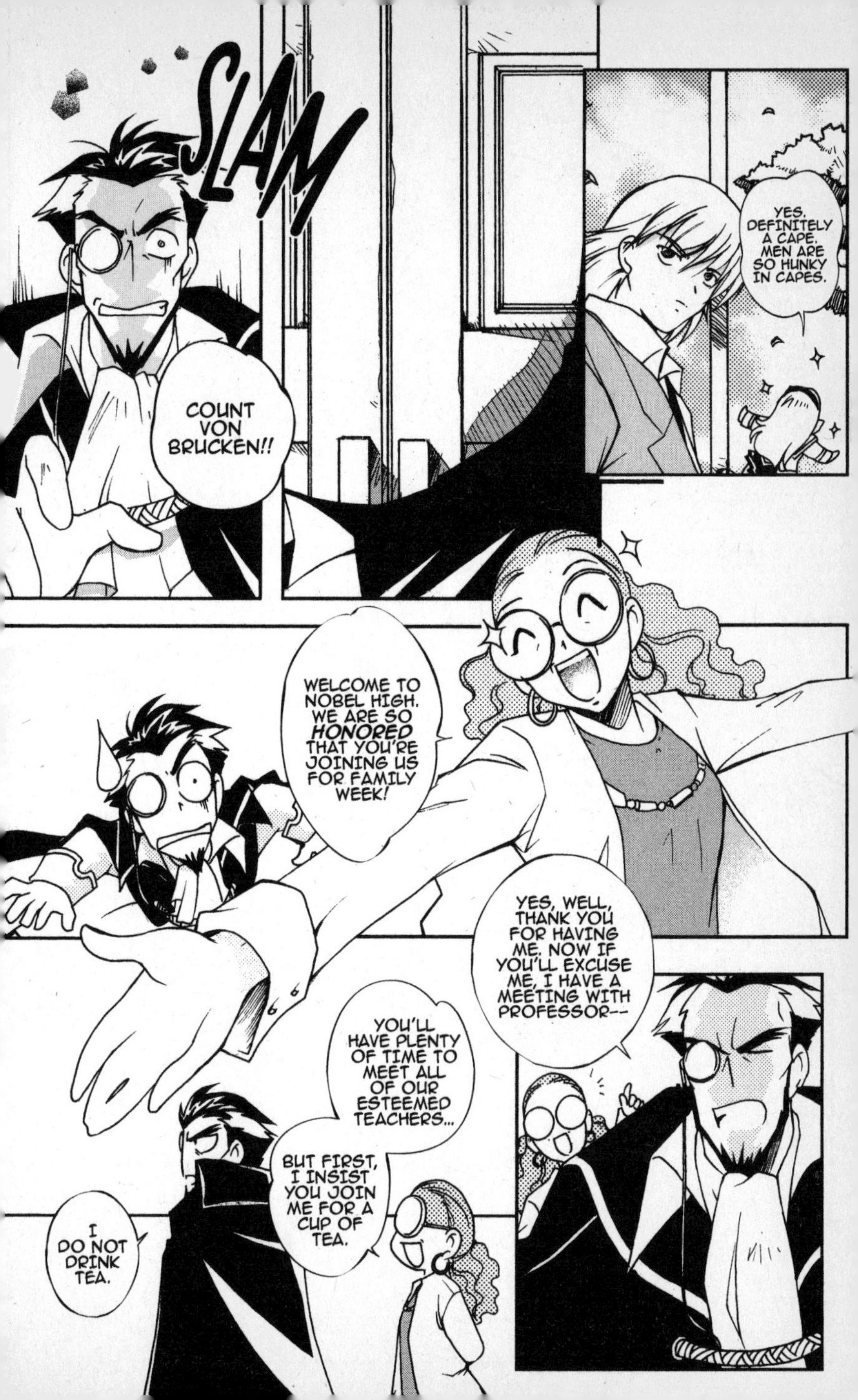
YES. DEFINITELY A CAPE. MEN ARE SO HUNKY IN CAPES.
SLAM
COUNT VON BRUCKEN!!
WELCOME TO NOBEL HIGH. WE ARE SO ***HONORED*** THAT YOU'RE JOINING US FOR FAMILY WEEK!
YES, WELL, THANK YOU FOR HAVING ME. NOW IF YOU'LL EXCUSE ME, I HAVE A MEETING WITH PROFESSOR--
YOU'LL HAVE PLENTY OF TIME TO MEET ALL OF OUR ESTEEMED TEACHERS...
BUT FIRST, I INSIST YOU JOIN ME FOR A CUP OF TEA.
I DO NOT DRINK TEA.

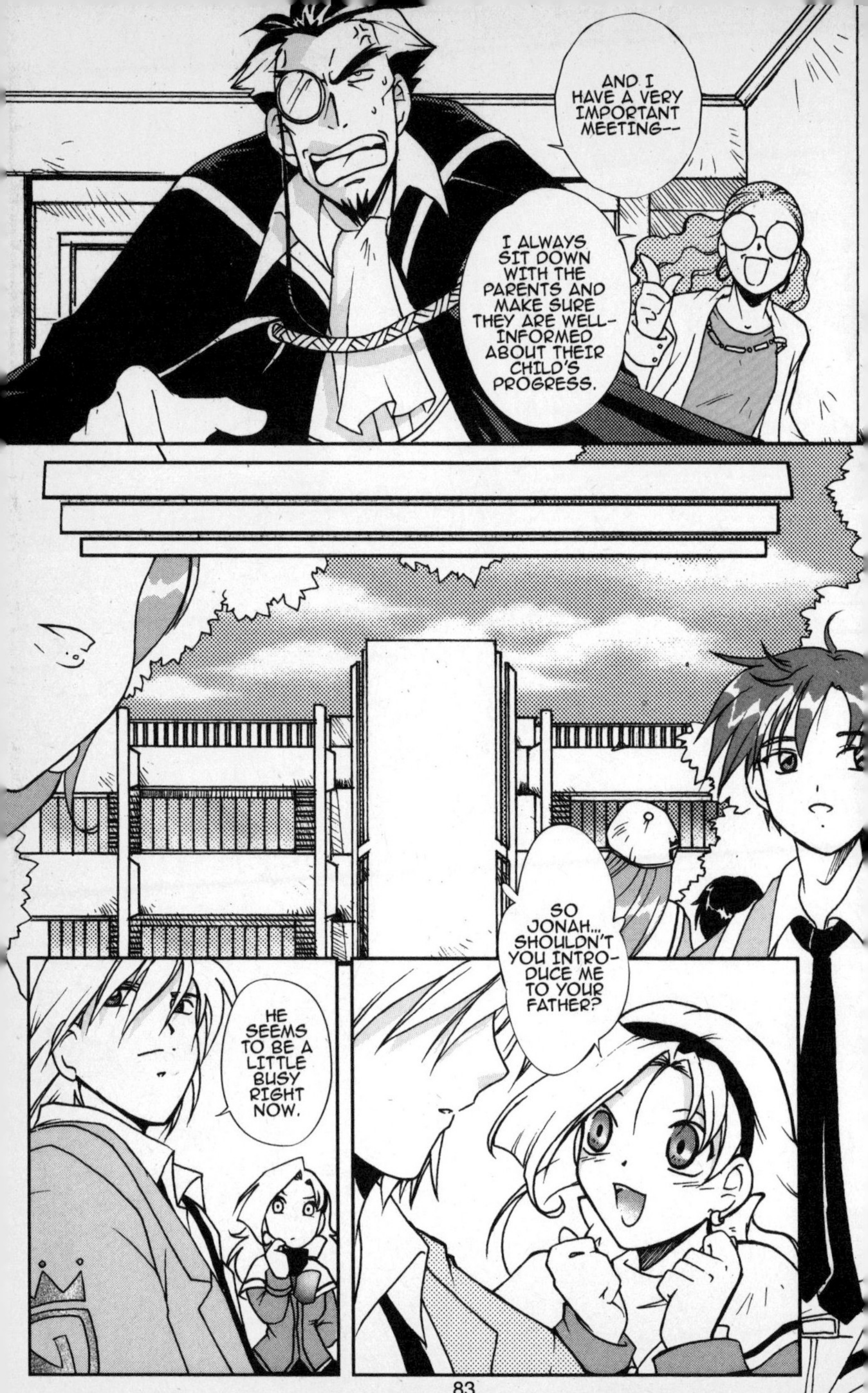
AND I HAVE A VERY IMPORTANT MEETING--
I ALWAYS SIT DOWN WITH THE PARENTS AND MAKE SURE THEY ARE WELL-INFORMED ABOUT THEIR CHILD'S PROGRESS.
SO JONAH... SHOULDN'T YOU INTRODUCE ME TO YOUR FATHER?
HE SEEMS TO BE A LITTLE BUSY RIGHT NOW.

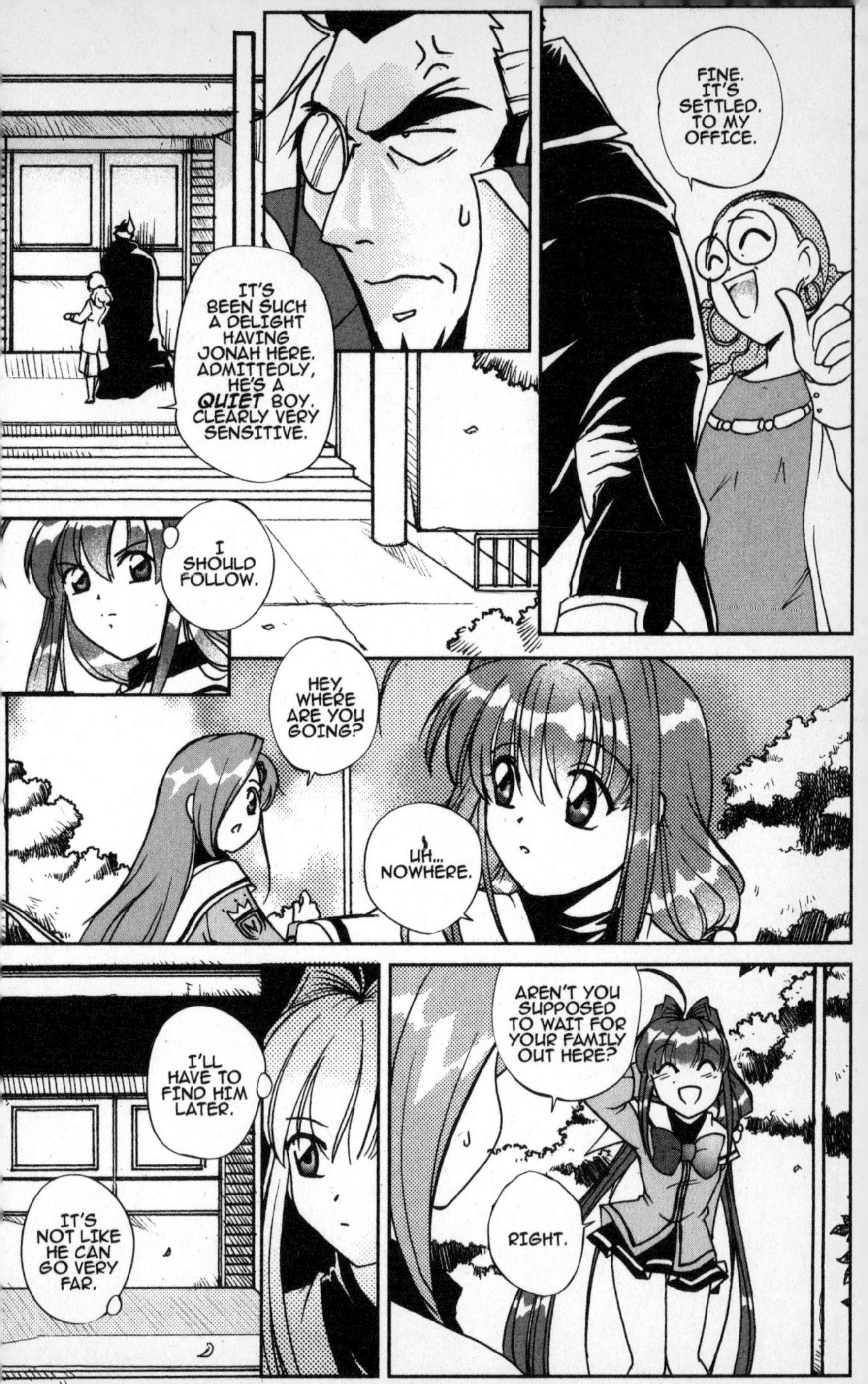
FINE. IT'S SETTLED. TO MY OFFICE.
IT'S BEEN SUCH A DELIGHT HAVING JONAH HERE. ADMITTEDLY, HE'S A **QUIET** BOY. CLEARLY VERY SENSITIVE.
I SHOULD FOLLOW.
HEY, WHERE ARE YOU GOING?
UH... NOWHERE.
AREN'T YOU SUPPOSED TO WAIT FOR YOUR FAMILY OUT HERE?
RIGHT.
I'LL HAVE TO FIND HIM LATER.
IT'S NOT LIKE HE CAN GO VERY FAR.

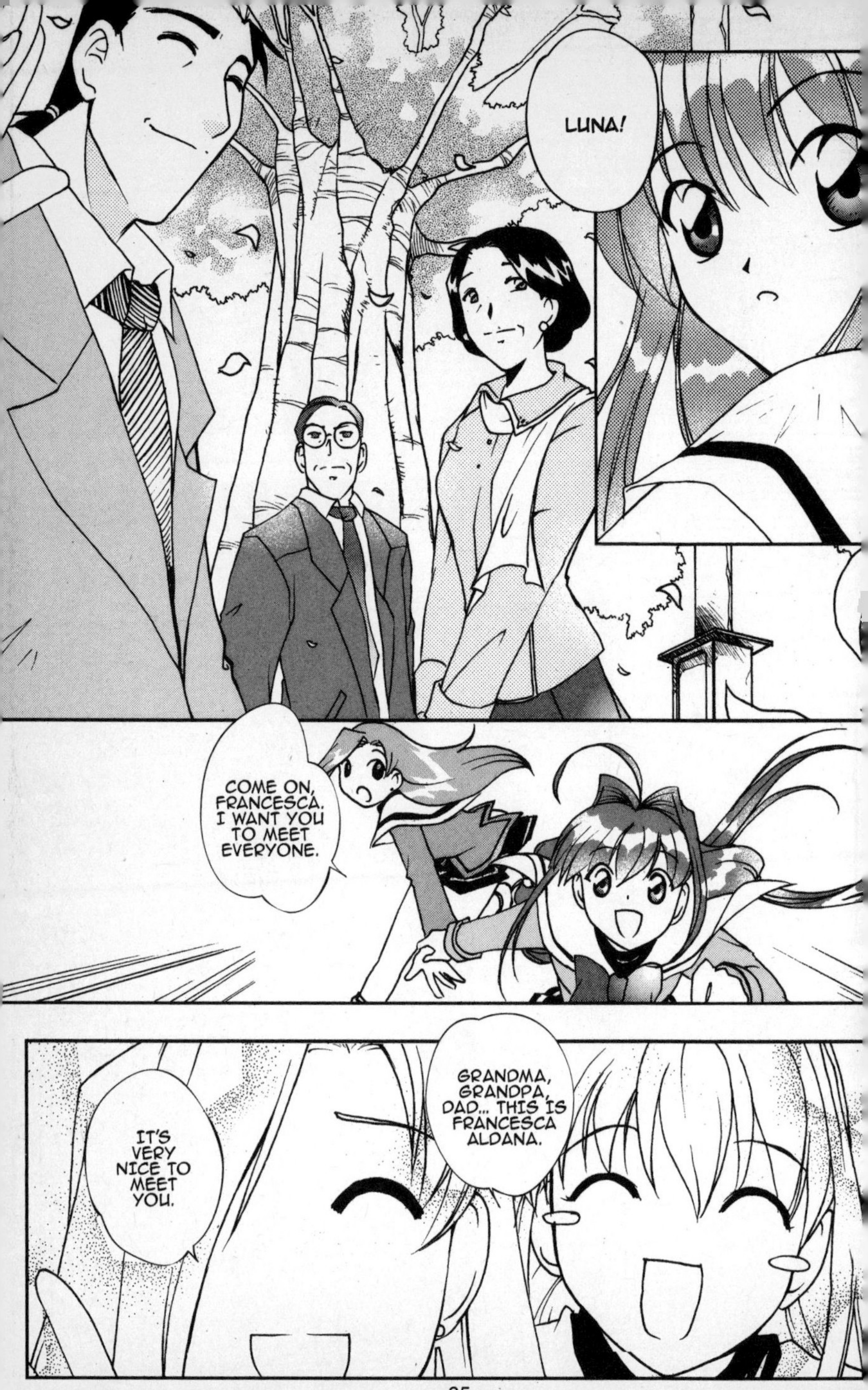
LUNA!
COME ON, FRANCESCA. I WANT YOU TO MEET EVERYONE.
GRANDMA, GRANDPA, DAD... THIS IS FRANCESCA ALDANA.
IT'S VERY NICE TO MEET YOU.

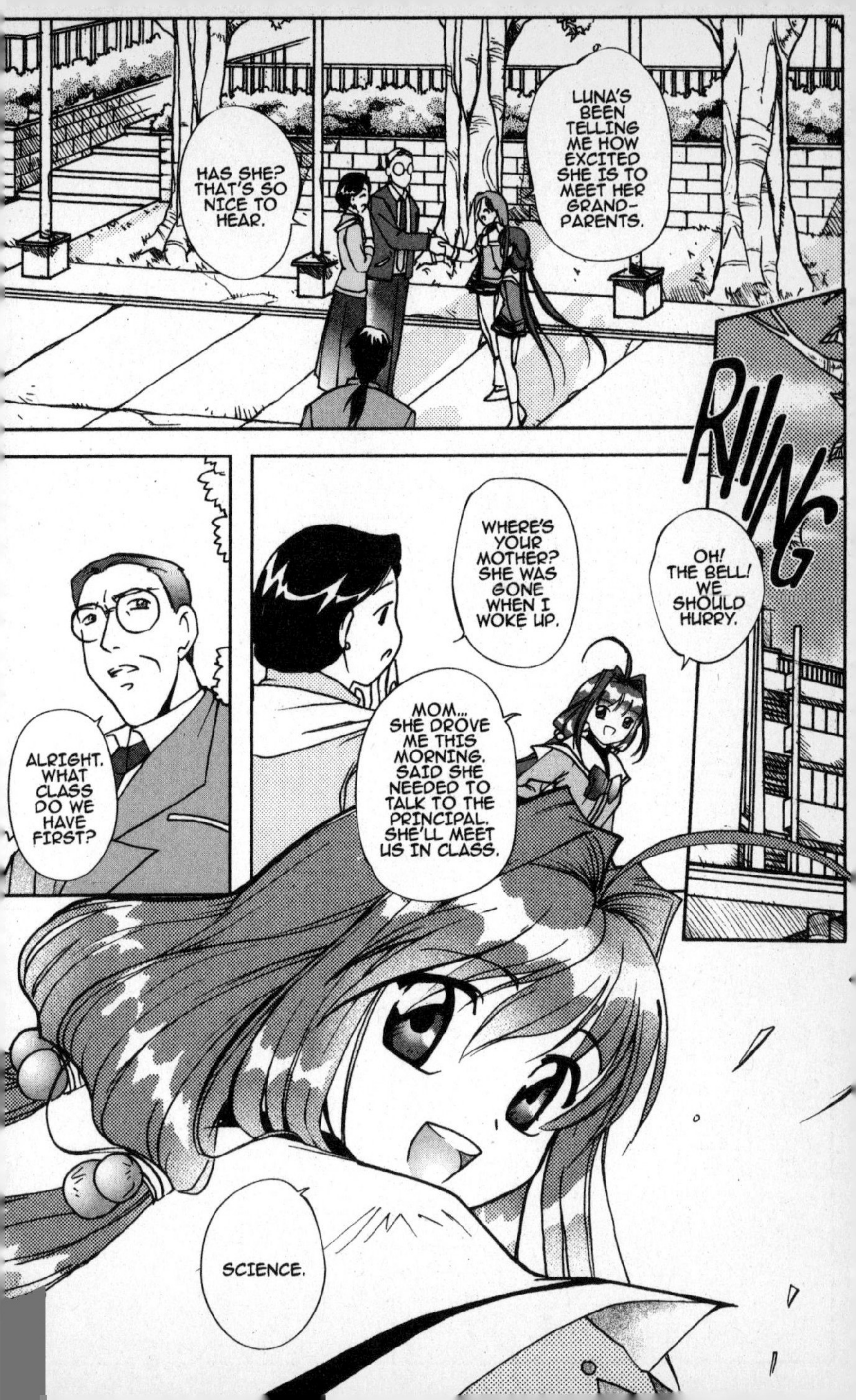
LUNA'S BEEN TELLING ME HOW EXCITED SHE IS TO MEET HER GRAND-PARENTS.
HAS SHE? THAT'S SO NICE TO HEAR.
RIING
OH! THE BELL! WE SHOULD HURRY.
WHERE'S YOUR MOTHER? SHE WAS GONE WHEN I WOKE UP.
MOM... SHE DROVE ME THIS MORNING. SAID SHE NEEDED TO TALK TO THE PRINCIPAL. SHE'LL MEET US IN CLASS.
ALRIGHT. WHAT CLASS DO WE HAVE FIRST?
SCIENCE.

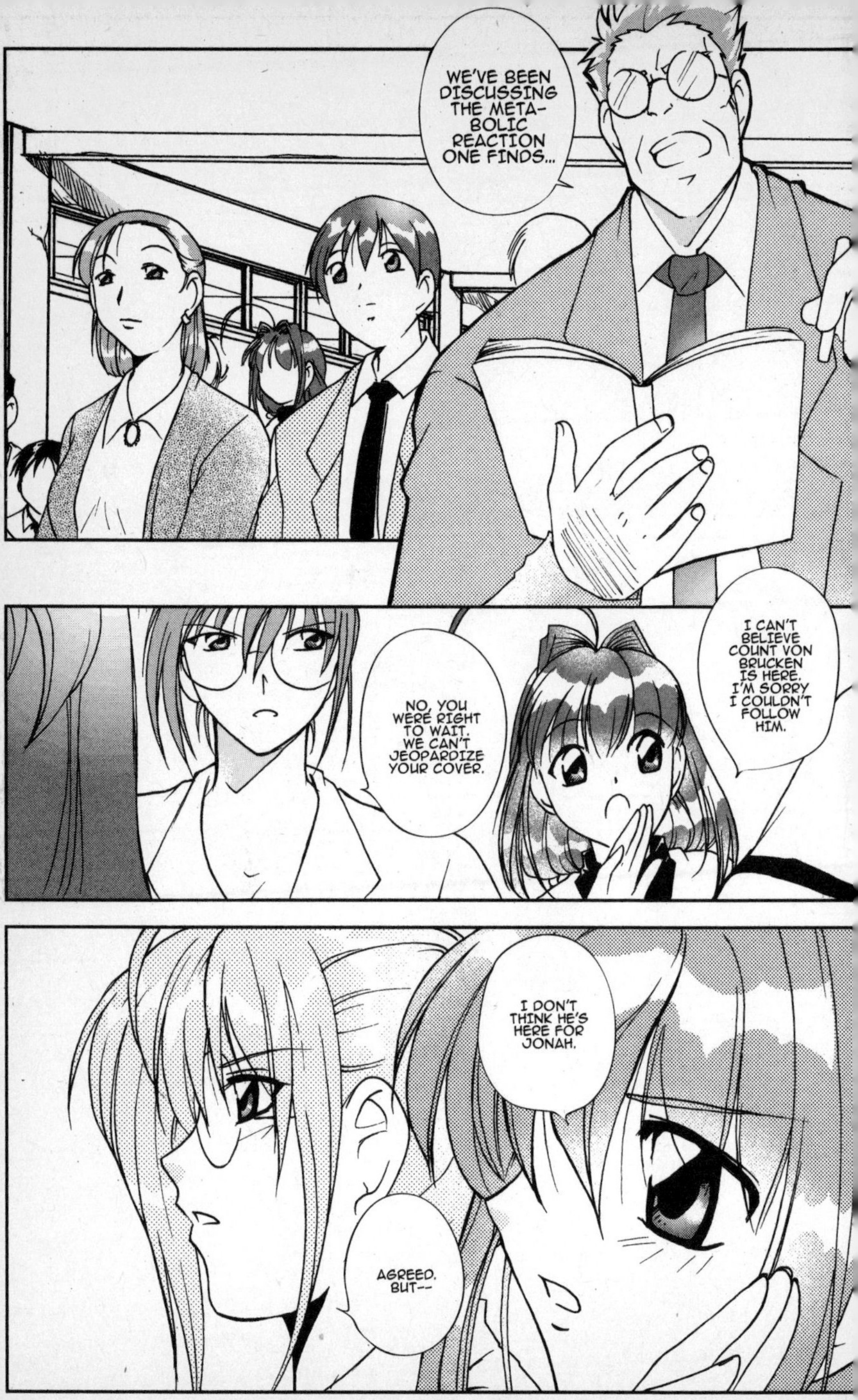
WE'VE BEEN DISCUSSING THE META-BOLIC REACTION ONE FINDS...
I CAN'T BELIEVE COUNT VON BRUCKEN IS HERE. I'M SORRY I COULDN'T FOLLOW HIM.
NO, YOU WERE RIGHT TO WAIT. WE CAN'T JEOPARDIZE YOUR COVER.
I DON'T THINK HE'S HERE FOR JONAH.
AGREED. BUT--

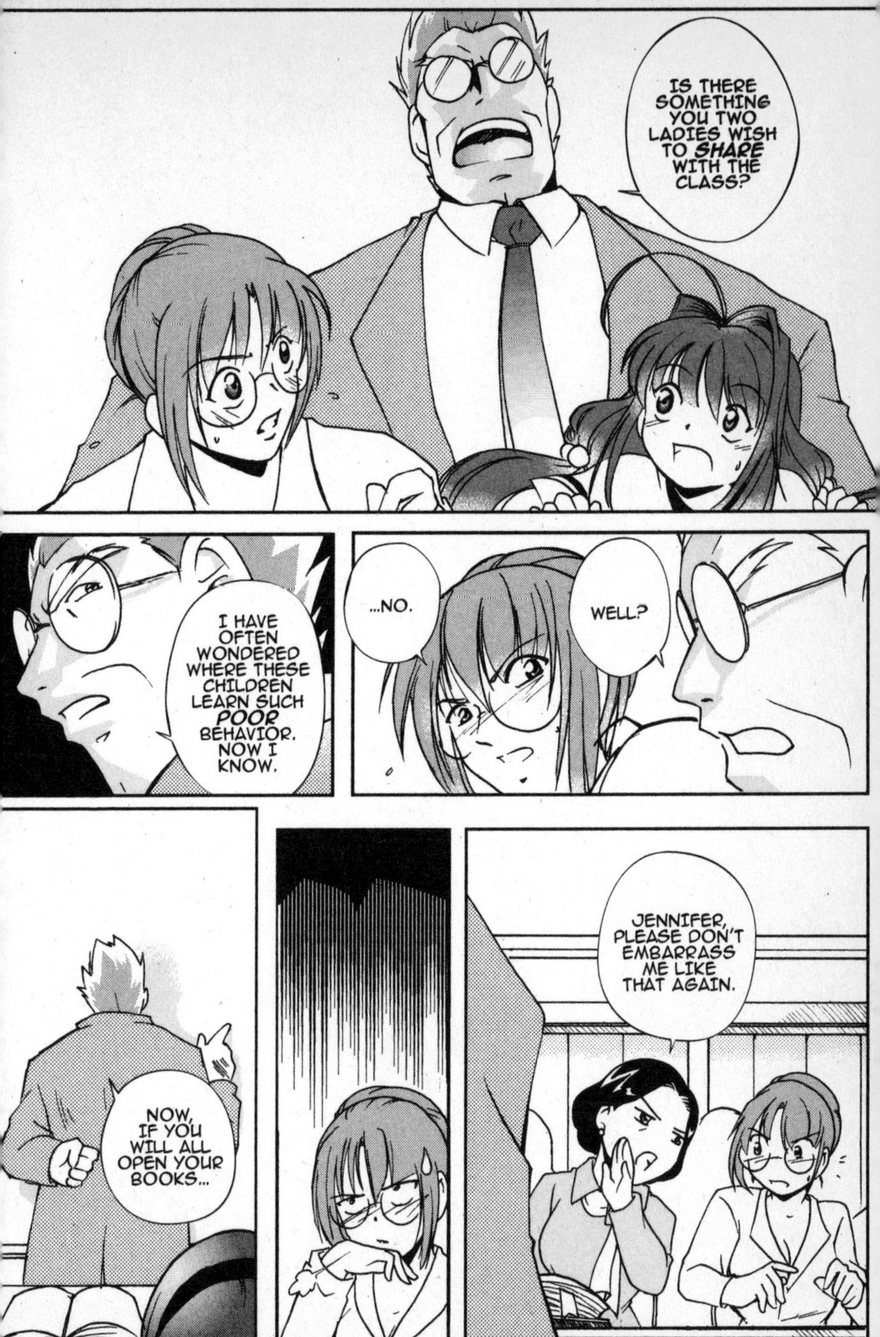
IS THERE SOMETHING YOU TWO LADIES WISH TO SHARE WITH THE CLASS?
WELL?
...NO.
I HAVE OFTEN WONDERED WHERE THESE CHILDREN LEARN SUCH POOR BEHAVIOR. NOW I KNOW.
JENNIFER, PLEASE DON'T EMBARRASS ME LIKE THAT AGAIN.
NOW, IF YOU WILL ALL OPEN YOUR BOOKS...

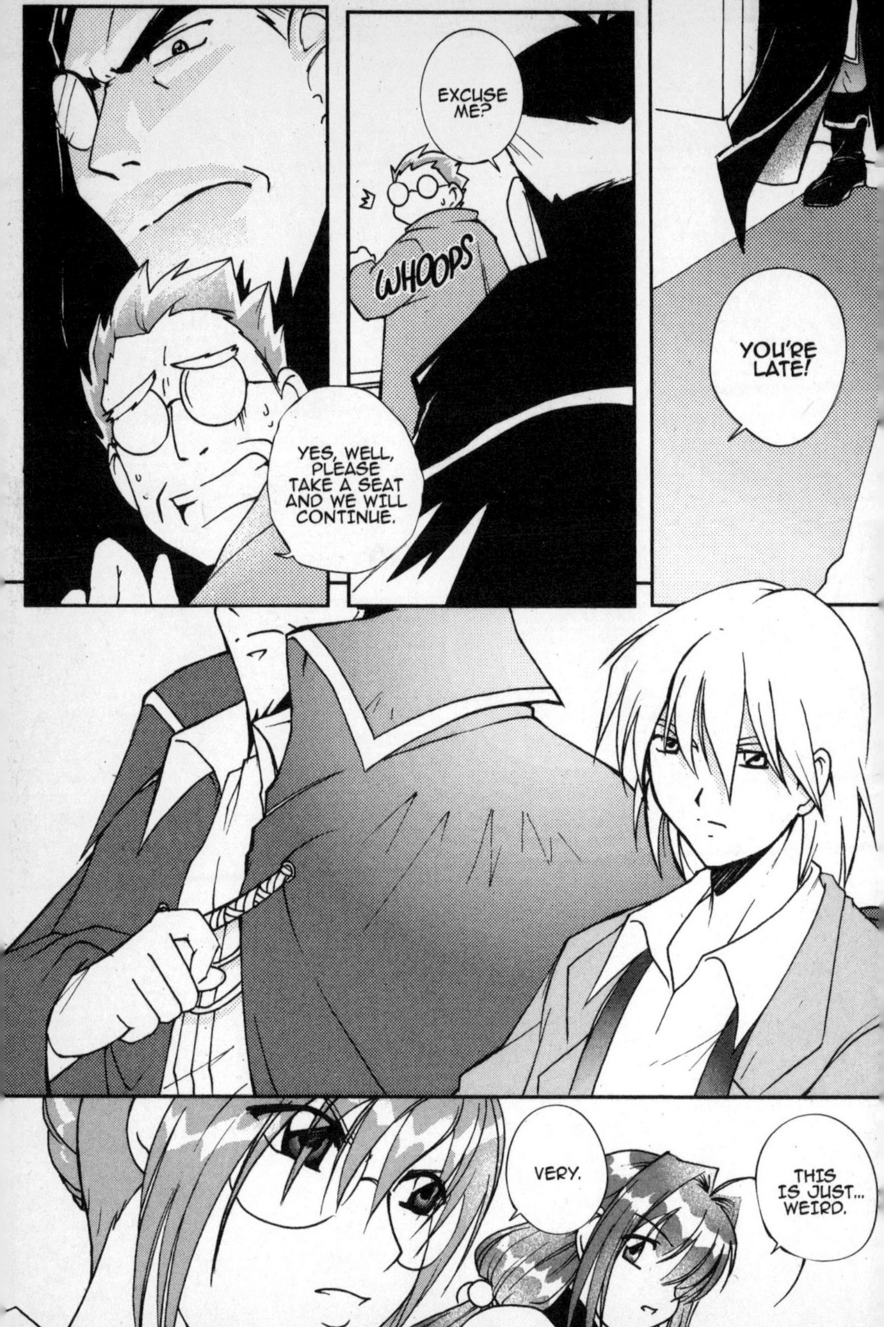
YOU'RE LATE!
EXCUSE ME?
WHOOPS
YES, WELL, PLEASE TAKE A SEAT AND WE WILL CONTINUE.
THIS IS JUST... WEIRD.
VERY.

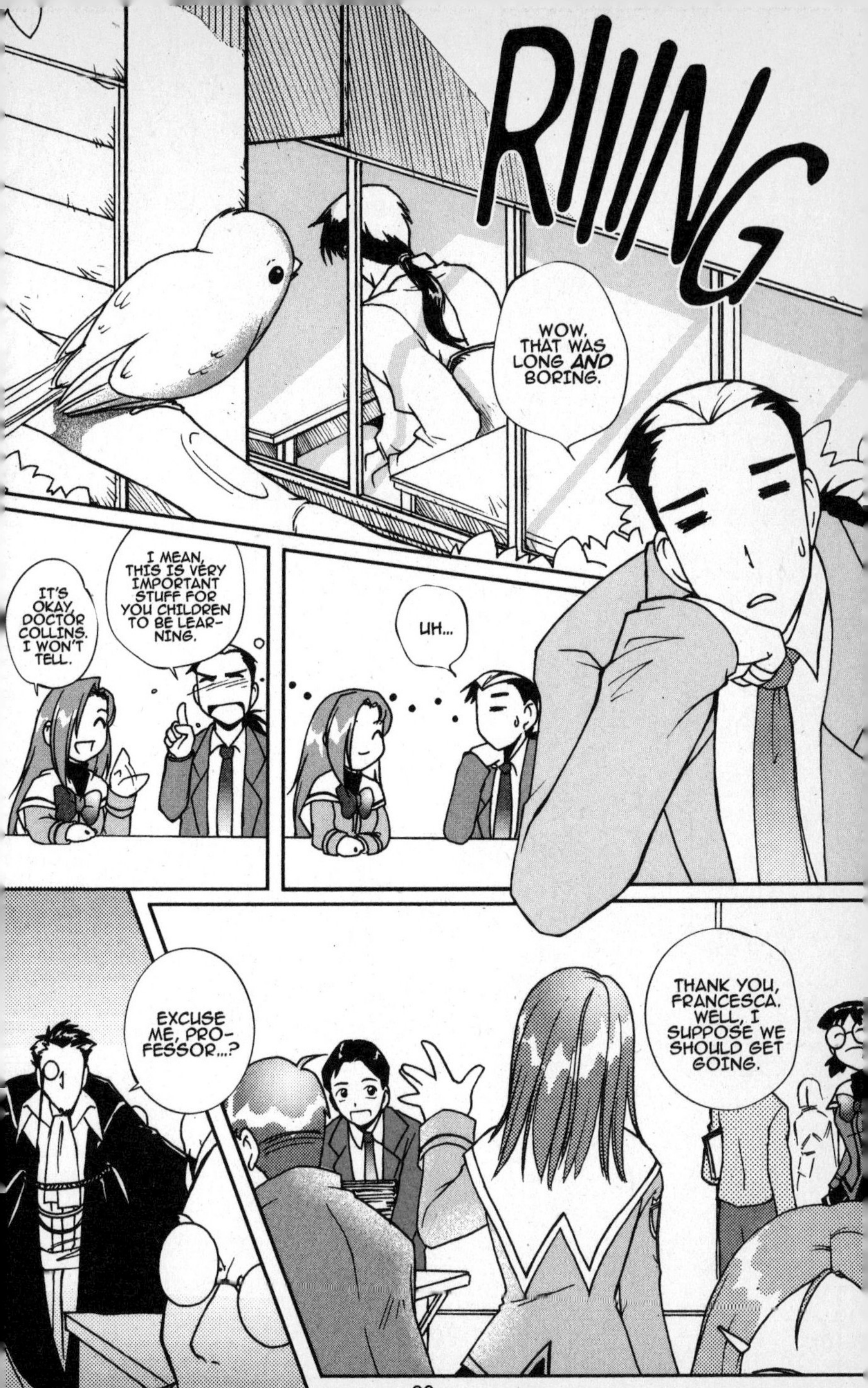
RIIING
WOW, THAT WAS LONG AND BORING.
UH...
I MEAN, THIS IS VERY IMPORTANT STUFF FOR YOU CHILDREN TO BE LEARNING.
IT'S OKAY, DOCTOR COLLINS. I WON'T TELL.
THANK YOU, FRANCESCA. WELL, I SUPPOSE WE SHOULD GET GOING.
EXCUSE ME, PROFESSOR...?

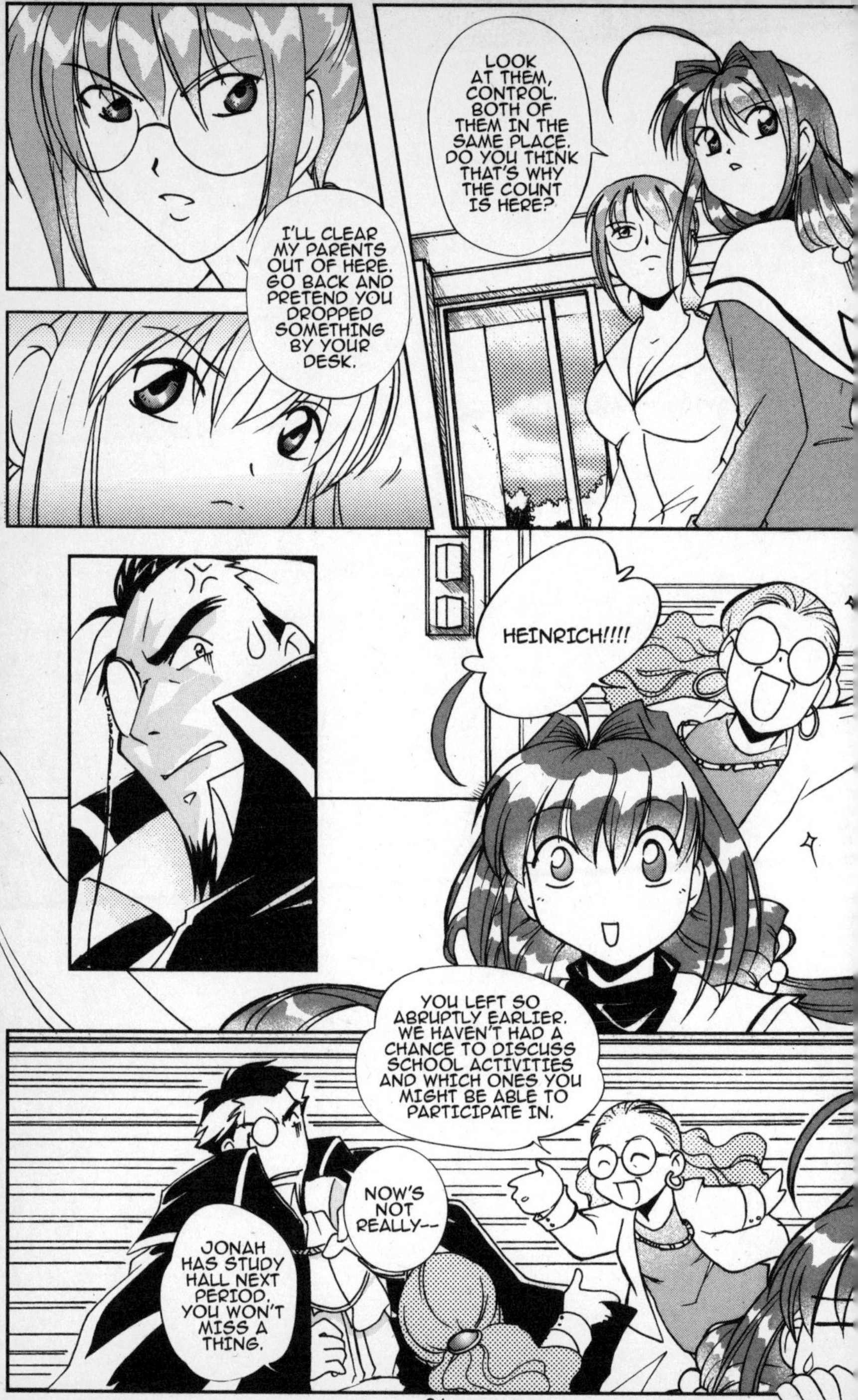
LOOK AT THEM, CONTROL. BOTH OF THEM IN THE SAME PLACE. DO YOU THINK THAT'S WHY THE COUNT IS HERE?
I'LL CLEAR MY PARENTS OUT OF HERE. GO BACK AND PRETEND YOU DROPPED SOMETHING BY YOUR DESK.
HEINRICH!!!!
YOU LEFT SO ABRUPTLY EARLIER. WE HAVEN'T HAD A CHANCE TO DISCUSS SCHOOL ACTIVITIES AND WHICH ONES YOU MIGHT BE ABLE TO PARTICIPATE IN.
NOW'S NOT REALLY--
JONAH HAS STUDY HALL NEXT PERIOD. YOU WON'T MISS A THING.

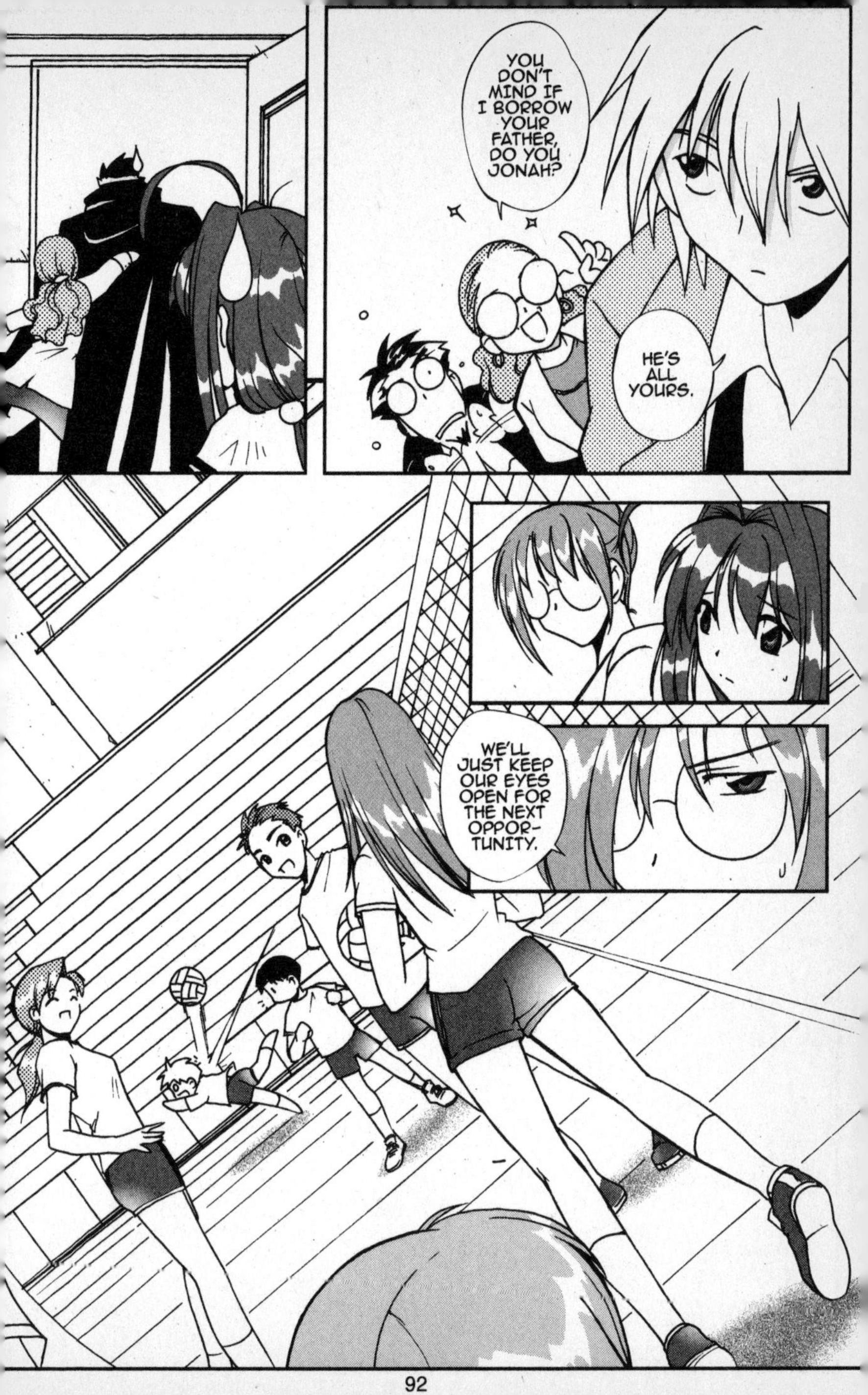
YOU DON'T MIND IF I BORROW YOUR FATHER, DO YOU JONAH?
HE'S ALL YOURS.
WE'LL JUST KEEP OUR EYES OPEN FOR THE NEXT OPPORTUNITY.

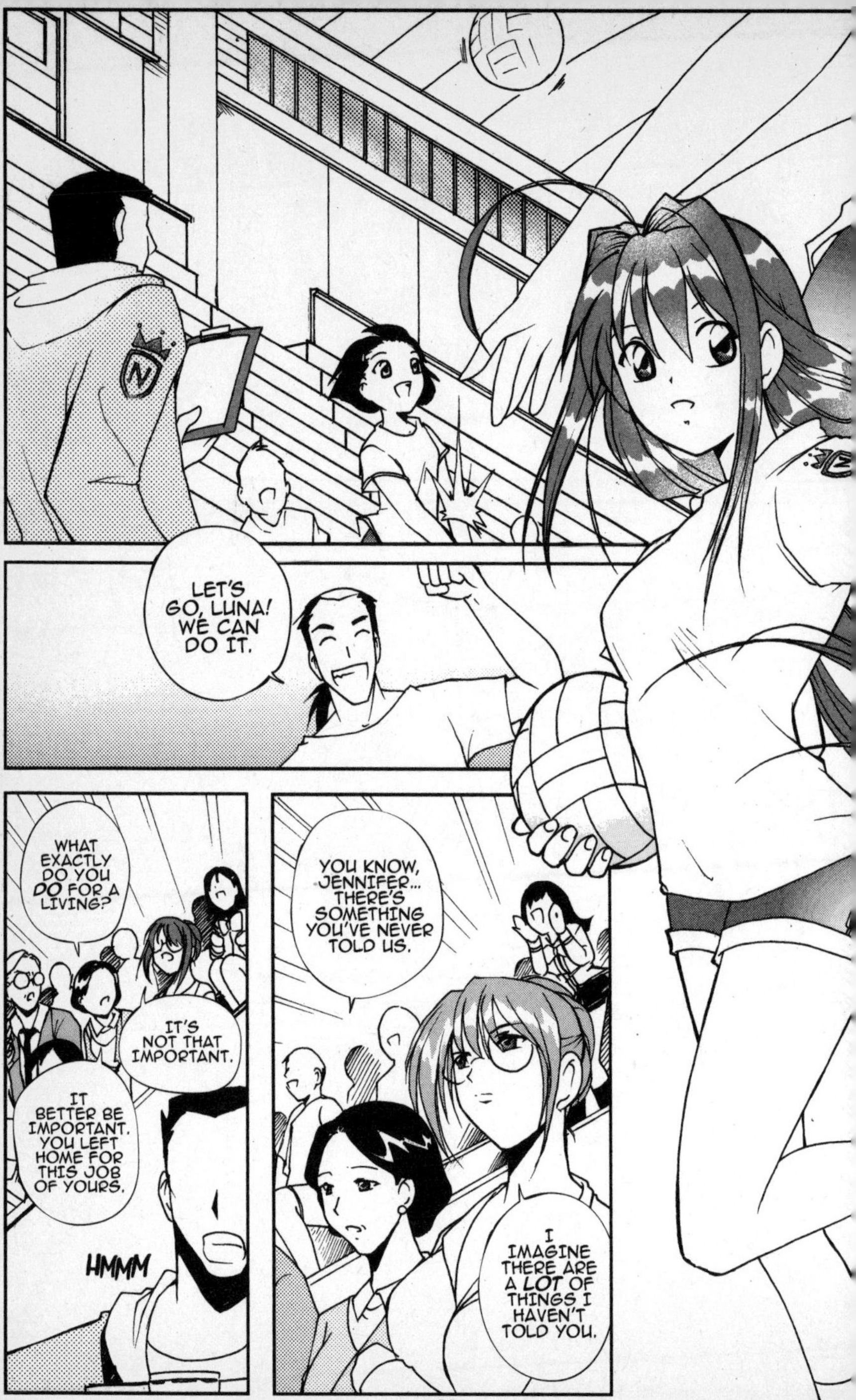
LET'S GO, LUNA! WE CAN DO IT.
YOU KNOW, JENNIFER... THERE'S SOMETHING YOU'VE NEVER TOLD US.
I IMAGINE THERE ARE A *LOT* OF THINGS I HAVEN'T TOLD YOU.
WHAT EXACTLY DO YOU *DO* FOR A LIVING?
IT'S NOT THAT IMPORTANT.
IT BETTER BE IMPORTANT. YOU LEFT HOME FOR THIS JOB OF YOURS.
HMMM

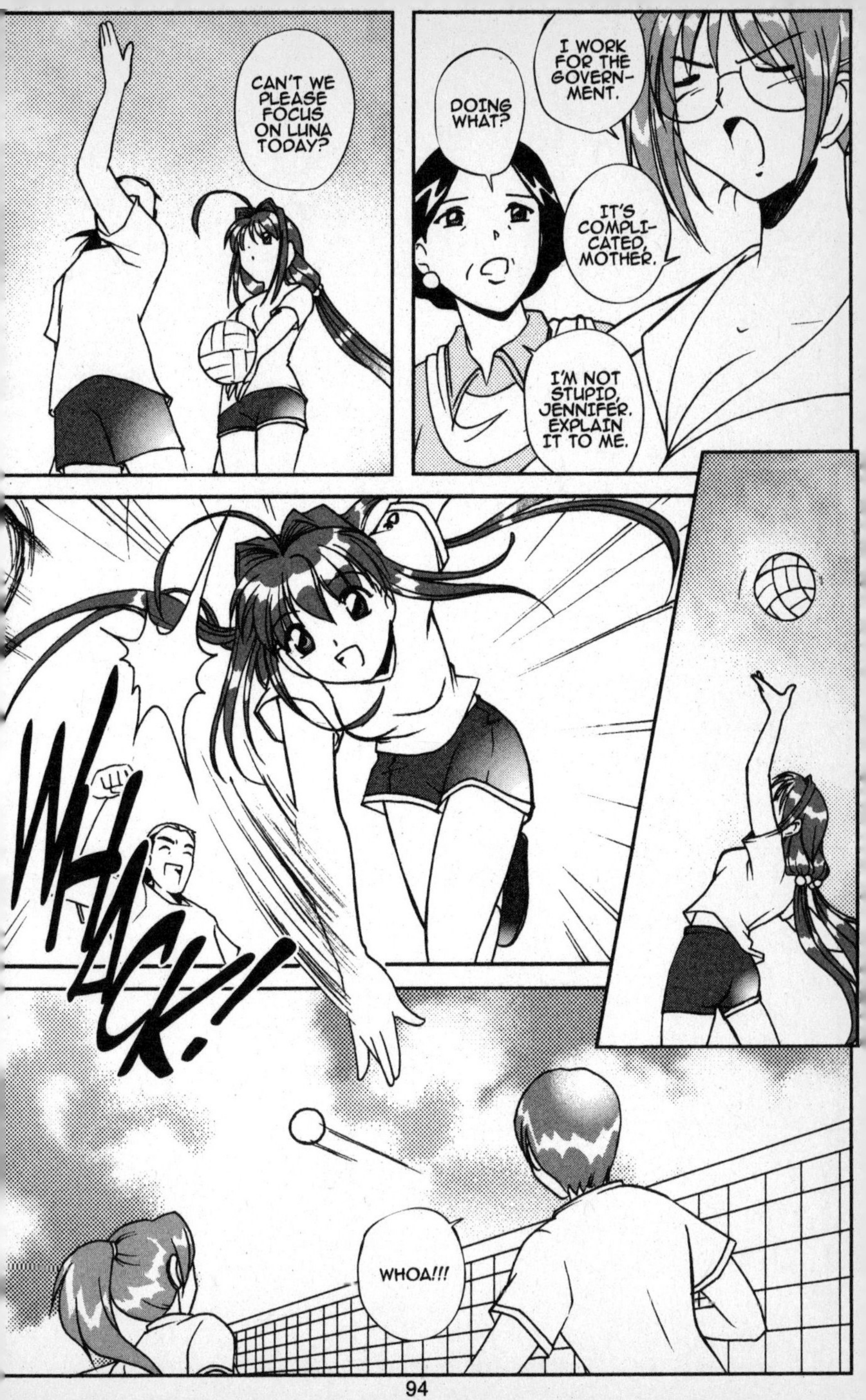
I WORK FOR THE GOVERNMENT.
DOING WHAT?
IT'S COMPLICATED, MOTHER.
I'M NOT STUPID, JENNIFER. EXPLAIN IT TO ME.
CAN'T WE PLEASE FOCUS ON LUNA TODAY?
WHACK!!
WHOA!!!

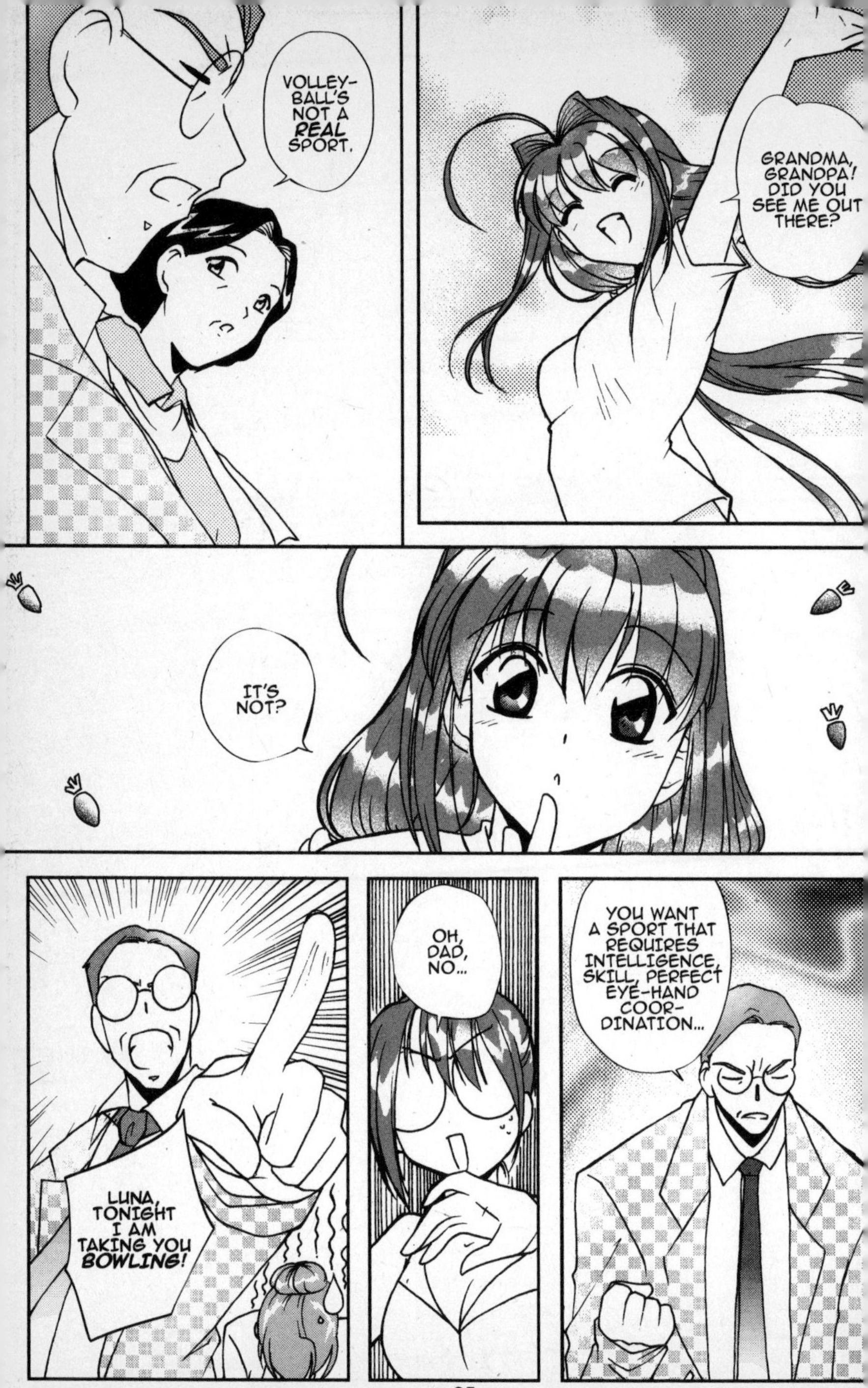
GRANDMA, GRANDPA! DID YOU SEE ME OUT THERE?
VOLLEY-BALL'S NOT A **REAL** SPORT.
IT'S NOT?
YOU WANT A SPORT THAT REQUIRES INTELLIGENCE, SKILL, PERFECT EYE-HAND COOR-DINATION...
OH, DAD, NO...
LUNA, TONIGHT I AM TAKING YOU **BOWLING**!

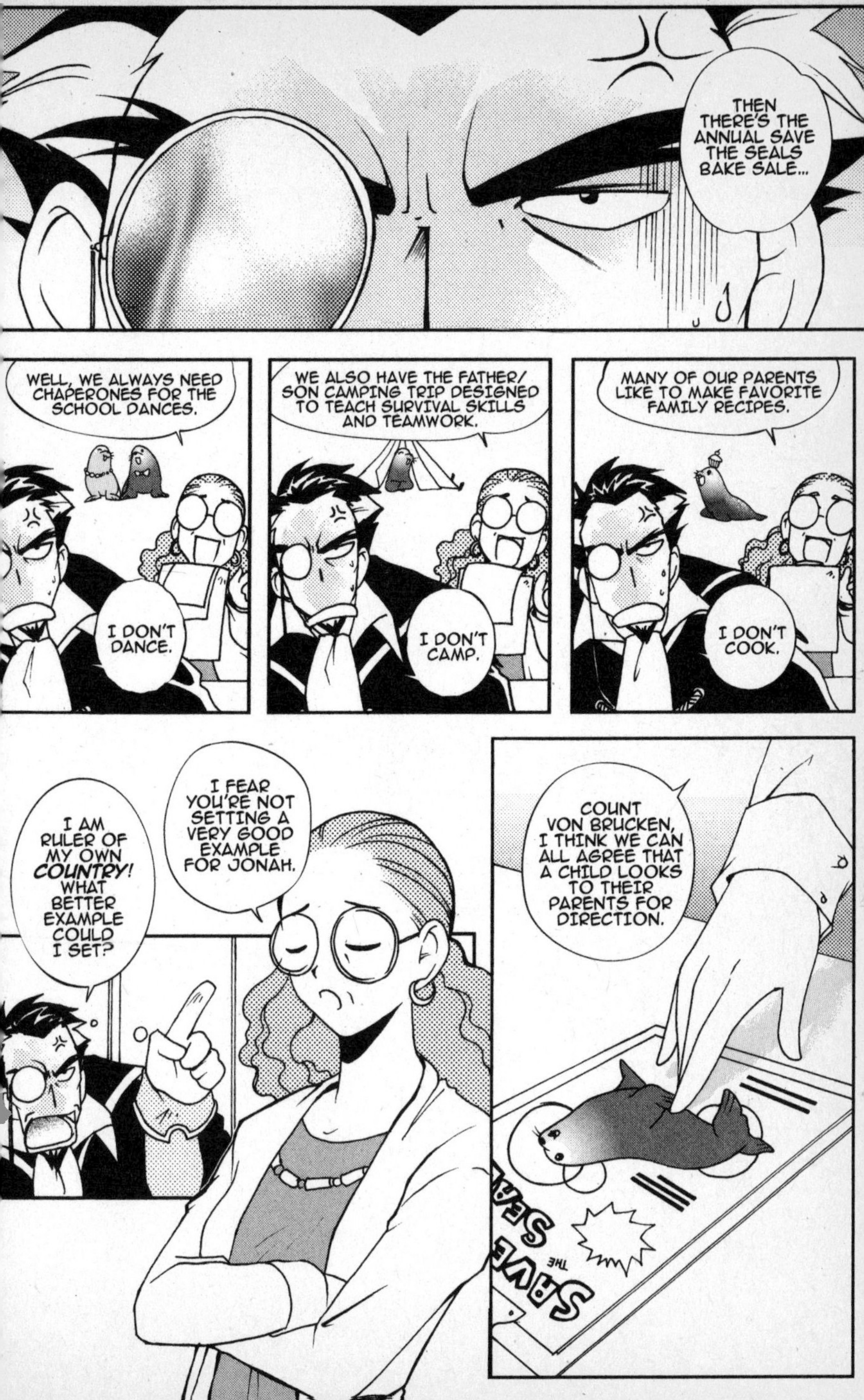
THEN THERE'S THE ANNUAL SAVE THE SEALS BAKE SALE...
MANY OF OUR PARENTS LIKE TO MAKE FAVORITE FAMILY RECIPES.
I DON'T COOK.
WE ALSO HAVE THE FATHER/SON CAMPING TRIP DESIGNED TO TEACH SURVIVAL SKILLS AND TEAMWORK.
I DON'T CAMP.
WELL, WE ALWAYS NEED CHAPERONES FOR THE SCHOOL DANCES.
I DON'T DANCE.
COUNT VON BRUCKEN, I THINK WE CAN ALL AGREE THAT A CHILD LOOKS TO THEIR PARENTS FOR DIRECTION.
I FEAR YOU'RE NOT SETTING A VERY GOOD EXAMPLE FOR JONAH.
I AM RULER OF MY OWN *COUNTRY*! WHAT BETTER EXAMPLE COULD I SET?

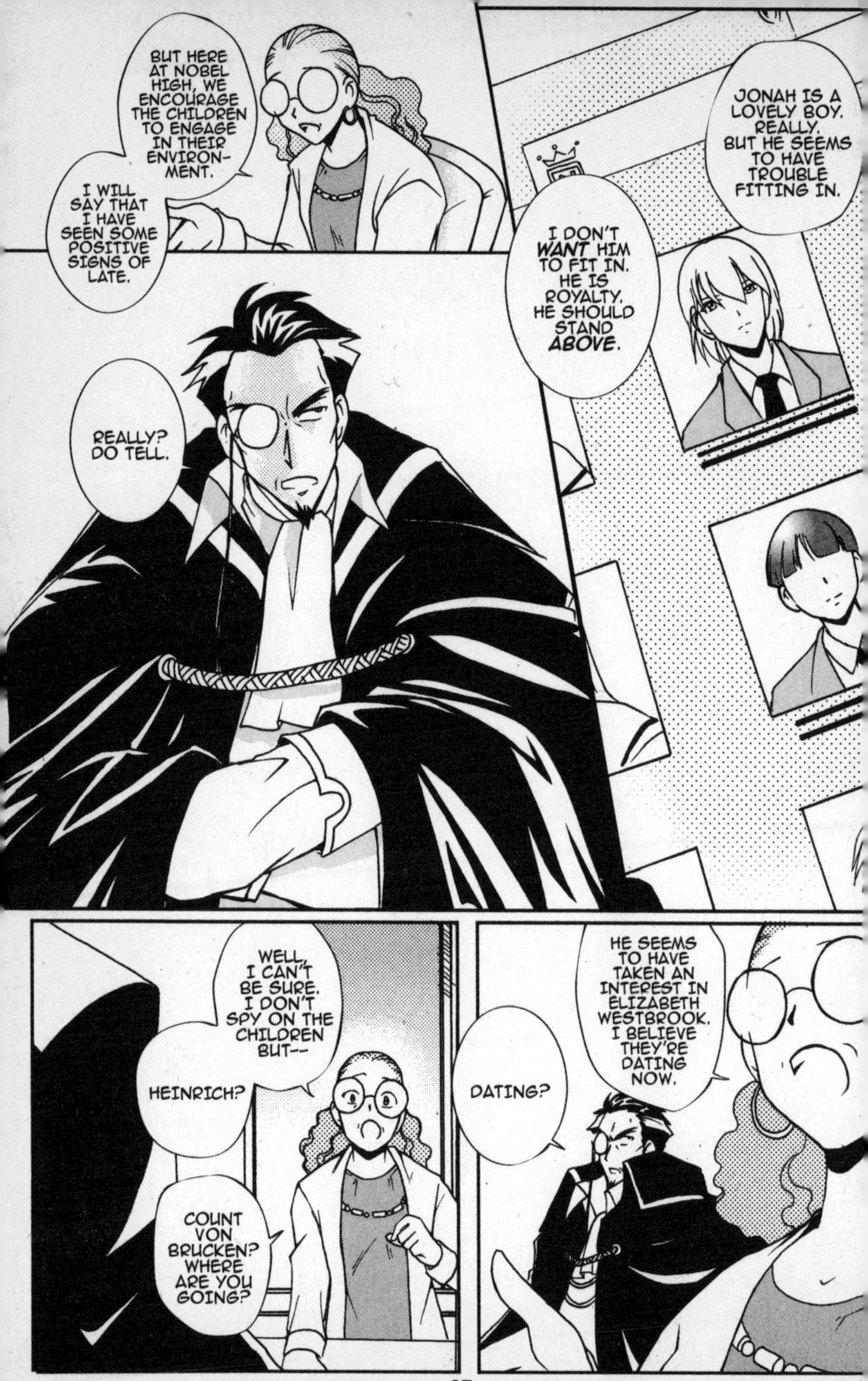
JONAH IS A LOVELY BOY. REALLY. BUT HE SEEMS TO HAVE TROUBLE FITTING IN.
I DON'T *WANT* HIM TO FIT IN. HE IS ROYALTY. HE SHOULD STAND *ABOVE*.
BUT HERE AT NOBEL HIGH, WE ENCOURAGE THE CHILDREN TO ENGAGE IN THEIR ENVIRON-MENT.
I WILL SAY THAT I HAVE SEEN SOME POSITIVE SIGNS OF LATE.
REALLY? DO TELL.
HE SEEMS TO HAVE TAKEN AN INTEREST IN ELIZABETH WESTBROOK. I BELIEVE THEY'RE DATING NOW.
DATING?
WELL, I CAN'T BE SURE. I DON'T SPY ON THE CHILDREN BUT--
HEINRICH?
COUNT VON BRUCKEN? WHERE ARE YOU GOING?

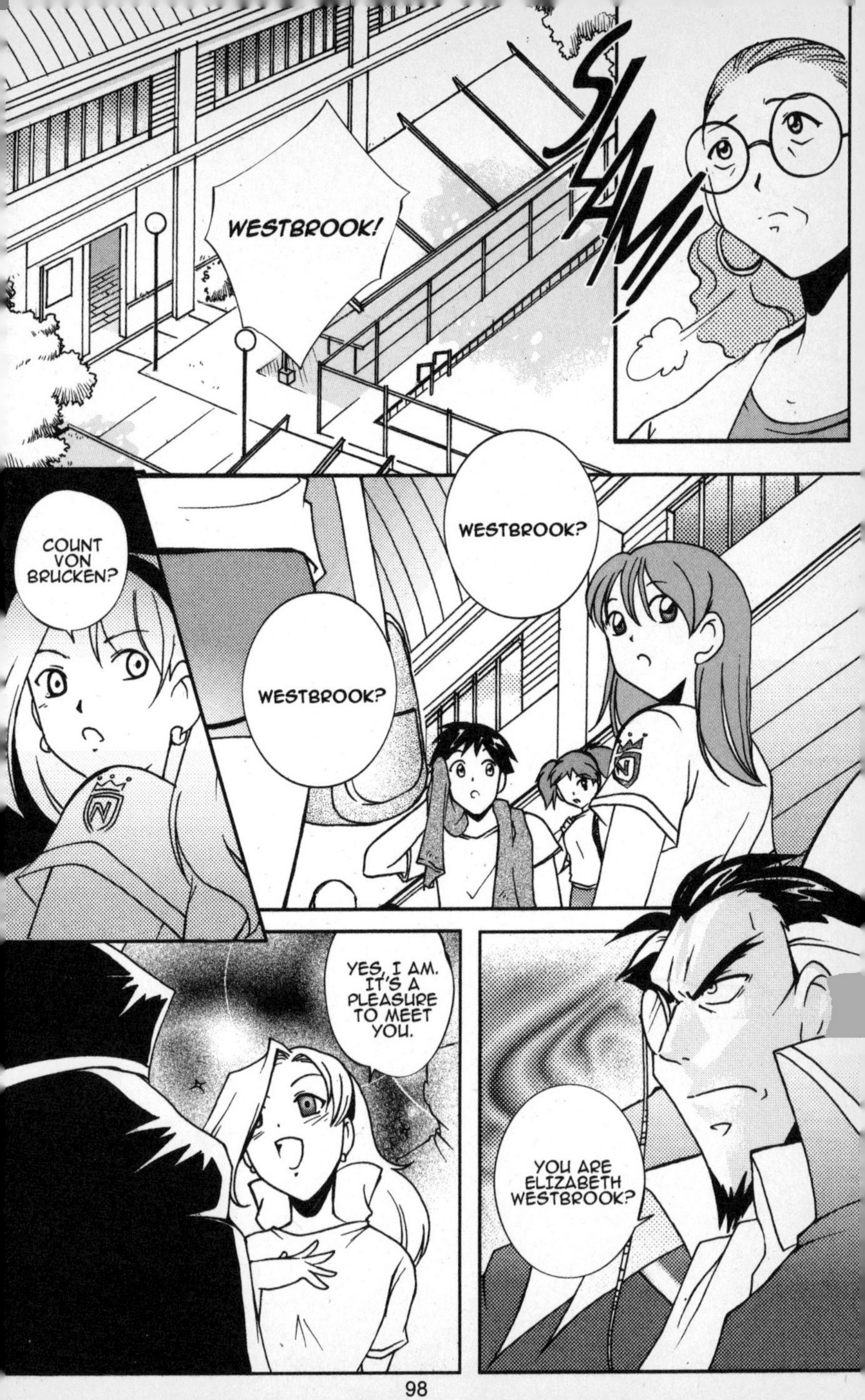
SLAM!
WESTBROOK!
WESTBROOK?
WESTBROOK?
COUNT VON BRUCKEN?
YOU ARE ELIZABETH WESTBROOK?
YES, I AM. IT'S A PLEASURE TO MEET YOU.

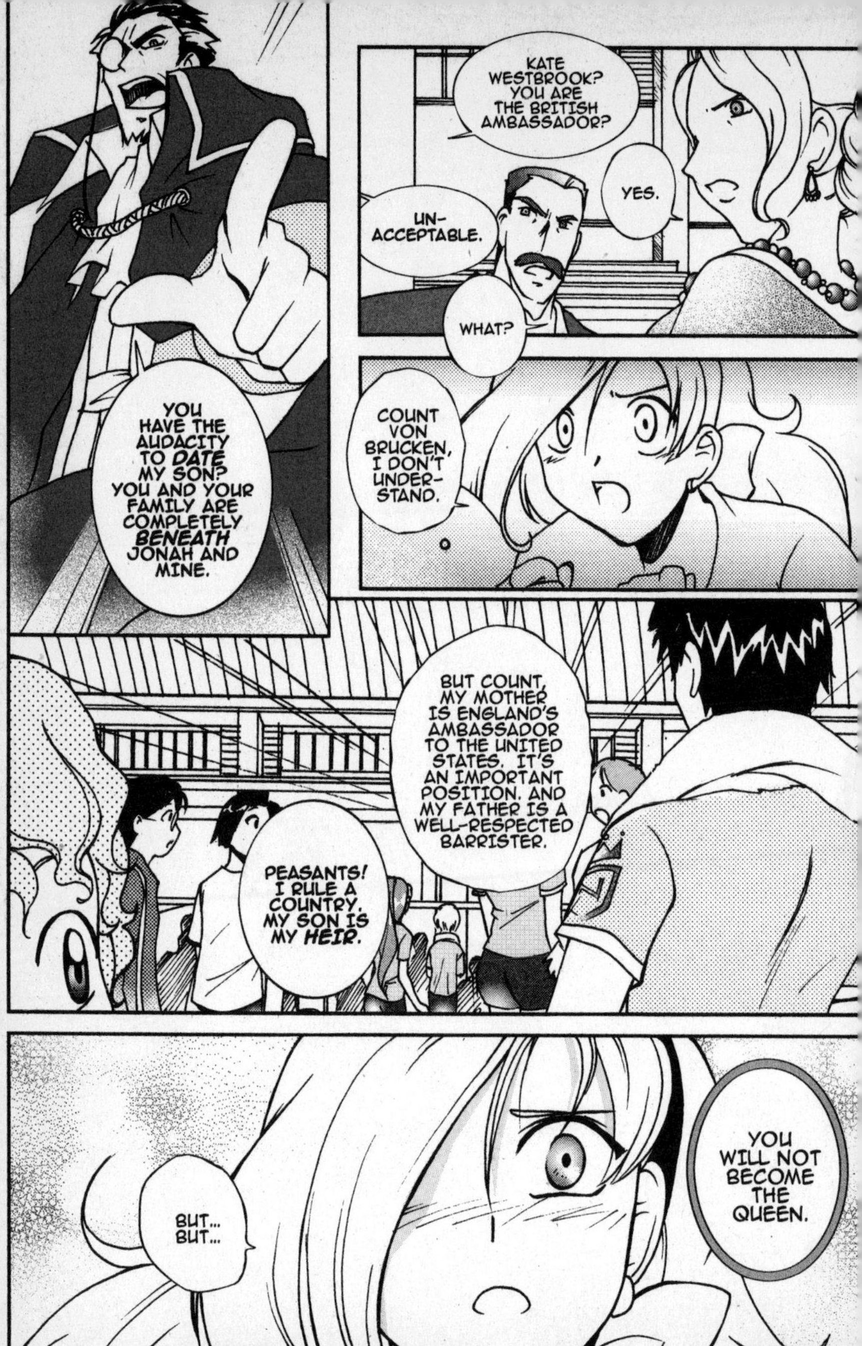
KATE WESTBROOK? YOU ARE THE BRITISH AMBASSADOR?
YES.
UN-ACCEPTABLE.
WHAT?
COUNT VON BRUCKEN, I DON'T UNDER-STAND.
YOU HAVE THE AUDACITY TO DATE MY SON? YOU AND YOUR FAMILY ARE COMPLETELY BENEATH JONAH AND MINE.
BUT COUNT, MY MOTHER IS ENGLAND'S AMBASSADOR TO THE UNITED STATES. IT'S AN IMPORTANT POSITION. AND MY FATHER IS A WELL-RESPECTED BARRISTER.
PEASANTS! I RULE A COUNTRY. MY SON IS MY HEIR.
YOU WILL NOT BECOME THE QUEEN.
BUT... BUT...

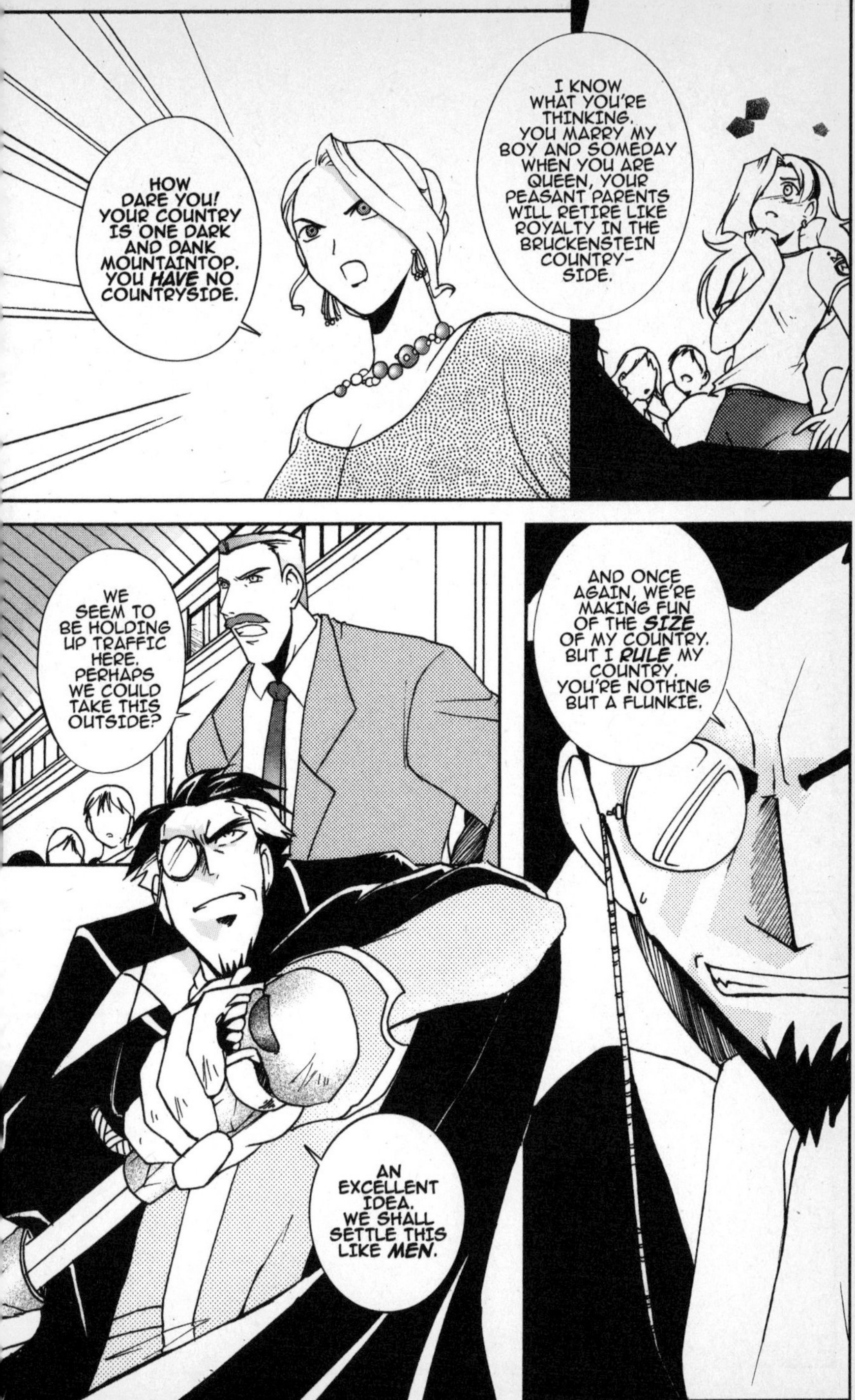
I KNOW WHAT YOU'RE THINKING. YOU MARRY MY BOY AND SOMEDAY WHEN YOU ARE QUEEN, YOUR PEASANT PARENTS WILL RETIRE LIKE ROYALTY IN THE BRUCKENSTEIN COUNTRY-SIDE.
HOW DARE YOU! YOUR COUNTRY IS ONE DARK AND DANK MOUNTAINTOP. YOU *HAVE* NO COUNTRYSIDE.
AND ONCE AGAIN, WE'RE MAKING FUN OF THE *SIZE* OF MY COUNTRY. BUT I *RULE* MY COUNTRY. YOU'RE NOTHING BUT A FLUNKIE.
WE SEEM TO BE HOLDING UP TRAFFIC HERE. PERHAPS WE COULD TAKE THIS OUTSIDE?
AN EXCELLENT IDEA. WE SHALL SETTLE THIS LIKE *MEN*.

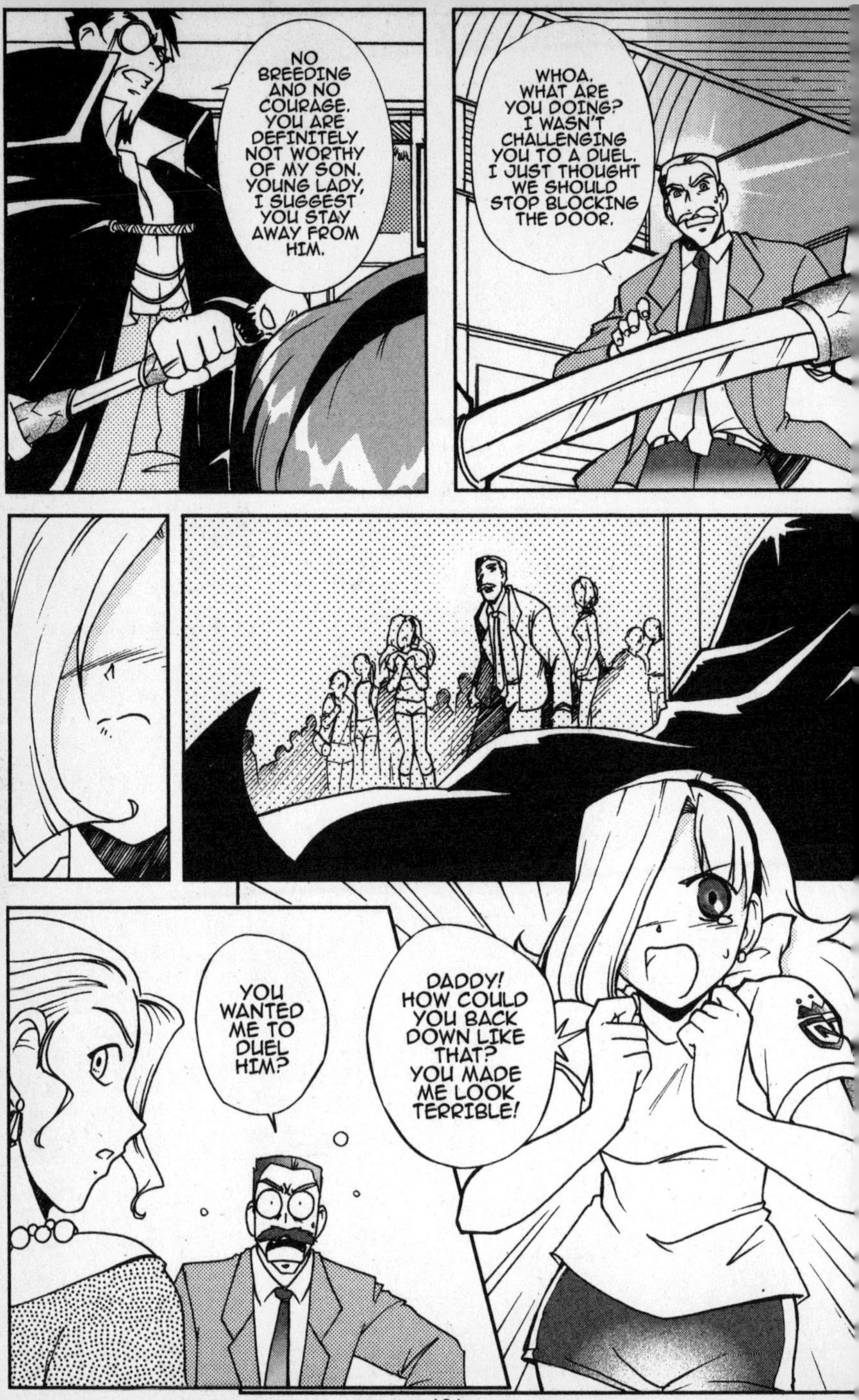
WHOA. WHAT ARE YOU DOING? I WASN'T CHALLENGING YOU TO A DUEL. I JUST THOUGHT WE SHOULD STOP BLOCKING THE DOOR.
NO BREEDING AND NO COURAGE. YOU ARE DEFINITELY NOT WORTHY OF MY SON. YOUNG LADY, I SUGGEST YOU STAY AWAY FROM HIM.
DADDY! HOW COULD YOU BACK DOWN LIKE THAT? YOU MADE ME LOOK TERRIBLE!
YOU WANTED ME TO DUEL HIM?

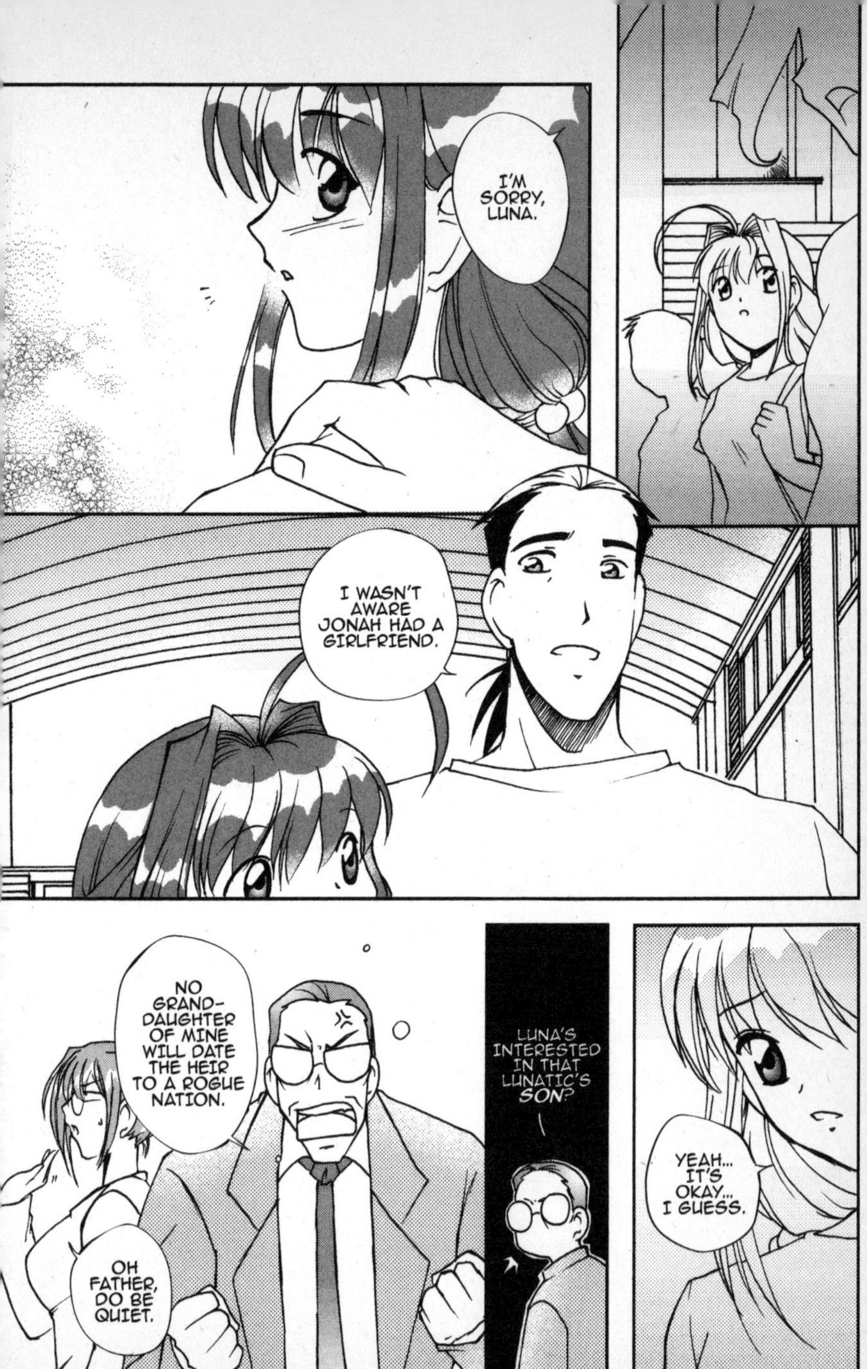
I'M SORRY, LUNA.
I WASN'T AWARE JONAH HAD A GIRLFRIEND.
YEAH... IT'S OKAY... I GUESS.
LUNA'S INTERESTED IN THAT LUNATIC'S *SON*?
NO GRAND-DAUGHTER OF MINE WILL DATE THE HEIR TO A ROGUE NATION.
OH FATHER, DO BE QUIET.

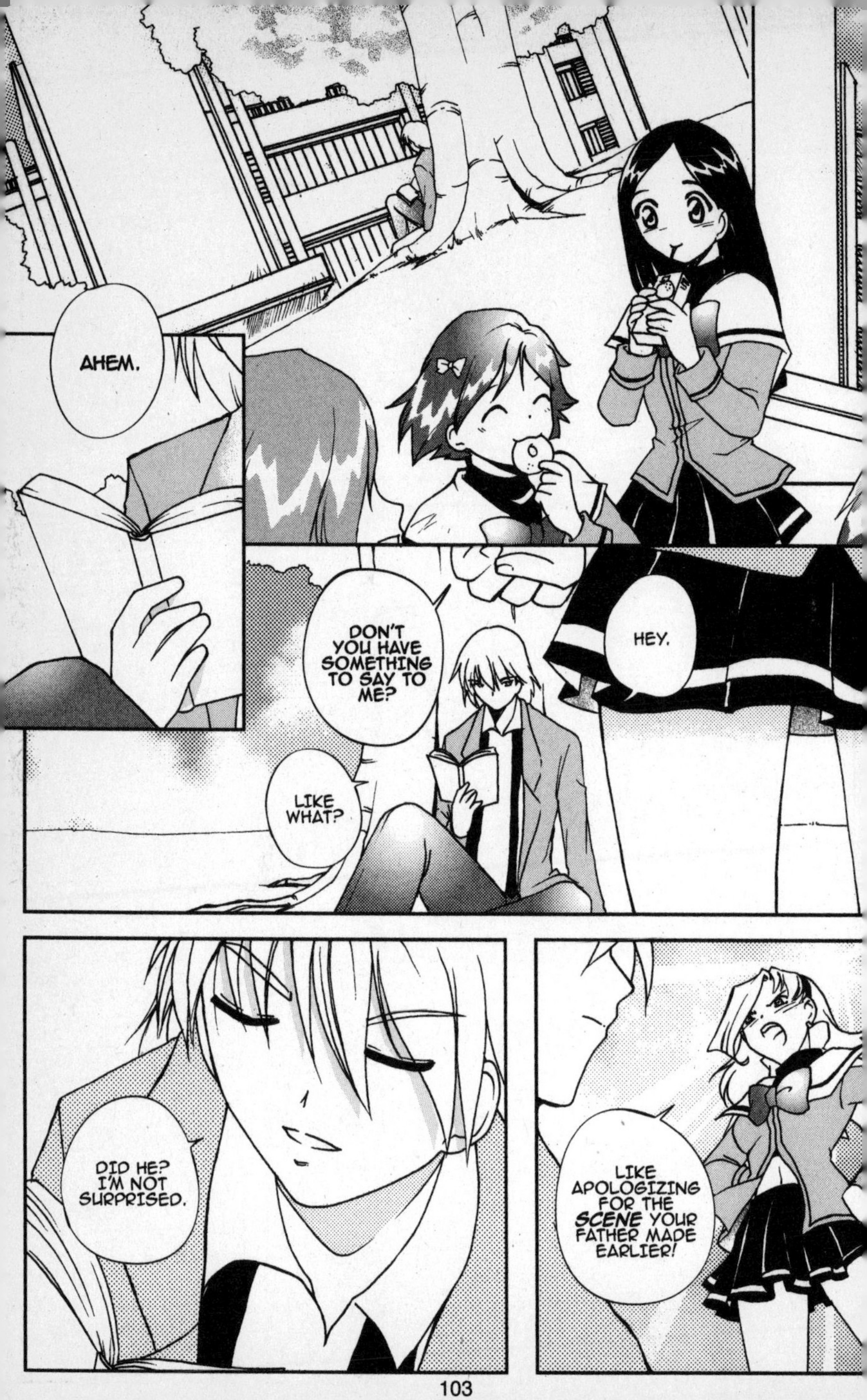
AHEM.
HEY.
DON'T YOU HAVE SOMETHING TO SAY TO ME?
LIKE WHAT?
LIKE APOLOGIZING FOR THE *SCENE* YOUR FATHER MADE EARLIER!
DID HE? I'M NOT SURPRISED.

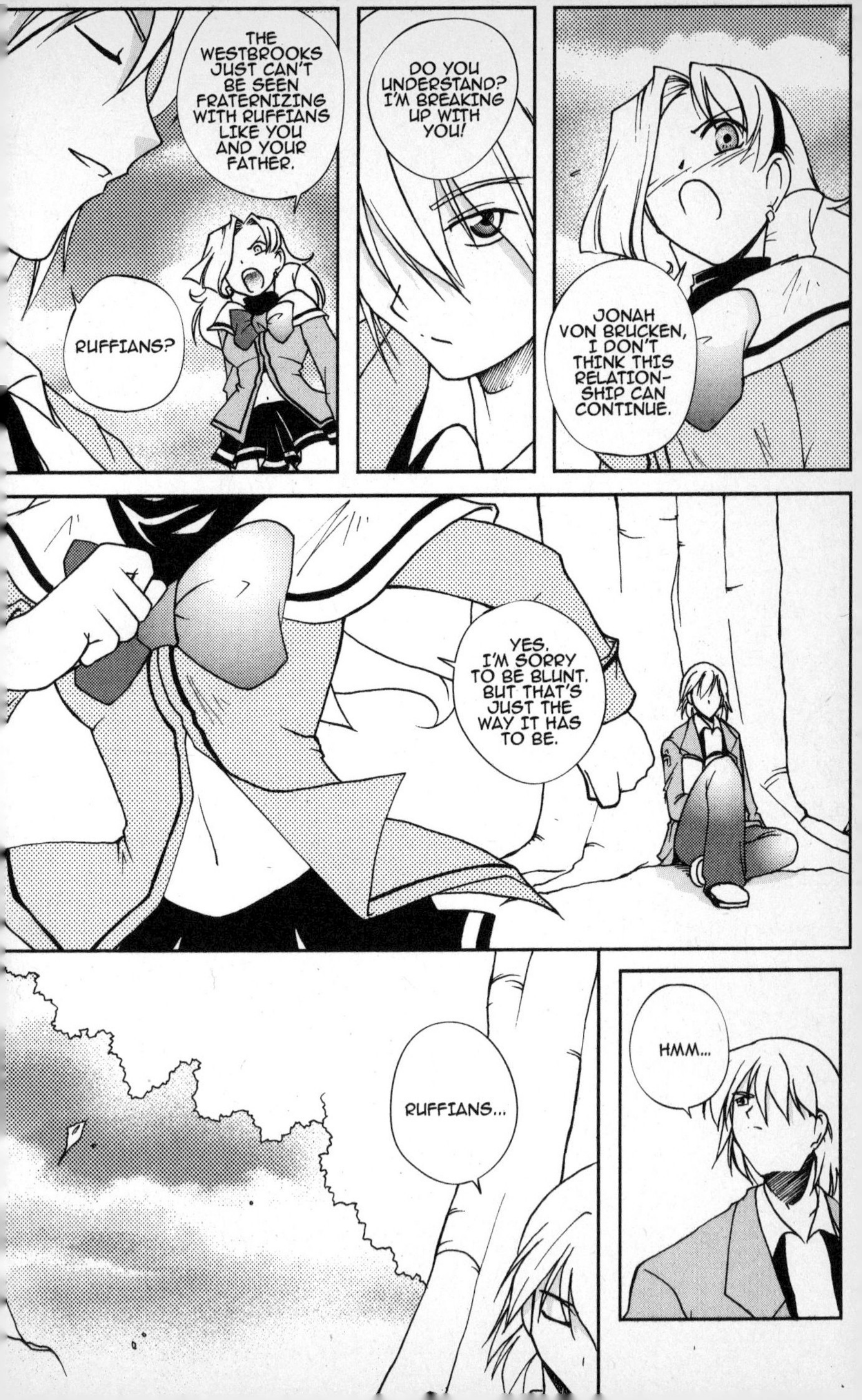
JONAH VON BRUCKEN, I DON'T THINK THIS RELATION-SHIP CAN CONTINUE.
DO YOU UNDERSTAND? I'M BREAKING UP WITH YOU!
THE WESTBROOKS JUST CAN'T BE SEEN FRATERNIZING WITH RUFFIANS LIKE YOU AND YOUR FATHER.
RUFFIANS?
YES. I'M SORRY TO BE BLUNT. BUT THAT'S JUST THE WAY IT HAS TO BE.
HMM...
RUFFIANS...

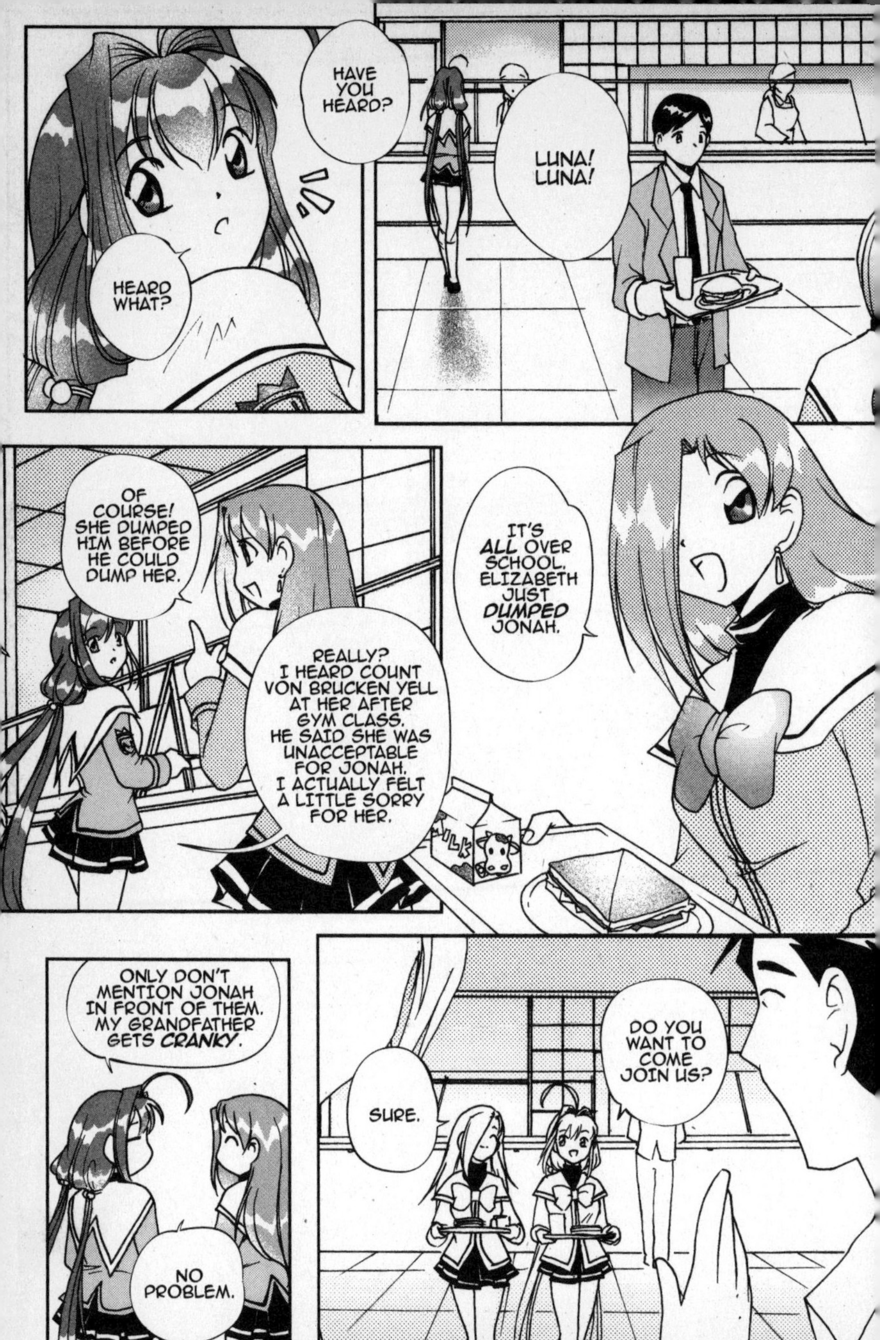
LUNA! LUNA!
HAVE YOU HEARD?
HEARD WHAT?
IT'S ALL OVER SCHOOL. ELIZABETH JUST DUMPED JONAH.
REALLY? I HEARD COUNT VON BRUCKEN YELL AT HER AFTER GYM CLASS. HE SAID SHE WAS UNACCEPTABLE FOR JONAH. I ACTUALLY FELT A LITTLE SORRY FOR HER.
OF COURSE! SHE DUMPED HIM BEFORE HE COULD DUMP HER.
DO YOU WANT TO COME JOIN US?
SURE.
ONLY DON'T MENTION JONAH IN FRONT OF THEM. MY GRANDFATHER GETS CRANKY.
NO PROBLEM.

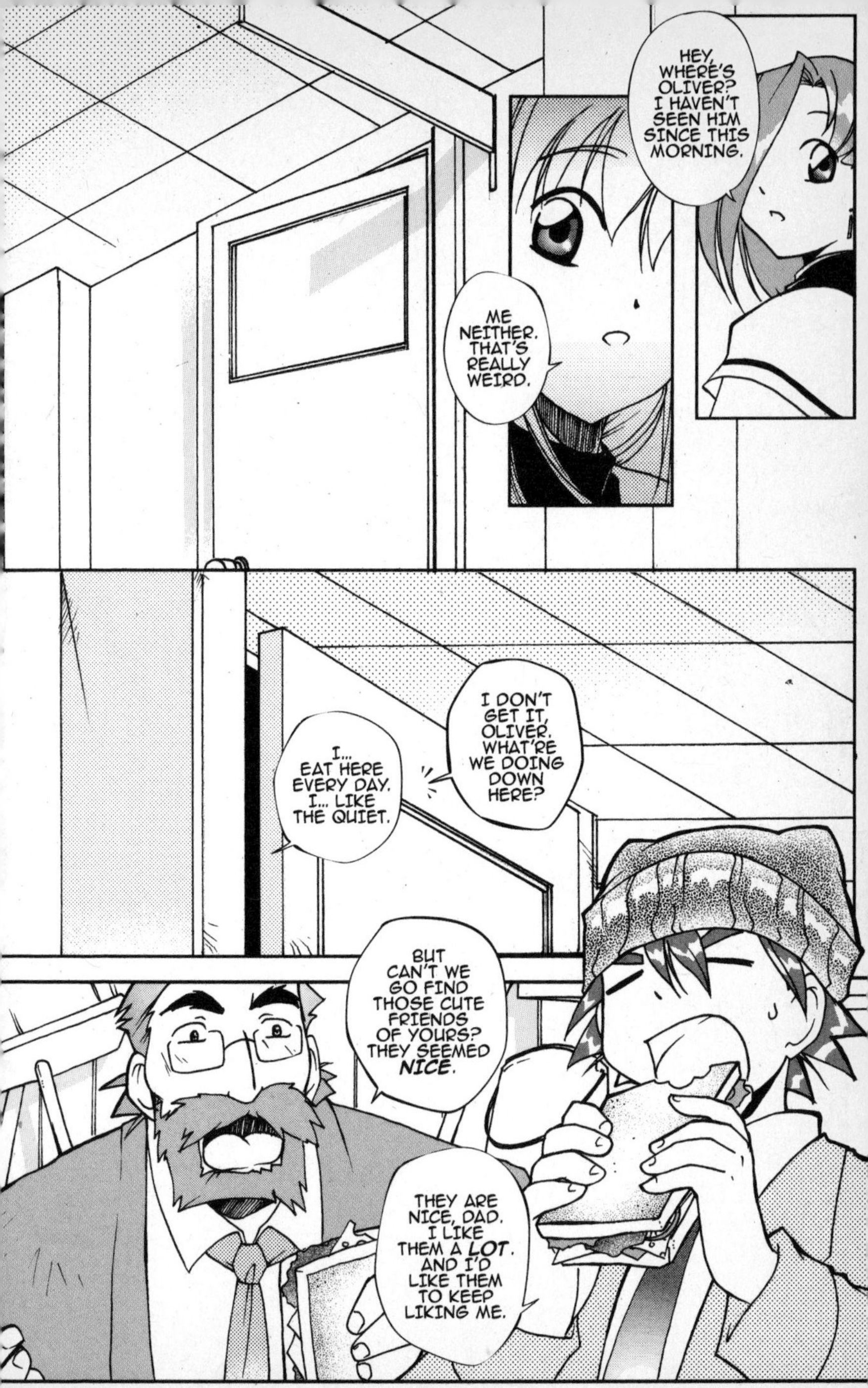
HEY, WHERE'S OLIVER? I HAVEN'T SEEN HIM SINCE THIS MORNING.
ME NEITHER. THAT'S REALLY WEIRD.
I DON'T GET IT, OLIVER. WHAT'RE WE DOING DOWN HERE?
I... EAT HERE EVERY DAY. I... LIKE THE QUIET.
BUT CAN'T WE GO FIND THOSE CUTE FRIENDS OF YOURS? THEY SEEMED ***NICE***.
THEY ARE NICE, DAD. I LIKE THEM A ***LOT***. AND I'D LIKE THEM TO KEEP LIKING ME.

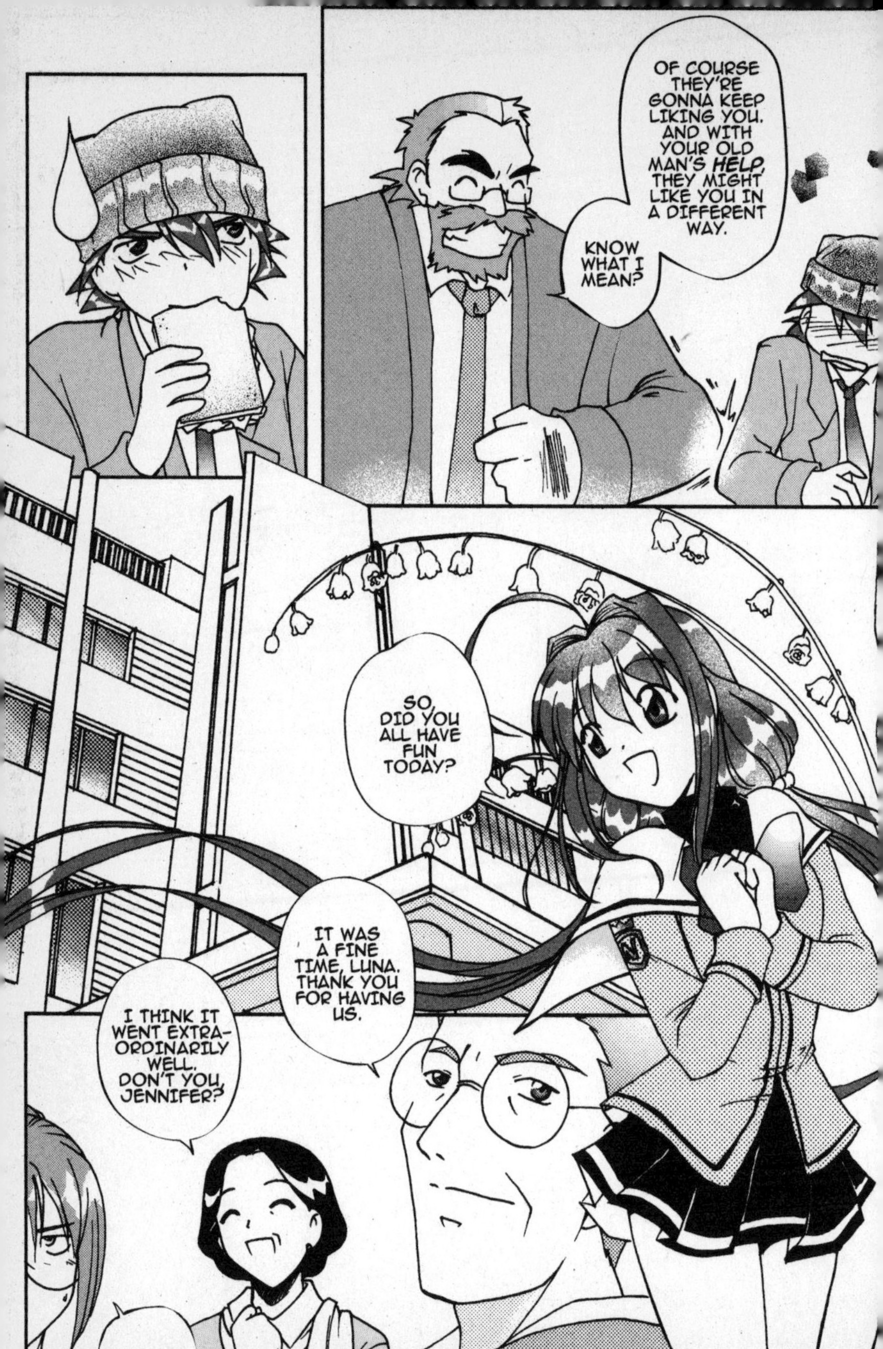
OF COURSE THEY'RE GONNA KEEP LIKING YOU. AND WITH YOUR OLD MAN'S *HELP*, THEY MIGHT LIKE YOU IN A DIFFERENT WAY.
KNOW WHAT I MEAN?
SO, DID YOU ALL HAVE FUN TODAY?
IT WAS A FINE TIME, LUNA. THANK YOU FOR HAVING US.
I THINK IT WENT EXTRA-ORDINARILY WELL. DON'T YOU, JENNIFER?
TERRIFIC.

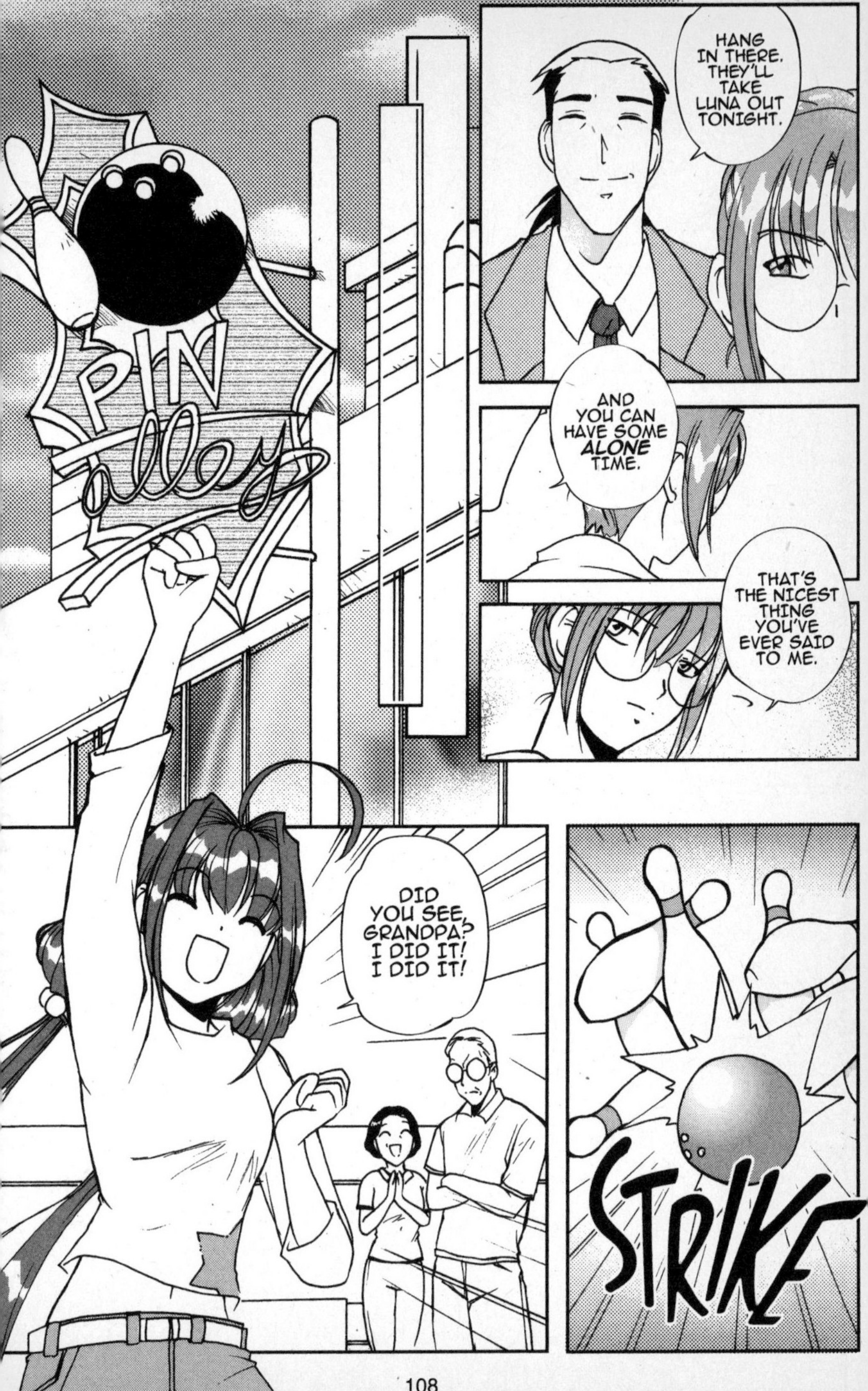
HANG IN THERE. THEY'LL TAKE LUNA OUT TONIGHT.
AND YOU CAN HAVE SOME ALONE TIME.
THAT'S THE NICEST THING YOU'VE EVER SAID TO ME.
PIN alley
STRIKE
DID YOU SEE, GRANDPA? I DID IT! I DID IT!

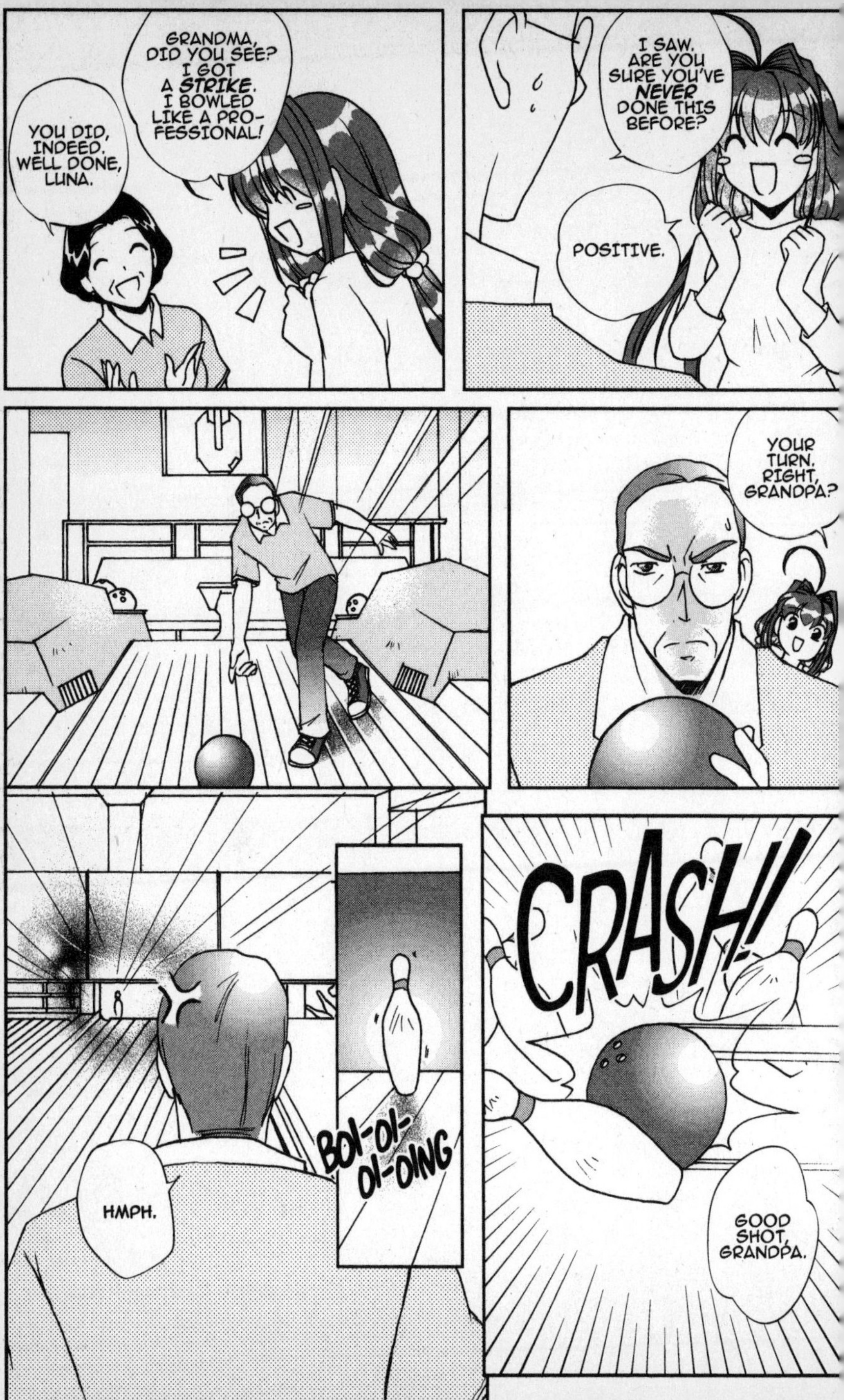
I SAW. ARE YOU SURE YOU'VE NEVER DONE THIS BEFORE?
POSITIVE.
GRANDMA, DID YOU SEE? I GOT A STRIKE. I BOWLED LIKE A PRO-FESSIONAL!
YOU DID, INDEED. WELL DONE, LUNA.
YOUR TURN. RIGHT, GRANDPA?
CRASH!!
GOOD SHOT, GRANDPA.
BOI-OI-OI-OING
HMPH.

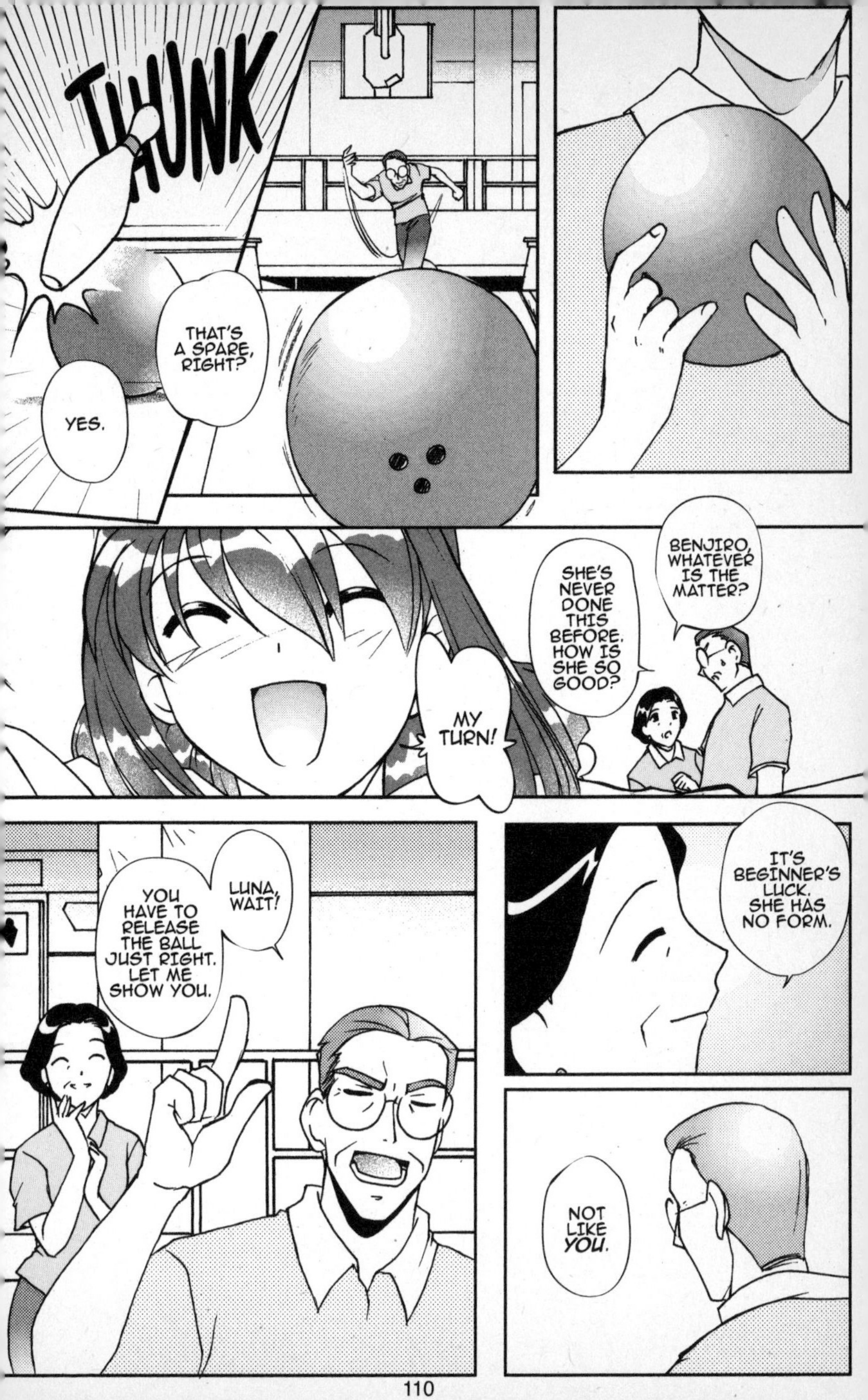
THUNK
THAT'S A SPARE, RIGHT?
YES.
BENJIRO, WHATEVER IS THE MATTER?
SHE'S NEVER DONE THIS BEFORE. HOW IS SHE SO GOOD?
MY TURN!
IT'S BEGINNER'S LUCK. SHE HAS NO FORM.
NOT LIKE *YOU*.
LUNA, WAIT!
YOU HAVE TO RELEASE THE BALL JUST RIGHT. LET ME SHOW YOU.

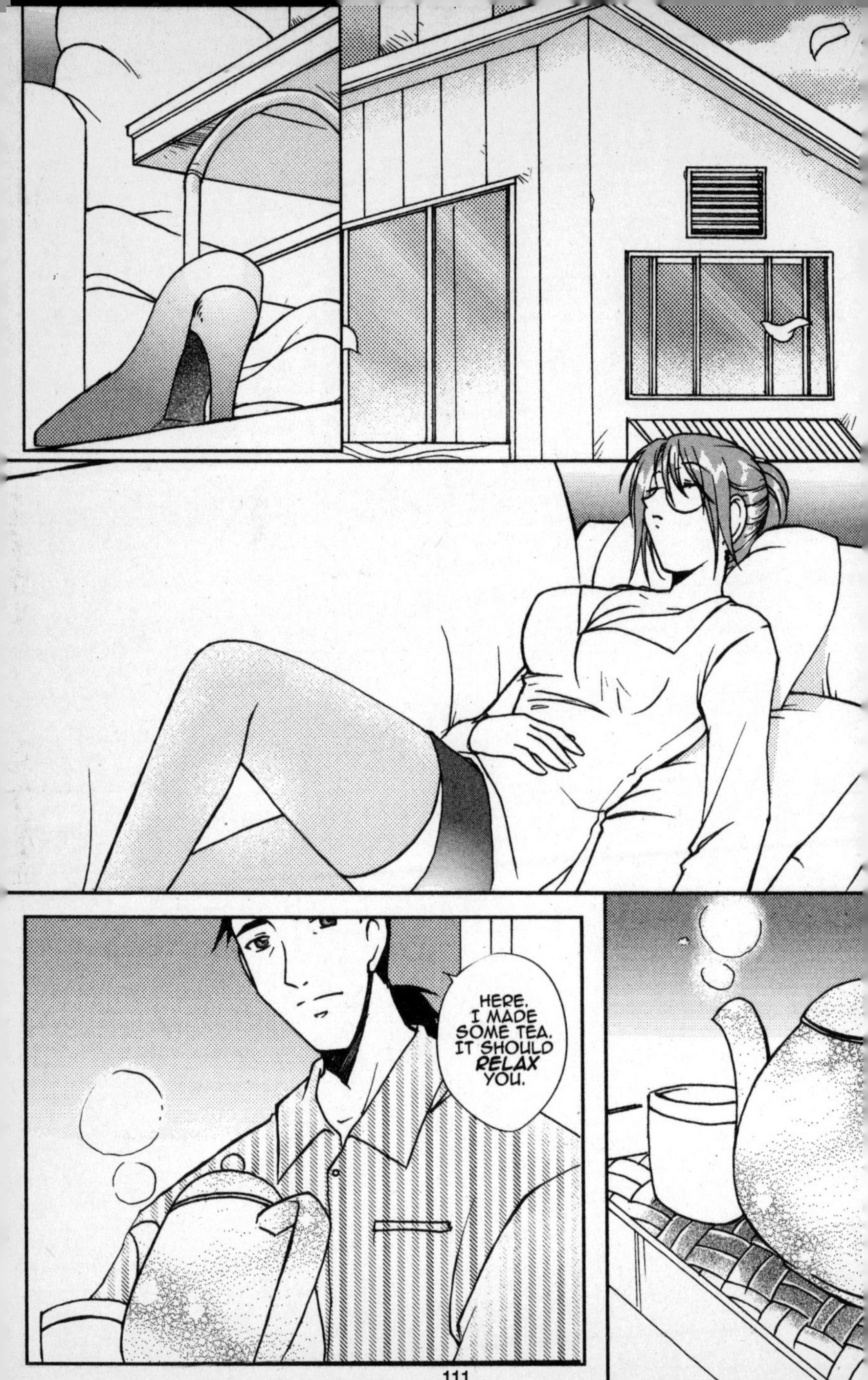
HERE, I MADE SOME TEA. IT SHOULD RELAX YOU.

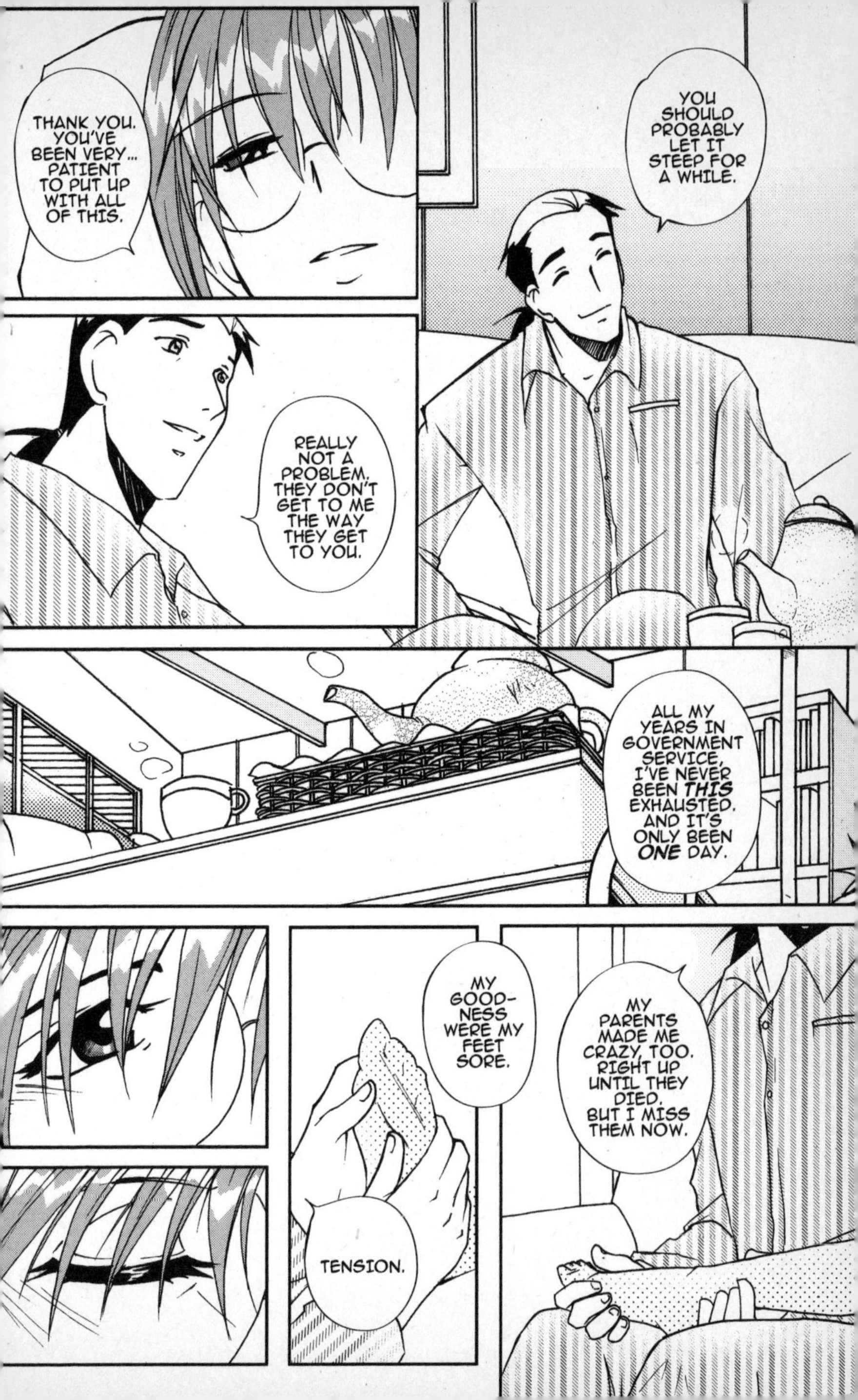
YOU SHOULD PROBABLY LET IT STEEP FOR A WHILE.
THANK YOU. YOU'VE BEEN VERY... PATIENT TO PUT UP WITH ALL OF THIS.
REALLY NOT A PROBLEM. THEY DON'T GET TO ME THE WAY THEY GET TO YOU.
ALL MY YEARS IN GOVERNMENT SERVICE, I'VE NEVER BEEN *THIS* EXHAUSTED. AND IT'S ONLY BEEN *ONE* DAY.
MY PARENTS MADE ME CRAZY, TOO. RIGHT UP UNTIL THEY DIED. BUT I MISS THEM NOW.
MY GOODNESS WERE MY FEET SORE.
TENSION.

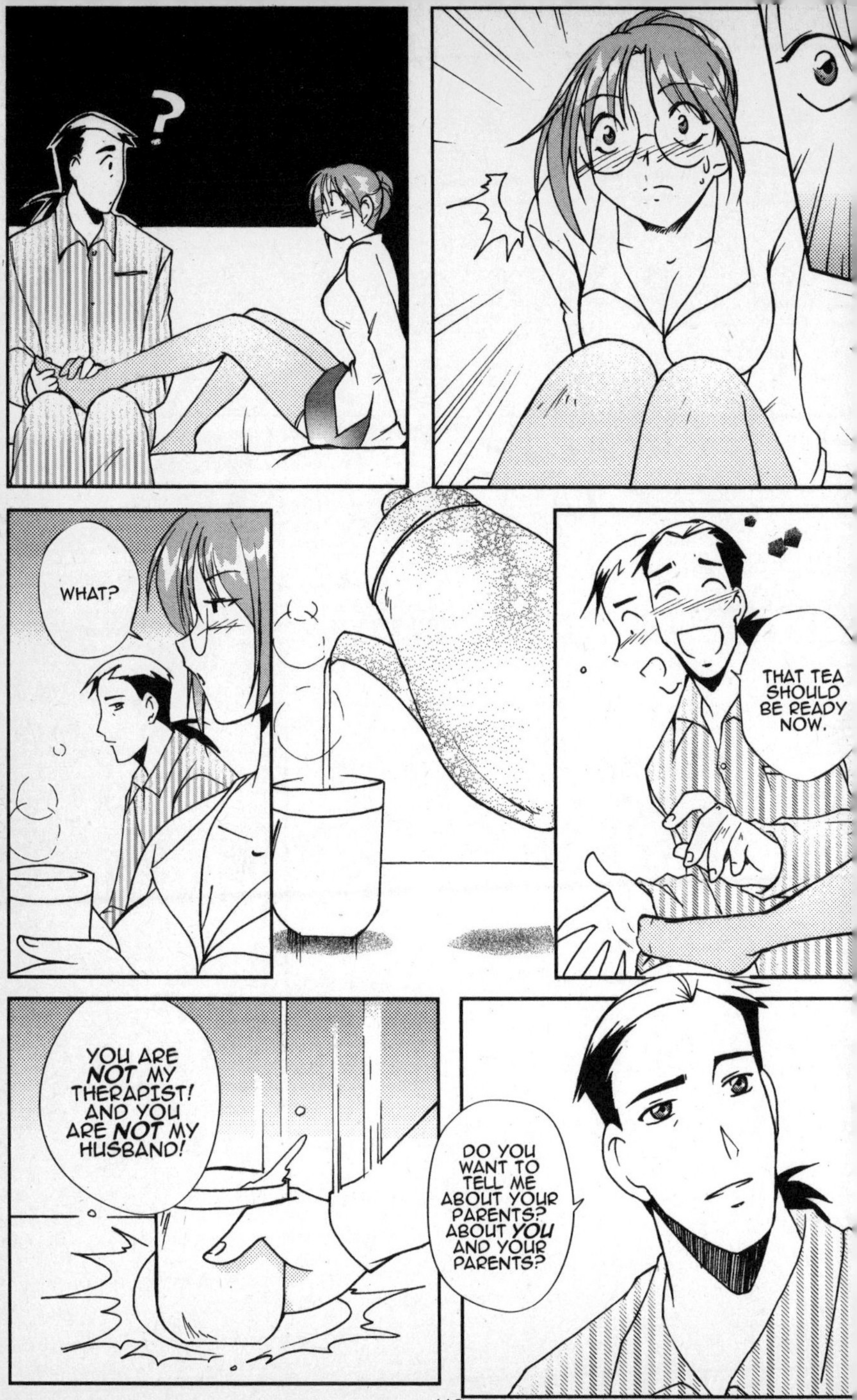
THAT TEA SHOULD BE READY NOW.
WHAT?
DO YOU WANT TO TELL ME ABOUT YOUR PARENTS? ABOUT YOU AND YOUR PARENTS?
YOU ARE NOT MY THERAPIST! AND YOU ARE NOT MY HUSBAND!

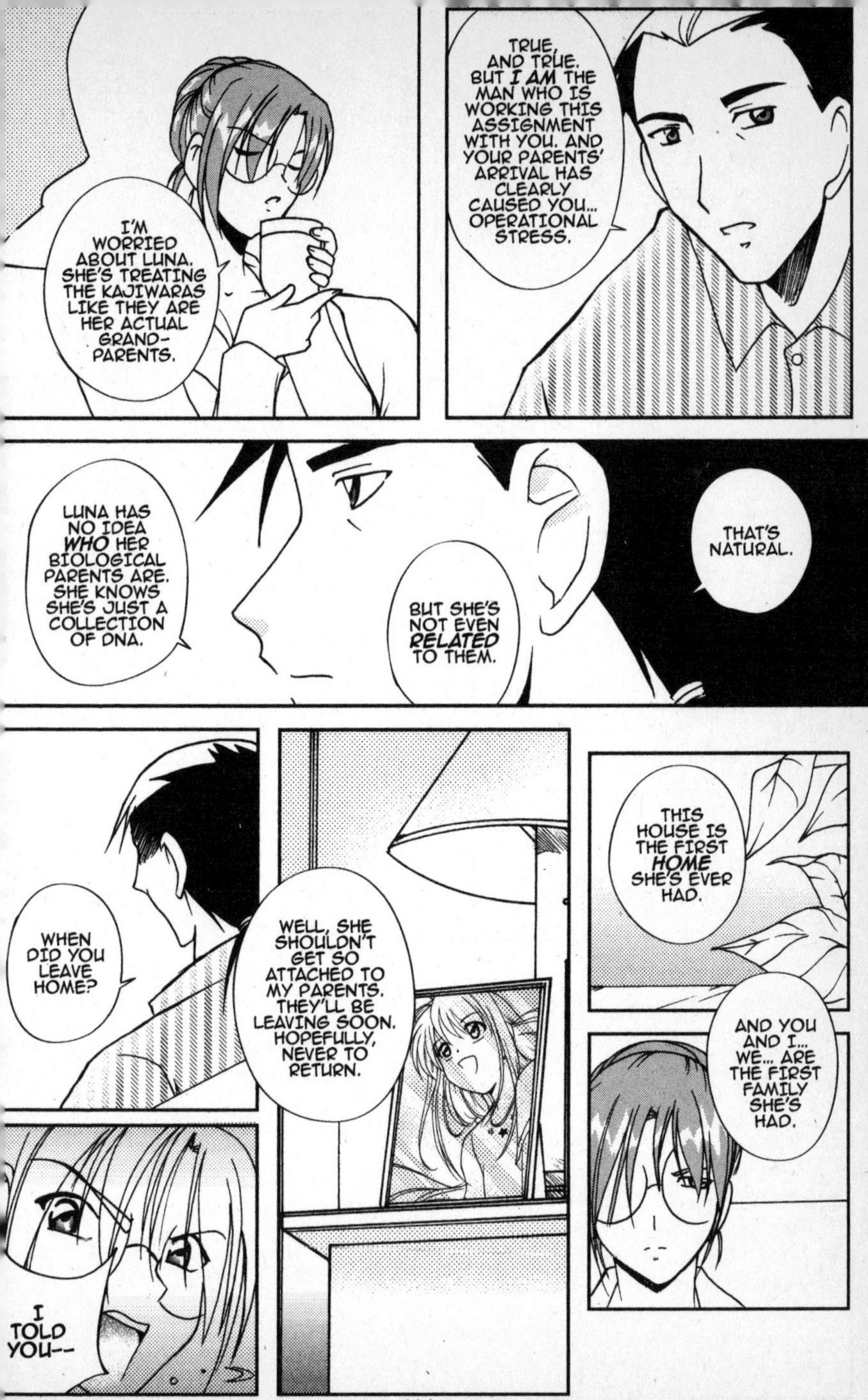
TRUE, AND TRUE. BUT *I AM* THE MAN WHO IS WORKING THIS ASSIGNMENT WITH YOU. AND YOUR PARENTS' ARRIVAL HAS CLEARLY CAUSED YOU... OPERATIONAL STRESS.
I'M WORRIED ABOUT LUNA. SHE'S TREATING THE KAJIWARAS LIKE THEY ARE HER ACTUAL GRAND-PARENTS.
THAT'S NATURAL.
BUT SHE'S NOT EVEN *RELATED* TO THEM.
LUNA HAS NO IDEA *WHO* HER BIOLOGICAL PARENTS ARE. SHE KNOWS SHE'S JUST A COLLECTION OF DNA.
THIS HOUSE IS THE FIRST *HOME* SHE'S EVER HAD.
AND YOU AND I... WE... ARE THE FIRST FAMILY SHE'S HAD.
WELL, SHE SHOULDN'T GET SO ATTACHED TO MY PARENTS. THEY'LL BE LEAVING SOON. HOPEFULLY, NEVER TO RETURN.
WHEN DID YOU LEAVE HOME?
I TOLD YOU--

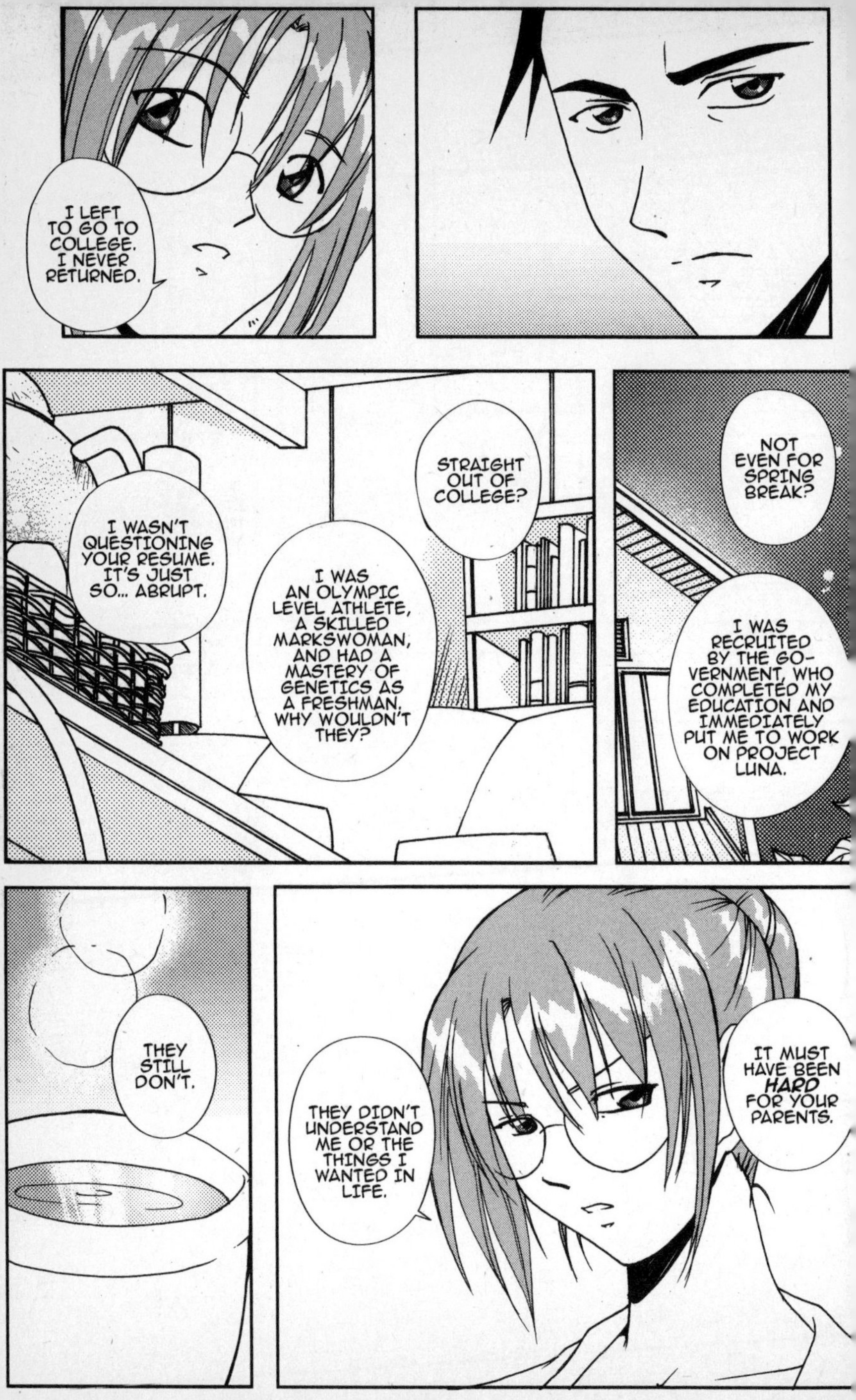
I LEFT TO GO TO COLLEGE. I NEVER RETURNED.
NOT EVEN FOR SPRING BREAK?
I WAS RECRUITED BY THE GO-VERNMENT, WHO COMPLETED MY EDUCATION AND IMMEDIATELY PUT ME TO WORK ON PROJECT LUNA.
STRAIGHT OUT OF COLLEGE?
I WAS AN OLYMPIC LEVEL ATHLETE, A SKILLED MARKSWOMAN, AND HAD A MASTERY OF GENETICS AS A FRESHMAN. WHY WOULDN'T THEY?
I WASN'T QUESTIONING YOUR RESUME. IT'S JUST SO... ABRUPT.
IT MUST HAVE BEEN *HARD* FOR YOUR PARENTS.
THEY DIDN'T UNDERSTAND ME OR THE THINGS I WANTED IN LIFE.
THEY STILL DON'T.

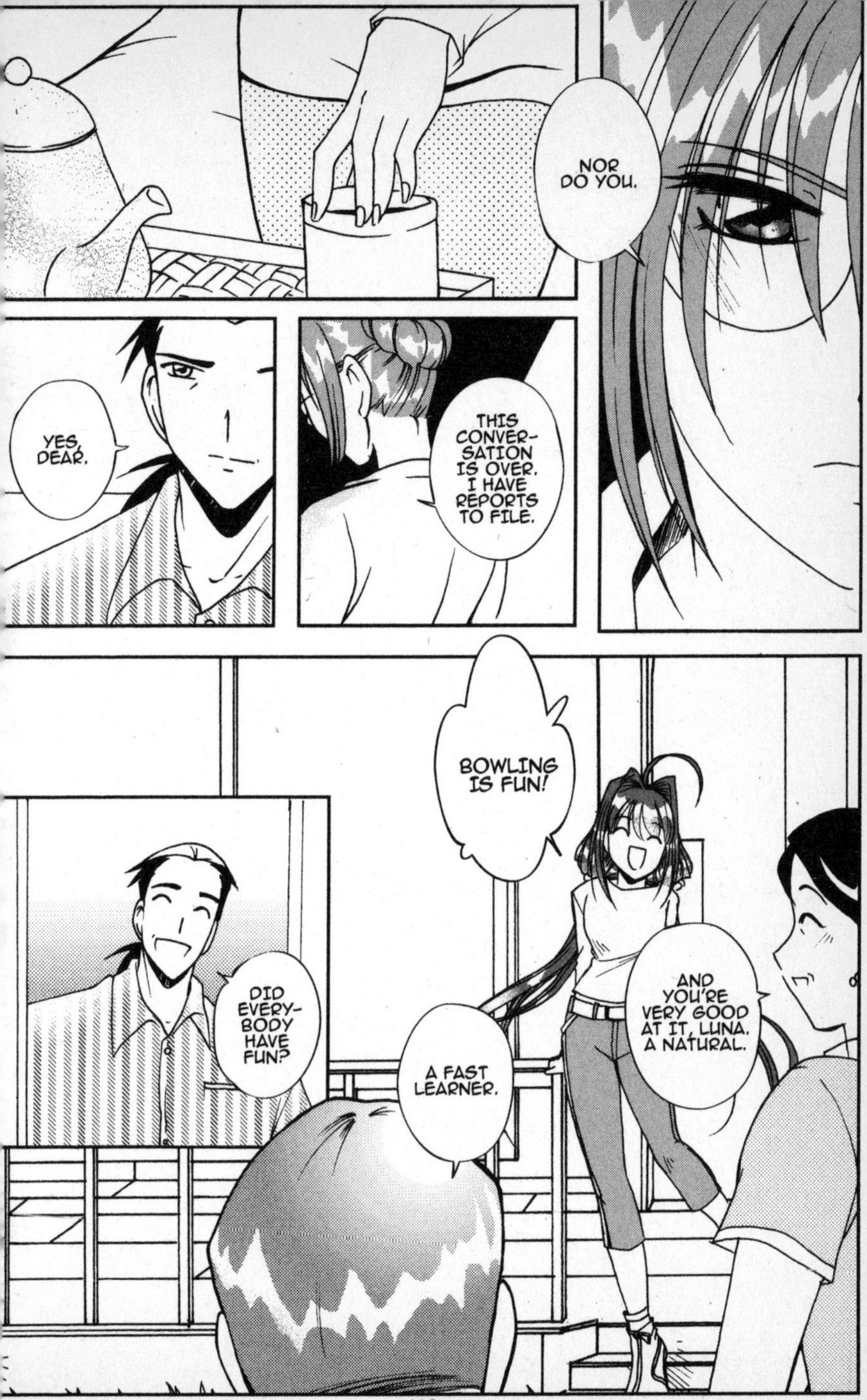
NOR DO YOU.
THIS CONVERSATION IS OVER. I HAVE REPORTS TO FILE.
YES, DEAR.
BOWLING IS FUN!
AND YOU'RE VERY GOOD AT IT, LUNA. A NATURAL.
A FAST LEARNER.
DID EVERYBODY HAVE FUN?

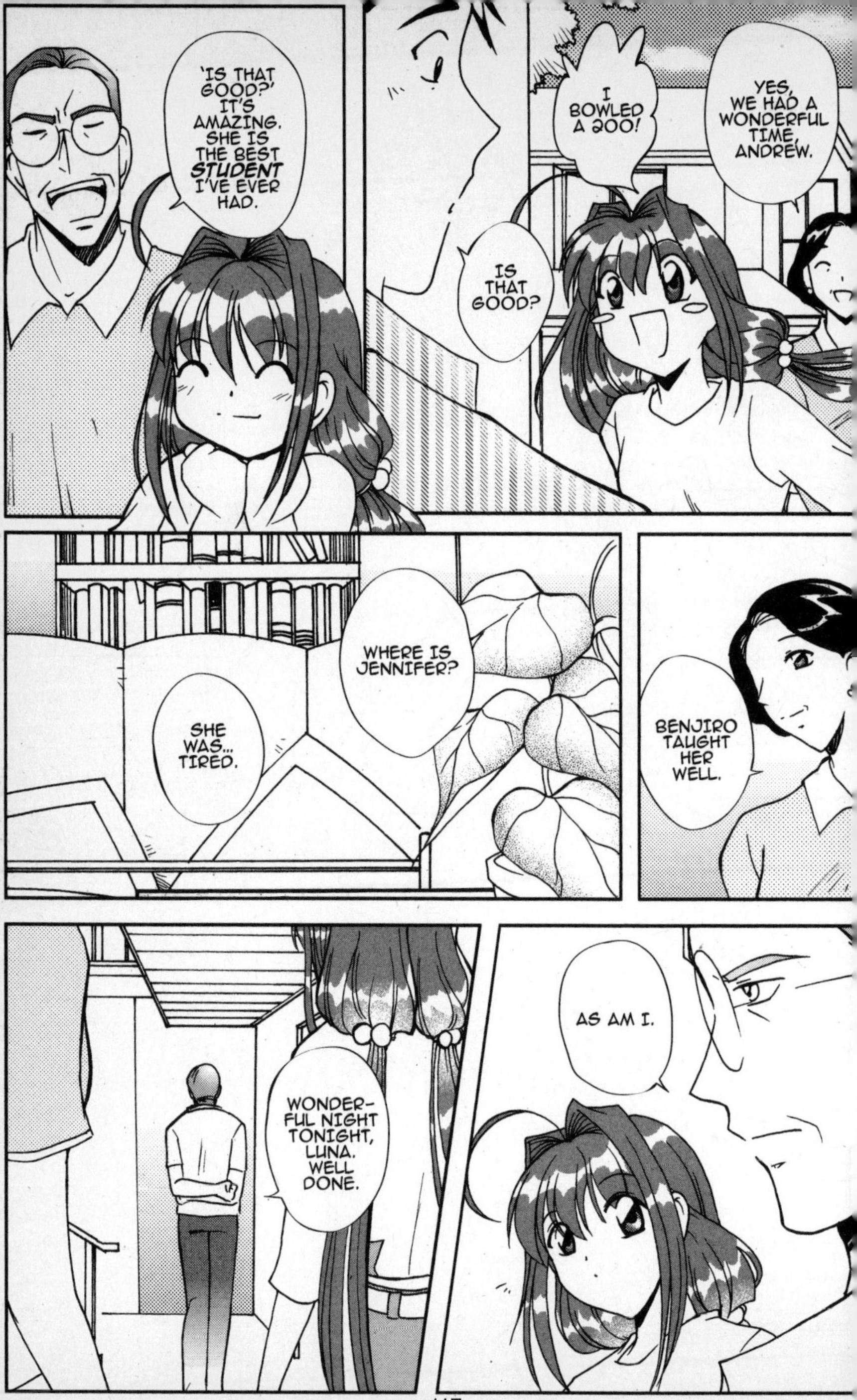
YES, WE HAD A WONDERFUL TIME, ANDREW.
I BOWLED A 200!
IS THAT GOOD?
'IS THAT GOOD?' IT'S AMAZING. SHE IS THE BEST **STUDENT** I'VE EVER HAD.
BENJIRO TAUGHT HER WELL.
WHERE IS JENNIFER?
SHE WAS... TIRED.
AS AM I.
WONDER-FUL NIGHT TONIGHT, LUNA. WELL DONE.

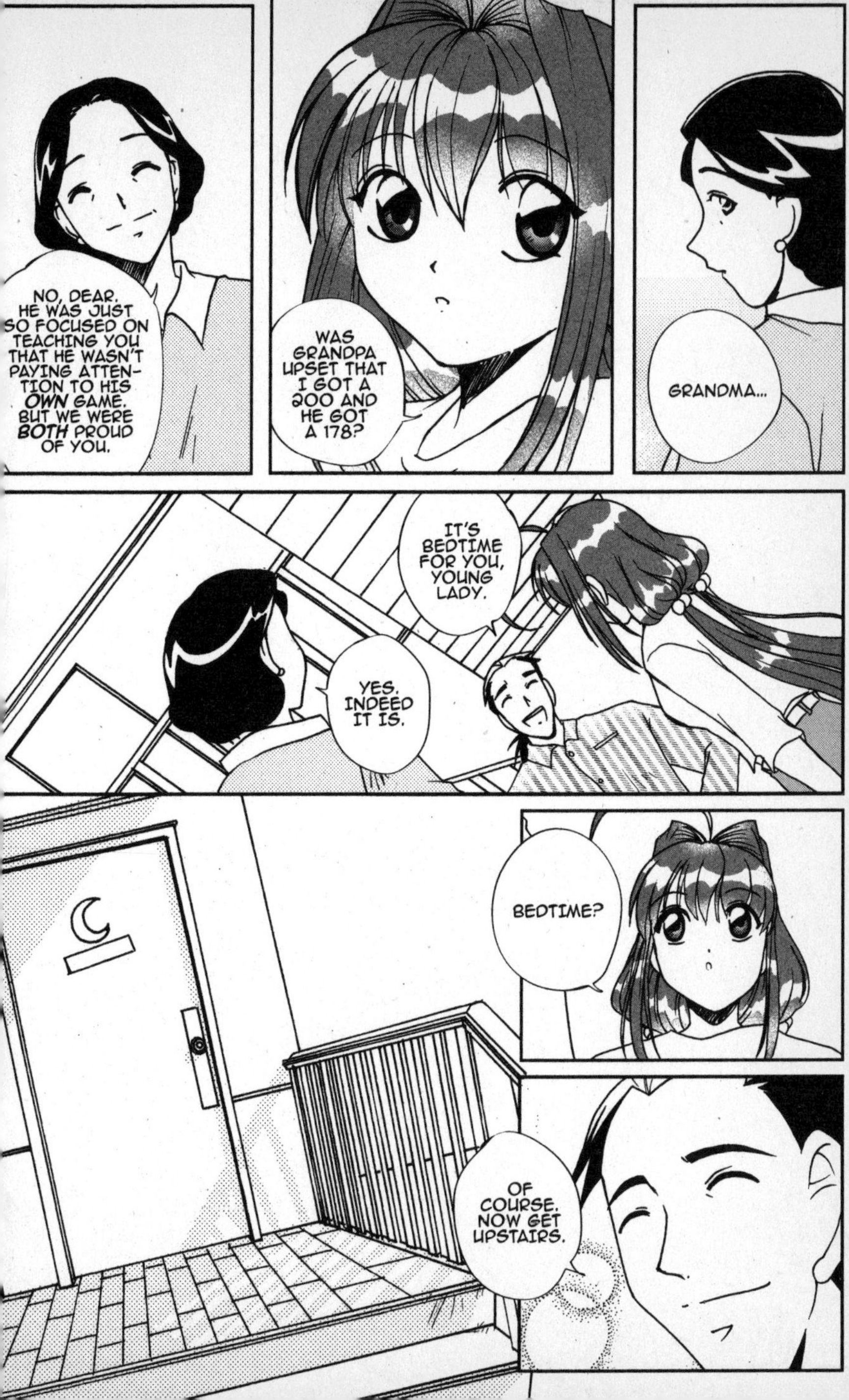
GRANDMA...
WAS GRANDPA UPSET THAT I GOT A 200 AND HE GOT A 178?
NO, DEAR. HE WAS JUST SO FOCUSED ON TEACHING YOU THAT HE WASN'T PAYING ATTENTION TO HIS *OWN* GAME. BUT WE WERE *BOTH* PROUD OF YOU.
IT'S BEDTIME FOR YOU, YOUNG LADY.
YES. INDEED IT IS.
BEDTIME?
OF COURSE. NOW GET UPSTAIRS.

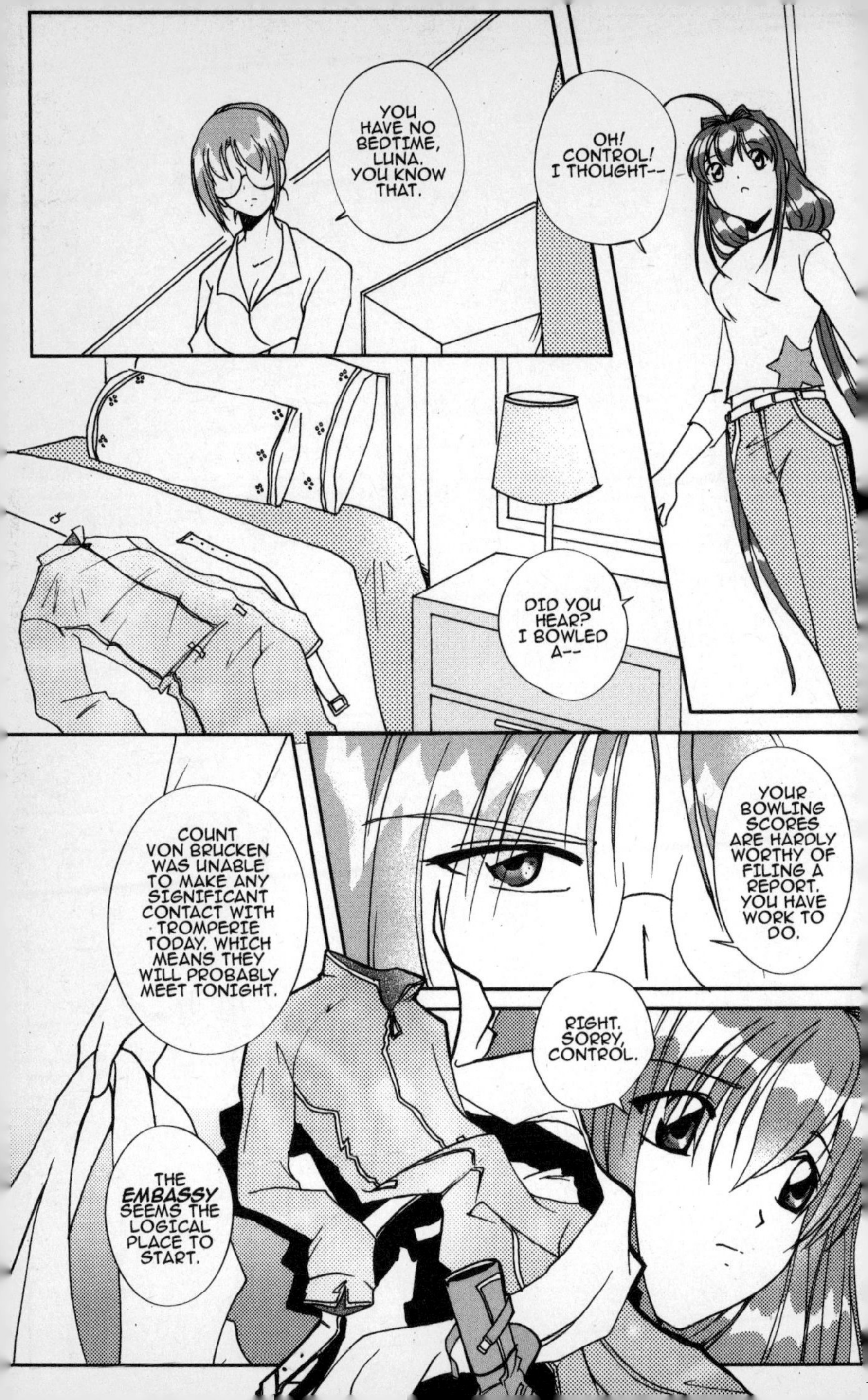

OH! CONTROL! I THOUGHT--
YOU HAVE NO BEDTIME, LUNA. YOU KNOW THAT.
DID YOU HEAR? I BOWLED A--
YOUR BOWLING SCORES ARE HARDLY WORTHY OF FILING A REPORT. YOU HAVE WORK TO DO.
COUNT VON BRUCKEN WAS UNABLE TO MAKE ANY SIGNIFICANT CONTACT WITH TROMPERIE TODAY, WHICH MEANS THEY WILL PROBABLY MEET TONIGHT.
RIGHT. SORRY, CONTROL.
THE *EMBASSY* SEEMS THE LOGICAL PLACE TO START.

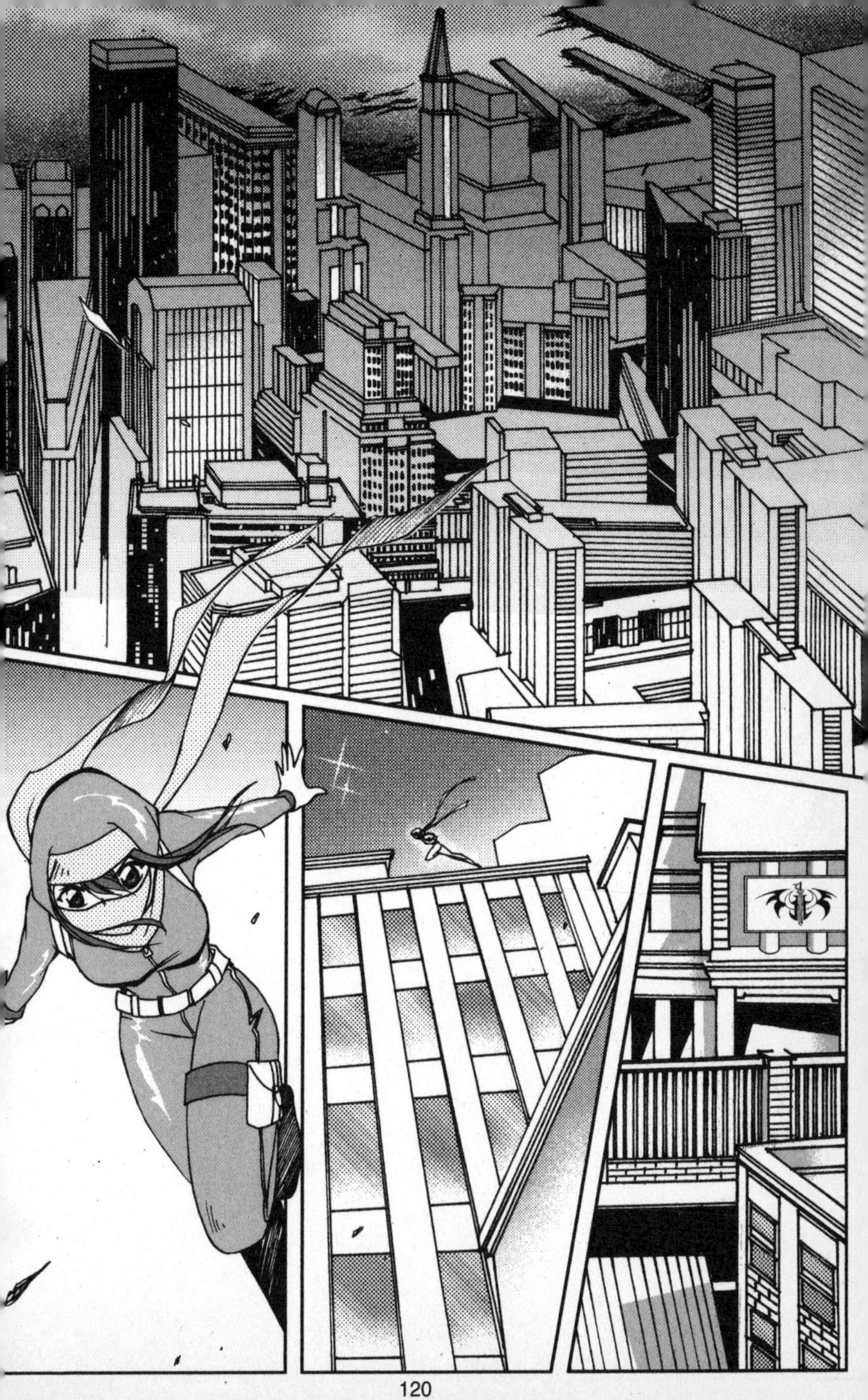

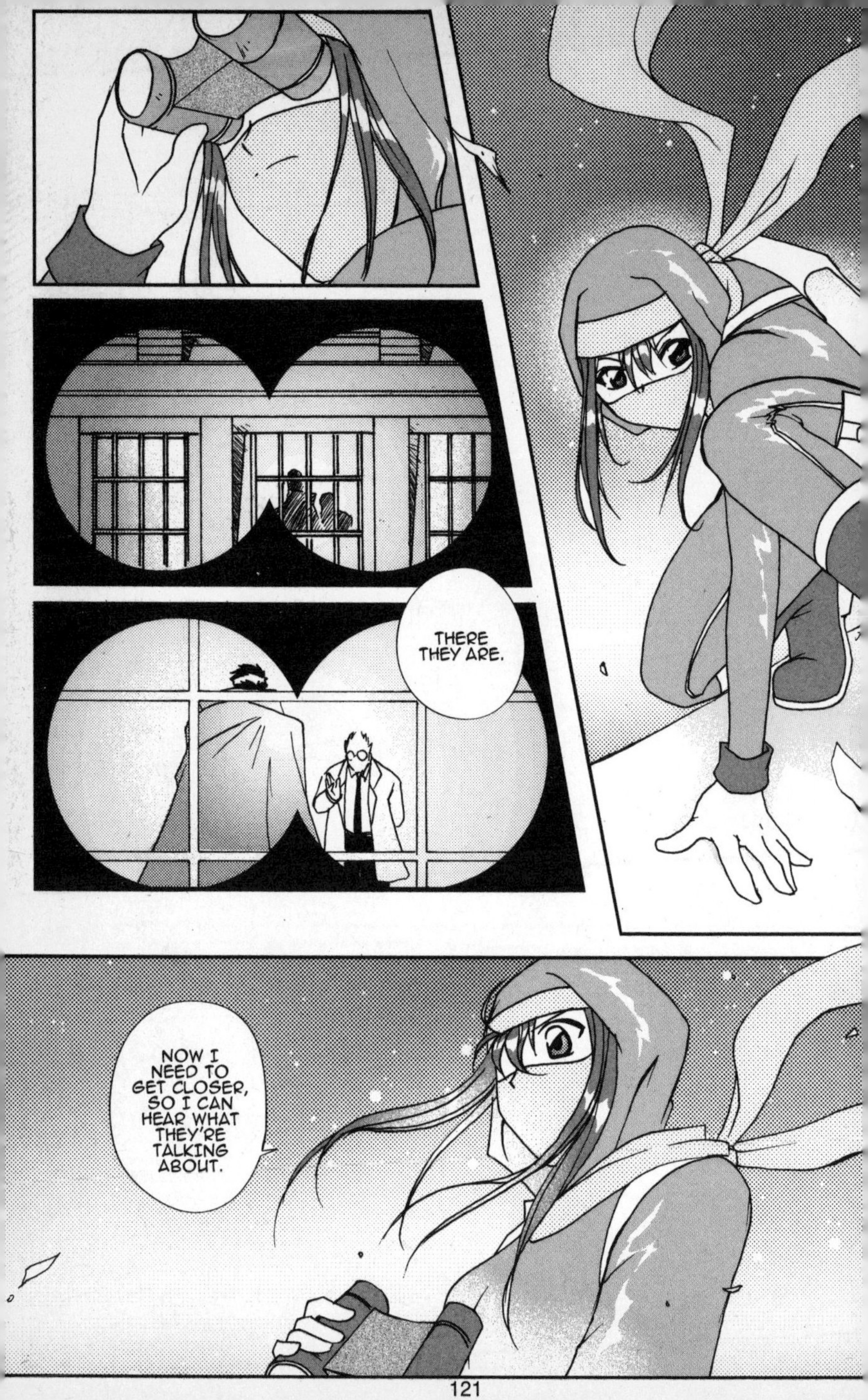
THERE THEY ARE.
NOW I NEED TO GET CLOSER, SO I CAN HEAR WHAT THEY'RE TALKING ABOUT.

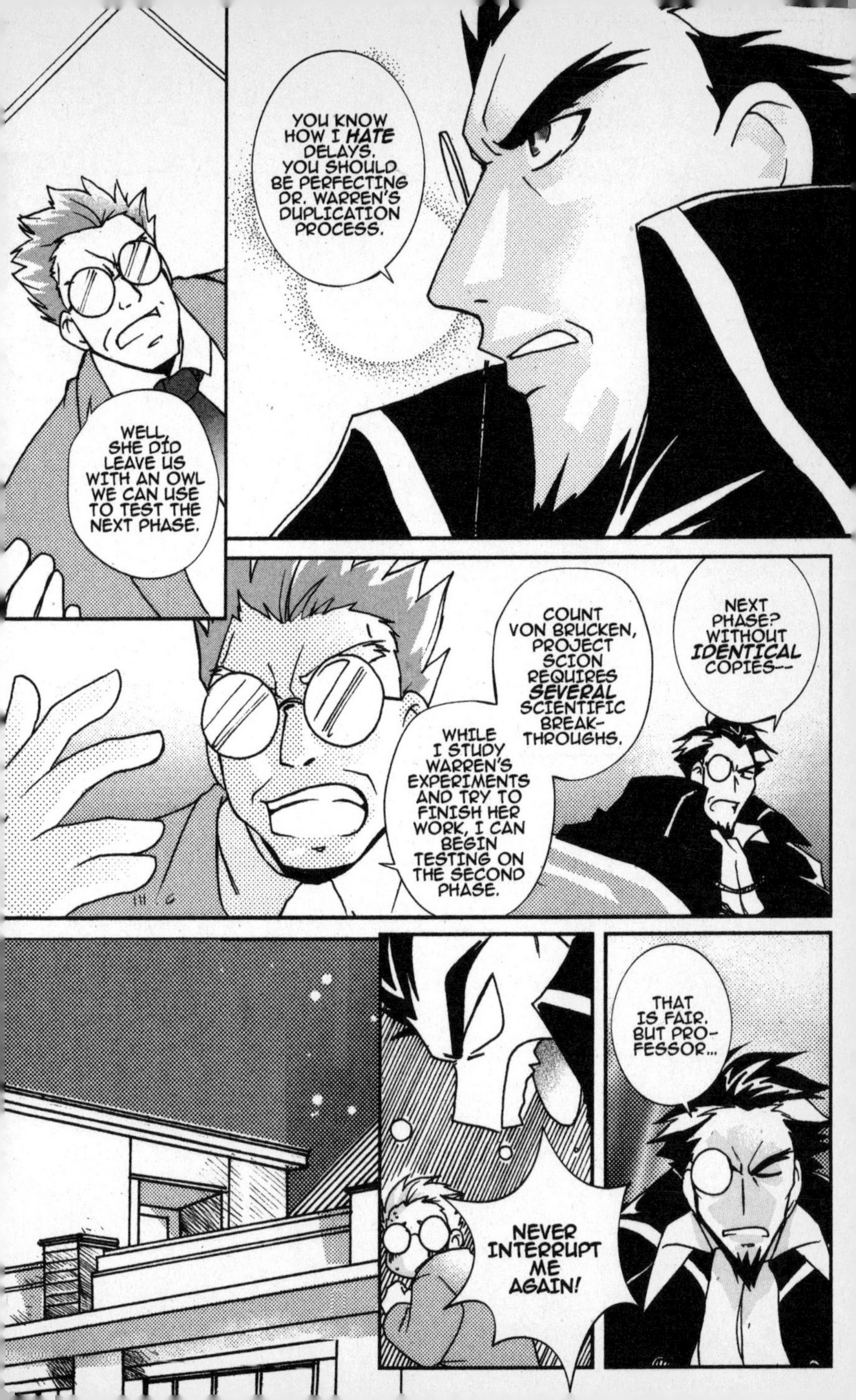
YOU KNOW HOW I HATE DELAYS. YOU SHOULD BE PERFECTING DR. WARREN'S DUPLICATION PROCESS.
WELL, SHE DID LEAVE US WITH AN OWL WE CAN USE TO TEST THE NEXT PHASE.
NEXT PHASE? WITHOUT IDENTICAL COPIES--
COUNT VON BRUCKEN, PROJECT SCION REQUIRES SEVERAL SCIENTIFIC BREAK-THROUGHS.
WHILE I STUDY WARREN'S EXPERIMENTS AND TRY TO FINISH HER WORK, I CAN BEGIN TESTING ON THE SECOND PHASE.
THAT IS FAIR. BUT PRO-FESSOR...
NEVER INTERRUPT ME AGAIN!

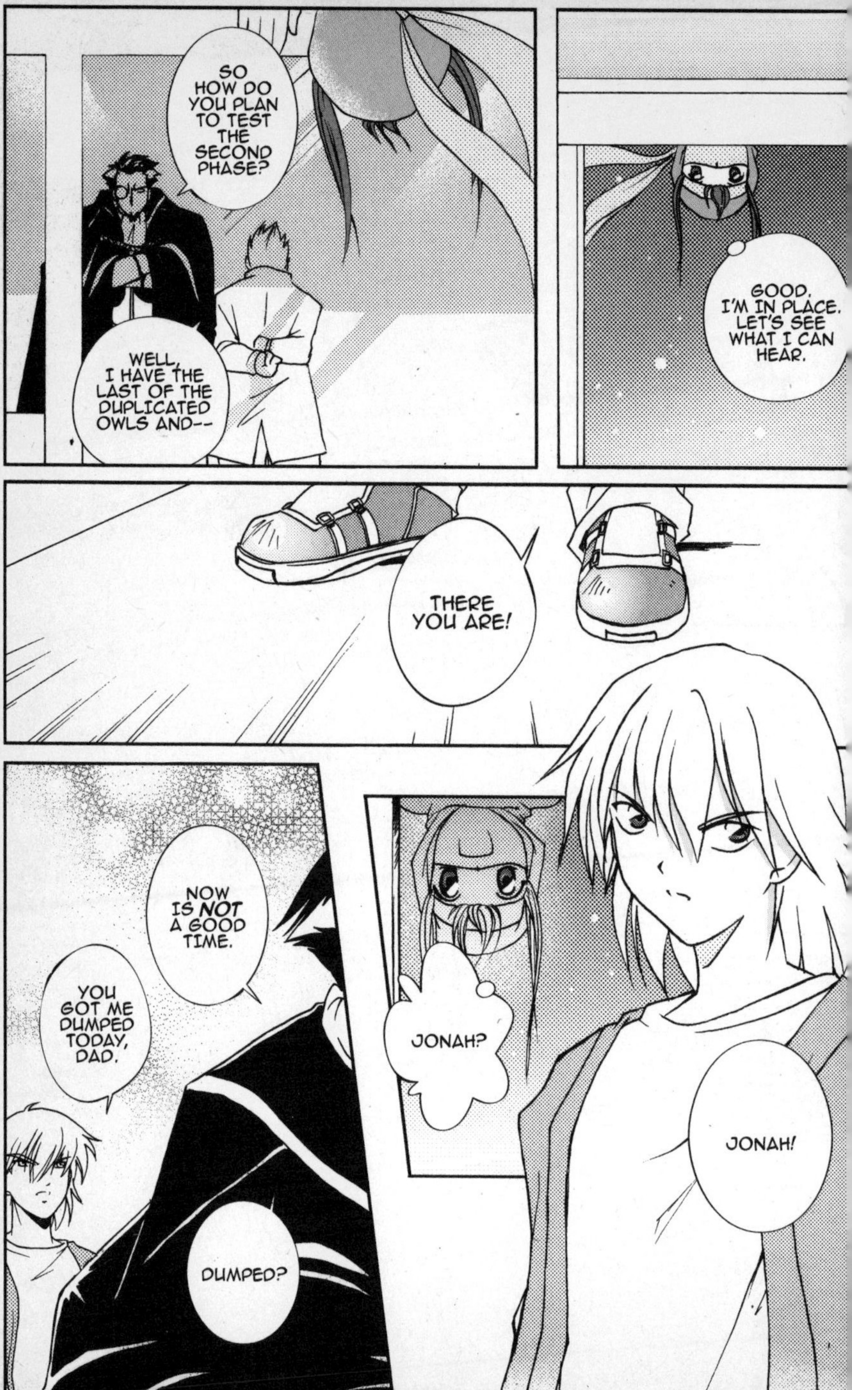
GOOD. I'M IN PLACE. LET'S SEE WHAT I CAN HEAR.
SO HOW DO YOU PLAN TO TEST THE SECOND PHASE?
WELL, I HAVE THE LAST OF THE DUPLICATED OWLS AND--
THERE YOU ARE!
JONAH?
JONAH!
NOW IS *NOT* A GOOD TIME.
YOU GOT ME DUMPED TODAY, DAD.
DUMPED?

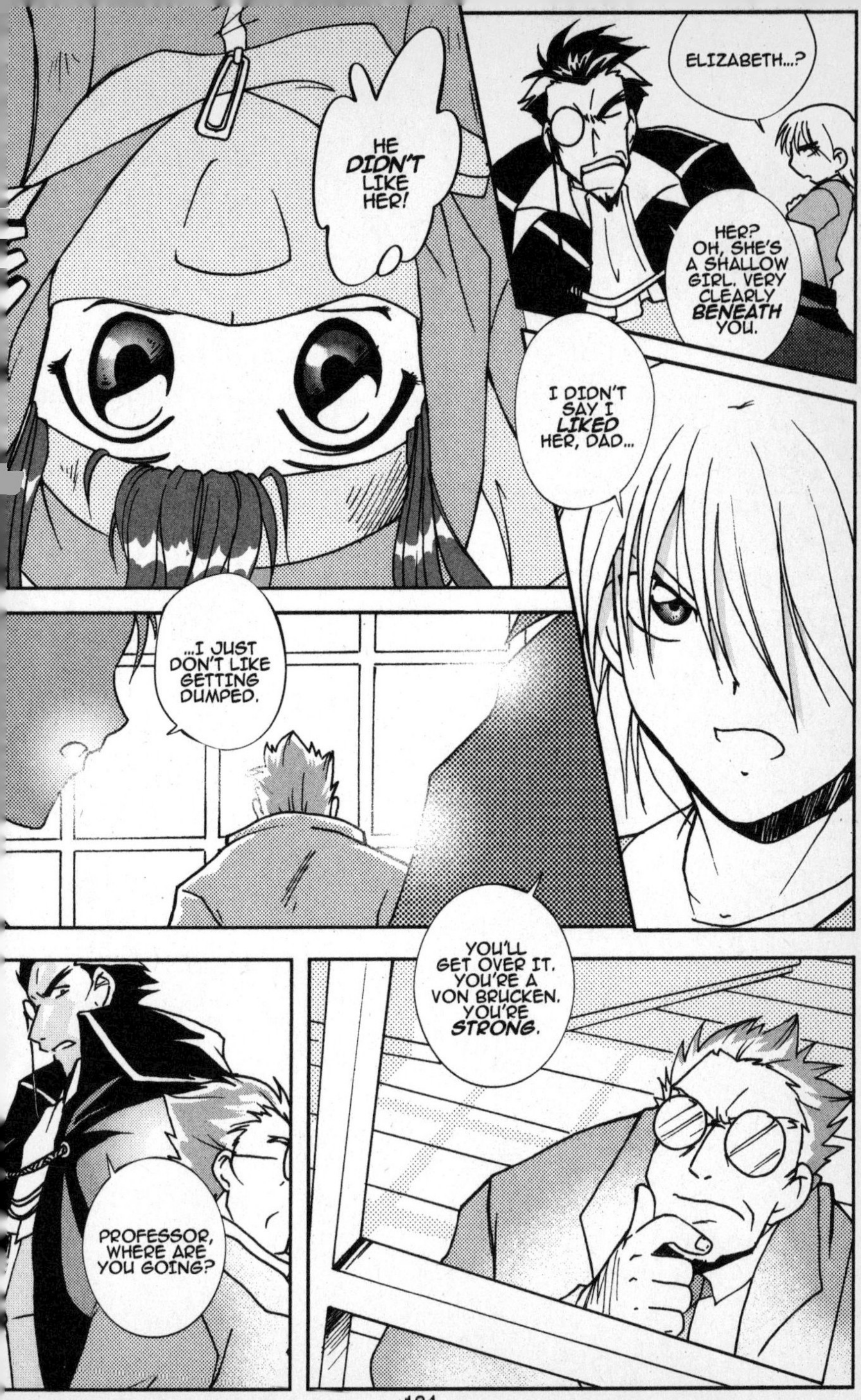

ELIZABETH...?
HER? OH, SHE'S A SHALLOW GIRL. VERY CLEARLY *BENEATH* YOU.
HE *DIDN'T* LIKE HER!
I DIDN'T SAY I *LIKED* HER, DAD...
...I JUST DON'T LIKE GETTING DUMPED.
YOU'LL GET OVER IT. YOU'RE A VON BRUCKEN. YOU'RE *STRONG*.
PROFESSOR, WHERE ARE YOU GOING?

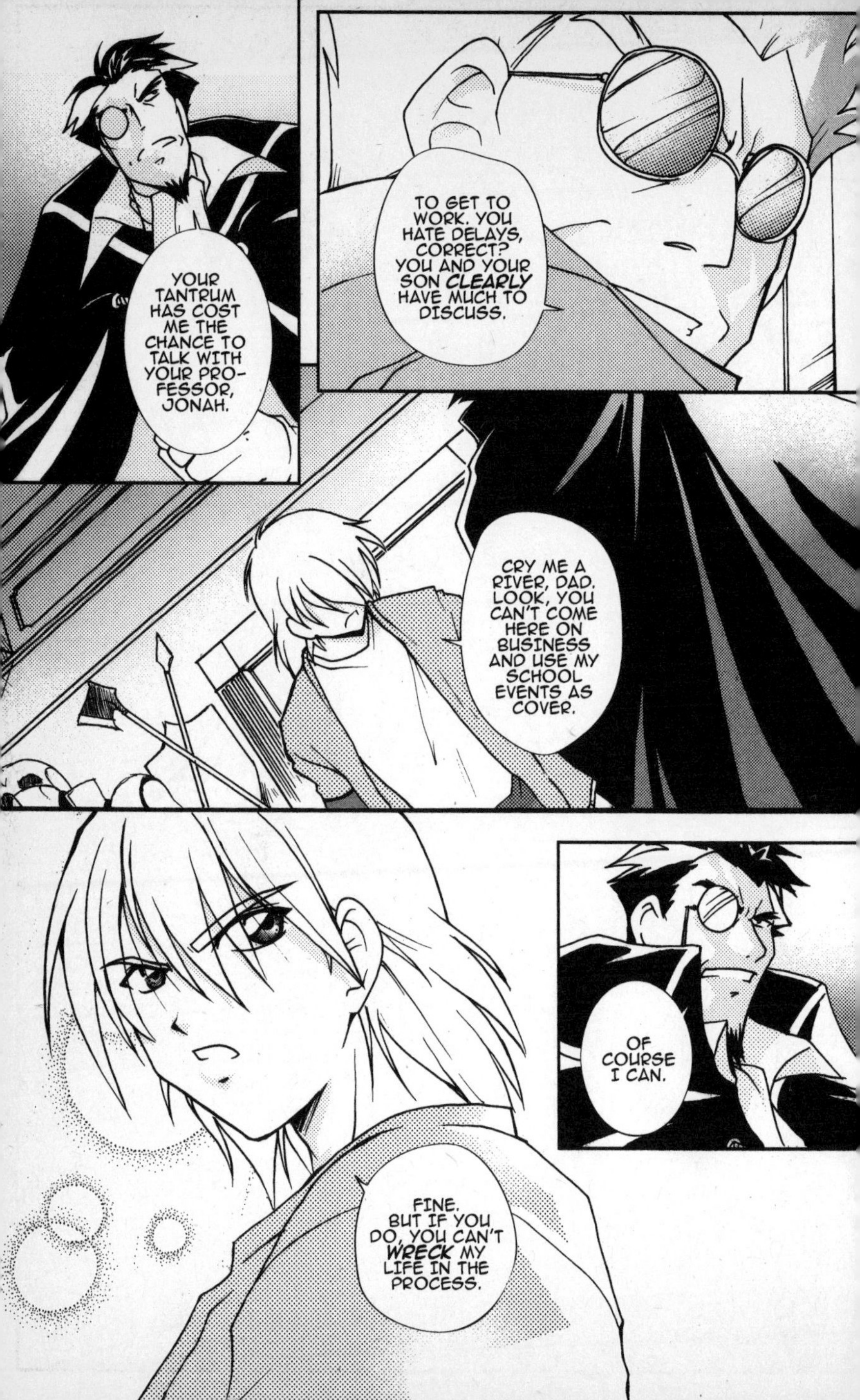
TO GET TO WORK. YOU HATE DELAYS, CORRECT? YOU AND YOUR SON CLEARLY HAVE MUCH TO DISCUSS.
YOUR TANTRUM HAS COST ME THE CHANCE TO TALK WITH YOUR PRO-FESSOR, JONAH.
CRY ME A RIVER, DAD. LOOK, YOU CAN'T COME HERE ON BUSINESS AND USE MY SCHOOL EVENTS AS COVER.
OF COURSE I CAN.
FINE. BUT IF YOU DO, YOU CAN'T WRECK MY LIFE IN THE PROCESS.

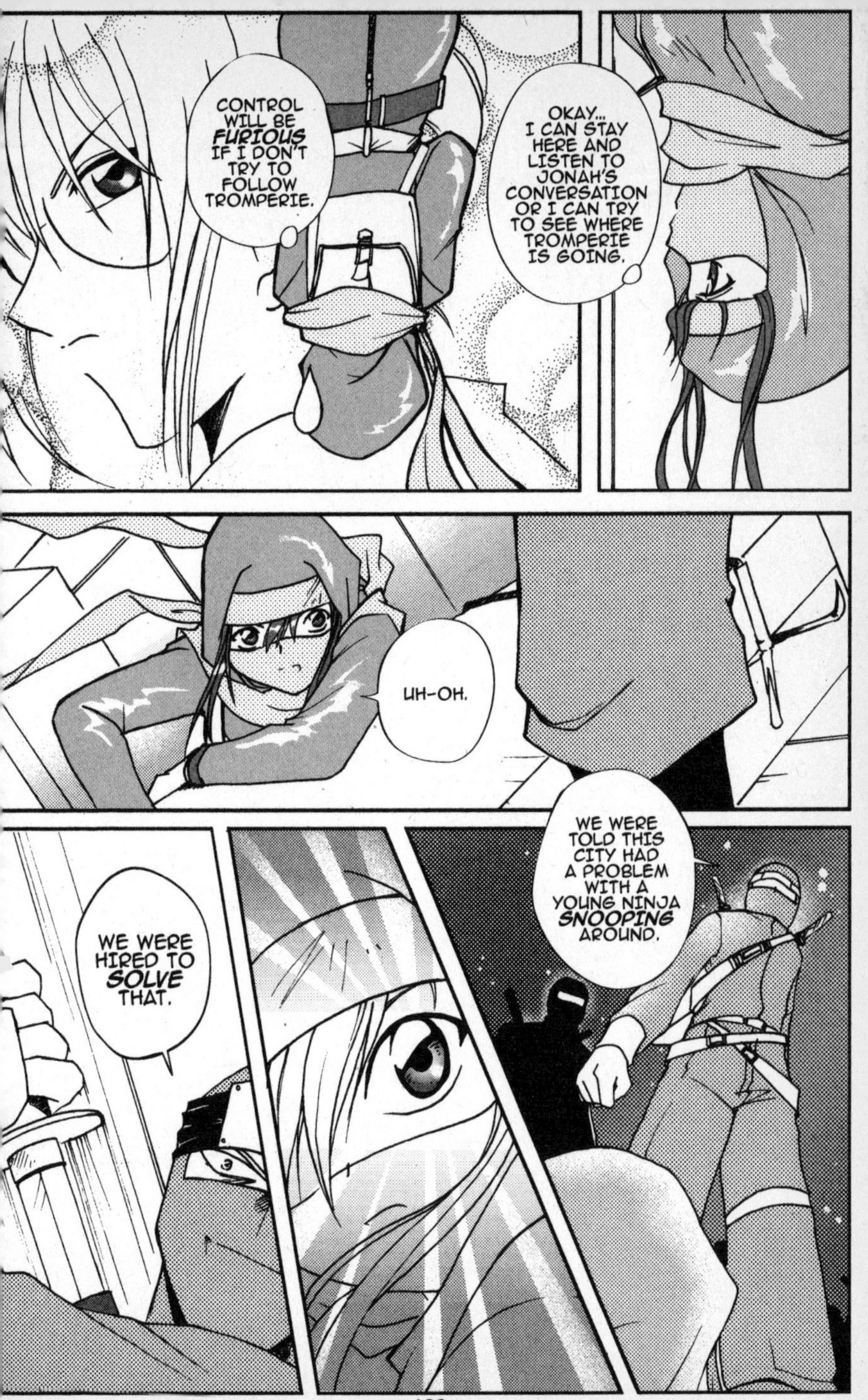
OKAY... I CAN STAY HERE AND LISTEN TO JONAH'S CONVERSATION OR I CAN TRY TO SEE WHERE TROMPERIE IS GOING.
CONTROL WILL BE *FURIOUS* IF I DON'T TRY TO FOLLOW TROMPERIE.
UH-OH.
WE WERE TOLD THIS CITY HAD A PROBLEM WITH A YOUNG NINJA *SNOOPING* AROUND.
WE WERE HIRED TO *SOLVE* THAT.

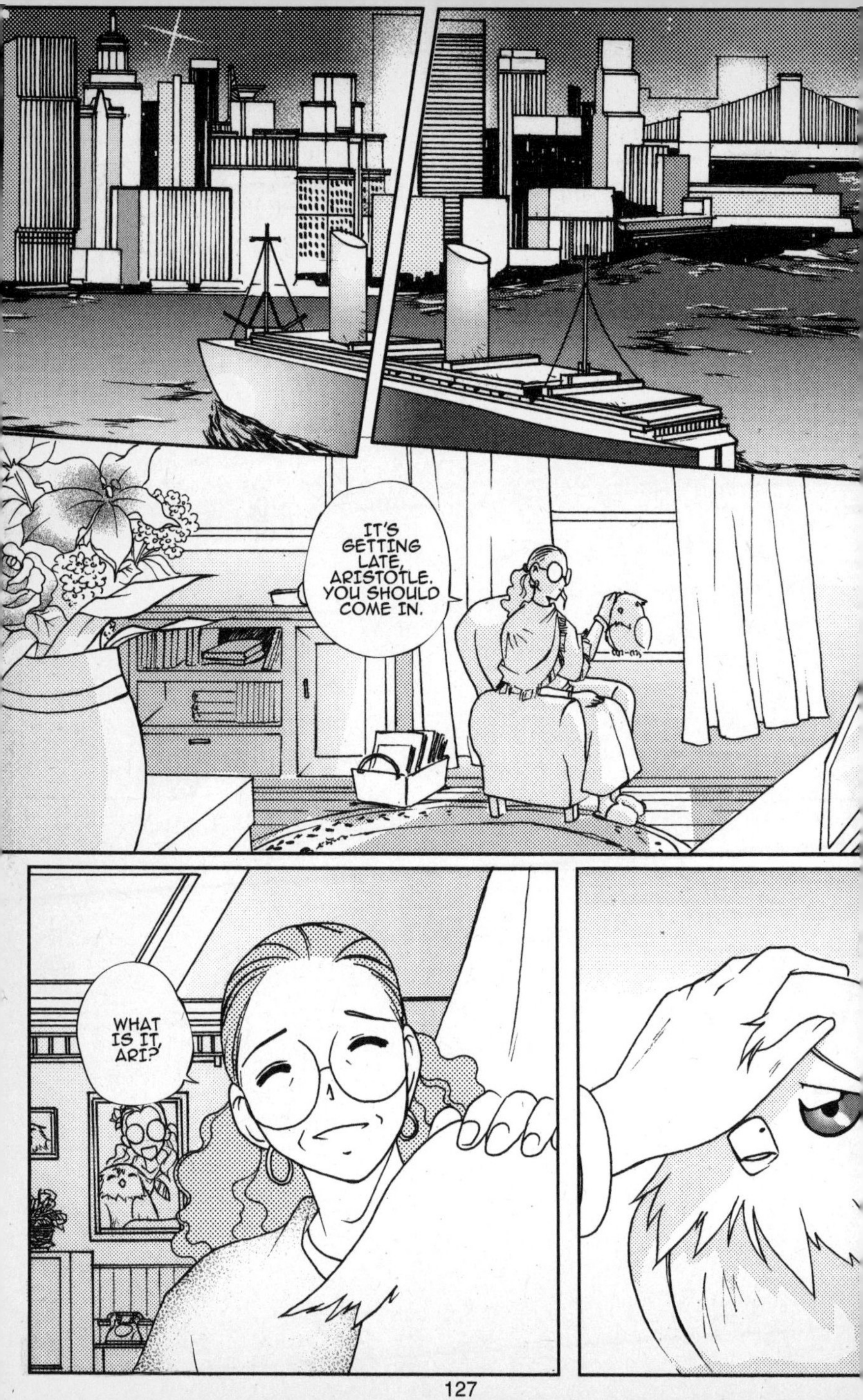
IT'S GETTING LATE, ARISTOTLE. YOU SHOULD COME IN.
WHAT IS IT, ARI?

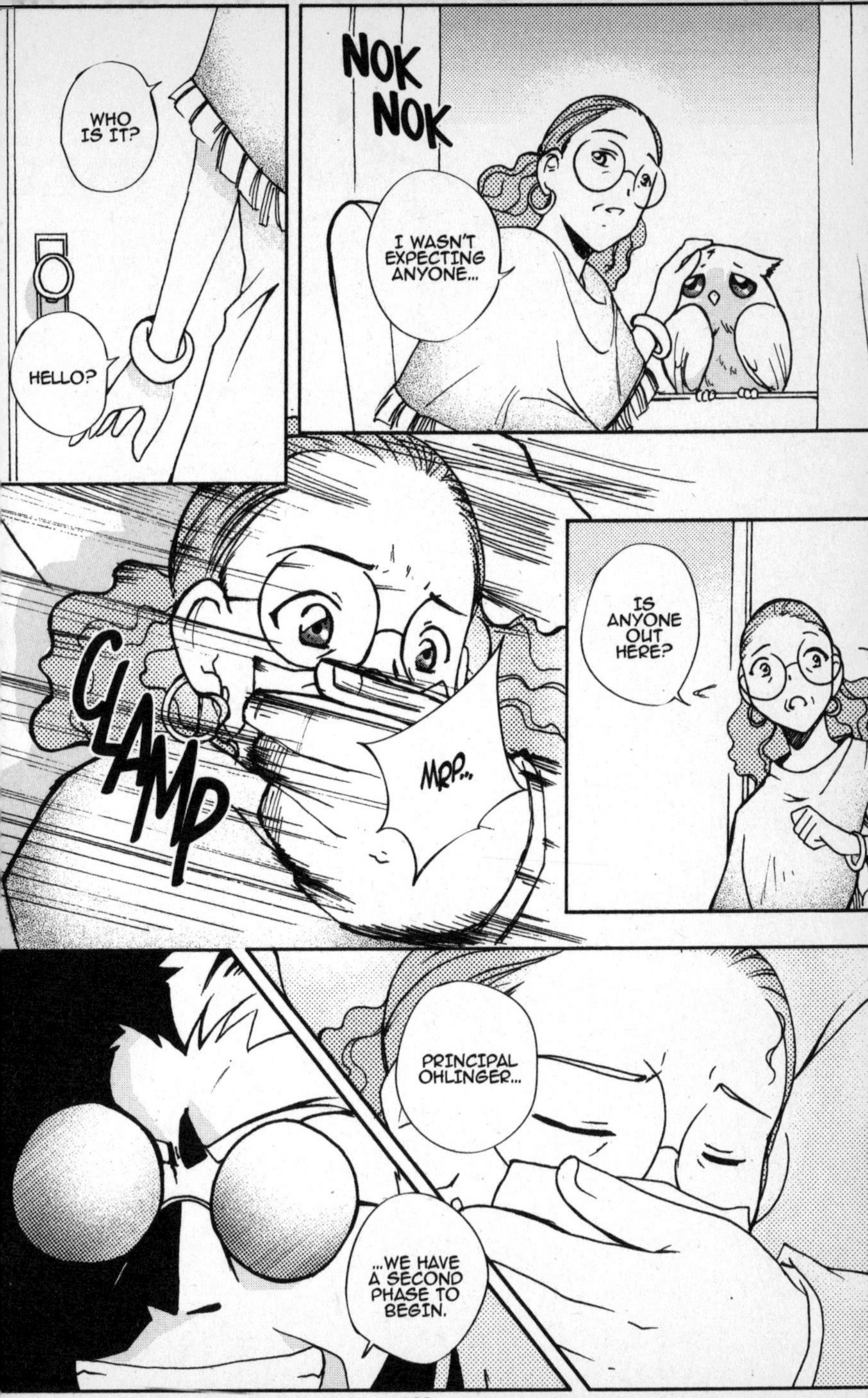
NOK NOK
I WASN'T EXPECTING ANYONE...
WHO IS IT?
HELLO?
IS ANYONE OUT HERE?
CLAMP
MRP...
PRINCIPAL OHLINGER...
...WE HAVE A SECOND PHASE TO BEGIN.

File 10
MEMORIES

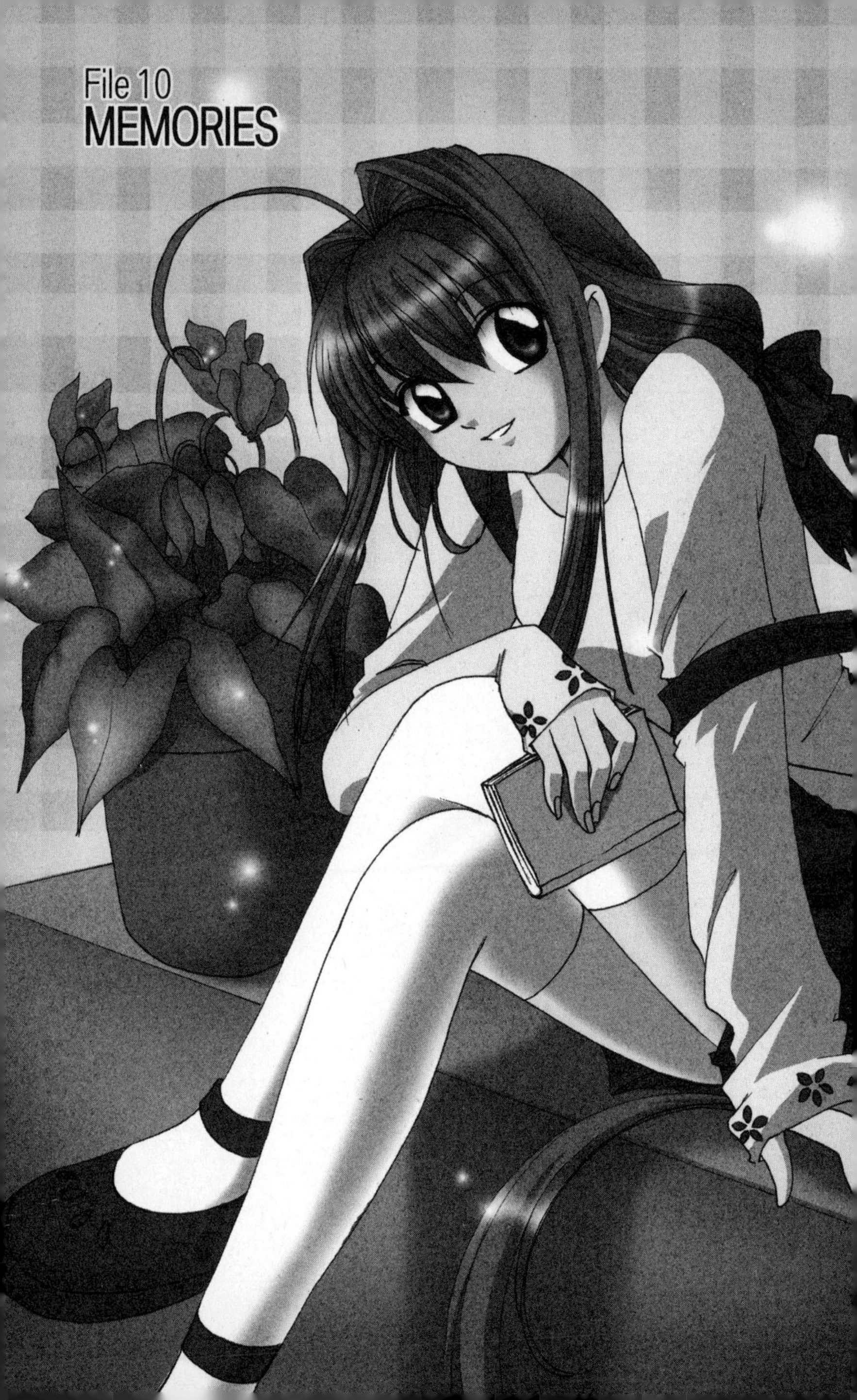

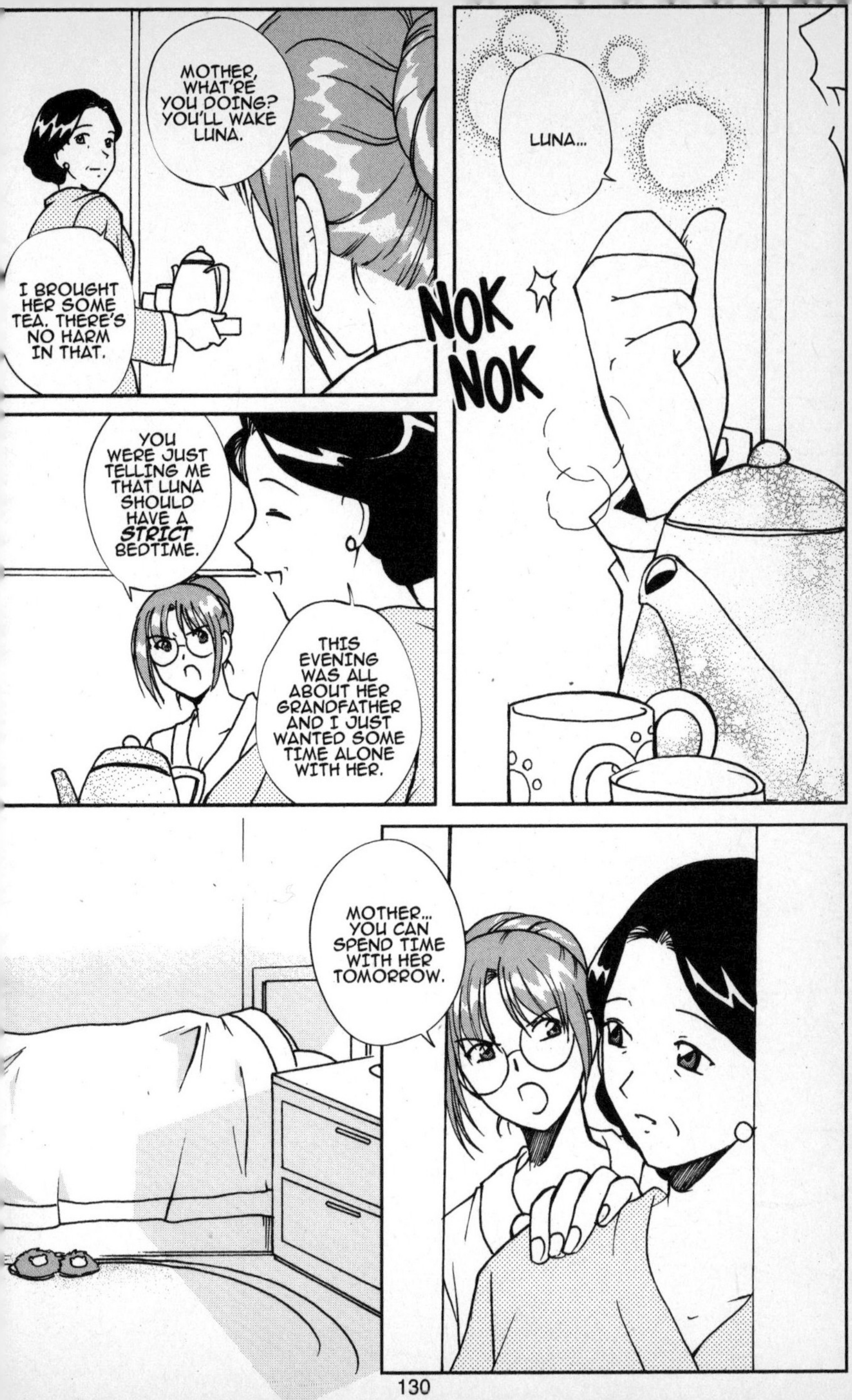
LUNA...
NOK NOK
MOTHER, WHAT'RE YOU DOING? YOU'LL WAKE LUNA.
I BROUGHT HER SOME TEA. THERE'S NO HARM IN THAT.
YOU WERE JUST TELLING ME THAT LUNA SHOULD HAVE A STRICT BEDTIME.
THIS EVENING WAS ALL ABOUT HER GRANDFATHER AND I JUST WANTED SOME TIME ALONE WITH HER.
MOTHER... YOU CAN SPEND TIME WITH HER TOMORROW.

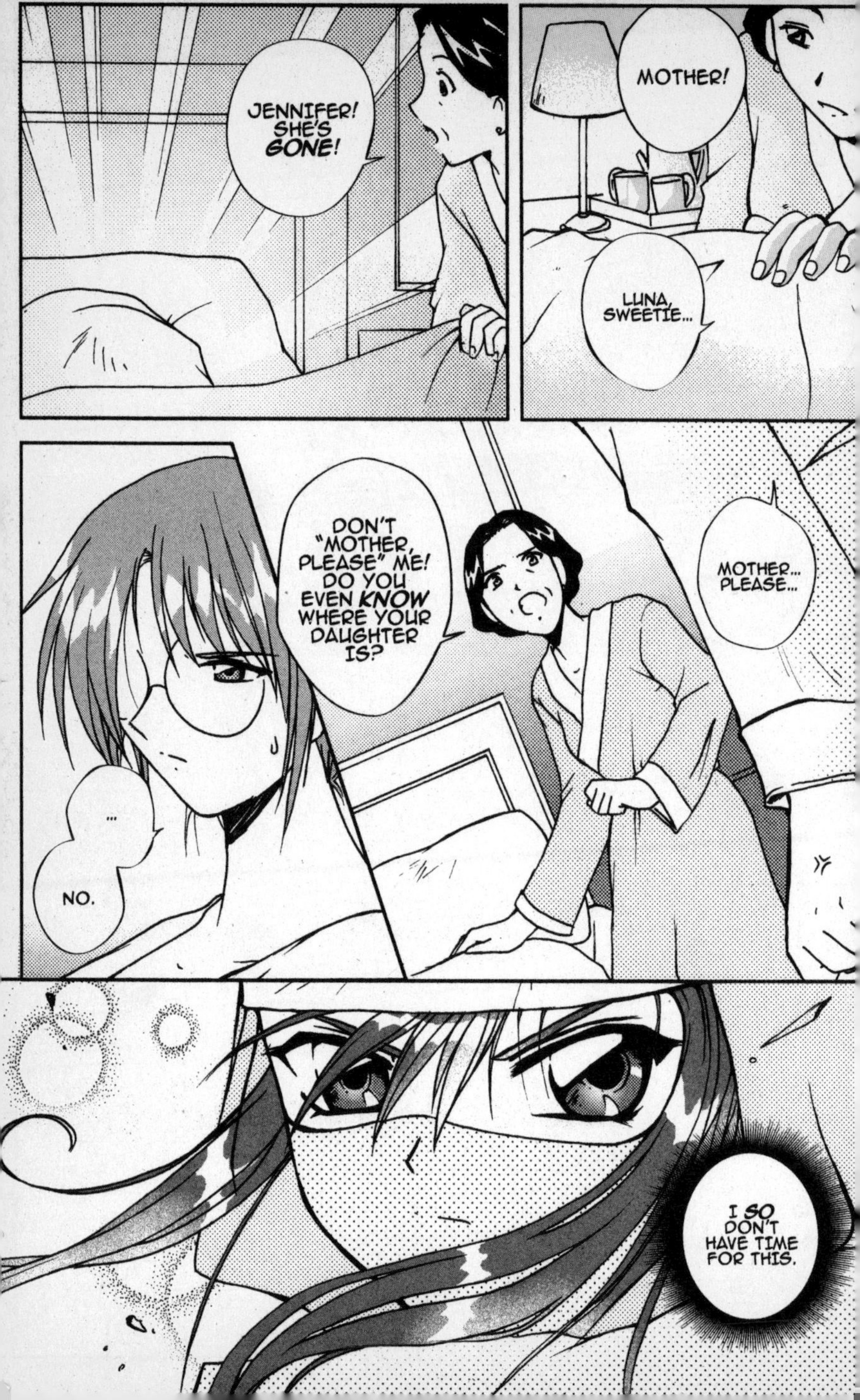
MOTHER!
LUNA, SWEETIE...
JENNIFER! SHE'S GONE!
MOTHER... PLEASE...
DON'T "MOTHER, PLEASE" ME! DO YOU EVEN KNOW WHERE YOUR DAUGHTER IS?
...
NO.
I SO DON'T HAVE TIME FOR THIS.

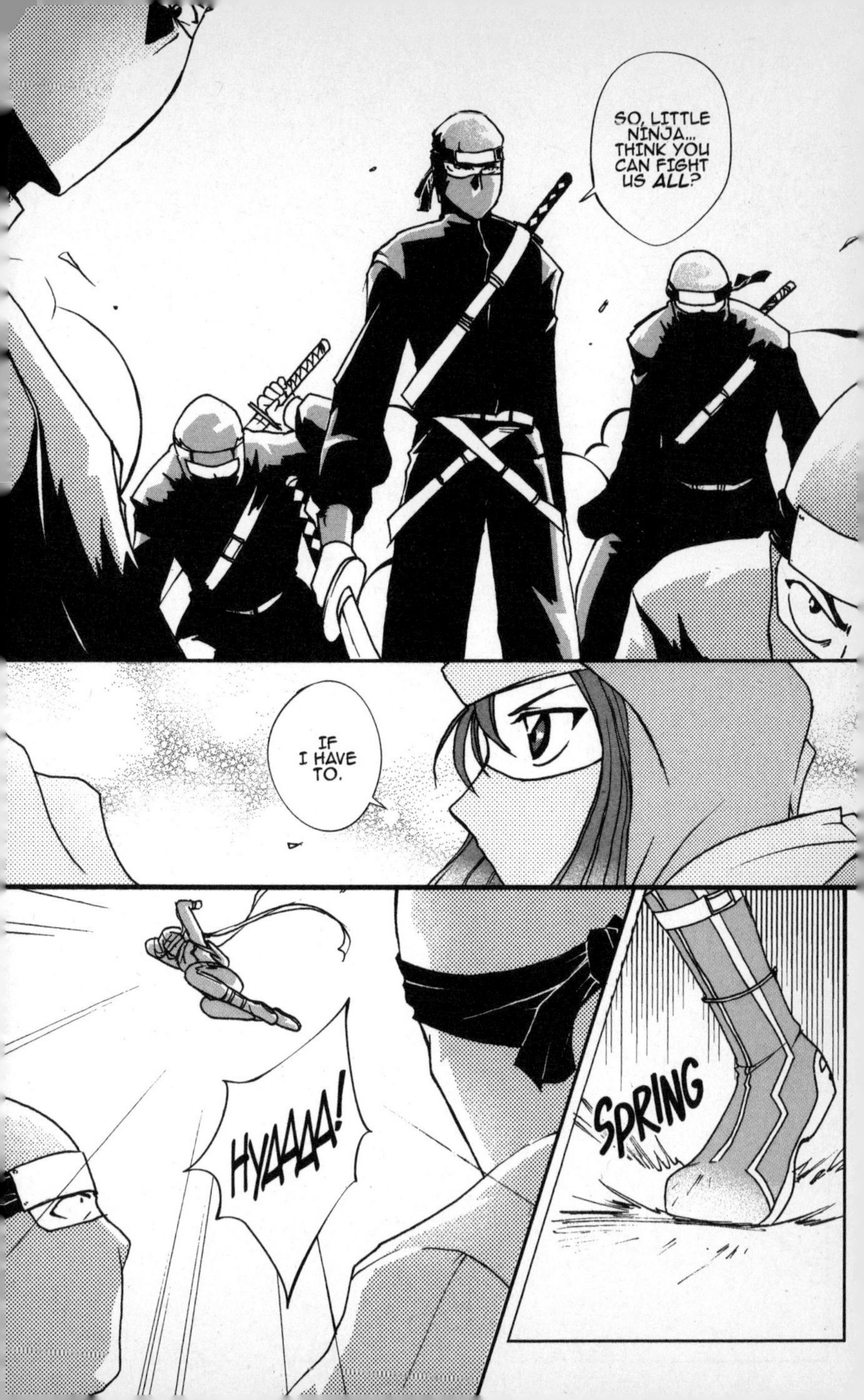
SO, LITTLE NINJA... THINK YOU CAN FIGHT US ALL?
IF I HAVE TO.
SPRING
HYAAAA!

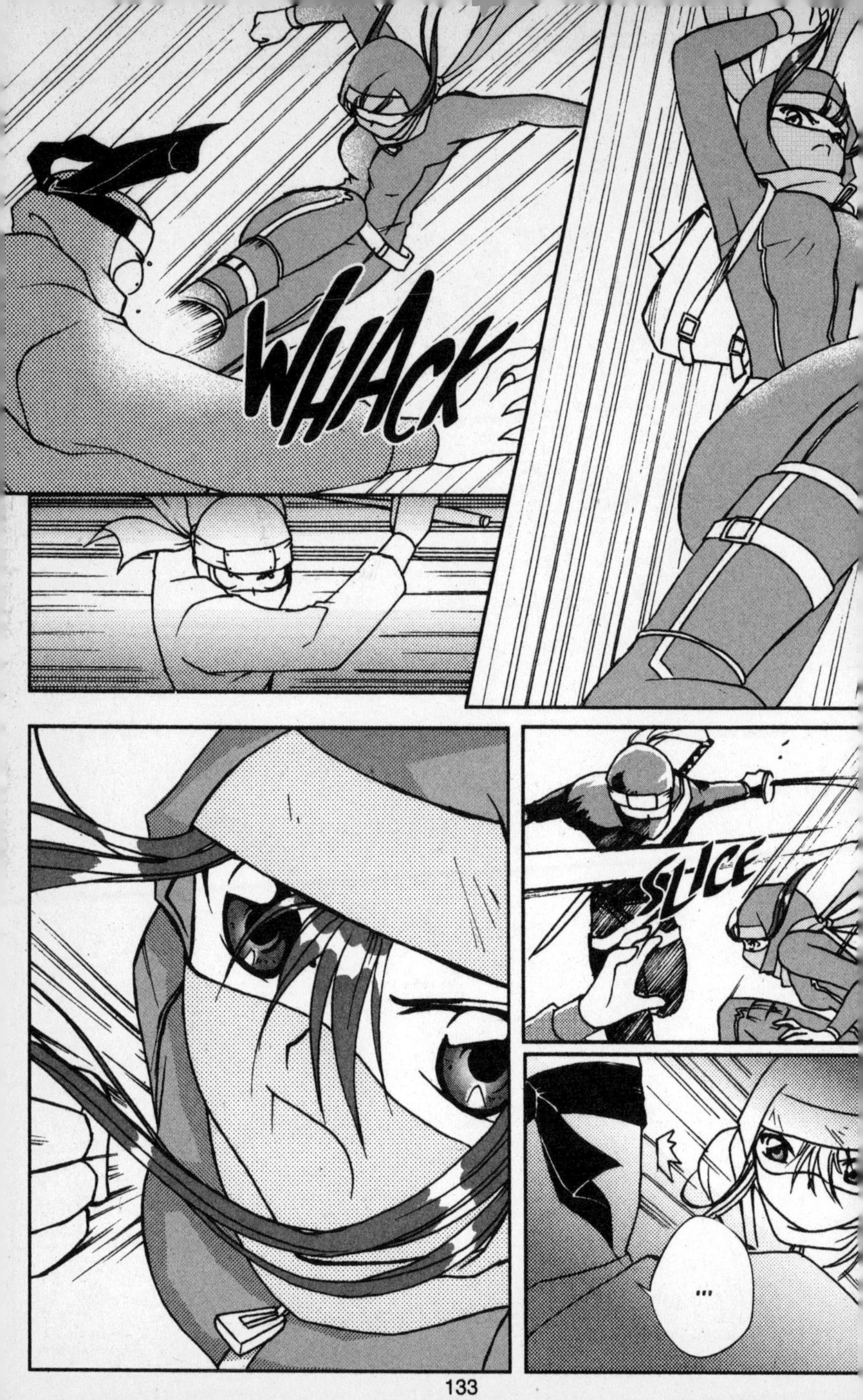
WHACK
SLICE
...

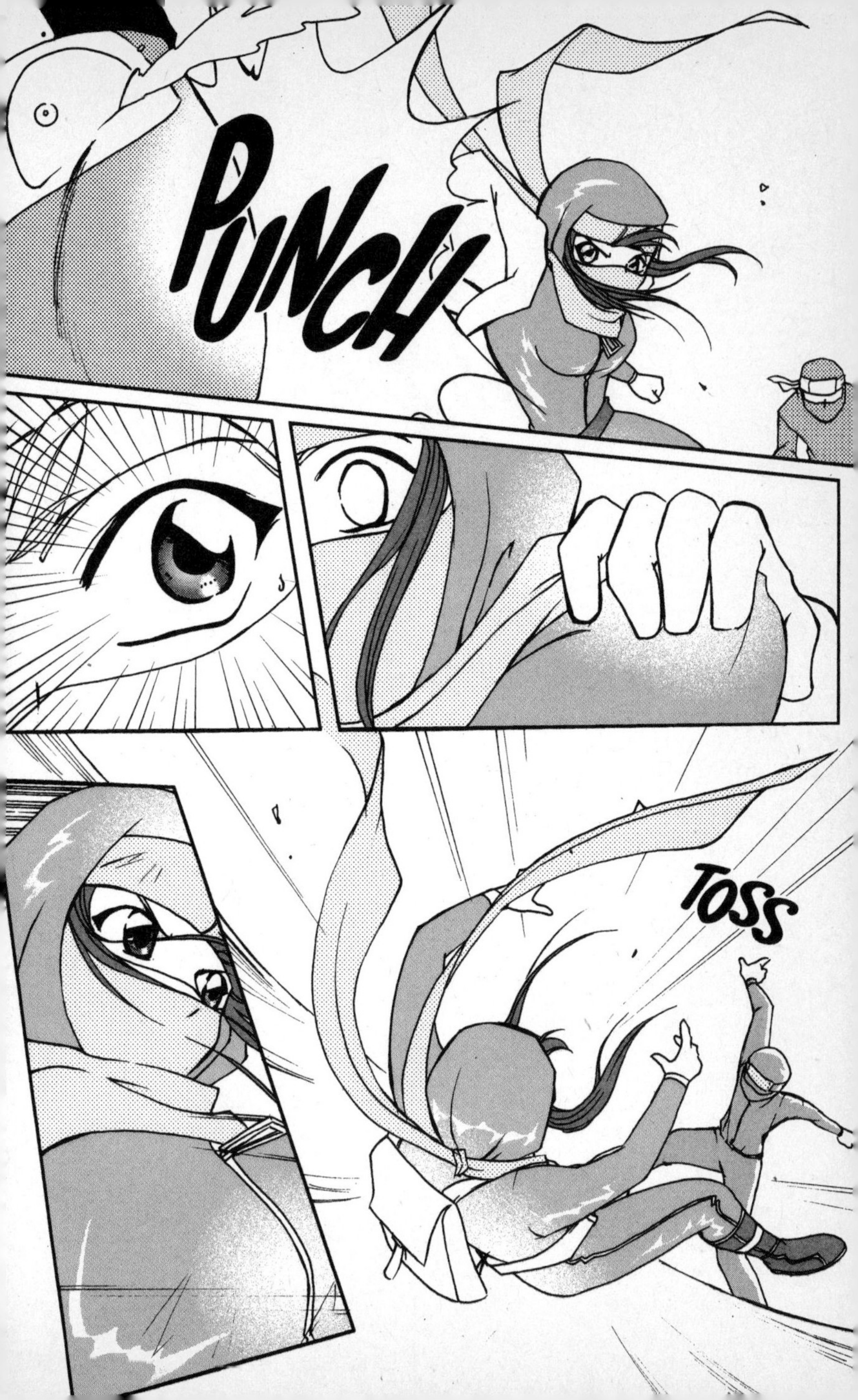
PUNCH
TOSS

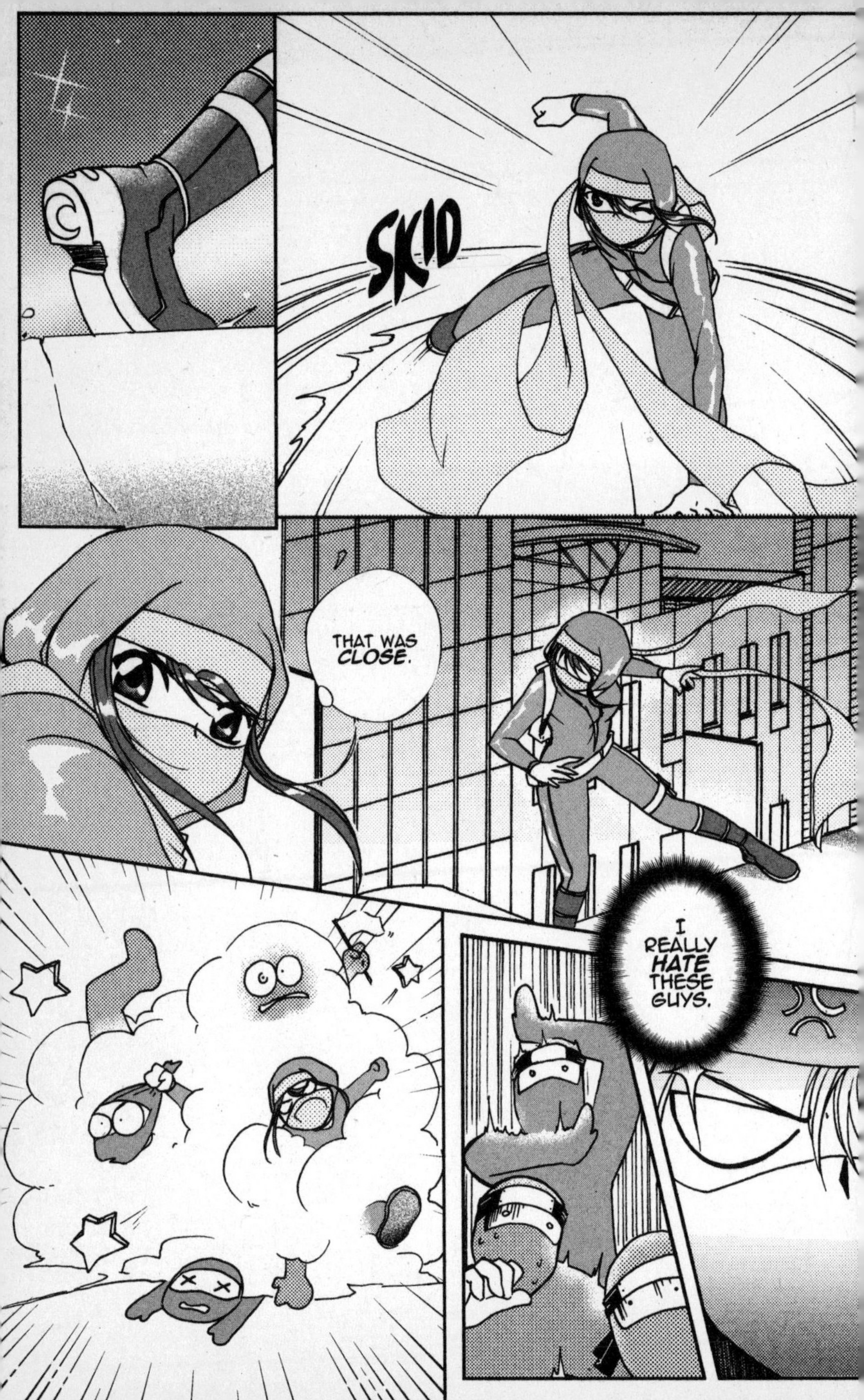
SKID
THAT WAS CLOSE.
I REALLY HATE THESE GUYS.

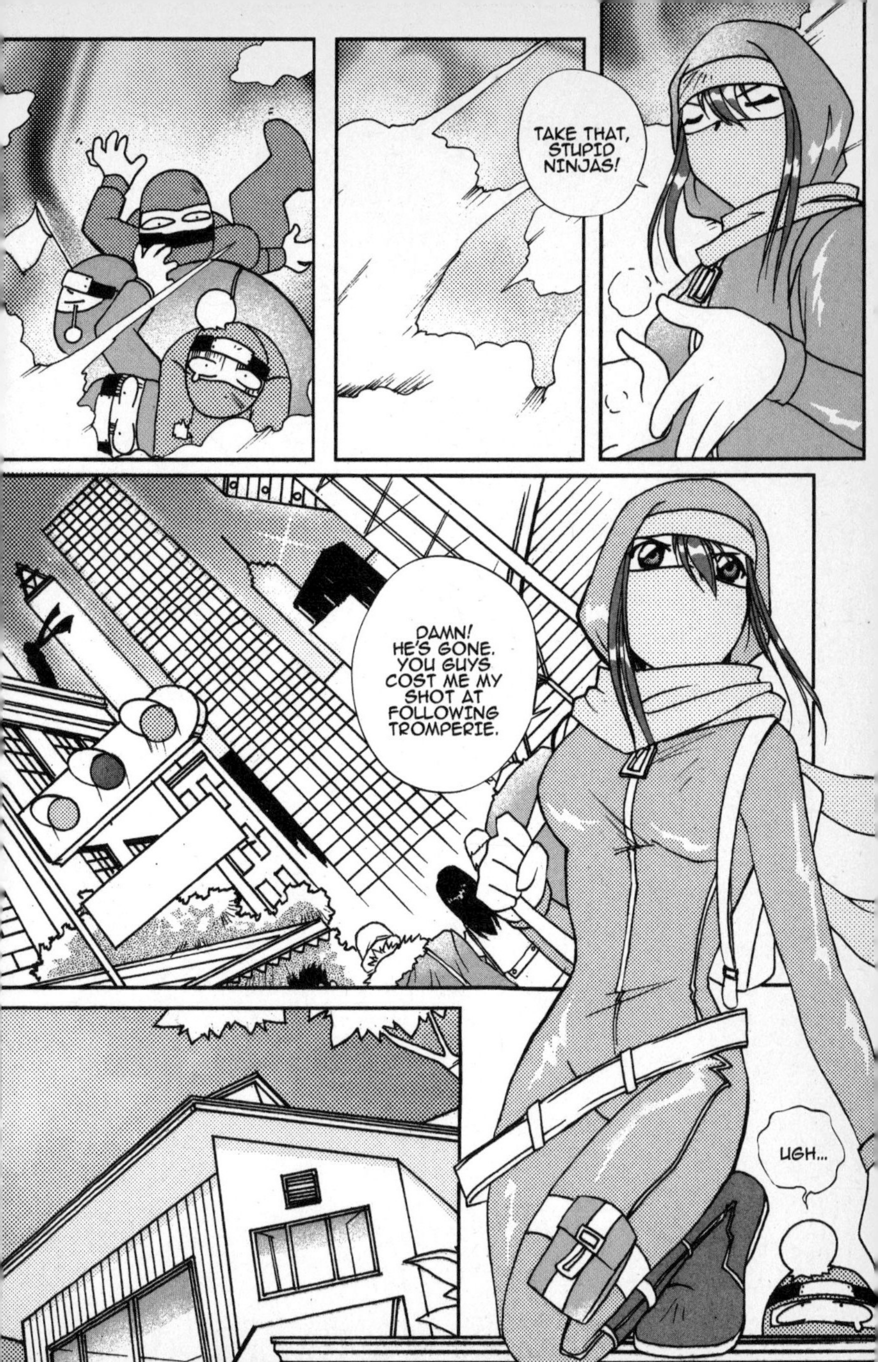
TAKE THAT, STUPID NINJAS!
DAMN! HE'S GONE. YOU GUYS COST ME MY SHOT AT FOLLOWING TROMPERIE.
UGH...

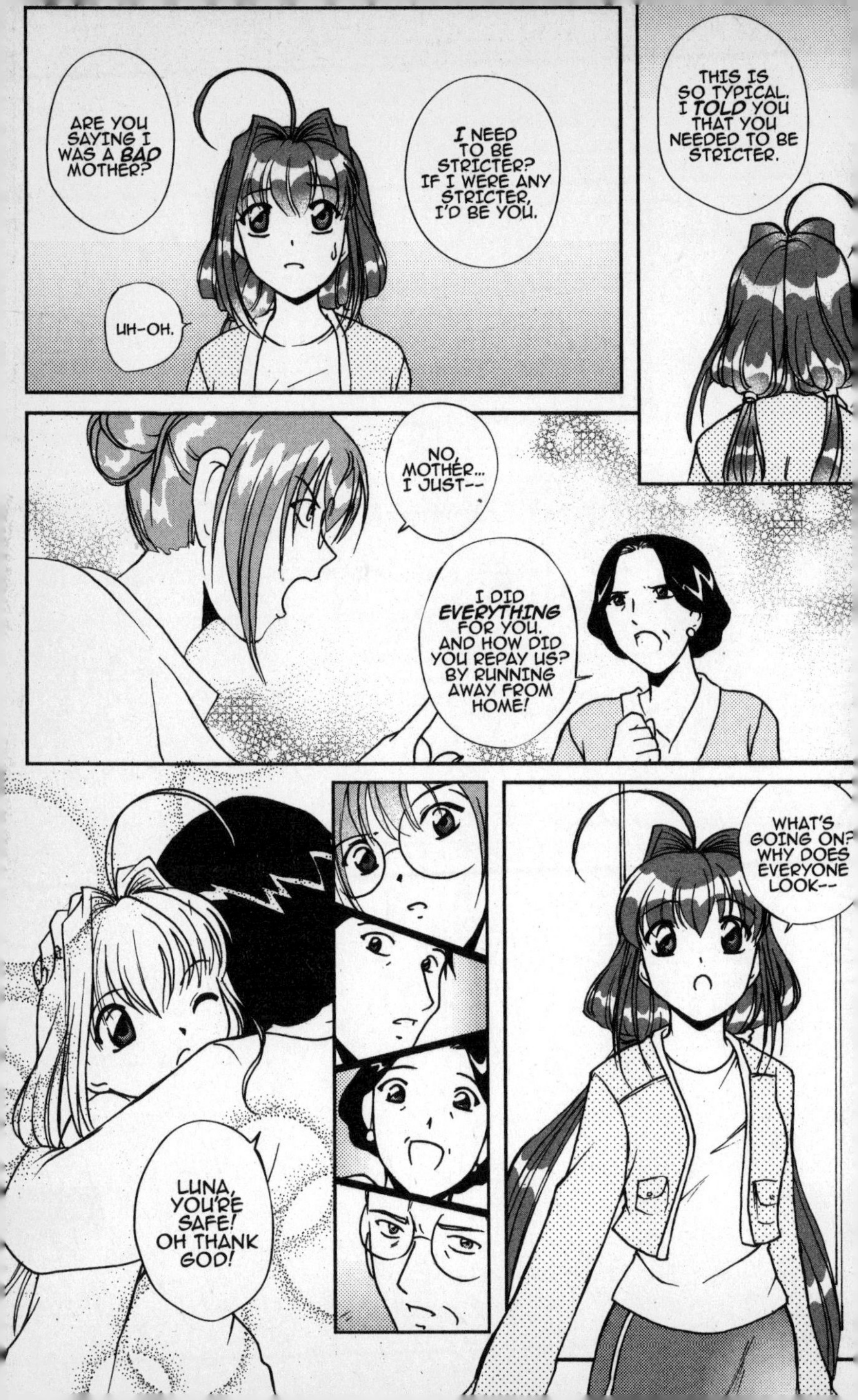
THIS IS SO TYPICAL. I TOLD YOU THAT YOU NEEDED TO BE STRICTER.
I NEED TO BE STRICTER? IF I WERE ANY STRICTER, I'D BE YOU.
ARE YOU SAYING I WAS A BAD MOTHER?
UH-OH.
NO, MOTHER... I JUST--
I DID EVERYTHING FOR YOU. AND HOW DID YOU REPAY US? BY RUNNING AWAY FROM HOME!
WHAT'S GOING ON? WHY DOES EVERYONE LOOK--
LUNA, YOU'RE SAFE! OH THANK GOD!

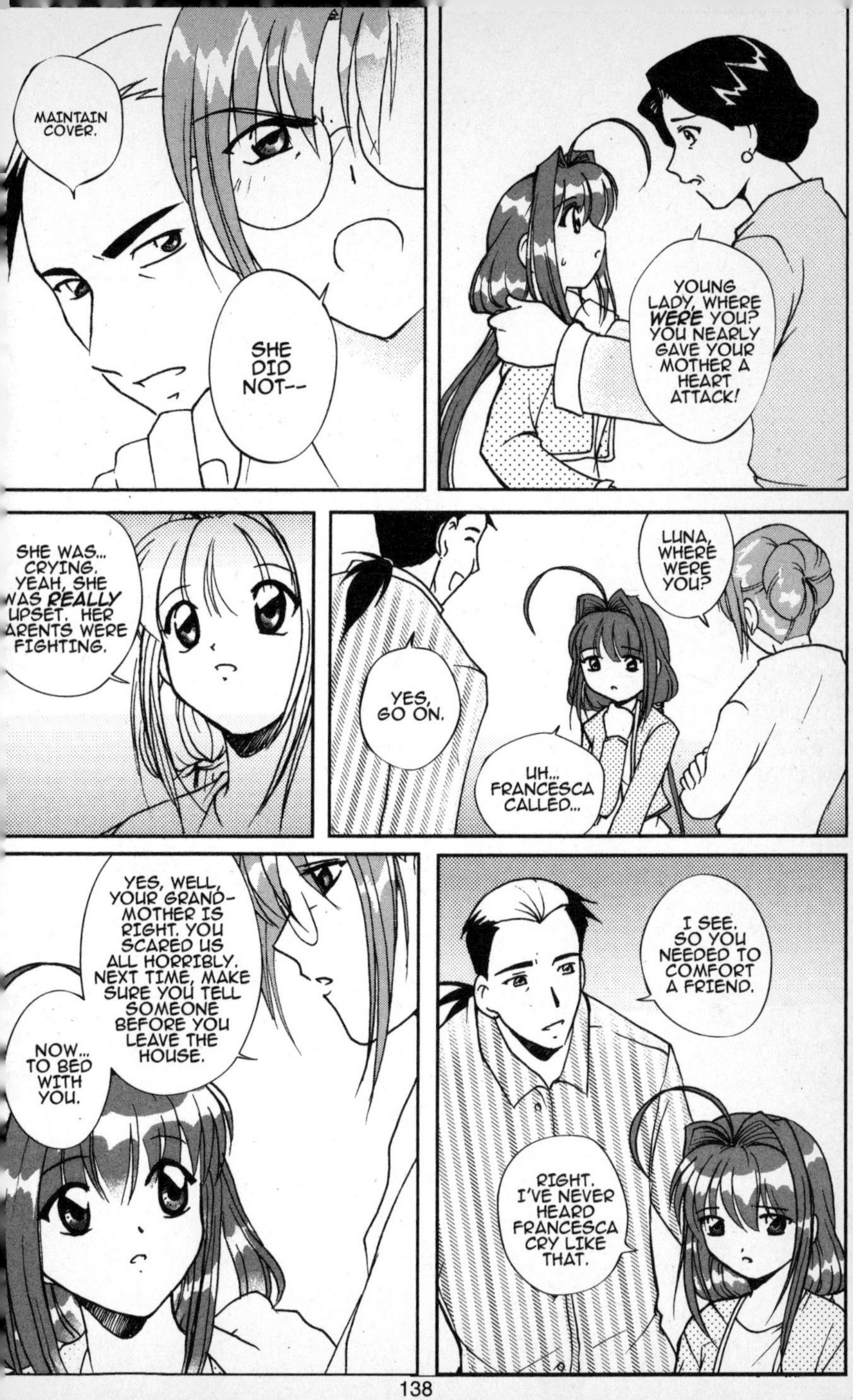
YOUNG LADY, WHERE *WERE* YOU? YOU NEARLY GAVE YOUR MOTHER A HEART ATTACK!
SHE DID NOT--
MAINTAIN COVER.
LUNA, WHERE WERE YOU?
UH... FRANCESCA CALLED...
YES, GO ON.
SHE WAS... CRYING. YEAH, SHE WAS *REALLY* UPSET. HER ARENTS WERE FIGHTING.
I SEE. SO YOU NEEDED TO COMFORT A FRIEND.
RIGHT. I'VE NEVER HEARD FRANCESCA CRY LIKE THAT.
YES, WELL, YOUR GRAND-MOTHER IS RIGHT. YOU SCARED US ALL HORRIBLY. NEXT TIME, MAKE SURE YOU TELL SOMEONE BEFORE YOU LEAVE THE HOUSE.
NOW... TO BED WITH YOU.

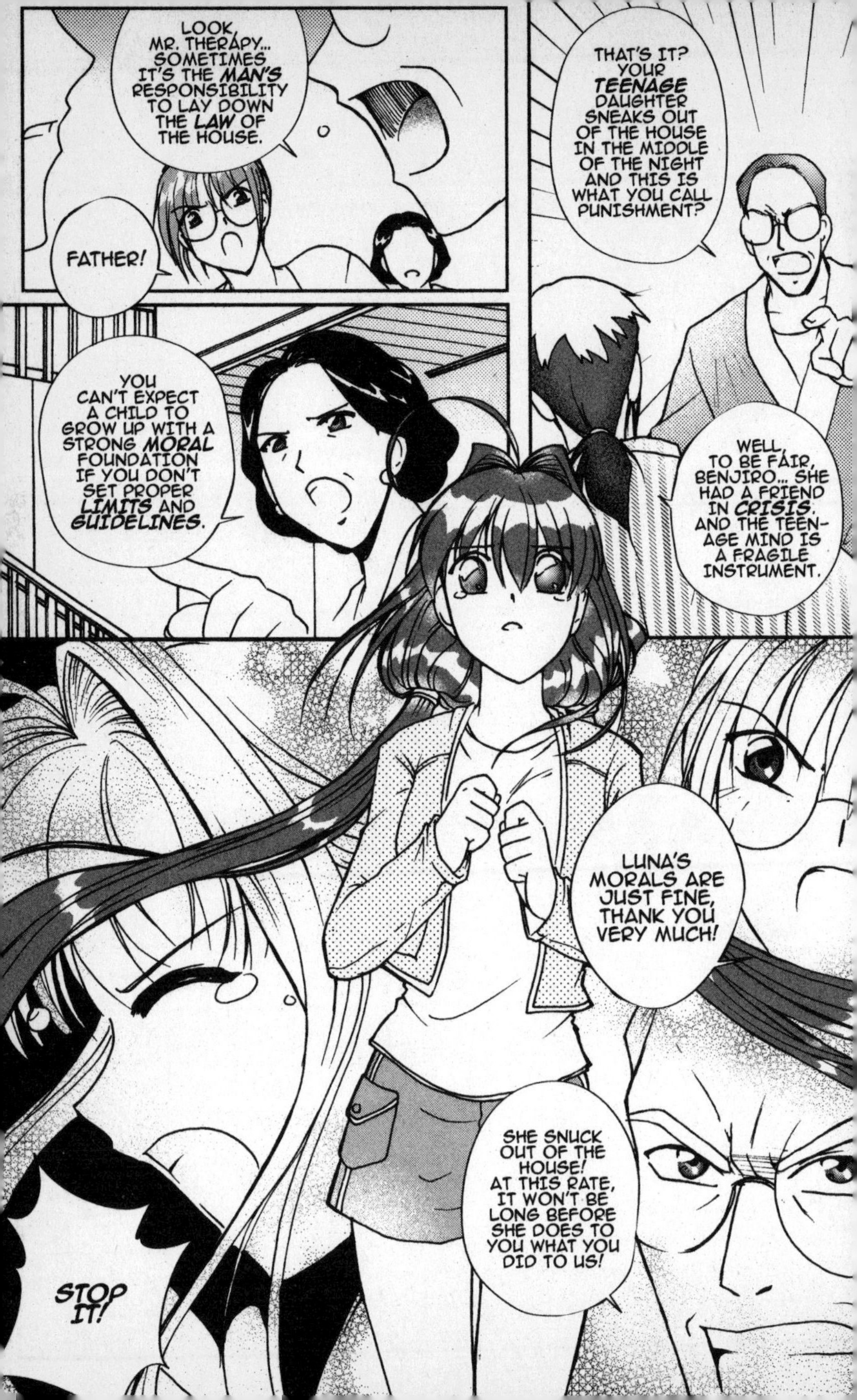
THAT'S IT? YOUR TEENAGE DAUGHTER SNEAKS OUT OF THE HOUSE IN THE MIDDLE OF THE NIGHT AND THIS IS WHAT YOU CALL PUNISHMENT?
WELL, TO BE FAIR, BENJIRO... SHE HAD A FRIEND IN CRISIS. AND THE TEEN-AGE MIND IS A FRAGILE INSTRUMENT.
LOOK, MR. THERAPY... SOMETIMES IT'S THE MAN'S RESPONSIBILITY TO LAY DOWN THE LAW OF THE HOUSE.
FATHER!
YOU CAN'T EXPECT A CHILD TO GROW UP WITH A STRONG MORAL FOUNDATION IF YOU DON'T SET PROPER LIMITS AND GUIDELINES.
LUNA'S MORALS ARE JUST FINE, THANK YOU VERY MUCH!
SHE SNUCK OUT OF THE HOUSE! AT THIS RATE, IT WON'T BE LONG BEFORE SHE DOES TO YOU WHAT YOU DID TO US!
STOP IT!

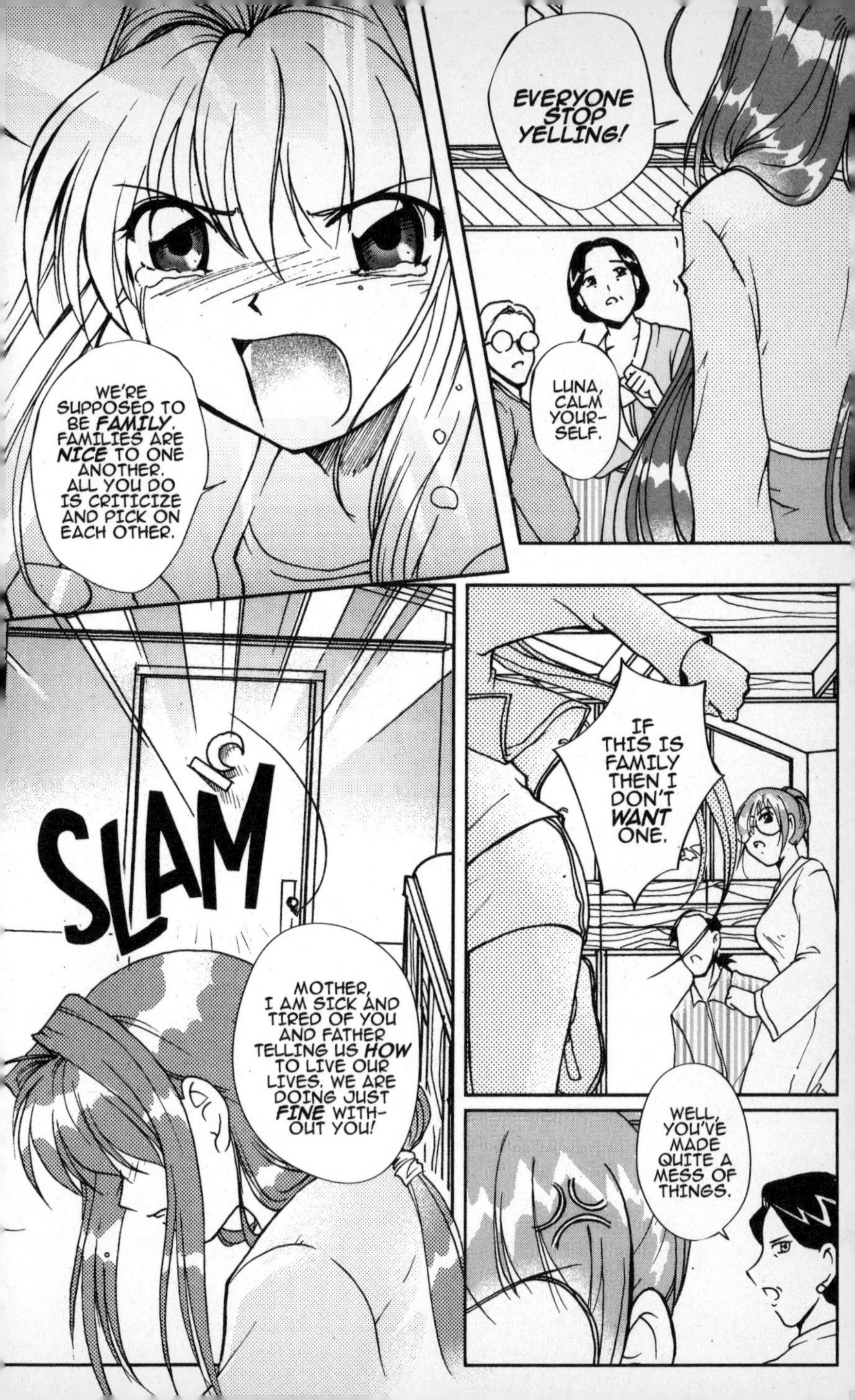
EVERYONE STOP YELLING!
LUNA, CALM YOURSELF.
WE'RE SUPPOSED TO BE *FAMILY*. FAMILIES ARE *NICE* TO ONE ANOTHER. ALL YOU DO IS CRITICIZE AND PICK ON EACH OTHER.
IF THIS IS FAMILY THEN I DON'T *WANT* ONE.
WELL, YOU'VE MADE QUITE A MESS OF THINGS.
SLAM
MOTHER, I AM SICK AND TIRED OF YOU AND FATHER TELLING US *HOW* TO LIVE OUR LIVES. WE ARE DOING JUST *FINE* WITHOUT YOU!

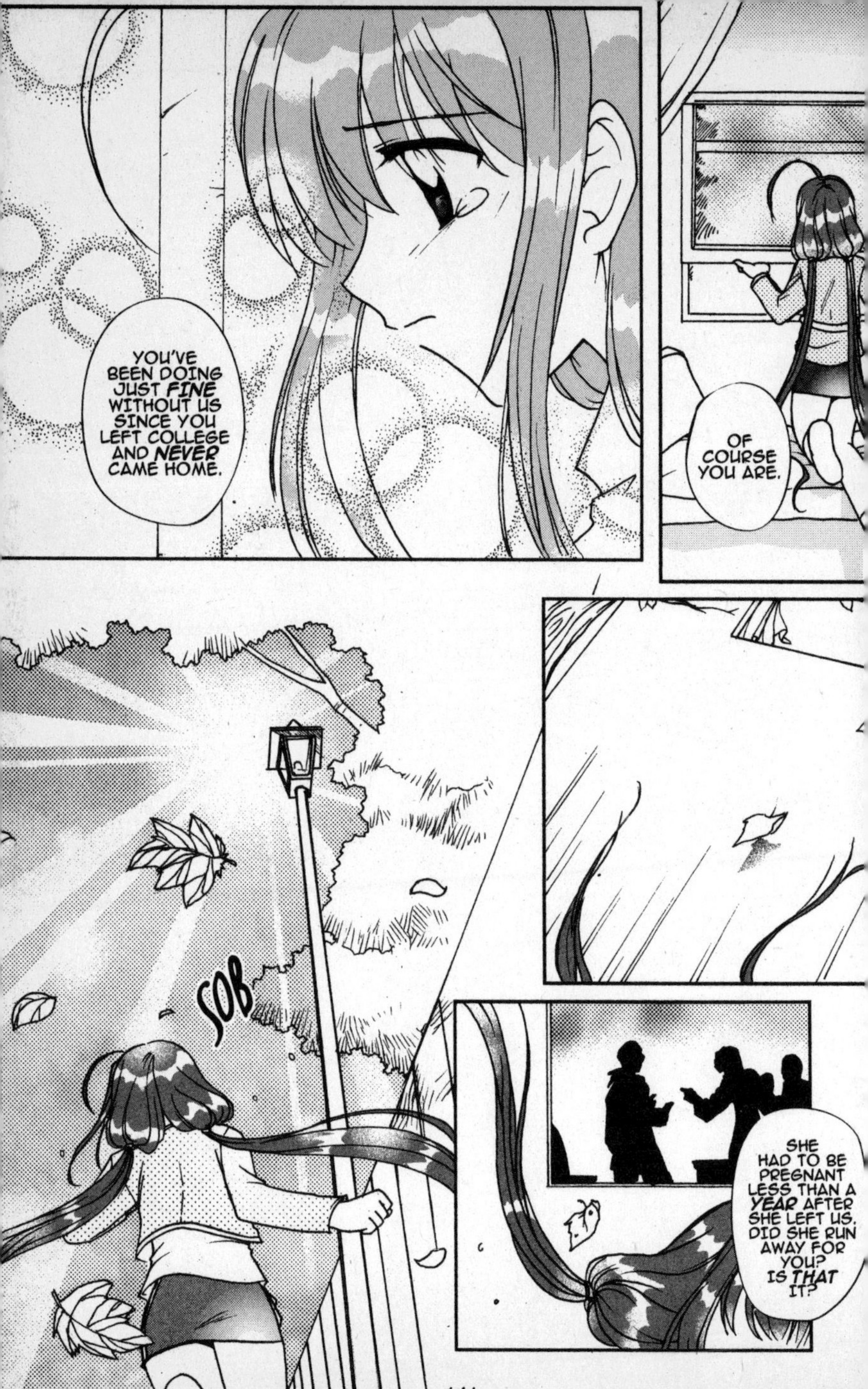
OF COURSE YOU ARE.
YOU'VE BEEN DOING JUST FINE WITHOUT US SINCE YOU LEFT COLLEGE AND NEVER CAME HOME.
SHE HAD TO BE PREGNANT LESS THAN A YEAR AFTER SHE LEFT US. DID SHE RUN AWAY FOR YOU? IS THAT IT?
SOB

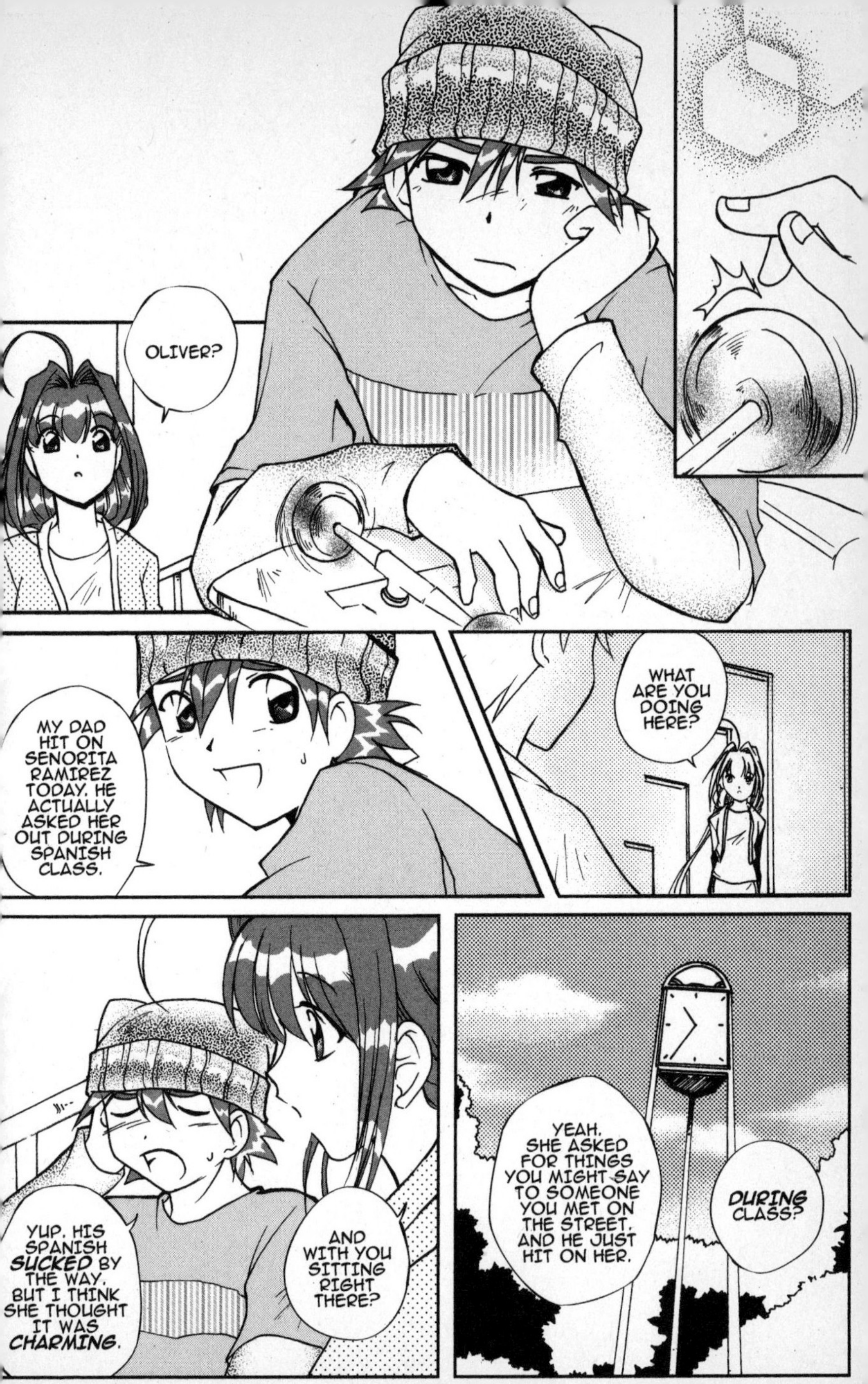
OLIVER?
WHAT ARE YOU DOING HERE?
MY DAD HIT ON SENORITA RAMIREZ TODAY. HE ACTUALLY ASKED HER OUT DURING SPANISH CLASS.
DURING CLASS?
YEAH. SHE ASKED FOR THINGS YOU MIGHT SAY TO SOMEONE YOU MET ON THE STREET. AND HE JUST HIT ON HER.
AND WITH YOU SITTING RIGHT THERE?
YUP. HIS SPANISH SUCKED BY THE WAY. BUT I THINK SHE THOUGHT IT WAS CHARMING.

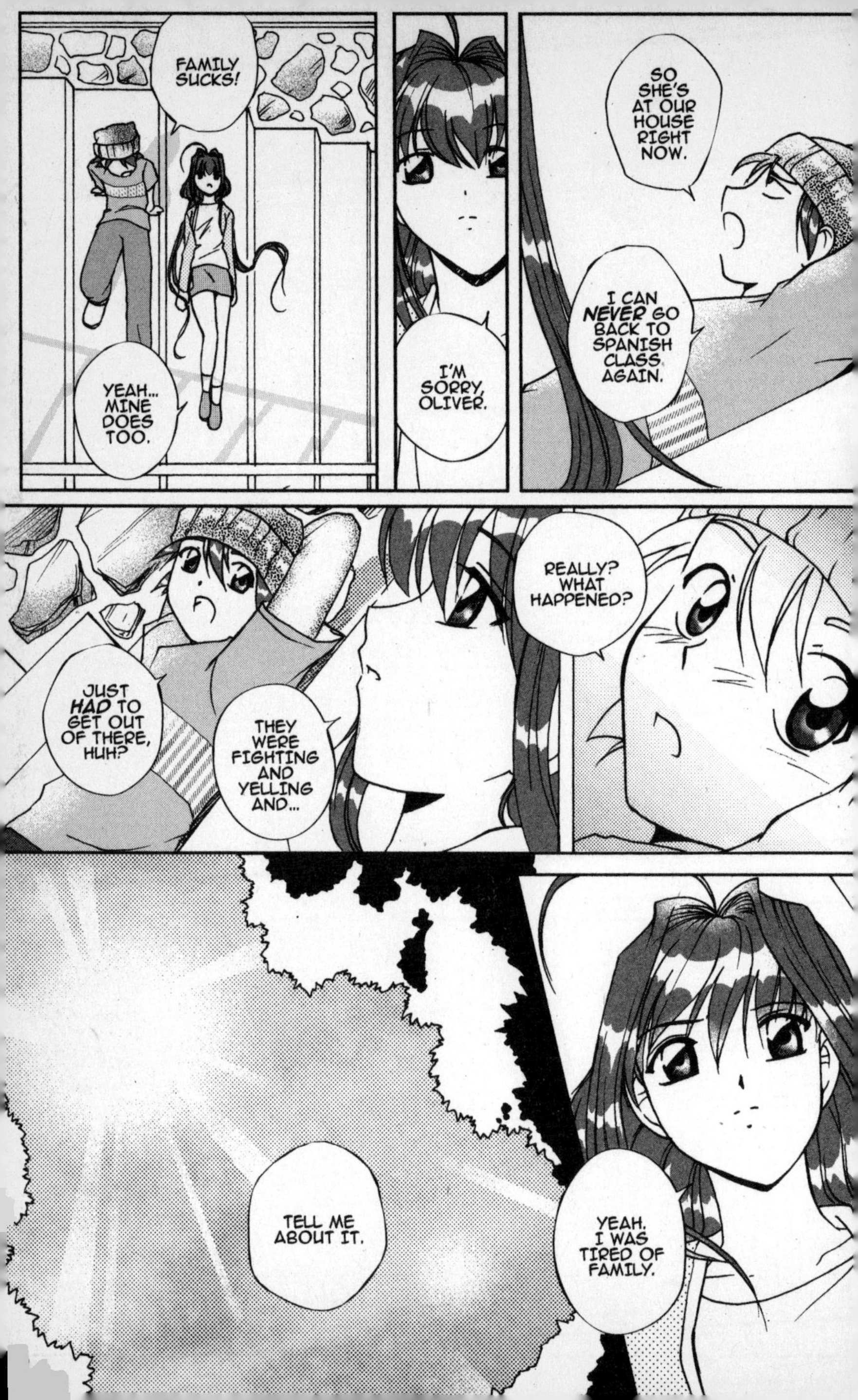
SO SHE'S AT OUR HOUSE RIGHT NOW.
I CAN NEVER GO BACK TO SPANISH CLASS AGAIN.
I'M SORRY, OLIVER.
FAMILY SUCKS!
YEAH... MINE DOES TOO.
REALLY? WHAT HAPPENED?
THEY WERE FIGHTING AND YELLING AND...
JUST HAD TO GET OUT OF THERE, HUH?
YEAH. I WAS TIRED OF FAMILY.
TELL ME ABOUT IT.

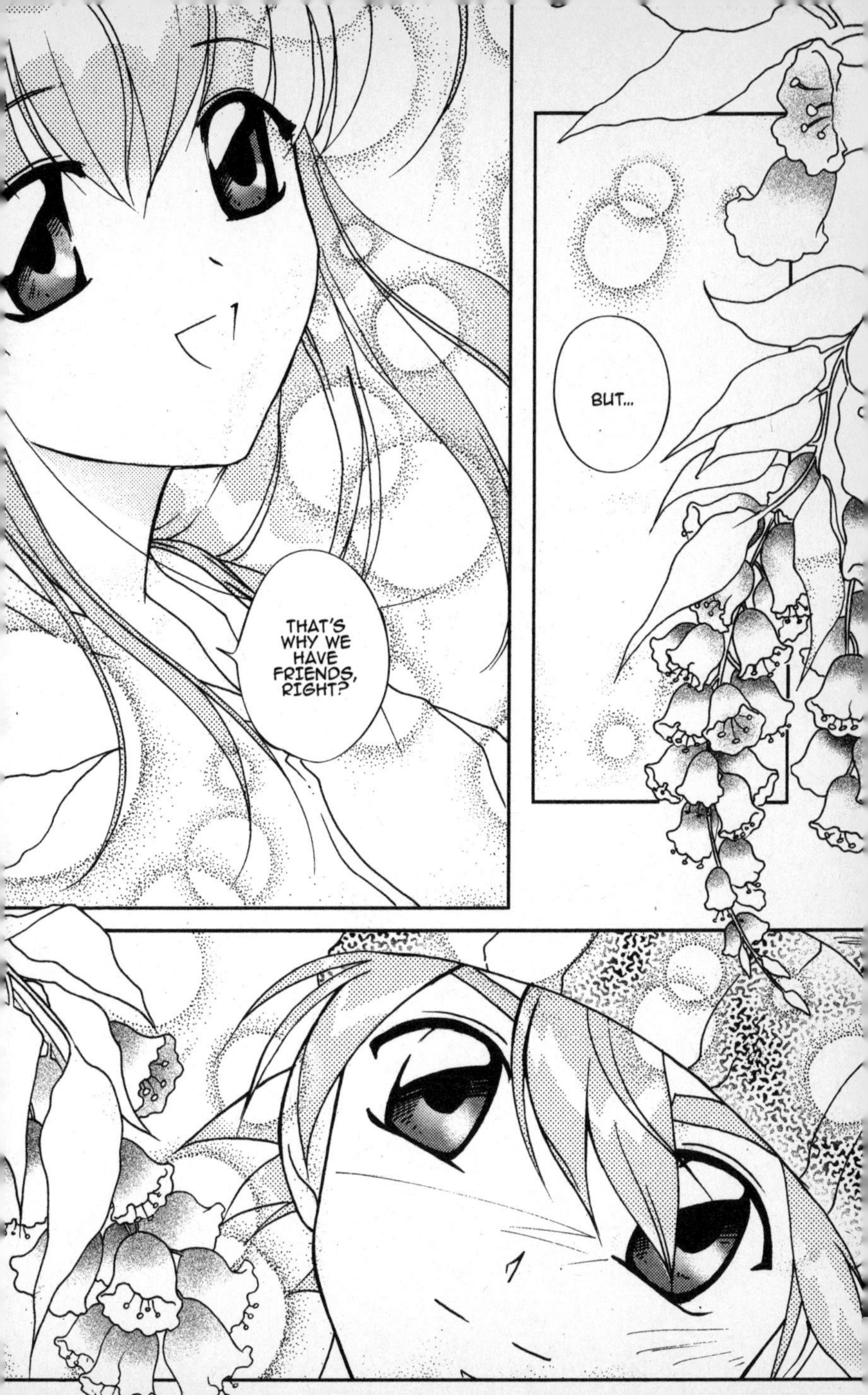
BUT...
THAT'S WHY WE HAVE FRIENDS, RIGHT?

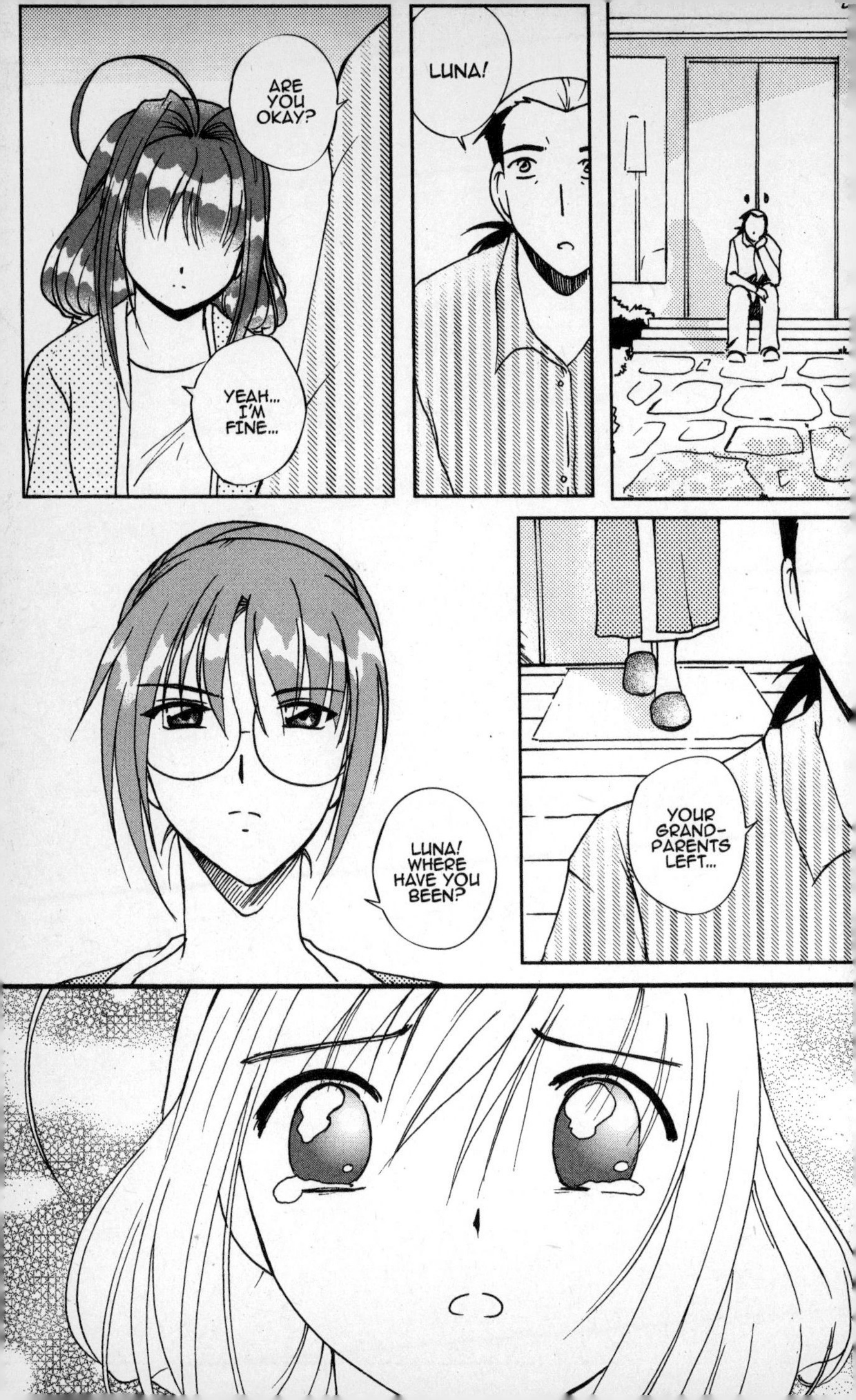
LUNA!
ARE YOU OKAY?
YEAH... I'M FINE...
YOUR GRAND-PARENTS LEFT...
LUNA! WHERE HAVE YOU BEEN?

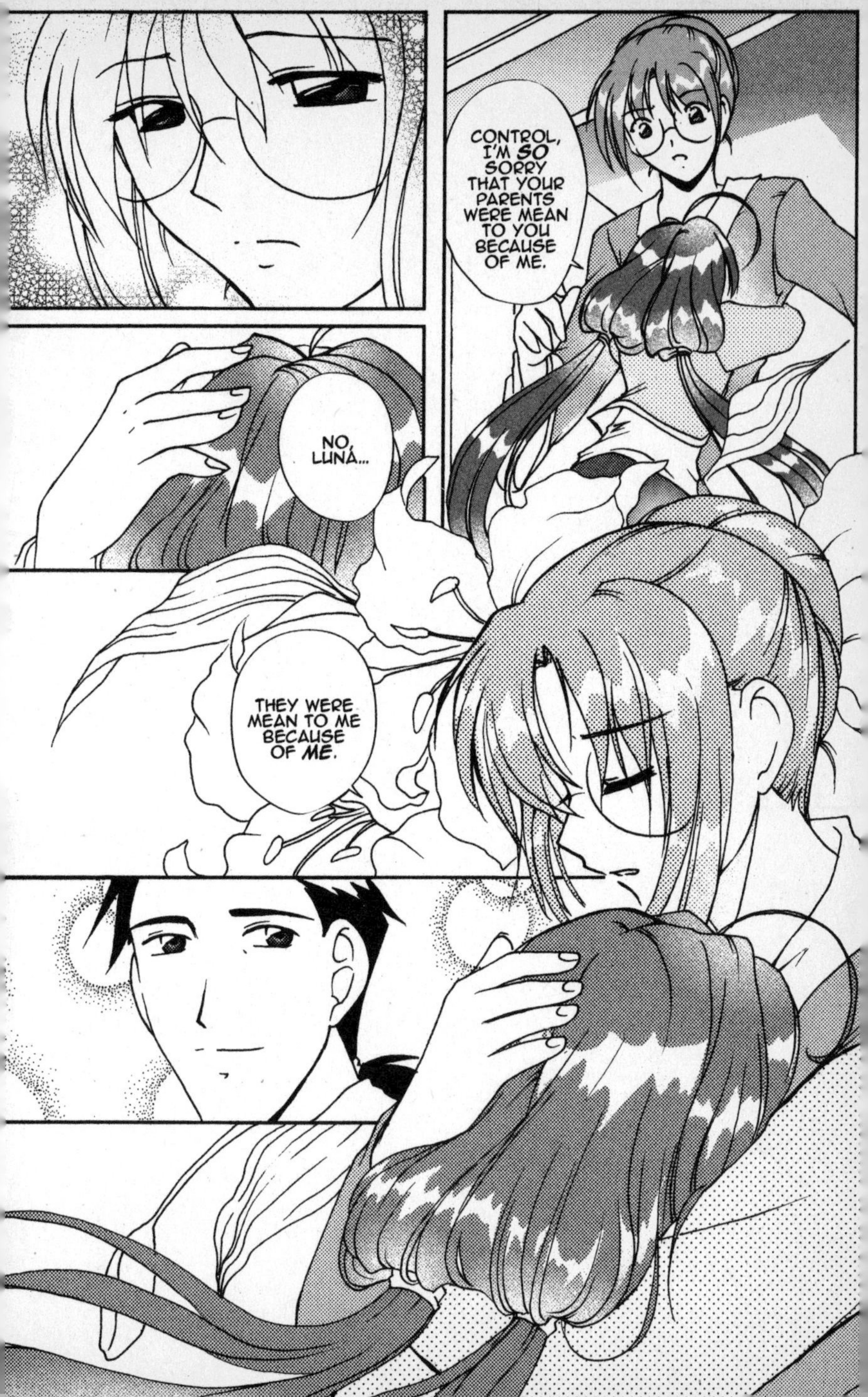
CONTROL, I'M *SO* SORRY THAT YOUR PARENTS WERE MEAN TO YOU BECAUSE OF ME.
NO, LUNA...
THEY WERE MEAN TO ME BECAUSE OF *ME*.

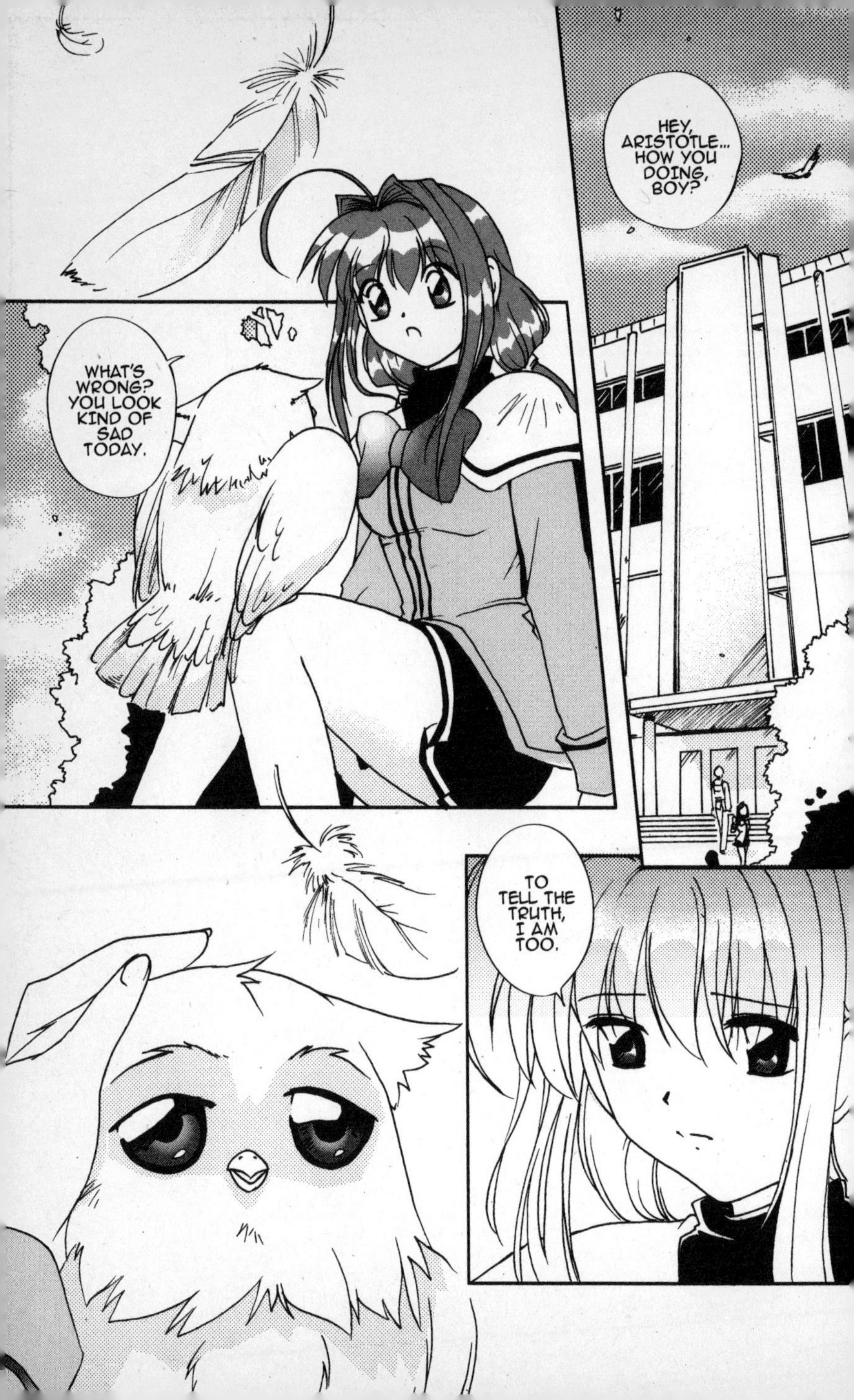
HEY, ARISTOTLE... HOW YOU DOING, BOY?
WHAT'S WRONG? YOU LOOK KIND OF SAD TODAY.
TO TELL THE TRUTH, I AM TOO.

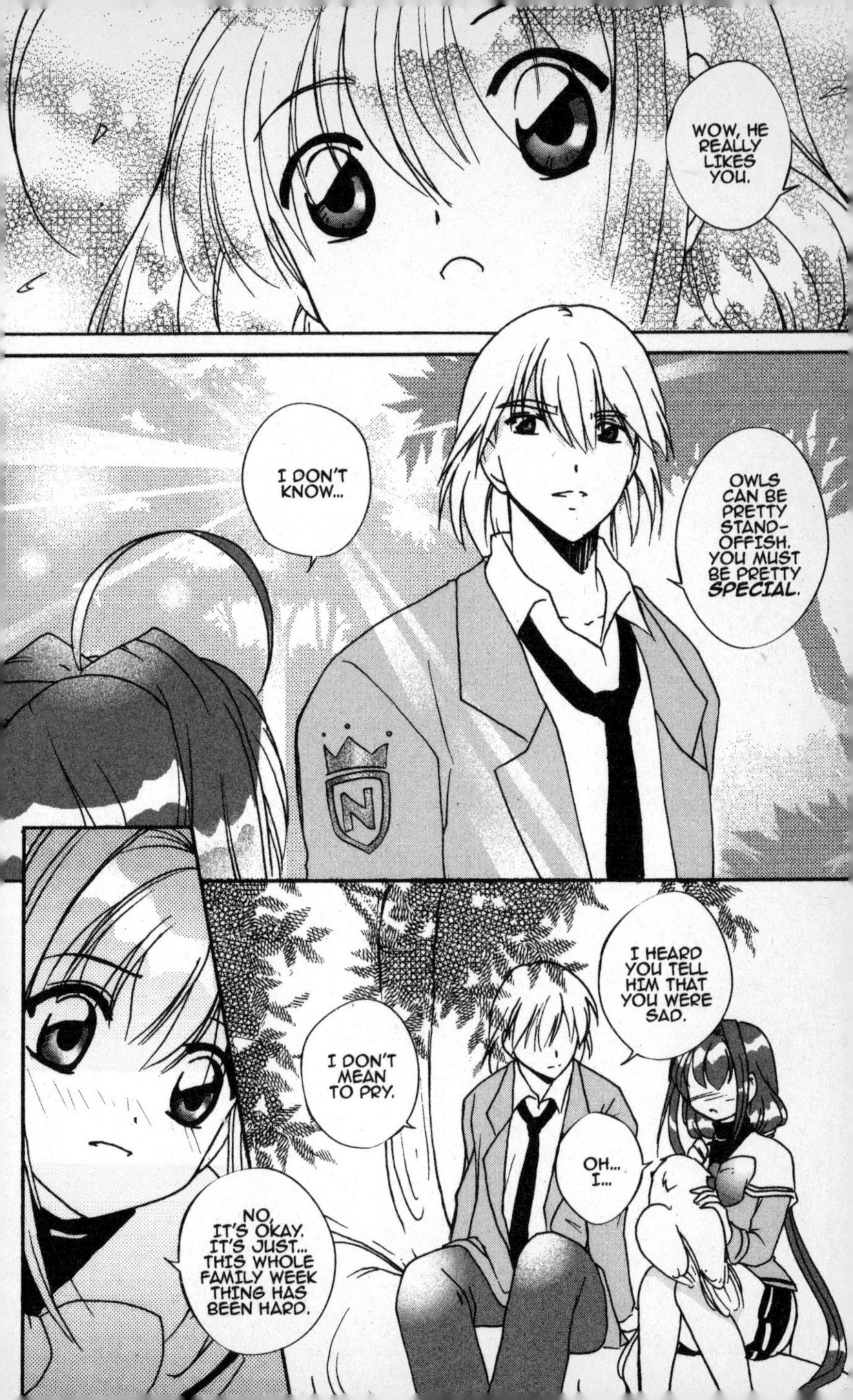
WOW, HE REALLY LIKES YOU.
OWLS CAN BE PRETTY STAND-OFFISH. YOU MUST BE PRETTY **SPECIAL**.
I DON'T KNOW...
I HEARD YOU TELL HIM THAT YOU WERE SAD.
I DON'T MEAN TO PRY.
OH... I...
NO, IT'S OKAY. IT'S JUST... THIS WHOLE FAMILY WEEK THING HAS BEEN HARD.

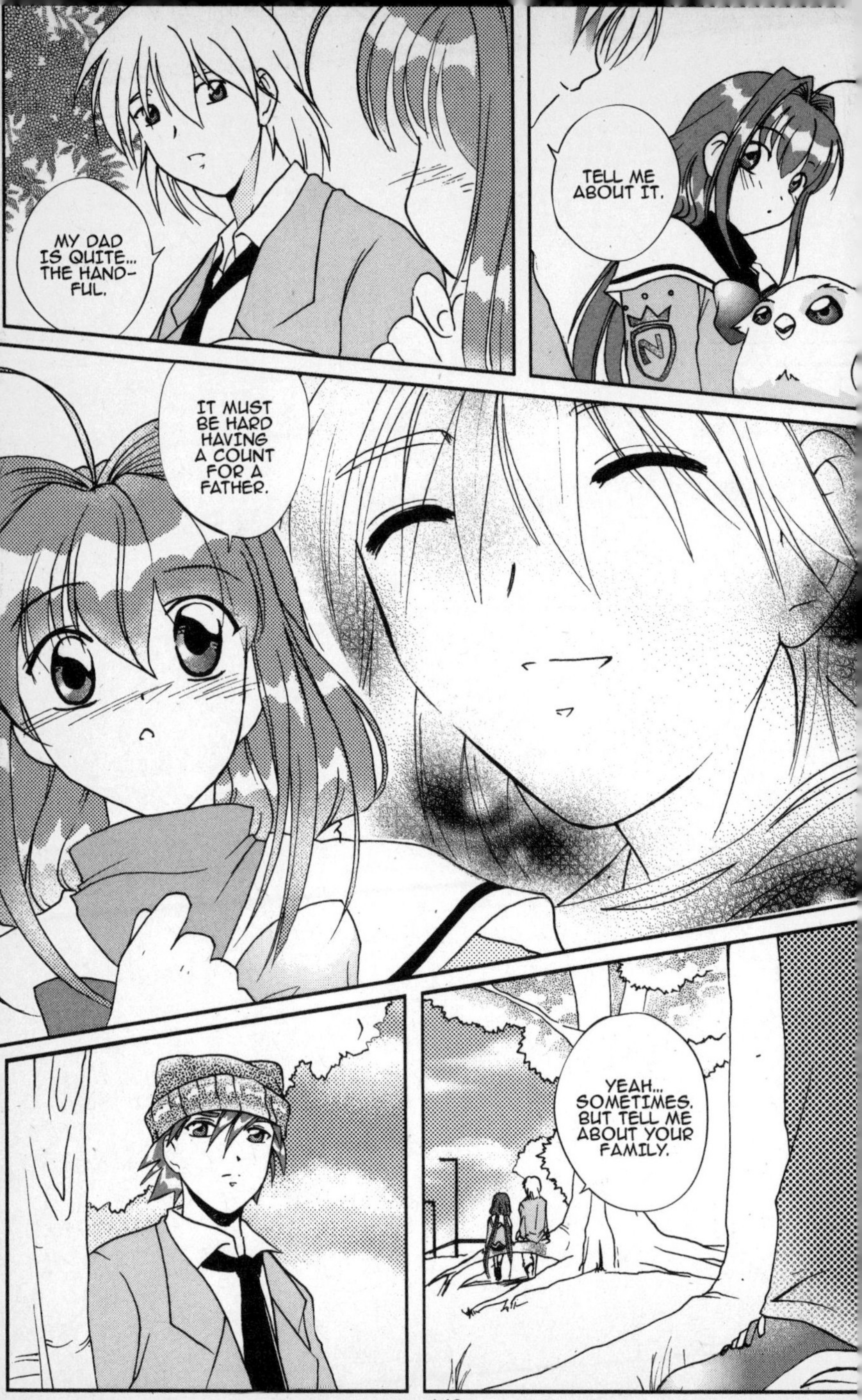
TELL ME ABOUT IT.
MY DAD IS QUITE... THE HAND-FUL.
IT MUST BE HARD HAVING A COUNT FOR A FATHER.
YEAH... SOMETIMES. BUT TELL ME ABOUT YOUR FAMILY.

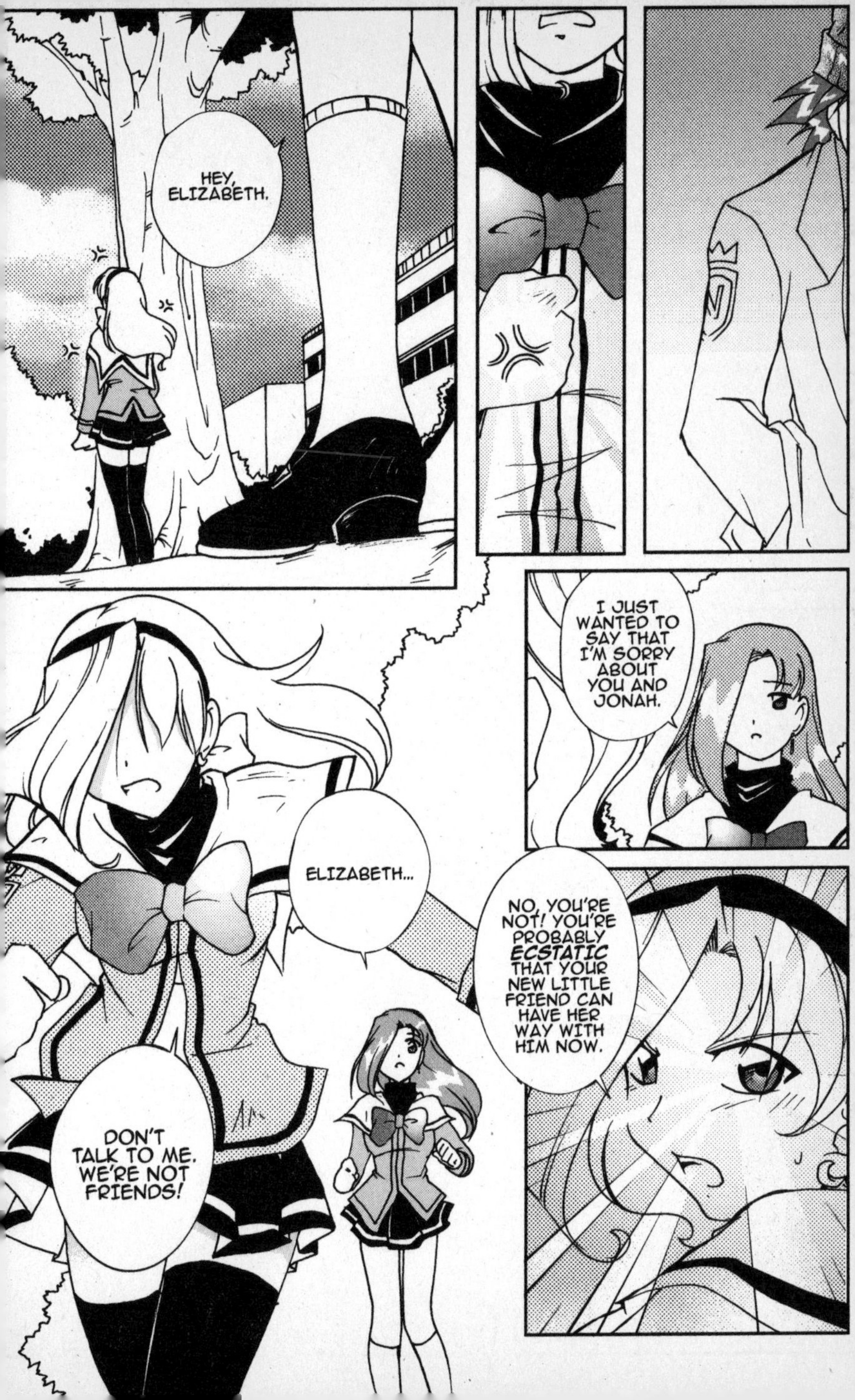
HEY, ELIZABETH.
I JUST WANTED TO SAY THAT I'M SORRY ABOUT YOU AND JONAH.
NO, YOU'RE NOT! YOU'RE PROBABLY *ECSTATIC* THAT YOUR NEW LITTLE FRIEND CAN HAVE HER WAY WITH HIM NOW.
ELIZABETH...
DON'T TALK TO ME. WE'RE NOT FRIENDS!

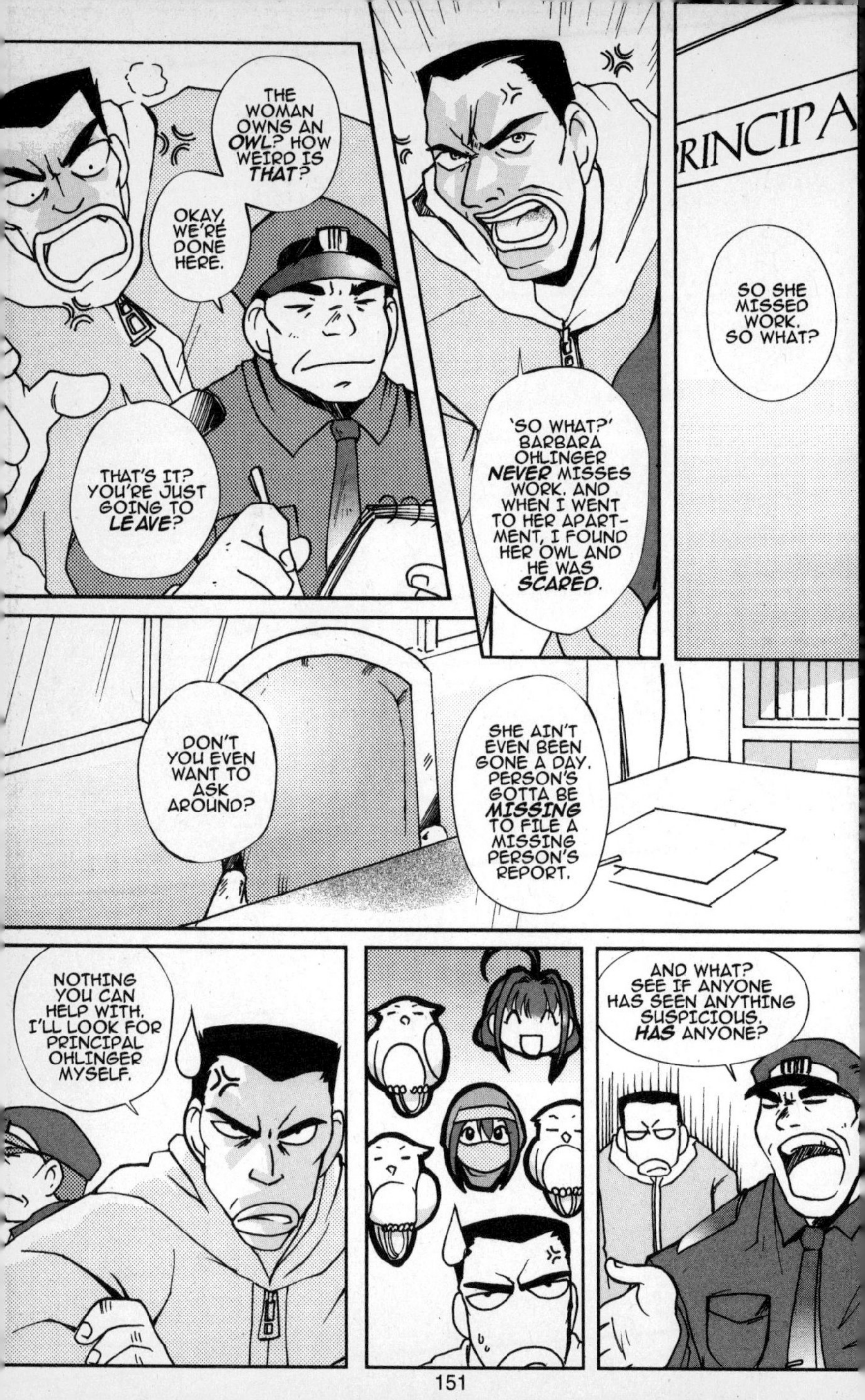
PRINCIPA
SO SHE MISSED WORK. SO WHAT?
'SO WHAT?' BARBARA OHLINGER **NEVER** MISSES WORK. AND WHEN I WENT TO HER APART-MENT, I FOUND HER OWL AND HE WAS **SCARED**.
THE WOMAN OWNS AN **OWL**? HOW WEIRD IS **THAT**?
OKAY, WE'RE DONE HERE.
THAT'S IT? YOU'RE JUST GOING TO **LEAVE**?
SHE AIN'T EVEN BEEN GONE A DAY. PERSON'S GOTTA BE **MISSING** TO FILE A MISSING PERSON'S REPORT.
DON'T YOU EVEN WANT TO ASK AROUND?
AND WHAT? SEE IF ANYONE HAS SEEN ANYTHING SUSPICIOUS. **HAS** ANYONE?
NOTHING YOU CAN HELP WITH. I'LL LOOK FOR PRINCIPAL OHLINGER MYSELF.

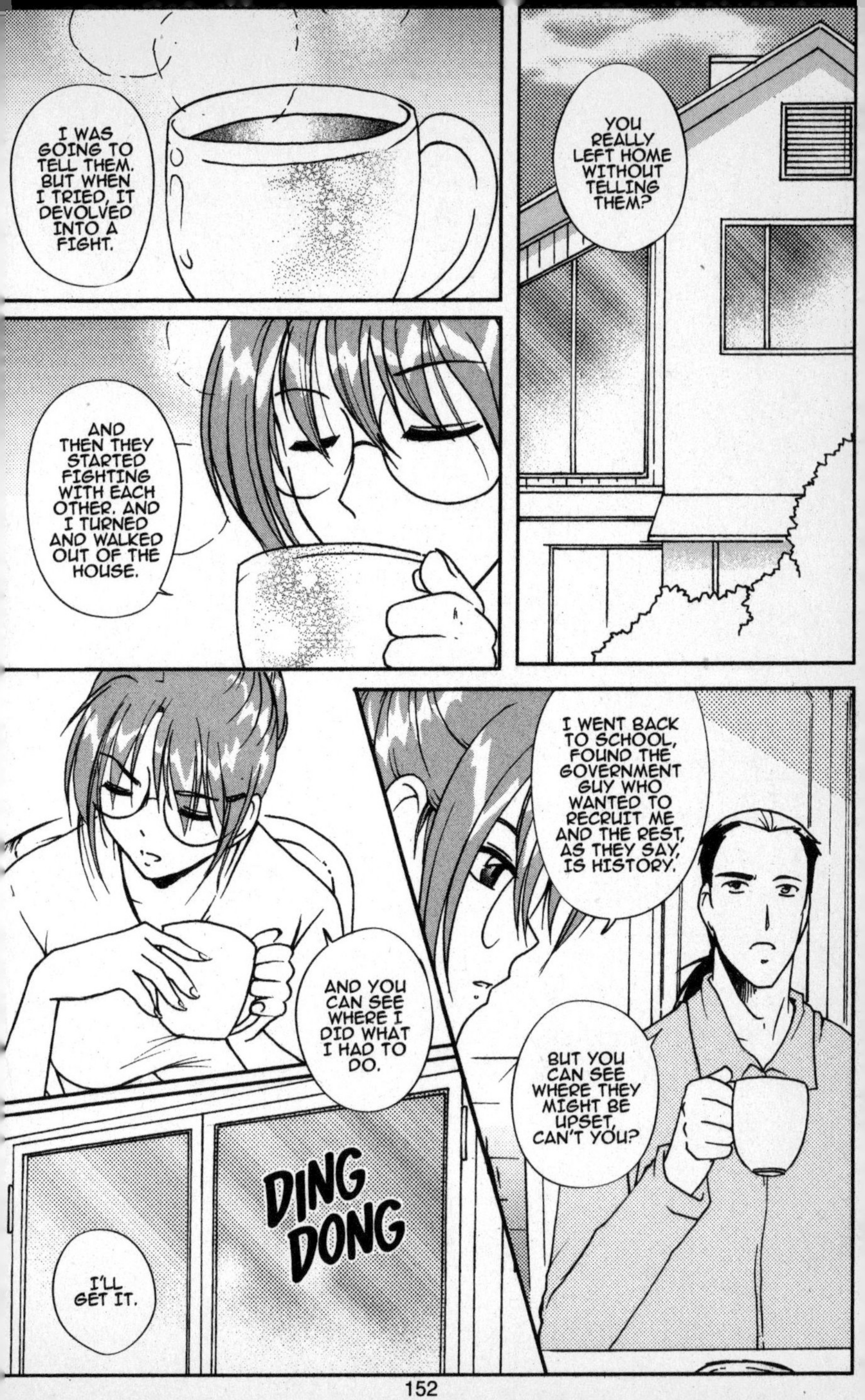
YOU REALLY LEFT HOME WITHOUT TELLING THEM?
I WAS GOING TO TELL THEM. BUT WHEN I TRIED, IT DEVOLVED INTO A FIGHT.
AND THEN THEY STARTED FIGHTING WITH EACH OTHER. AND I TURNED AND WALKED OUT OF THE HOUSE.
I WENT BACK TO SCHOOL, FOUND THE GOVERNMENT GUY WHO WANTED TO RECRUIT ME AND THE REST, AS THEY SAY, IS HISTORY.
BUT YOU CAN SEE WHERE THEY MIGHT BE UPSET, CAN'T YOU?
AND YOU CAN SEE WHERE I DID WHAT I HAD TO DO.
DING DONG
I'LL GET IT.

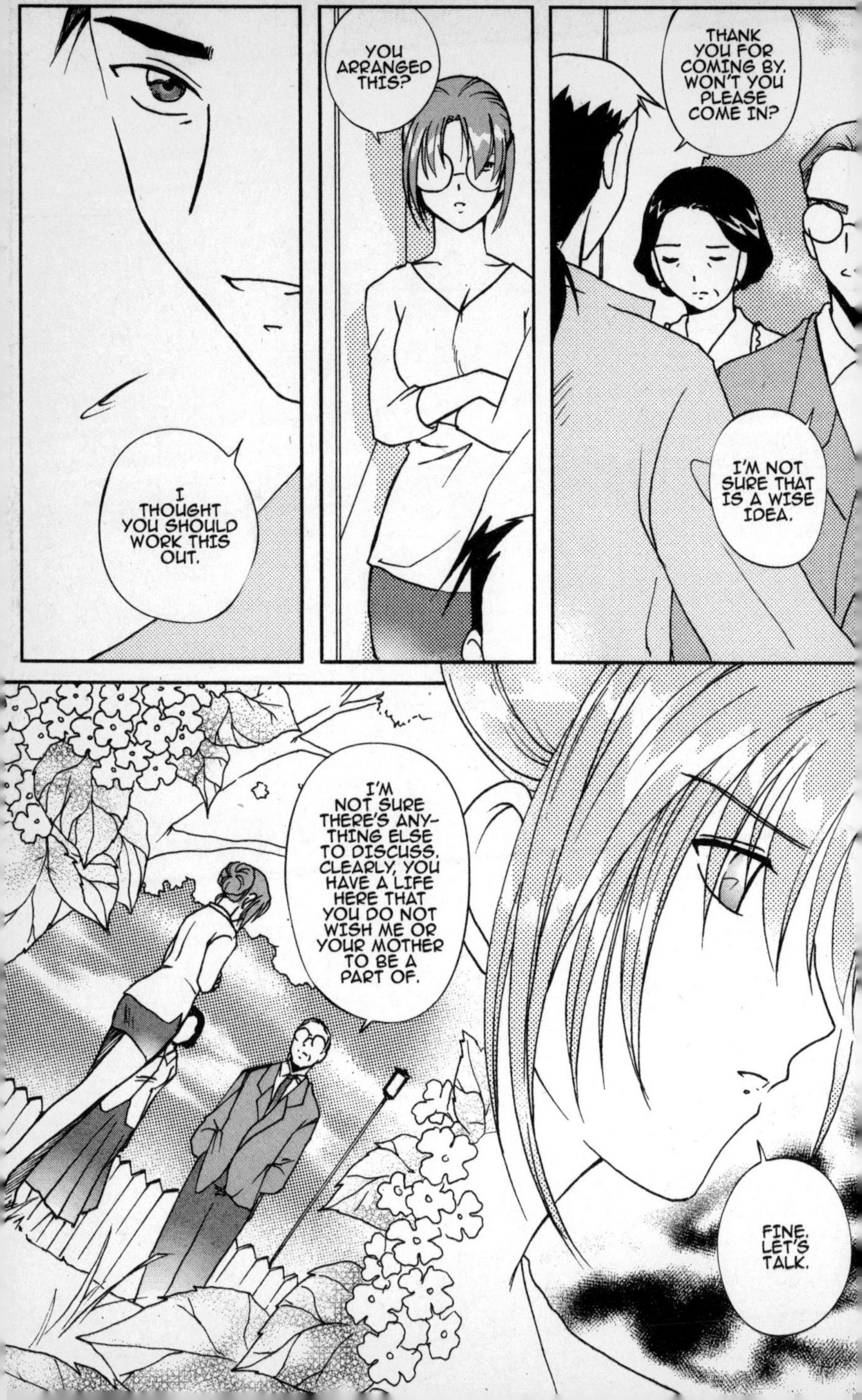
THANK YOU FOR COMING BY. WON'T YOU PLEASE COME IN?
I'M NOT SURE THAT IS A WISE IDEA.
YOU ARRANGED THIS?
I THOUGHT YOU SHOULD WORK THIS OUT.
I'M NOT SURE THERE'S ANYTHING ELSE TO DISCUSS. CLEARLY, YOU HAVE A LIFE HERE THAT YOU DO NOT WISH ME OR YOUR MOTHER TO BE A PART OF.
FINE. LET'S TALK.

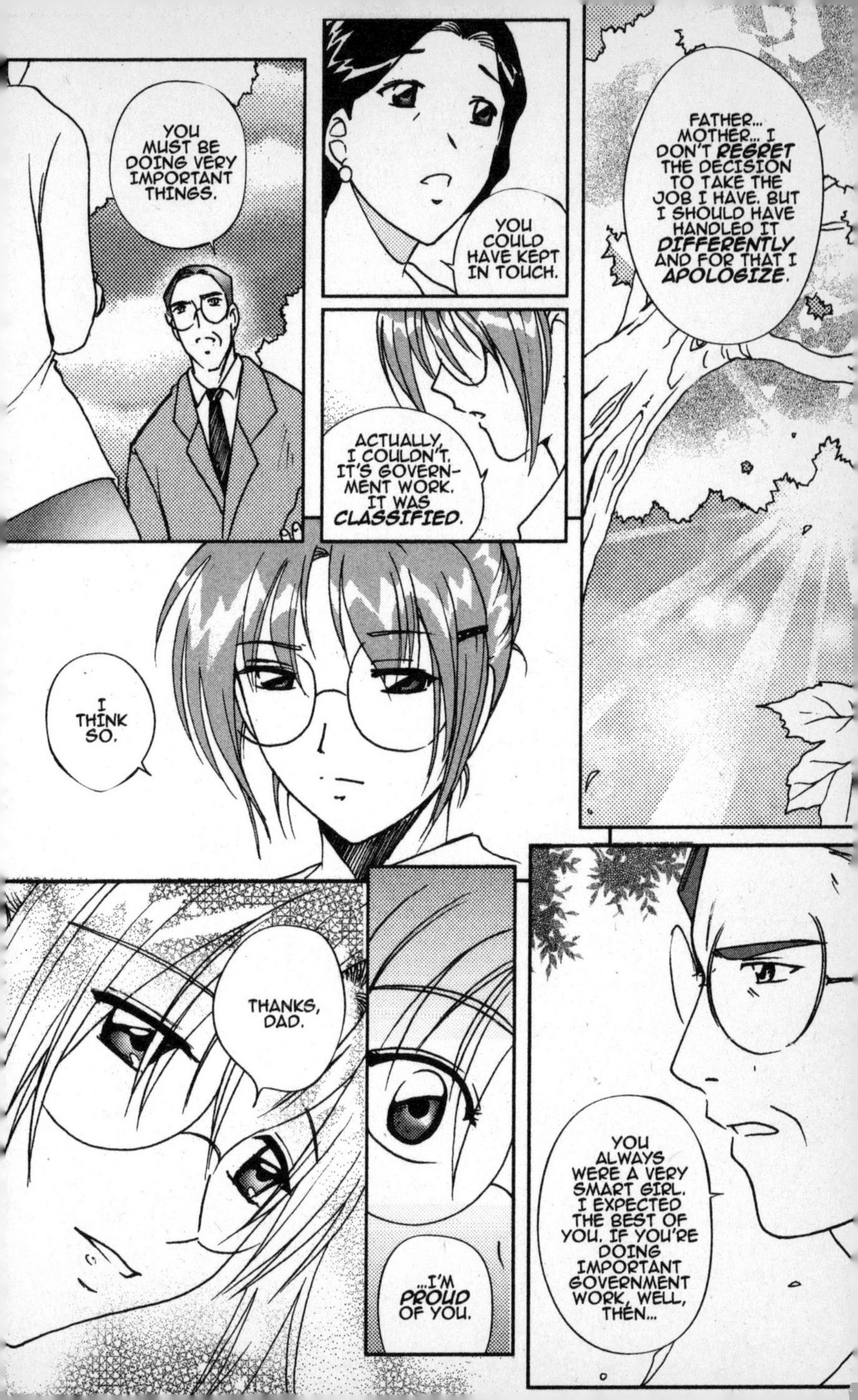
FATHER... MOTHER... I DON'T **REGRET** THE DECISION TO TAKE THE JOB I HAVE. BUT I SHOULD HAVE HANDLED IT **DIFFERENTLY** AND FOR THAT I **APOLOGIZE**.
YOU COULD HAVE KEPT IN TOUCH.
ACTUALLY, I COULDN'T. IT'S GOVERN-MENT WORK. IT WAS **CLASSIFIED**.
YOU MUST BE DOING VERY IMPORTANT THINGS.
I THINK SO.
YOU ALWAYS WERE A VERY SMART GIRL. I EXPECTED THE BEST OF YOU. IF YOU'RE DOING IMPORTANT GOVERNMENT WORK, WELL, THEN...
...I'M **PROUD** OF YOU.
THANKS, DAD.

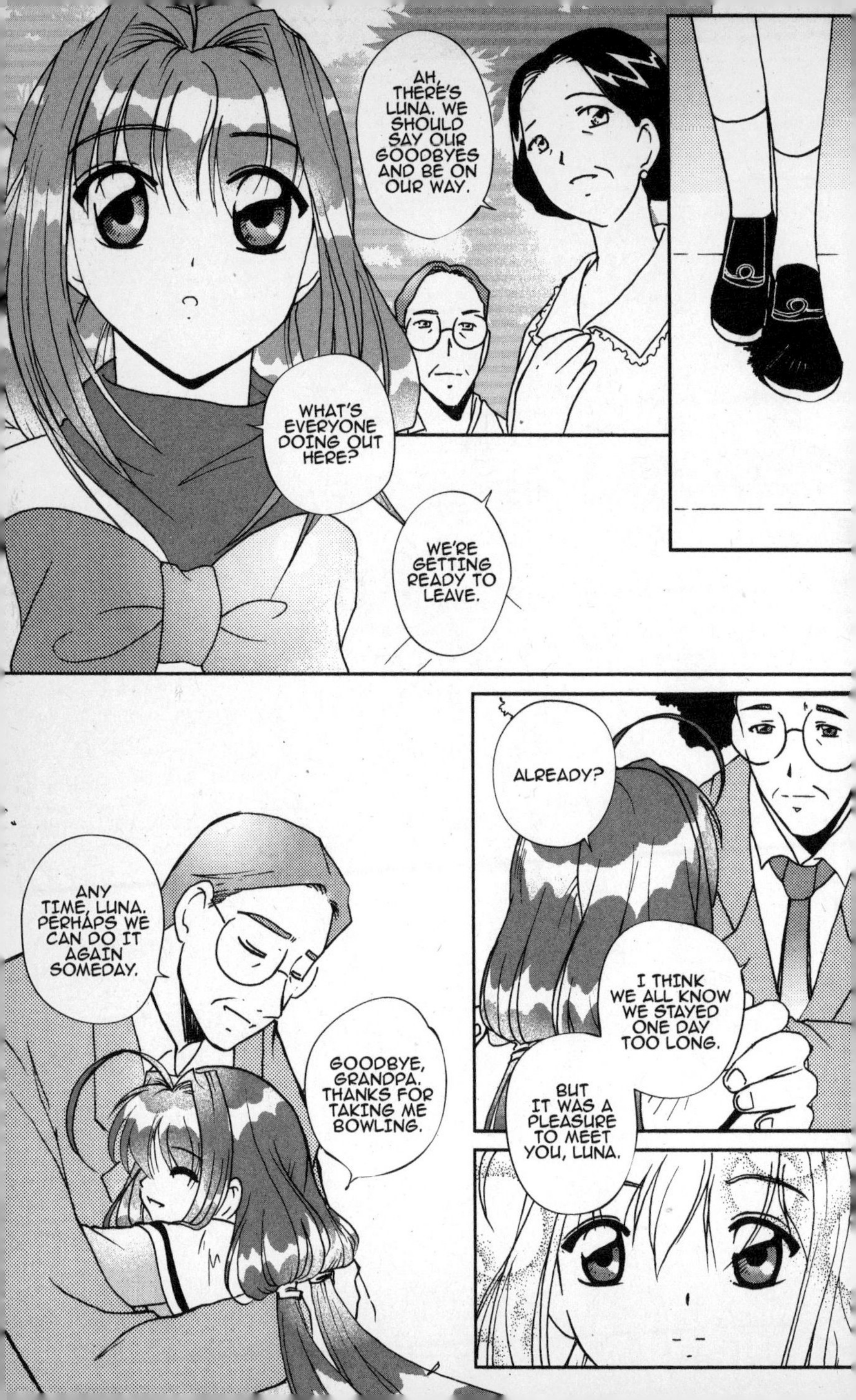
AH, THERE'S LUNA. WE SHOULD SAY OUR GOODBYES AND BE ON OUR WAY.
WHAT'S EVERYONE DOING OUT HERE?
WE'RE GETTING READY TO LEAVE.
ALREADY?
I THINK WE ALL KNOW WE STAYED ONE DAY TOO LONG.
BUT IT WAS A PLEASURE TO MEET YOU, LUNA.
GOODBYE, GRANDPA. THANKS FOR TAKING ME BOWLING.
ANY TIME, LUNA. PERHAPS WE CAN DO IT AGAIN SOMEDAY.

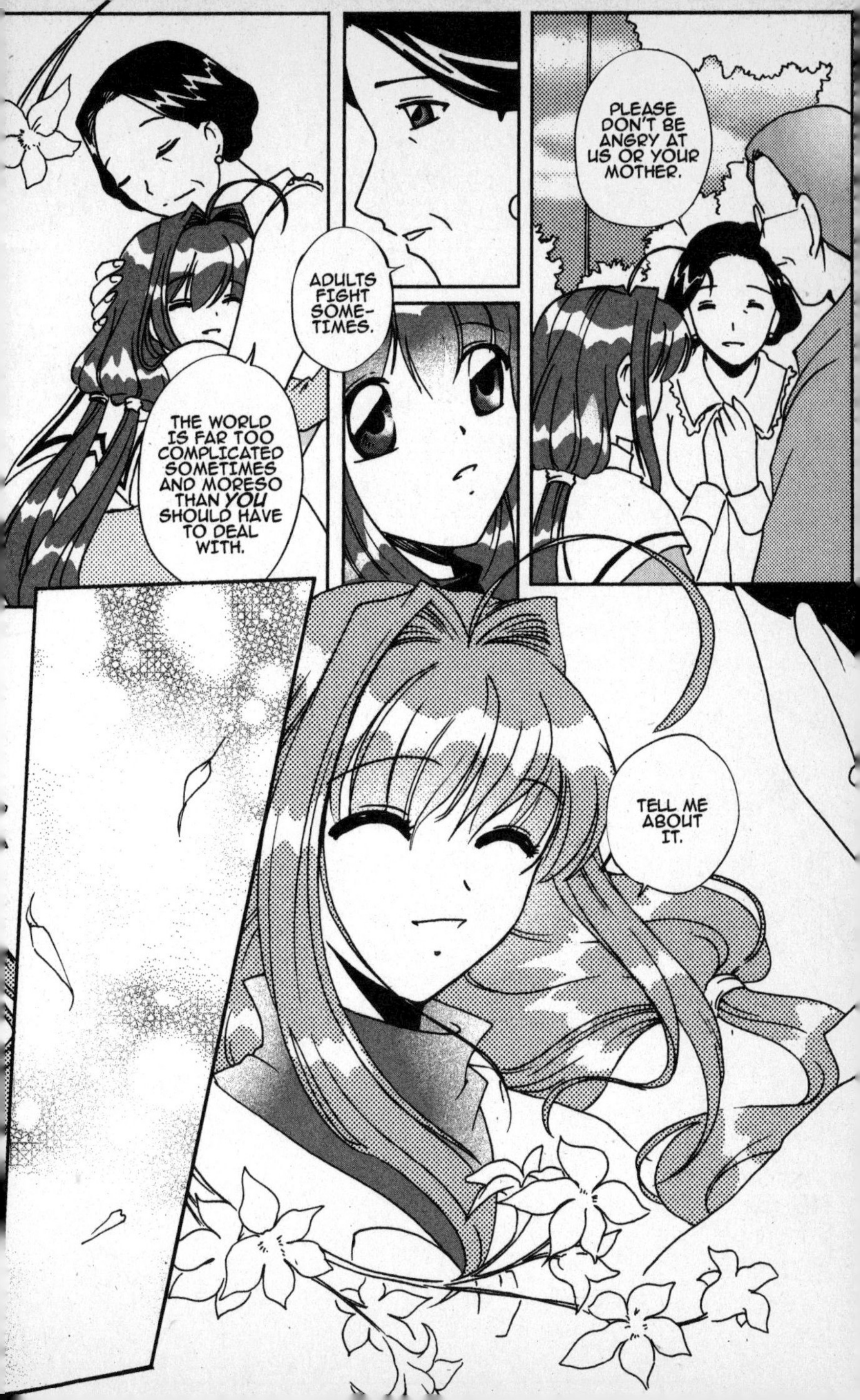
PLEASE DON'T BE ANGRY AT US OR YOUR MOTHER.
ADULTS FIGHT SOME-TIMES.
THE WORLD IS FAR TOO COMPLICATED SOMETIMES AND MORESO THAN *YOU* SHOULD HAVE TO DEAL WITH.
TELL ME ABOUT IT.

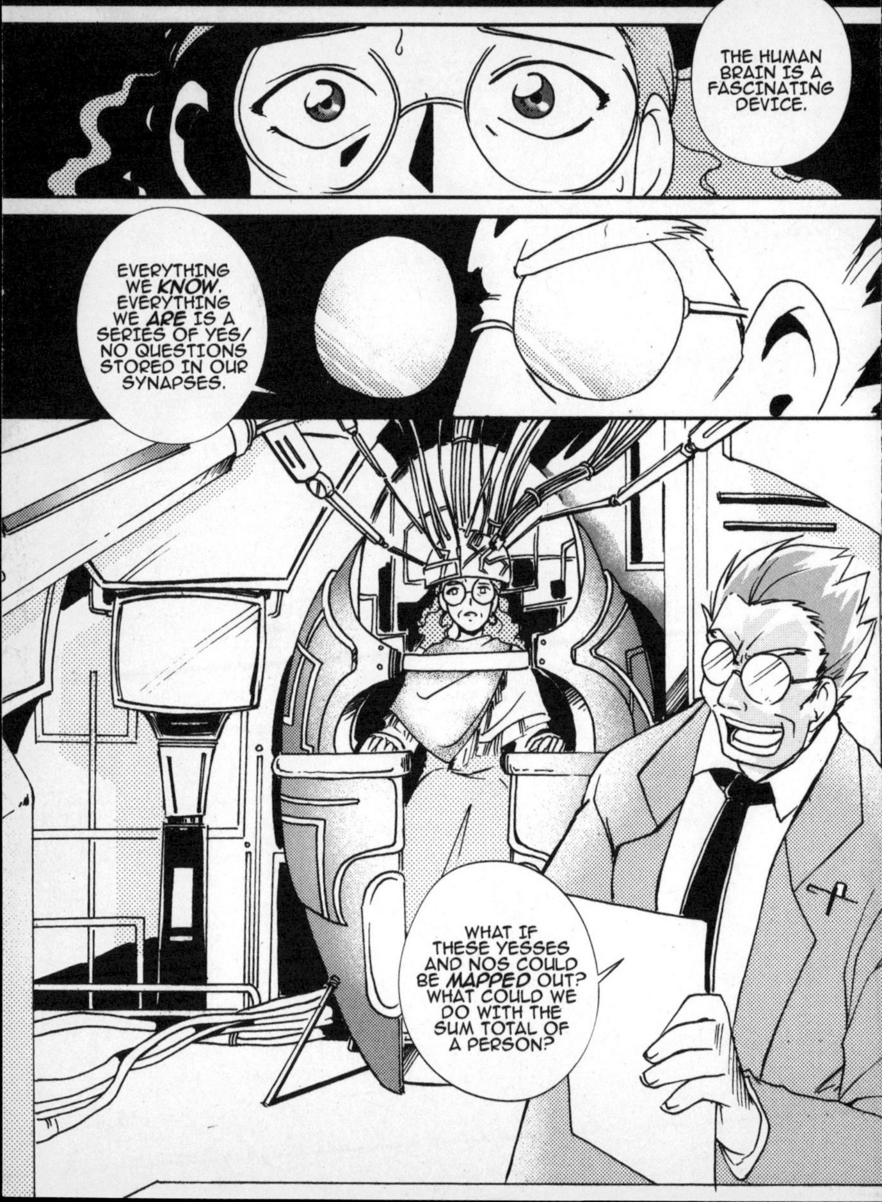
THE HUMAN BRAIN IS A FASCINATING DEVICE.
EVERYTHING WE *KNOW*. EVERYTHING WE *ARE* IS A SERIES OF YES/NO QUESTIONS STORED IN OUR SYNAPSES.
WHAT IF THESE YESSES AND NOS COULD BE *MAPPED* OUT? WHAT COULD WE DO WITH THE SUM TOTAL OF A PERSON?

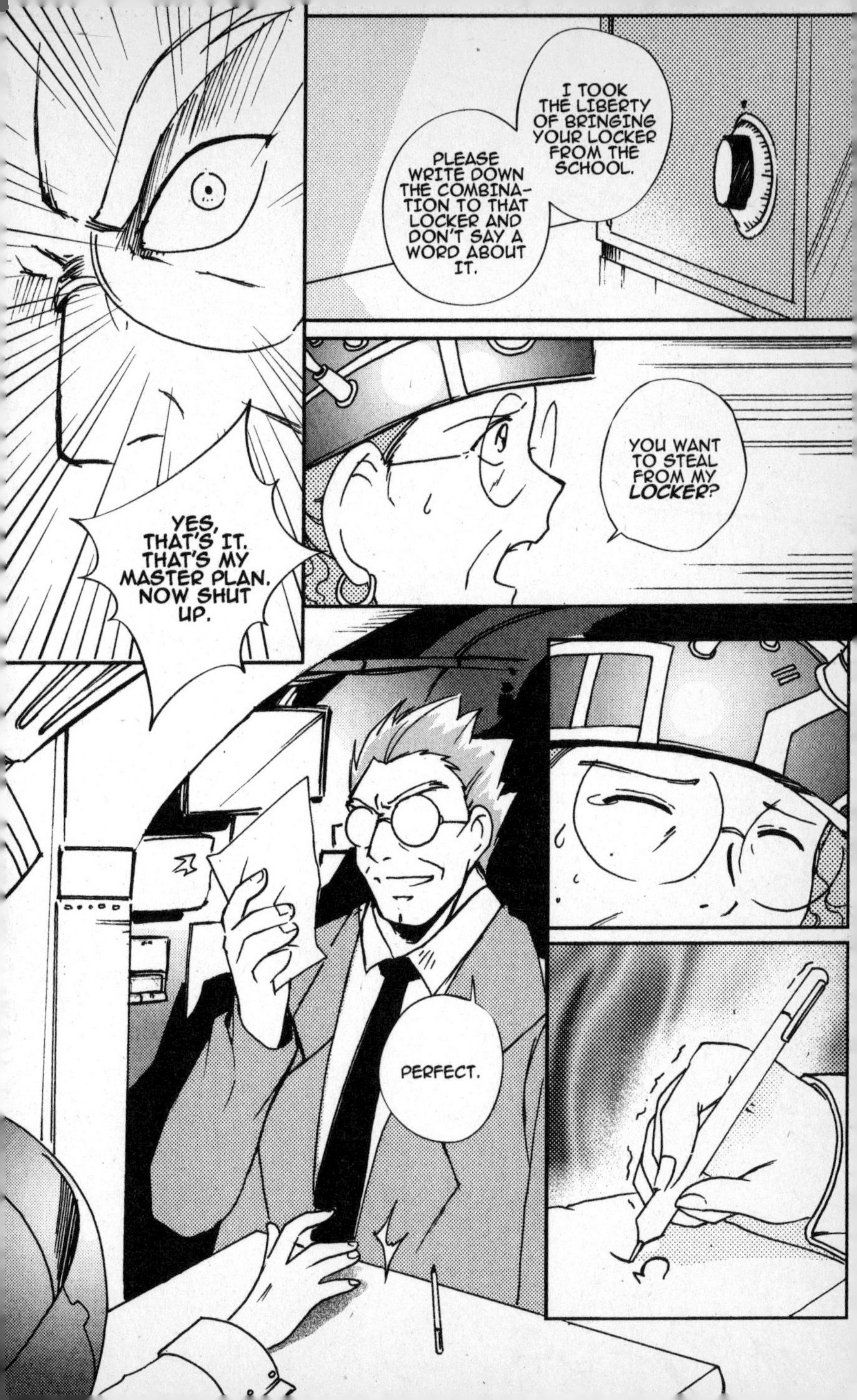
I TOOK THE LIBERTY OF BRINGING YOUR LOCKER FROM THE SCHOOL.
PLEASE WRITE DOWN THE COMBINATION TO THAT LOCKER AND DON'T SAY A WORD ABOUT IT.
YOU WANT TO STEAL FROM MY *LOCKER*?
YES, THAT'S IT. THAT'S MY MASTER PLAN. NOW SHUT UP.
PERFECT.

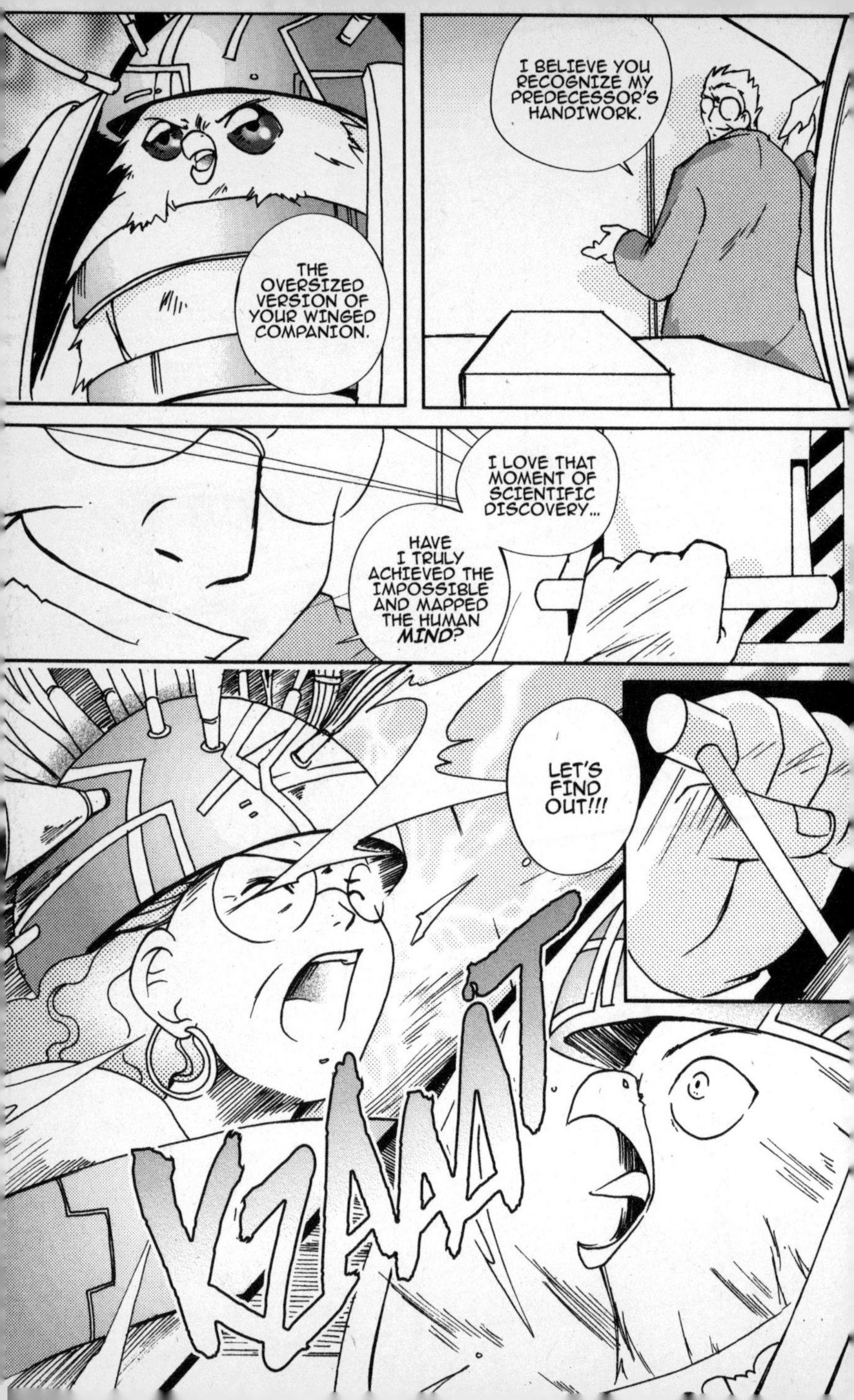
I BELIEVE YOU RECOGNIZE MY PREDECESSOR'S HANDIWORK.
THE OVERSIZED VERSION OF YOUR WINGED COMPANION.
I LOVE THAT MOMENT OF SCIENTIFIC DISCOVERY...
HAVE I TRULY ACHIEVED THE IMPOSSIBLE AND MAPPED THE HUMAN *MIND*?
LET'S FIND OUT!!!

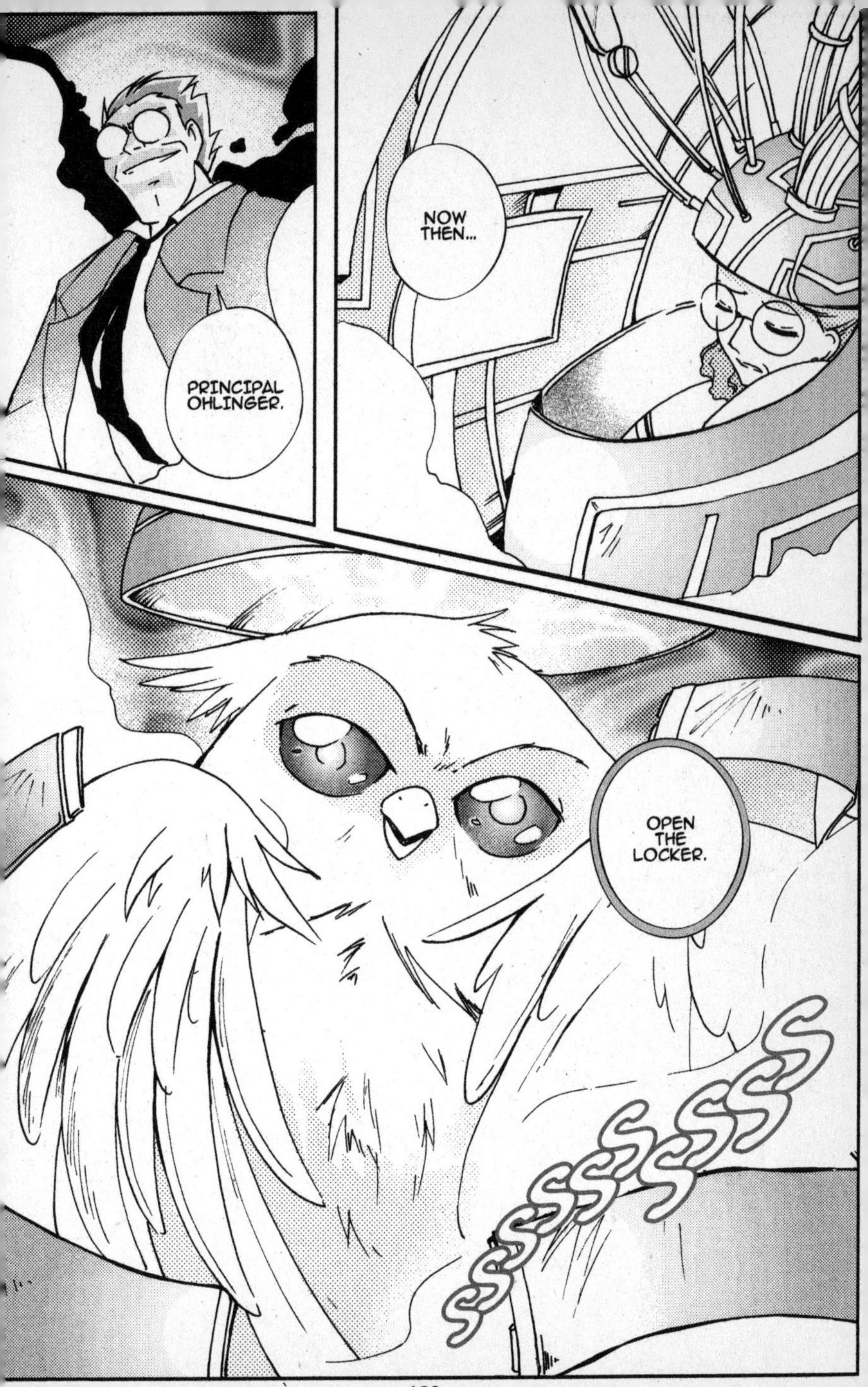
NOW THEN...
PRINCIPAL OHLINGER.
OPEN THE LOCKER.
SSSSSSSSSS

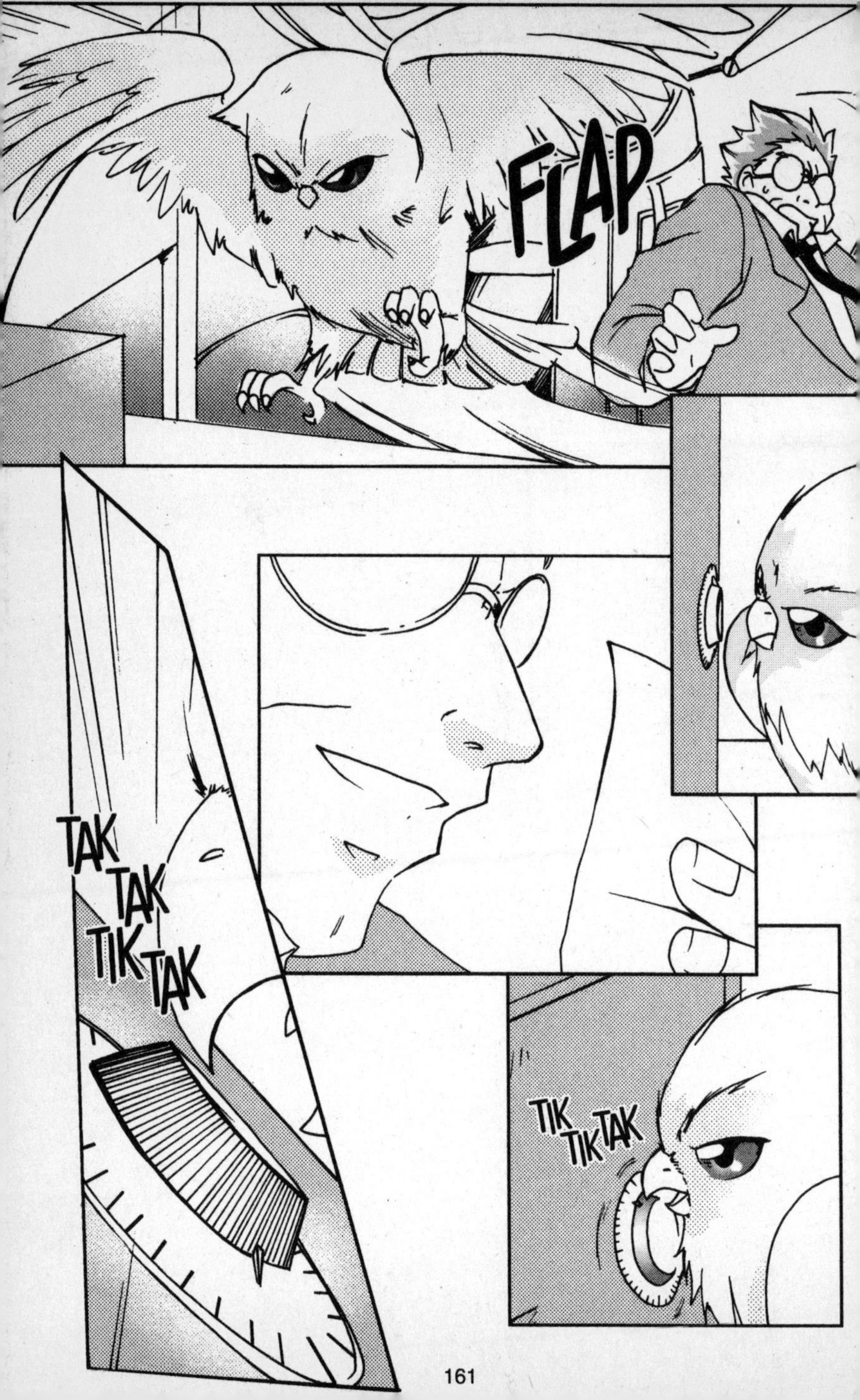
FLAP
TIK TIK TAK
TAK TAK TIK TAK

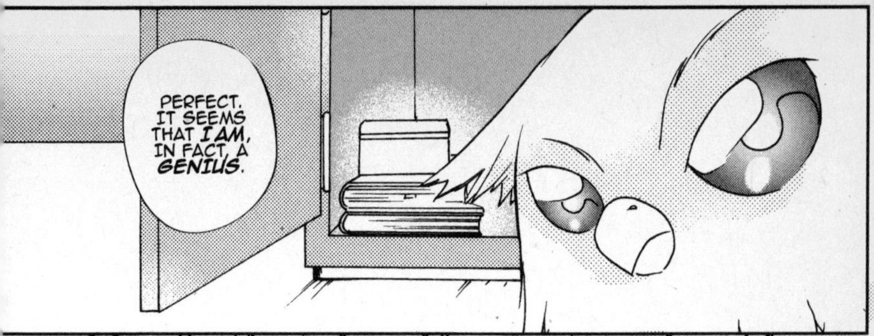
PERFECT. IT SEEMS THAT I AM, IN FACT, A GENIUS.

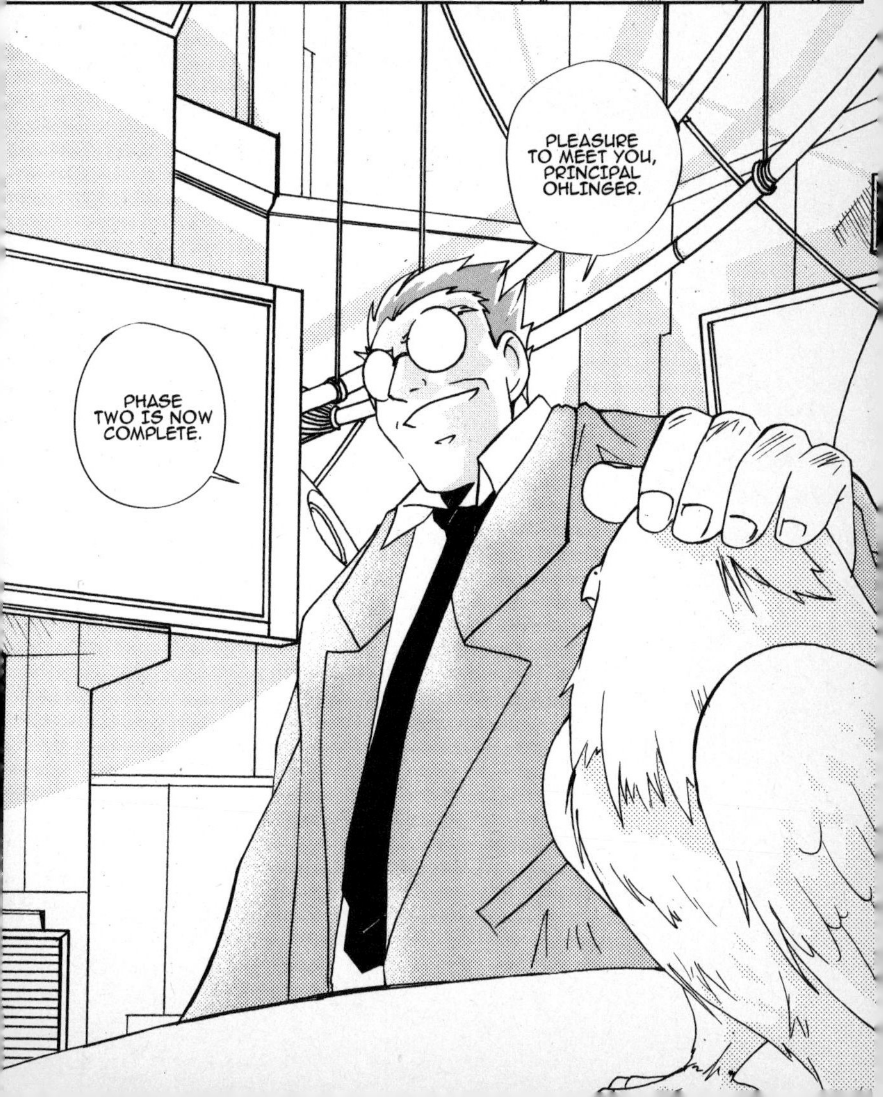
PLEASURE TO MEET YOU, PRINCIPAL OHLINGER.
PHASE TWO IS NOW COMPLETE.

Welcome aboard the second voyage of the good ship we call Seven Seas.

Thank you for hopping aboard to catch our second wave of manga! If you've been here before, then it sure is swell to see you again; and if this is your first time onboard, then get ready for a wild ride! You see, at Seven Seas, we're not here to play things safe. We're all about doing things *differently*, pushing past boundaries, and creating a whole new and original concept of manga.

If orange juice isn't just for breakfast anymore, then manga surely ain't just for or by Japanese anymore. It's for all of us. It's become a *world* art form. Past generations may have grown up with Mickey Mouse or Bugs Bunny, but we're being weaned on manga and anime characters. They have become OUR mythology, and we're now creating that mythology ourselves. In fact, the great manga icons of tomorrow may very well be found within these pages.

It's been a great first year for Seven Seas. We've come out with seven new original series so far, and have lots more thrilling manga on the way! Our web site, **www.gomanga.com**, has grown tremendously, as we continue to provide free web manga and lots of other great manga-related content. Plus, our online forum has been growing exponentially, and has become a place where thousands of manga and anime fans like you come daily to talk shop.

And since we're all about doing stuff *our* way, we've made some radical innovations in a relatively short period of time, like: 1) being the first manga company in history to make our manga downloadable to the Sony PSP, 2) releasing the first ever J-Pop style theme song for our web manga, *Aoi House*, and 3) creating a flash animation short based on our very own *No Man's Land*. Again, you can check out all this and more at **www.gomanga.com**. And believe me, we're just gettin' warmed up. The best is yet to come...

Hearty cheer and pirate songs from the crew at

Seven Seas

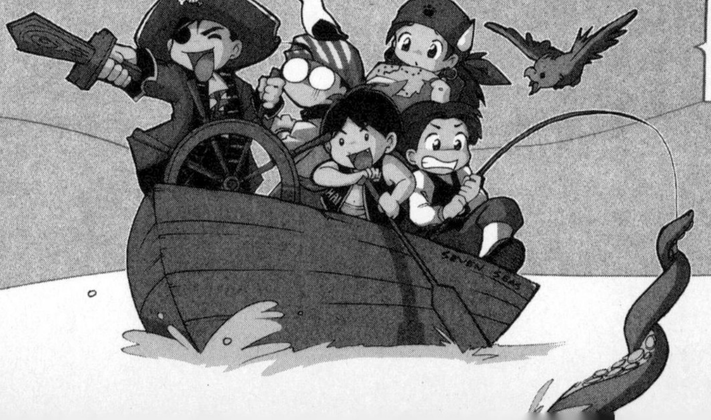
SEVEN SEAS

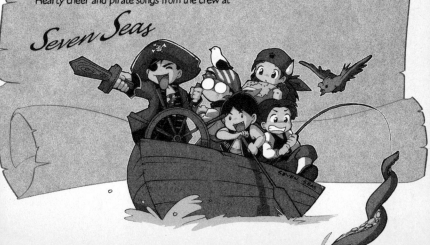

Amazing_Agent

LUNA

VOLUME 3

Luna's undercover life as a high school student and her real life as a secret agent are about to collide. The principal is missing, the gym teacher is on the verge of discovering her secret, Oliver finds himself caught up in sinister doings, and the only one who knows what's really going on is the mysterious bad boy Jonah Von Brucken. Will Luna sort out her two lives before they both come crumbling down?

Seven Seas

Look for it in early '06!

NEW WORLDS AT YOUR FINGER
www.gomanga.co

MEMORANDUM

TO: OUR READERS
FROM: NUNZIO DEFILIPPIS AND CHRISTINA WEIR
RE: AMAZING AGENT LUNA

Hi everyone and welcome back to Amazing Agent Luna, Volume Two. Hope you all have enjoyed reading it as much as we've enjoyed writing it. Honestly, we think this project has been the most fun of any we've ever worked on.

But now we find ourselves facing a dilemma.

It comes as no secret that Jonah was planned as a love interest for Luna. He's dark, he's handsome, he's got the mysterious broody thing going on. Of course, Oliver has his eyes on Luna, but when we started writing this, he didn't stand much of a chance. Luna and Jonah were the couple – either they'd work out, or they'd be doomed to be apart. Either way, Oliver was meant to pine in the corner for the girl of his dreams.

Enter Shiei. We have discovered that our immensely talented artist has a soft spot for young Oliver. She desperately wants Oliver (or Ollie, as she calls him, though he'd never call himself that) to be the one who winds up with Luna. And we want our artist to be happy, don't we?

So we've got ourselves an honest to goodness triangle going on here. Which in and of itself isn't a problem. The love triangle has long since served as a great dramatic device. But who will Luna wind up with? The tall, dark and handsome bad boy or the sweet, ever charming if slightly goofy boy next door?

We hope you'll stay tuned to see what happens next. For all you Oliver fans out there (and that includes you, Shiei), Volume 3 is going to shed a little more light on him and his life. And by the time that book is done, Oliver's life will never be the same!

Of course, Jonah's not leaving Nobel High or taking his eyes off Luna for a long time, either.

Yep, definitely a dilemma. Stay with us as we (and Luna) figure out what to do with it.

Family
Album

This book belongs to

Luna Collins

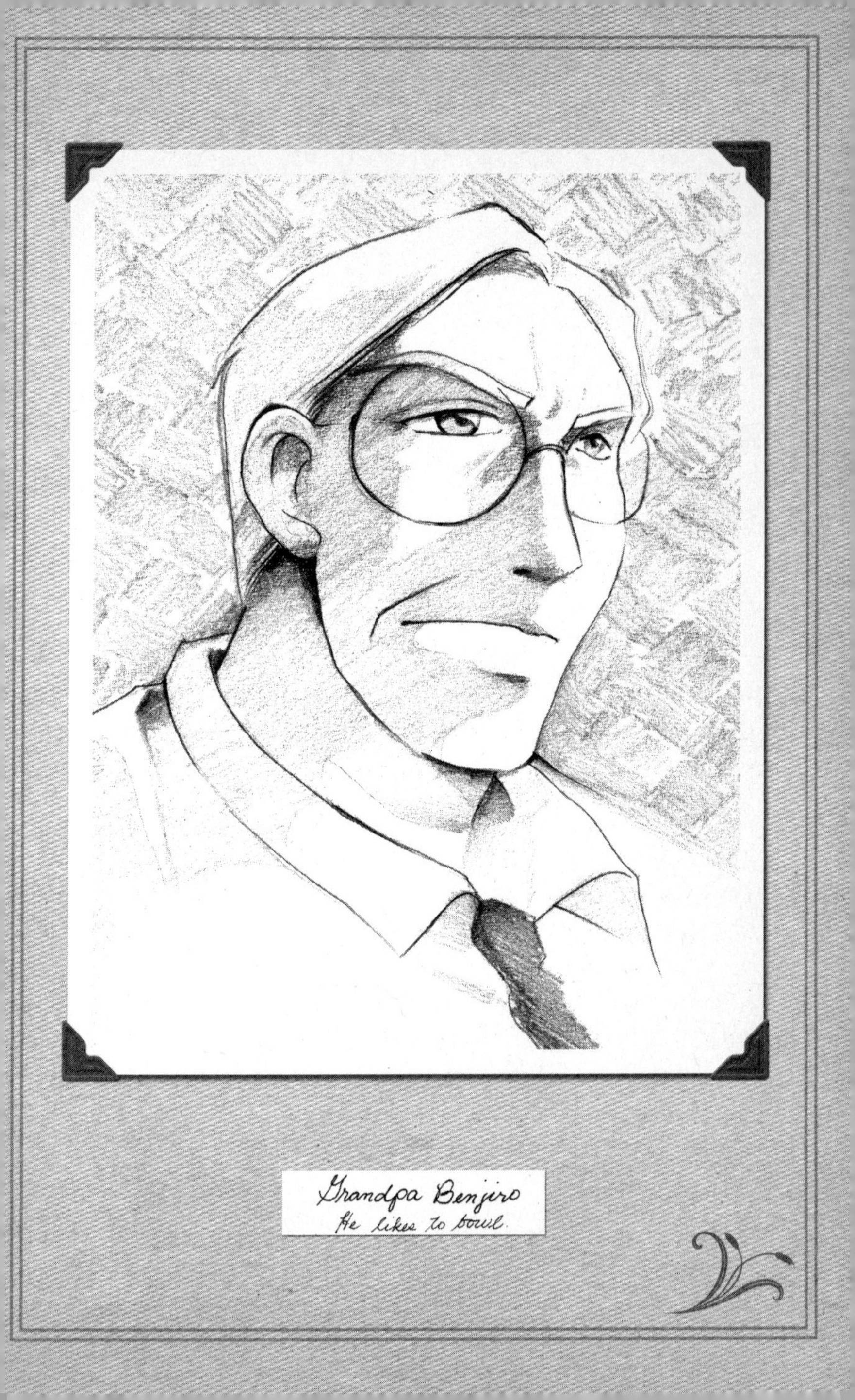

Grandpa Benjiro
He likes to bowl.

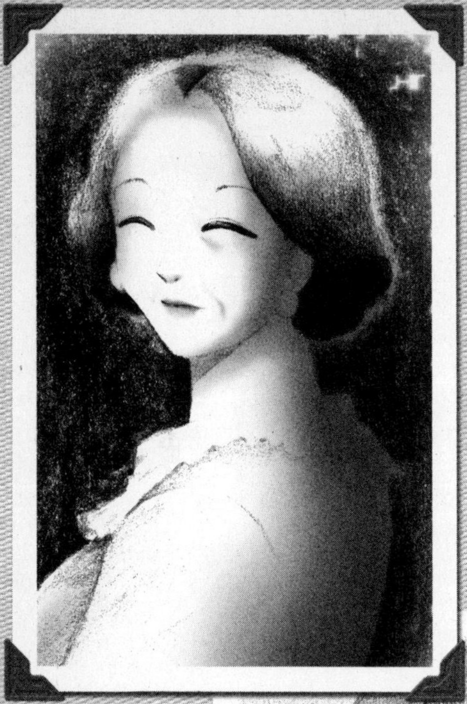

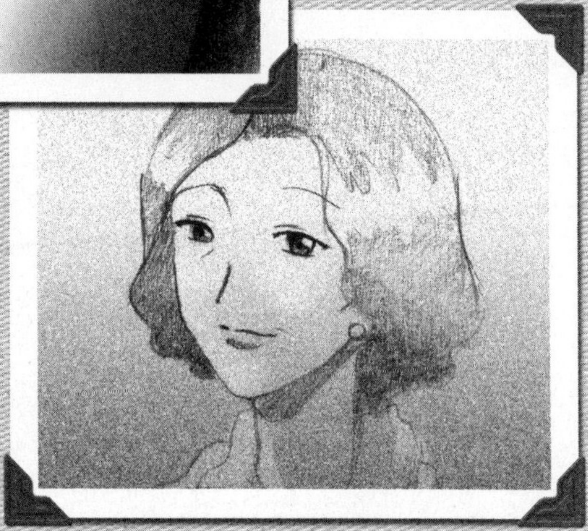

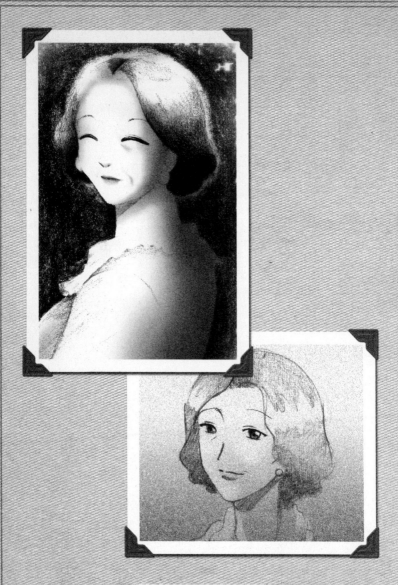

Grandma Emily

Now and when she was younger!

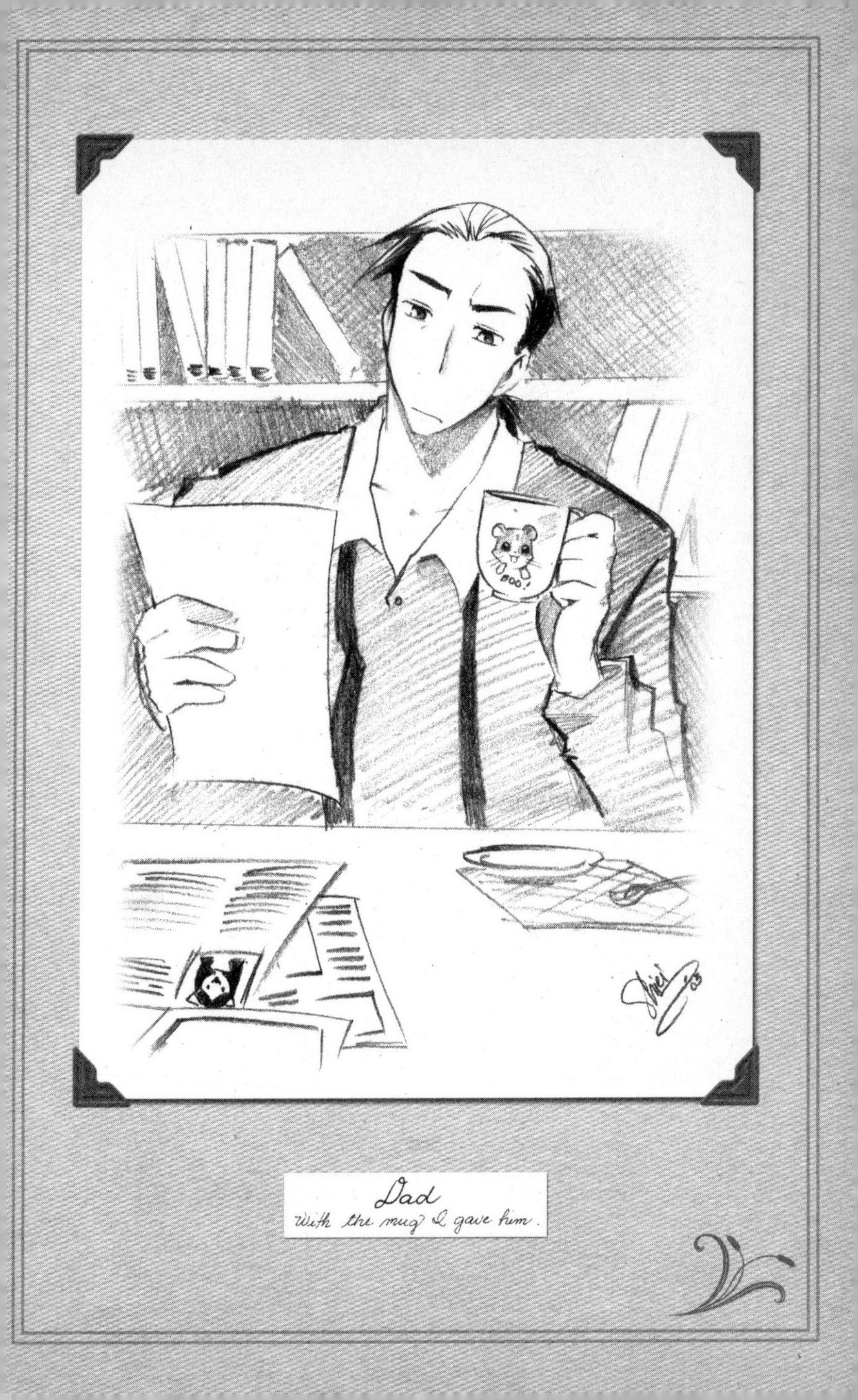
BOO!

Dad

With the mug I gave him.

Mom
When she was in college

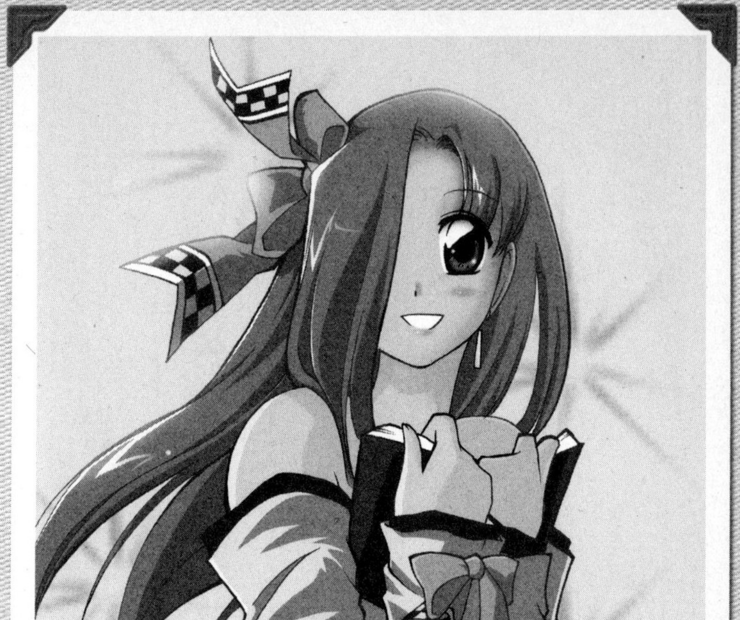
Shiei '05

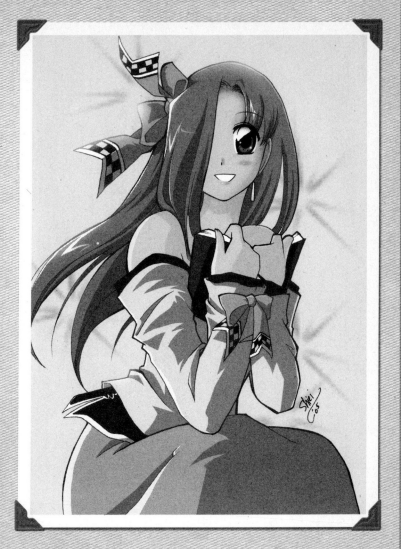

My Bestfriend
Francesca

Francesca
all dressed up

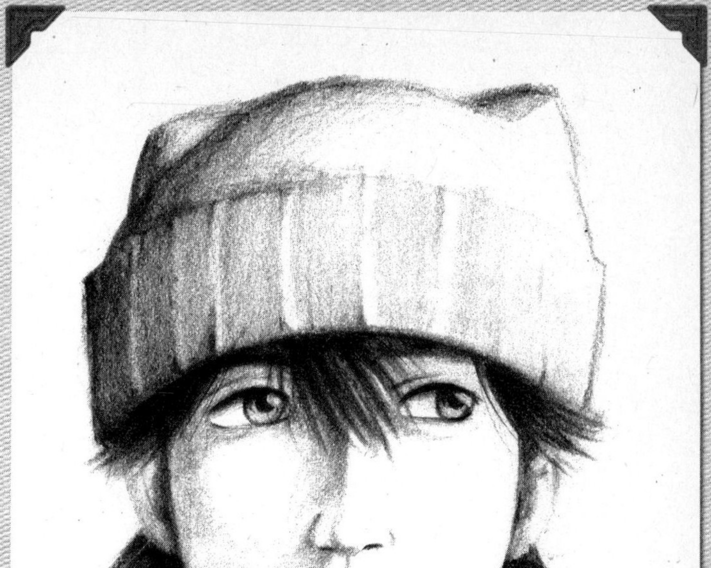
Shiei

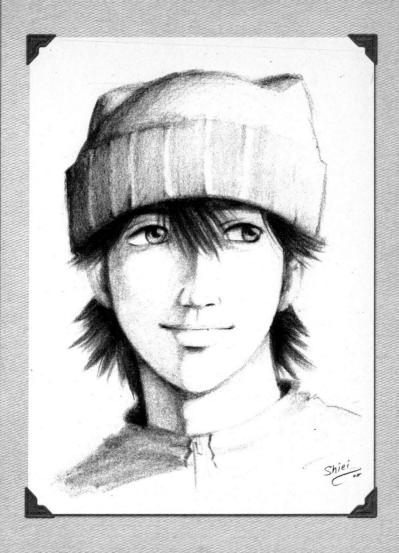

My first friend Oliver

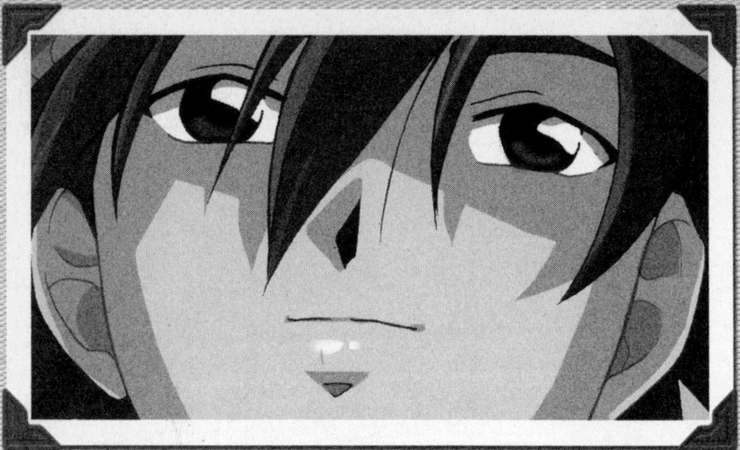

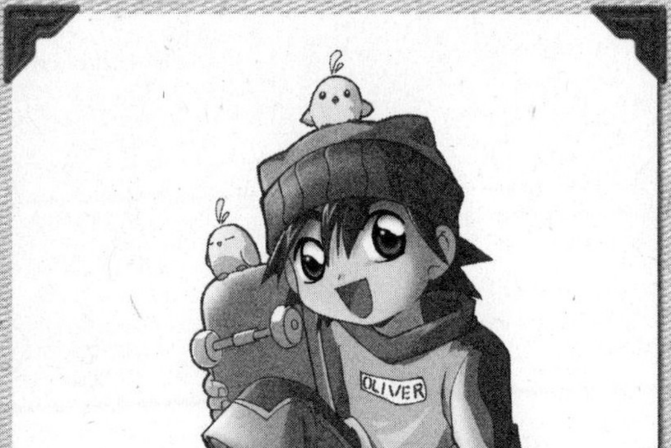
OLIVER

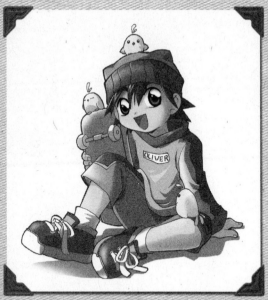

Oliver gave me "lots" of pictures of himself. I wonder why...

This is Jonah I like him.

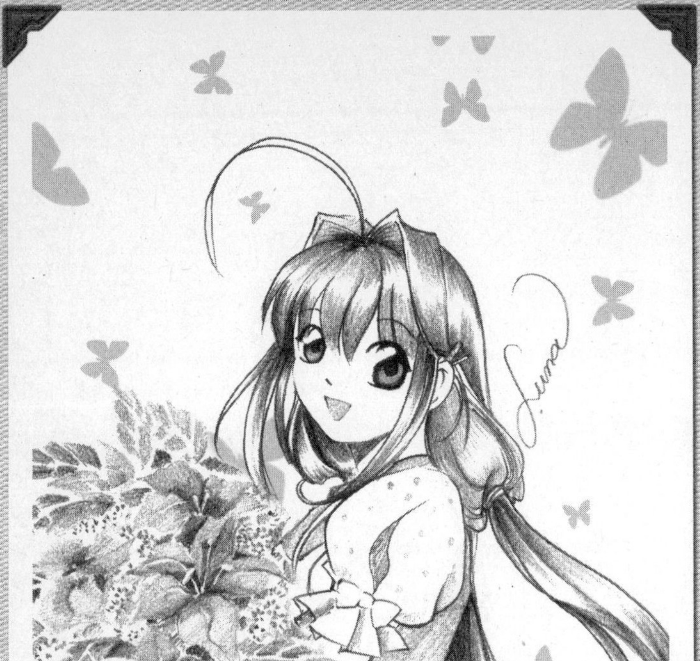
Luna
Shei '05

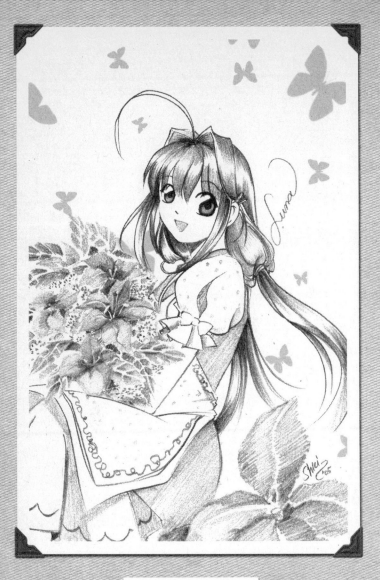

This is Me!

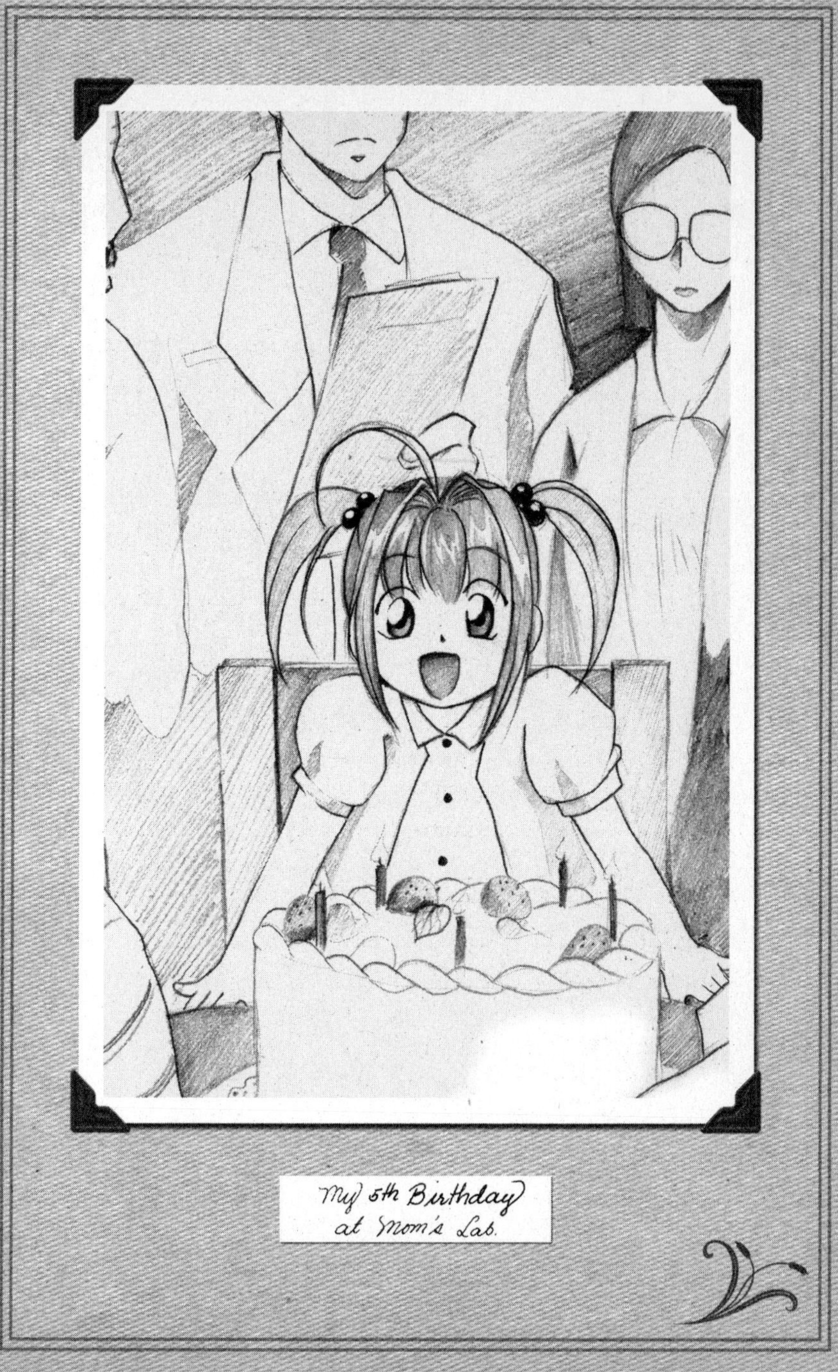
My 5th Birthday
at Mom's Lab.

My costume for
next Halloween !

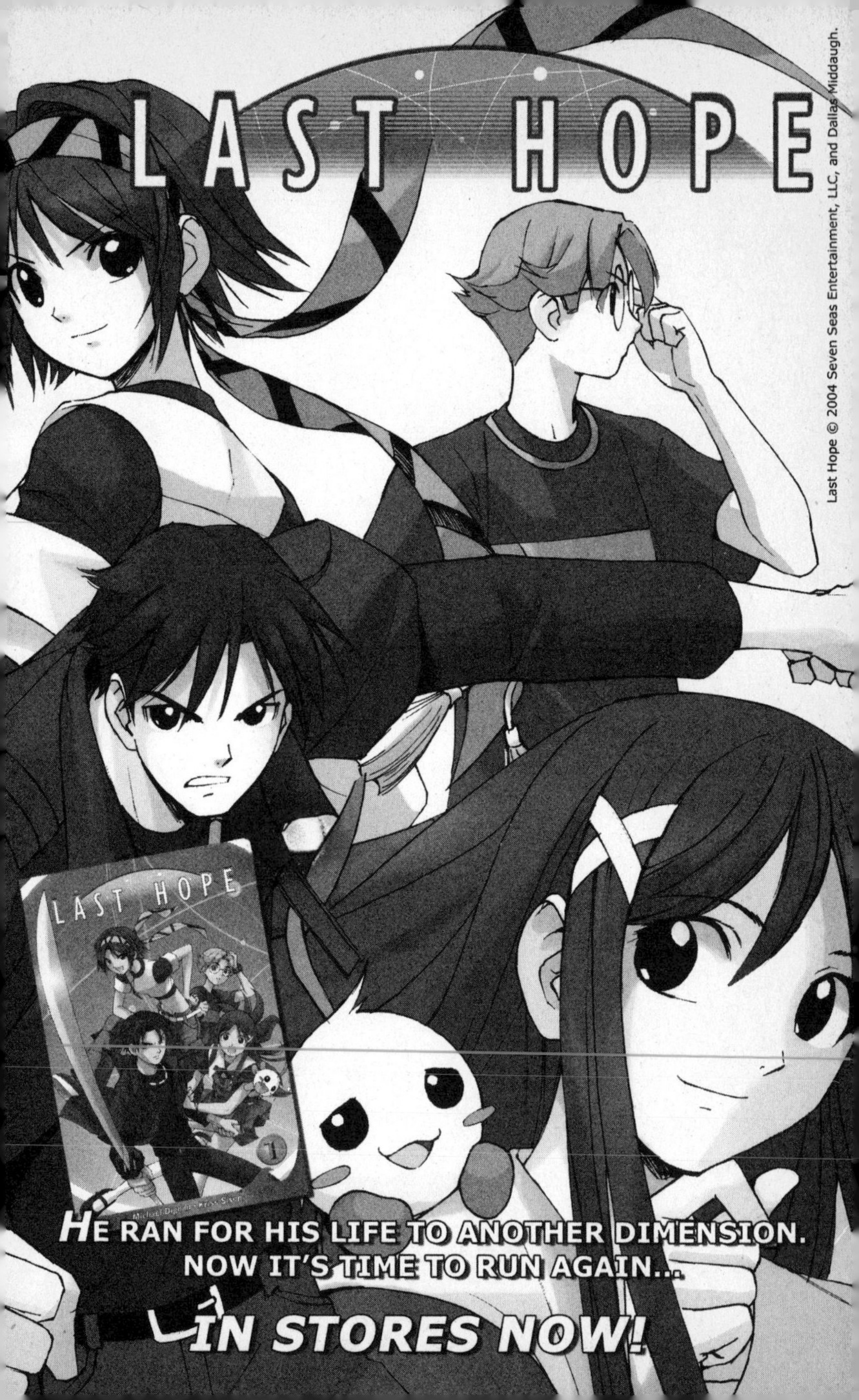
LAST HOPE
Last Hope © 2004 Seven Seas Entertainment, LLC, and Dallas Middaugh.
LAST HOPE
HE RAN FOR HIS LIFE TO ANOTHER DIMENSION.
NOW IT'S TIME TO RUN AGAIN...
IN STORES NOW!

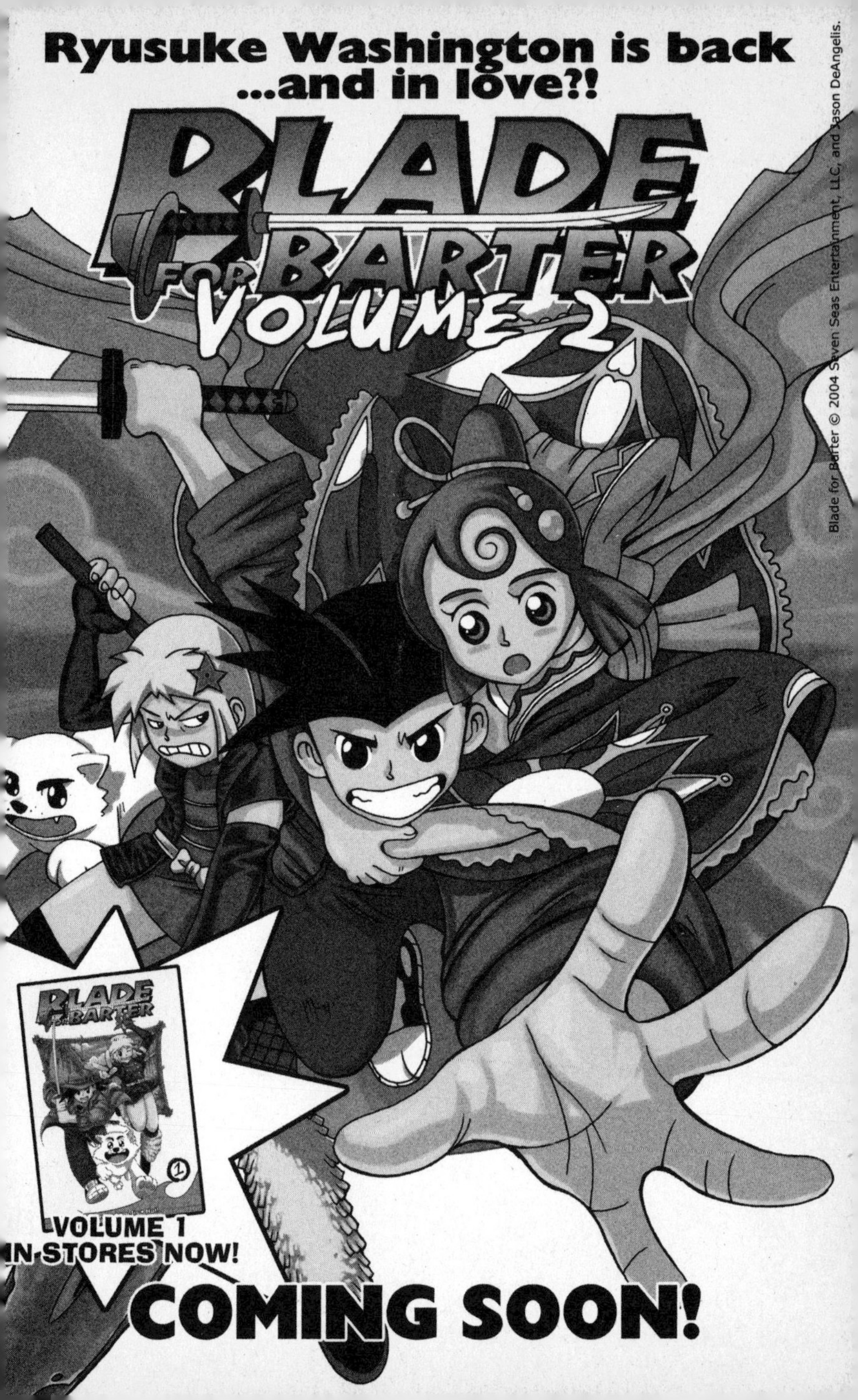
Ryusuke Washington is back
...and in love?!
BLADE FOR BARTER
VOLUME 2
BLADE FOR BARTER
VOLUME 1
IN STORES NOW!
COMING SOON!
Blade for Barter © 2004 Seven Seas Entertainment, LLC, and Jason DeAngelis.

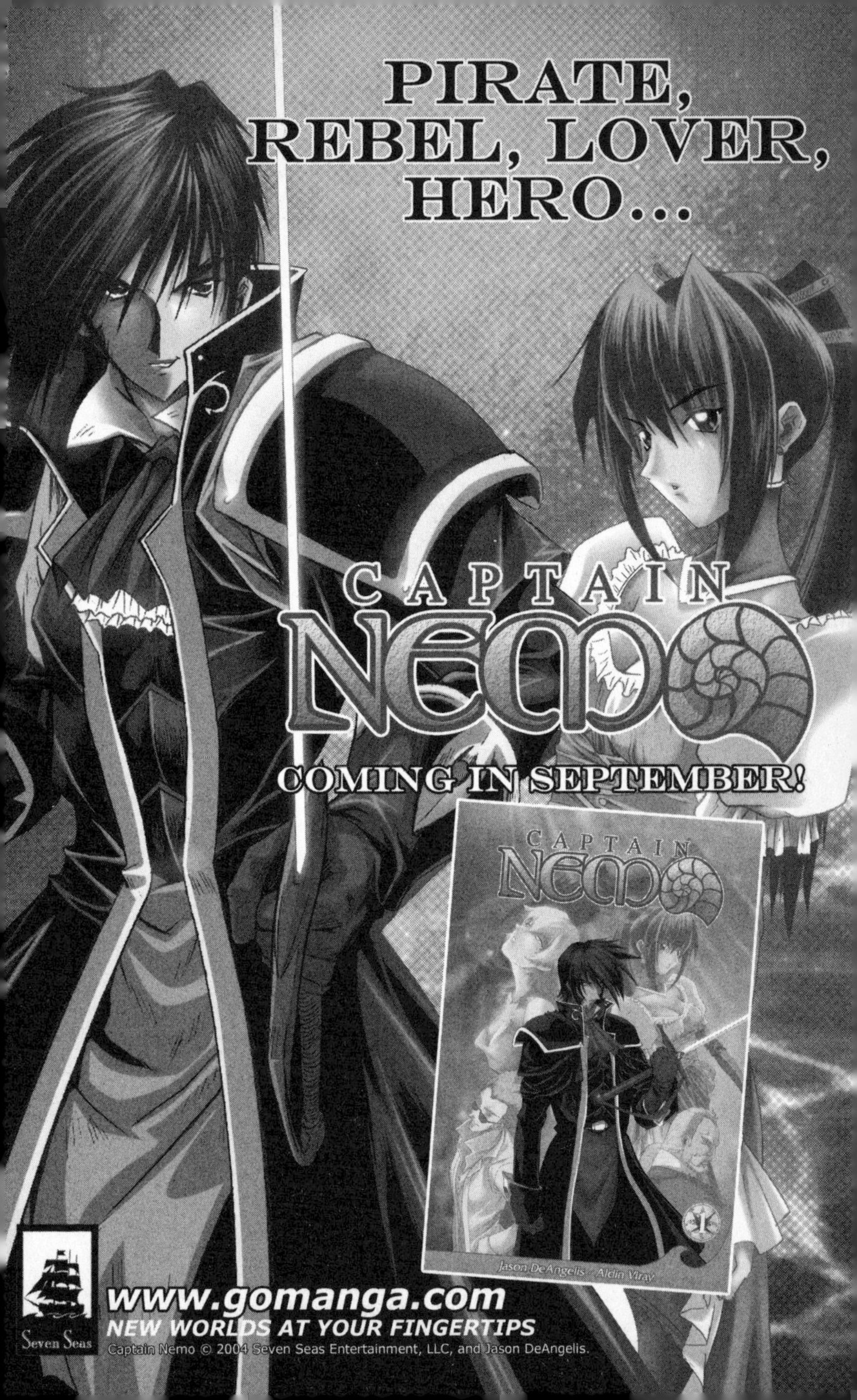
PIRATE, REBEL, LOVER, HERO...
CAPTAIN NEMO
COMING IN SEPTEMBER!
CAPTAIN NEMO
Jason DeAngelis · Aldin Viray
Seven Seas
www.gomanga.com
NEW WORLDS AT YOUR FINGERTIPS
Captain Nemo © 2004 Seven Seas Entertainment, LLC, and Jason DeAngelis.

Amazing Agent Luna Omake

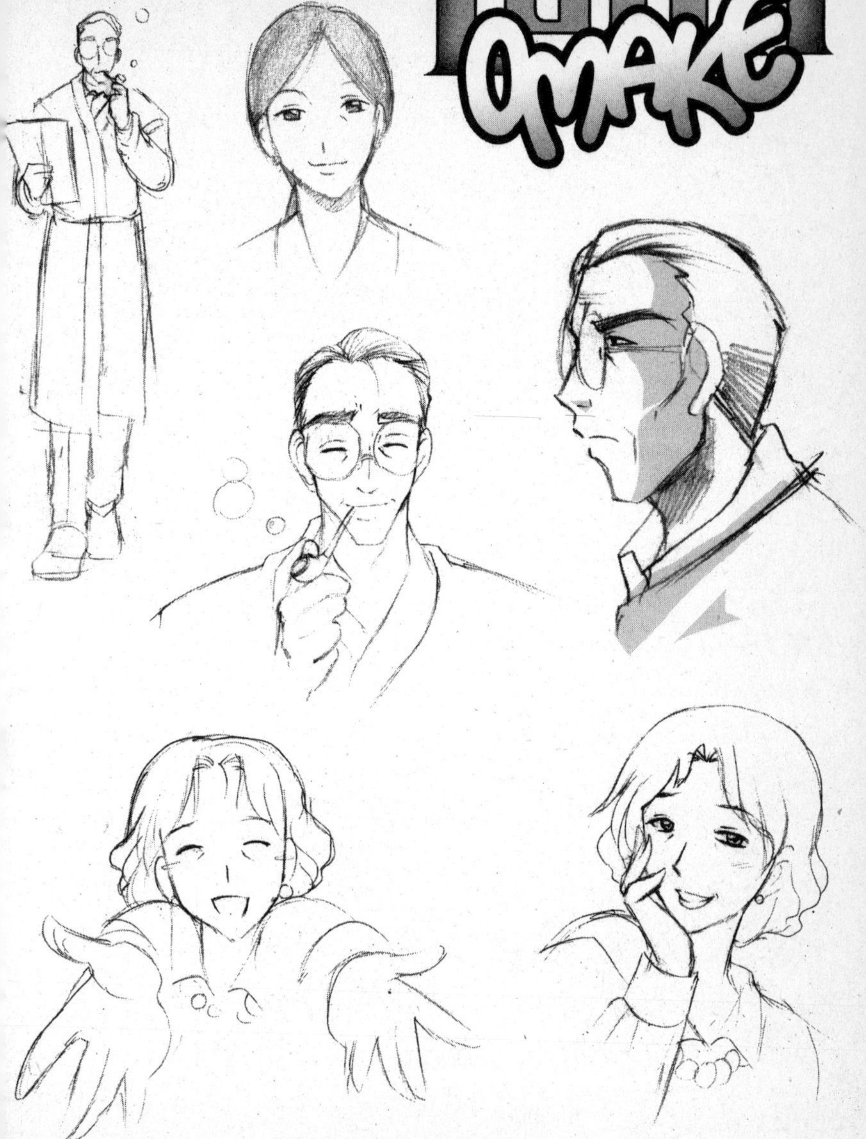

Mr. and Mrs. Kajiwara

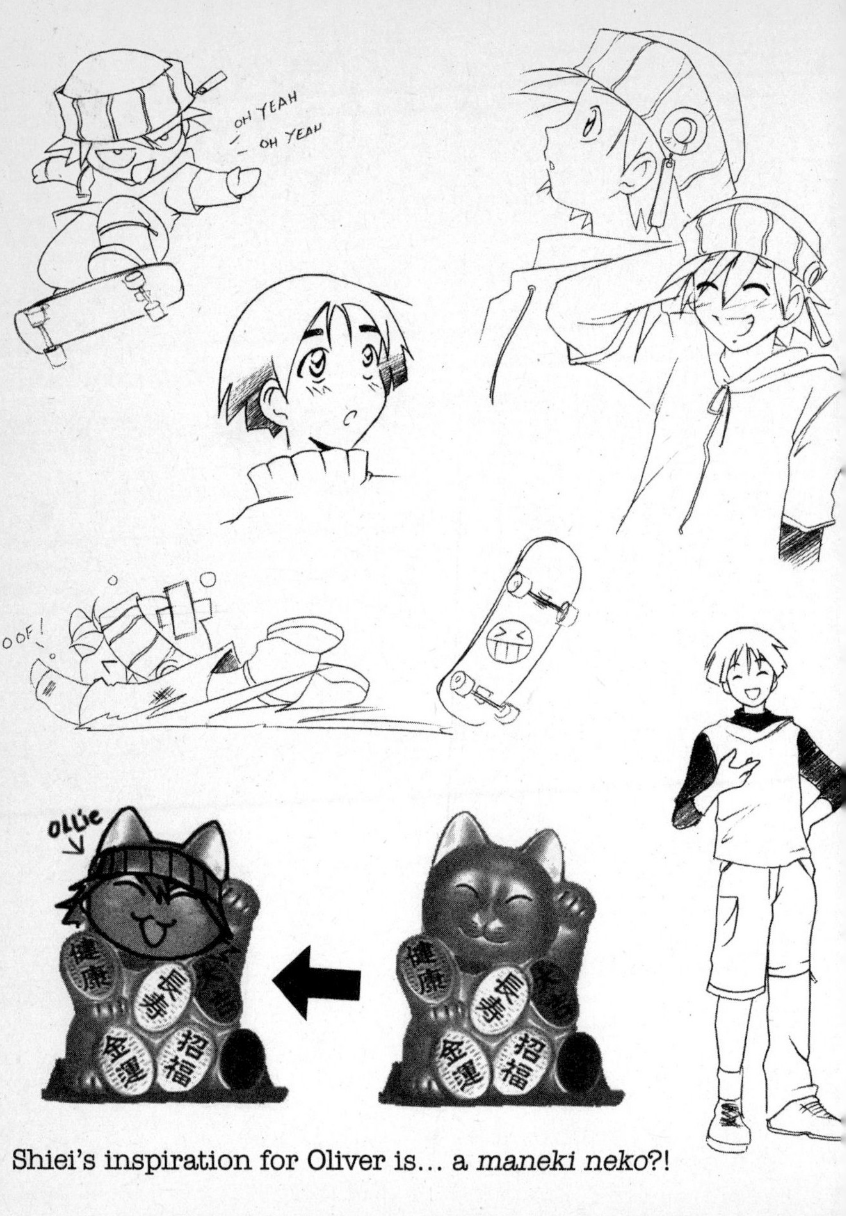
OH YEAH
OH YEAH
OOF!
Ollie
健康
長寿
金運
招福

Shiei's inspiration for Oliver is… a *maneki neko*?!

It's all about...
Control.

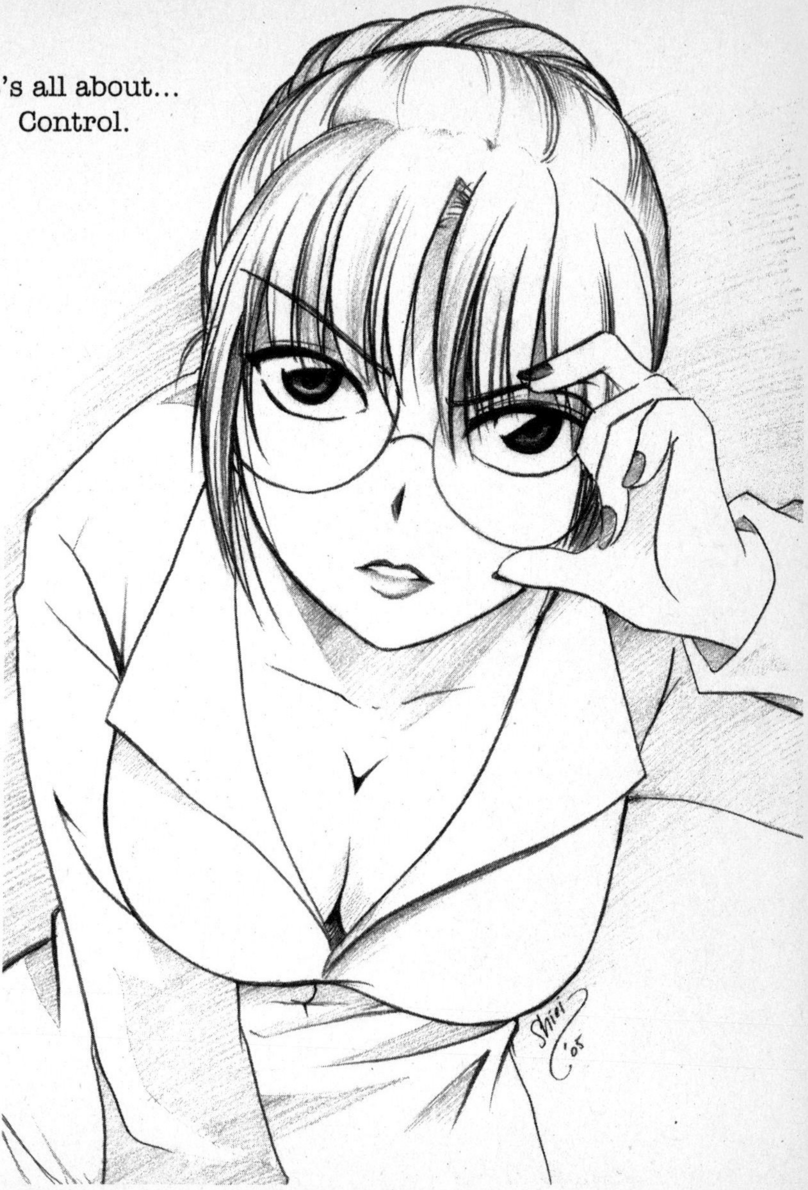
Shiei '05

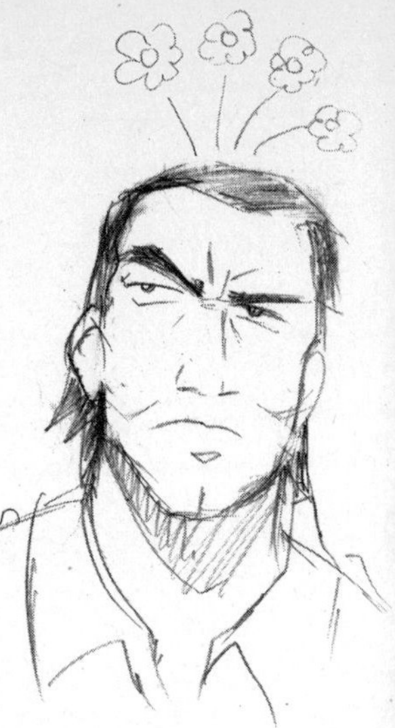

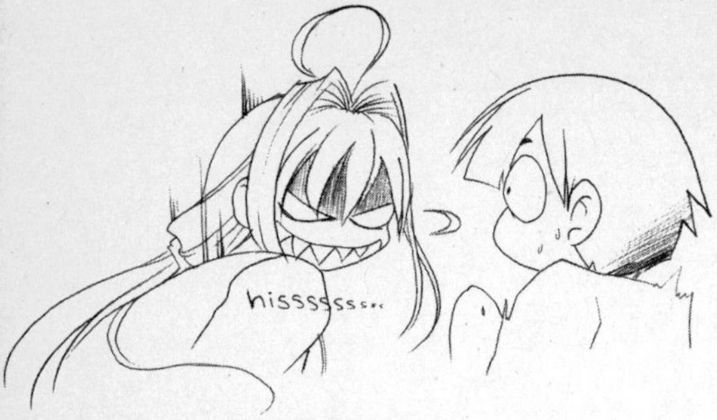
hisssssss...

Oliver's dad: early sketches

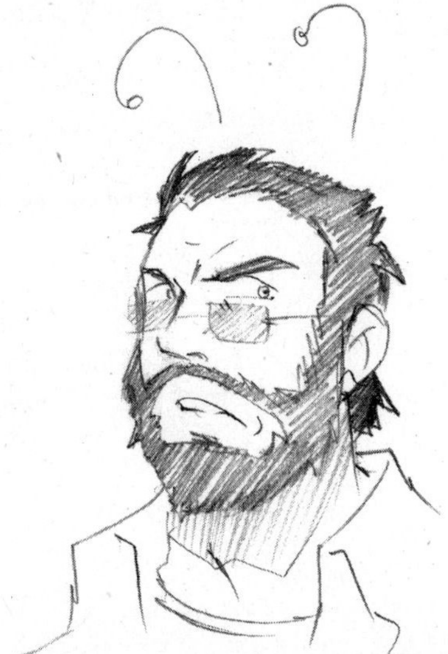

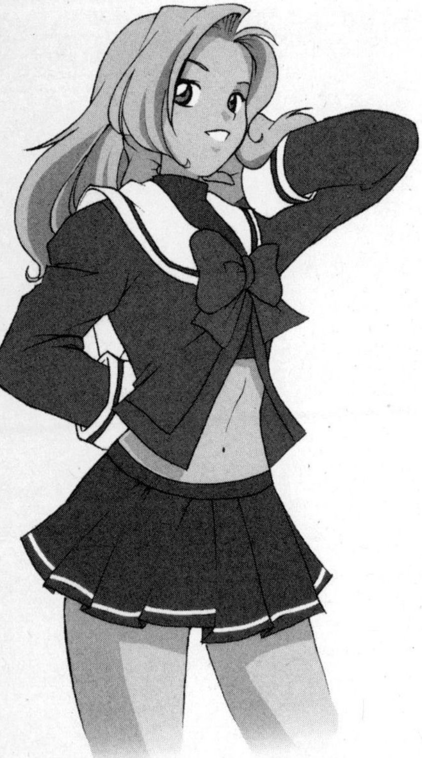

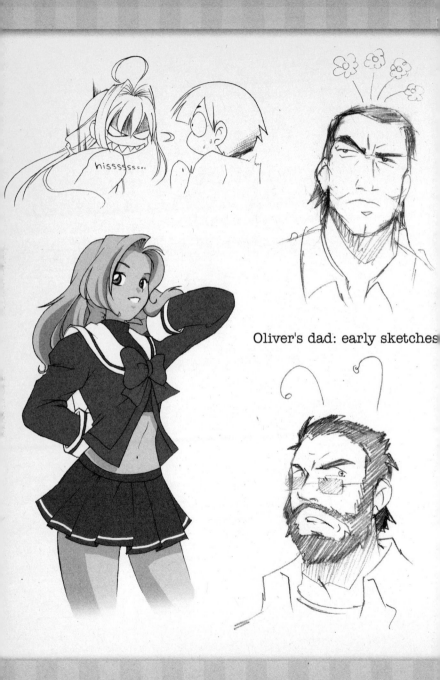

Amazing_Agent Luna FanArt

In February 2005, Seven Seas Entertainment unleashed a *fanart* contest of *fan*tabulous proportions: the Gomanga Fanfare Contest! Entrants were given the chance to flex their artistic muscle by choosing their favorite character or characters from any existing Seven Seas title.

We posted all the entries in our forum at Gomanga.com and allowed members to vote on their favorite pieces of artwork across three categories. The top eight pictures then proceeded to the finals where they went before a special panel of judges. In the end, four entrants emerged victorious, with two grand prize winners, who received original art from the artist whose work they emulated, and two runners-up, who received an autographed manga.

It turned out that three of the four winners did fan art from Amazing Agent Luna, so here they are! Congratulations, all!

GRAND PRIZE WINNER
Sally Lei, 15
San Francisco, California

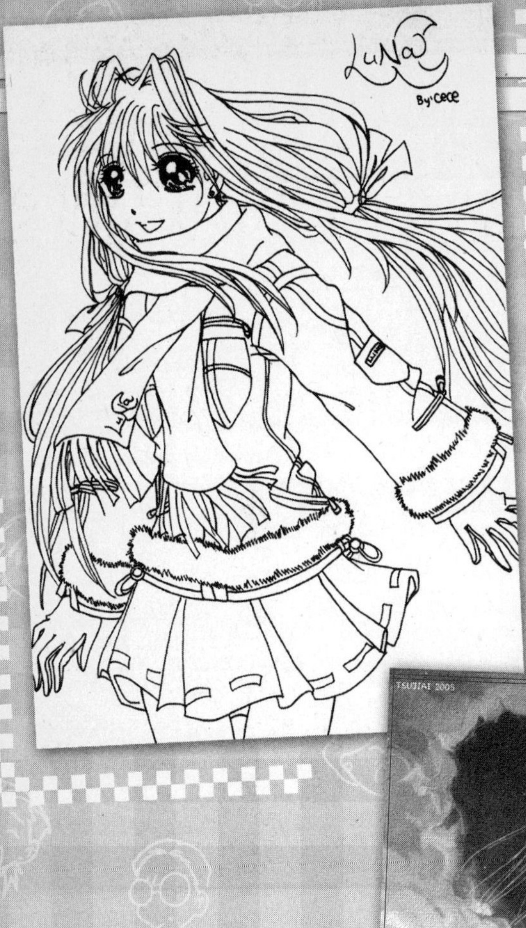
LuNa
By: cece

GRAND PRIZE WINNER
Cece Chu, 13
Fremont, California

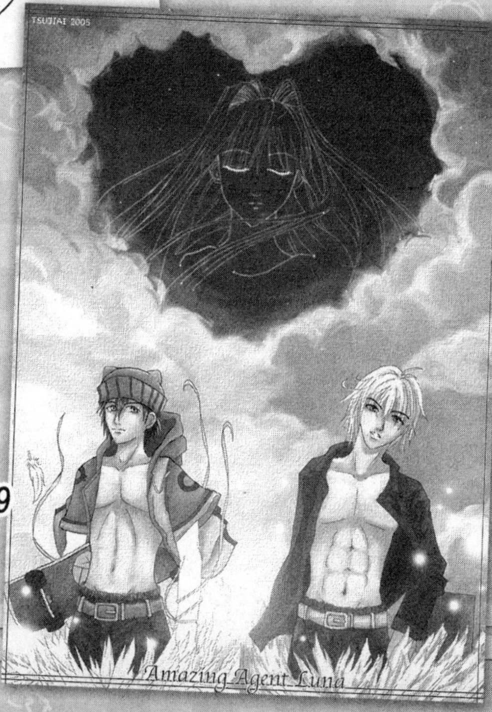
TSUJIAI 2005
Amazing Agent Luna

RUNNER-UP
John Philip Gatchalian, 19
New York, New York

THE END

YOU'RE READING THE WRONG WAY

This is the last page of
Amazing Agent Luna Volume 2.

This book reads from right to left, Japanese style. To read from the beginning, flip the book over to the other side, start with the top right panel, and take it from there.

If this is your first time reading manga, just follow the diagram. It may seem backwards at first, but you'll get used to it! Have fun!